Bibliography of
New Religious Movements
in Primal Societies

Volume II: North America

Bibliography of
New Religious Movements in Primal Societies

Volume II: North America

HAROLD W. TURNER

George Prior Publishers, London, England

G.K.HALL&CO.
70 LINCOLN STREET, BOSTON, MASS.

Available for sale in the British Commonwealth from
George Prior Publishers, 37-41 Bedford Row, London, W.C.1, England
ISBN (U.K.)   0 86043 303 4

Library of Congress Cataloging in Publication Data (Revised)
Turner, Harold W
  Bibliography of new religious movements in primal societies.

  (Bibliographies and guides in African studies)
  Bibliography: p.
  Includes indexes.
  CONTENTS: v. 1. Black Africa. — v. 2. North America.
  1. Religion — Bibliography.   2. Religion, Primitive —
Bibliography.   I. Title.   II. Series.
Z7833.T87   016.2   77-4732
ISBN 0-8161-7927-1   (v. 1)   0-8161-7928-X   (v. 2)

Contents

Introduction

This is the second of a bibliographic series of four volumes on new religious movements in primal societies. The first, on Black or sub-saharan Africa, appeared in 1977, and the series will continue with further volumes covering Asia with Oceania, and Latin America with the Caribbean. The religious movements dealt with in this bibliographic series are defined as those which arise in the interaction of a primal society with another society where there is a great disparity of power or sophistication; the subject has been dealt with systematically in items 99 and 101 in this volume.

These four volumes draw upon the extensive bibliographic and documentary resources of the Project for the Study of New Religious Movements in Primal Societies established in the Department of Religious Studies of the University of Aberdeen, Scotland, in 1973. These resources are continually being up-dated beyond the points where the published volumes have to stop, and also contain unpublished information; there are therefore known North American movements on which no publications have been discovered but about which something is known in the Project--for instance, recent syncretistic developments among the Narragansetts, a Sioux ex-Roman Catholic church, and the Hopis' Hotevilla Gospel Church.

The area covered by the term "North America" includes the Indian peoples of northern Mexico, those of the United States, Canada and Alaska, and the Eskimos of Alaska, Canada, and Greenland. It might be expected that the Black population of these areas would also make a substantial contribution to this volume, but Black prophets, millennial movements and independent churches, and Black Islam have been excluded for several reasons. These would require a volume on their own, and in any case they have already been included in the large number of bibliographies covering the Black population and Black religion that have appeared in the last two decades. In addition the phenomena are very complex: on the one hand the independent churches would be difficult to distinguish from the overall ecclesiastical history of North America (as is true now for some of the independent churches in Africa, see Volume I, p. viii); on the other hand the interaction processes for the Black population have occurred under the

peculiar circumstances of transplantation, of the intermingling of
many different African cultures in the situation of slavery, and of a
long acculturation during several centuries of the distinctive history
of European settlement in North America. In the final volume, however, on Latin America with the Caribbean, it is proposed to include
movements of Black as well as of Indian origin; for whatever reasons,
these movements are more akin to the phenomena in Black Africa itself,
and to those in the rest of these volumes.

Two other groups have also been excluded from this volume--the
mixed-blood Metis of Canada, who form a distinctive group with a different history, and the Mexican-Americans or Chicanos who are securing
their own bibliographies and whose religion tends to the folk form
rather than that with which these volumes are concerned; a few new
movements among Mexican-Americans have, however, been included for
comparative purposes--see Alianza and the Allelujahs. Some Indian
movements in the United States, such as the Buzzard cult, the Sun
Dance and Yuwipi, might seem to be primal religions rather than new
movements; they have been included in view of a certain amount of syncretism in some cases, and in order not to prejudge the issue where
the evidence is scanty or uncertain.

The classification is broadly geographical-political, with some
exceptions in each case; within the United States individual movements
or groups of movements have been classified by the names most commonly
used, although all the minor movements, and literature dealing with
more than one movement, have been placed in the preceding General
section. Movements that straddle geographical or political boundaries
have been placed in the area of their origin; some found in Canada are
therefore placed under United States. Material of theoretical value
may be found at many points, but items primarily focussed in this way
will be found in the opening section on Theory.

Since this is the first major attempt at covering the North
American materials, the bibliography is more comprehensive than selec-
tive, and thus differs from the previous volume. Many items are
popular in nature and many references are rather incidental, but these
can have their own value in revealing attitudes towards or neglect of
the subject; similarly the nature of the treatment, the context, and
who the author is can each be of independent significance; the annotations sometimes draw attention to these points. Dissertations have
been omitted if well represented in the later publications of the same
author. A few review articles or even briefer reviews of important
books have been included, likewise archival or unpublished materials
or reports of which the existence ought to be known, together with
their location. Certain "classic" items in the theory section of
Volume I have been repeated here, especially when of North American
origin, thus making this volume somewhat more self-contained; on the
other hand there are a few cross references back to material in
Volume I. The brief index of films and records is indicative rather
than comprehensive.

Introduction

As in the first volume, annotations are not provided where titles are sufficiently indicative of contents, or where it has not been possible to examine an item and further information has not been available. Annotations are mostly descriptive of contents, but some evaluation has been allowed where merits or demerits are unmistakeable and in a few other instances which will be obvious to most users.

It is tempting to embark on a comparison between the material available for the African movements and that presented here for those in North America. The African phenomena are clearly much more closely allied to the Christian tradition both in form and content, being for the most part independent churches in some sense. This category is a comparatively minor one among the wide range of North American forms, which relate more closely to the primal religious background. This again reflects the striking expansion of the Christian faith in Black Africa and the equally striking failure of Christian missions in North America when compared with other parts of the world, a failure we have explored in item 100. At the same time it must be remembered that the extensive range of movements represented in the literature of this volume forms an impressive reaction to the meeting with the Western and Christian traditions, albeit at the opposite end of the spectrum to their counterparts in Africa.

Not unconnected with the above difference is the contrast between the scholars who have contributed the major studies in the two continents. In Africa these have been mainly churchmen--missionaries, missiologists, theologians and historians; in North America the major studies have come overwhelmingly from anthropologists and to a lesser extent from historians and others not directly concerned with the relation of the movements to the Christian cause. Travellers, administrators and military officers also appear more prominently in the American materials, especially for the earlier movements. On the other hand it could be said that both continents have been affected by current concerns to re-examine the histories of their indigenous peoples through greater attention to Indian and to African sources and viewpoints. In Africa these sources include the publications of the new movements themselves (see especially in the Ghanaian and Nigerian sections of Volume I), whereas the American movements have very little to offer in this way, and for reasons that would not be far to seek.

In introducing the previous volume the limitations imposed upon a compiler were freely confessed. These limitations have been felt still more keenly in the preparation of this volume, during a time of increased academic austerity and in a place so far removed from many of the sources. There are sure to be formal inconsistencies and factual errors, but it is hoped that users will not be led astray in any matters of consequence, and that some will be generous enough to inform the compiler, both as to these matters and on the more important question of serious omissions.

ix

Introduction

Much of the earlier material was examined through the highly pro-
fessional assistance of the inter-library loan department of the
Woodruff Library of Emory University in 1970-72. Since 1973 the staff
of the same department in the King's College library of the University
of Aberdeen have been tireless in handling my endless requests, and
have produced items from as far afield as the library of the Navajo
Community College, all the way from Arizona to Aberdeen. Indeed, none
can strain the inter-library loan services more than a bibliographer,
and I am deeply appreciative both of the system and of those who have
so willingly joined me in the search for elusive items. I hope this
volume on the shelves of their own library will be some visible return
for their labours.

Until the end of 1977 Dr. Jocelyn Murray, Spalding Research Fellow
for the Project in Aberdeen, continued to handle new acquisitions, to
check bibliographical details, and to transform my own raw cards,
often written under divers and difficult circumstances, into type-
written bibliographical form; her assistance has been especially
valuable in solving the problems of style and presentation that make
up so much of the bibliographical task. My wife, Maude, has done much
of the library and other checking and filing, undertook the remaining
typing tasks, and has made the final preparation and indexing manage-
able; she is now cheerfully immune to the sight of yet another bunch
of 5" by 3" cards, and this is the best augury that the two remaining
volumes will not be too long delayed.

Bibliography of New Religious Movements in Primal Societies
Volume II: North America

Theory

Volume I contains ninety-two items of theoretical value, and a very few of these have been repeated here because of special relevance to North America. Otherwise this volume contains some theoretical items of world-wide application that have appeared since Volume I, together with material of special significance to North America since based on data or studies from this area. The remaining items have been included here, rather than in either of the two subsequent volumes, simply because written by North American scholars or published in this region. Further theoretical material connected in any of these ways will appear in the later collections on Asia/Pacific and Latin America/Caribbean movements. There is of course a vast literature on subjects such as acculturation and syncretism, but the items included here have either an explicit reference to our special field or some important focus that seems helpful for its study.

1   ABERLE, David F[riend]. A note on relative deprivation theory as applied to millenarian and other cult-movements, in S. Thrupp (ed.), 1962; repr. in P. Hammond (ed.), <u>Cultural and social anthropology</u>. New York and London: Macmillan/ Collier Macmillan 1964, 338-342.

2   ABERLE, David F[riend]. <u>The peyote religion among the Navaho</u> (Viking Fund Publications in Anthropology, 42). Chicago: Aldine Press 1966, xxvi + 469 p., illus., bibl.
     [Pp. 315-333, a classification of social movements. See also as item 771.]

3   ALEXANDER, H[artley] B[urr]. Incarnation (American), in J. Hastings (ed.), <u>Encyclopaedia of Religion and Ethics</u> vol. 7, 1914, 184a-186b.
     [P. 186, brief references of Tenskwatawa and the Ghost Dance as having antecedents in certain features of Indian religion; based on J. Mooney, item 508.]

4   BAER, Hans Albert. <u>The Levites of Utah: the development of and conversion to a small millenarian sect</u>. University of Utah, Ph.D. dissertation (anthropology) 1976, 377 p.

[The Aaronic Order which emerged from the Mormons in the 1930s; studies in terms of church-sect typology and of Wallace's revitalization theory and the deprivation model. Useful for comparative purposes.]

5   BARKUN, Michael (ed.). Millenarian change: movements of total transformation. American Behavioral Scientist 16 (2), 1972, 143-288, bibls.
      [Special theme for the whole issue: see M. Barkun, item 6; R. M. Kanter, item 52; T. S. Lebra, item 63; G. Rosen, item 81; J. F. Zygmunt, item 126.]

6   BARKUN, Michael. Movements of total transformation: an introduction, in M. Barkun (ed.), item 5, 145-151.
      [On the issues involved in defining and interpreting millennialisms.]

7   BARKUN, Michael. Disaster and the millennium. New Haven: Yale University Press 1974, 246 p., bibl.
      [See index for "millenarian movements"; p. 94, Indian Shakers; pp. 15-16, 42, 92, Ghost Dance; pp. 109, 115, Handsome Lake — all set in a theoretical context.]

8   BARNETT, H[omer] G[arner]. Innovation: the basis of cultural change (McGraw-Hill Series in Sociology and Anthropology). New York: McGraw-Hill 1953, 462 p., illus.
      [See index for messianic cults, Ghost Dance, Palauans (Modekne cult), and especially Shaker cult--numerous references.]

9   BARRETT, Stanley R. The use of models in anthropological fieldwork. Journal of Anthropological Research (Albuquerque) 32 (2), 1976, 161-181.
      [On the false interpretation of a famous Nigerian new religious community due to his initial rigid sociological deductive method; his four successive interpretations as he gave greater attention to historical and religious factors, with a more inductive anthropological approach.]

10   BARTH, Frederik. On the study of social change. American Anthropologist 69, 1967, 661-669.
      [Typological and comparative approaches are less useful than studies of ongoing process, especially as seen in allocations of time and resources.]

11   BASTIDE, Roger. Le millénarisme comme stratégie de la recherche d'une nouvelle identité et dignité, in his Le sacré sauvage et autres essais. Paris: Payot 1975, 151-162, bibl.

[An interpretation of new religious movements among peoples facing the superiorities of Western societies. (Many other items by Bastide, both theoretical and case studies, will appear in Vol. 4.)]

12 BATESON, Gregory. Culture contact and schismogenesis. <u>Man</u> 35 (art. no. 199) 1935, 178-183.
[A critique of the Memorandum of the Social Sciences Research Council (<u>idem</u> art. no. 162) on study of culture contact, with his own methodological suggestions.]

13 BEAN, Lowell John and VANE, Sylvia Brakke. Cults and their transformations, in R. F. Heizer (ed.), <u>California: Handbook of North American Indians</u>, 8 (gen. ed. W. C. Sturtevant). Washington, D.C.: Smithsonian Institution 1978, 662-672.

14 BENZ, Ernst. Traum, Hallucination, Vision. <u>Offene Tore</u> (Zurich, Swedenborg Verlag) Marz 1966; Eng. trans., <u>Dreams, hallucinations, visions</u>. New York: Swedenborg Foundation 1968, 46 p.
[An eminent historian of religion surveys dreams and visions from the viewpoint of religious experience, examines their revelatory potential, and distinguishes them from the pathological and the hallucinatory emphasized in medical and psychological studies; of theoretical importance.]

15 BERKHOFER, Robert F., Jr. Faith and factionalism among the Senecas: theory and ethnohistory. <u>Ethnohistory</u> 12 (2), 1965, 99-112.
[Critical of Wallace's revitalization theory; applies Smelser's model (see item 86) to the explanation of the dual response of the Seneca both to Handsome Lake and to the Quaker and Presbyterian missions. Handsome Lake religion as only one faction, employing "antagonistic acculturation".]

16 BIDNEY, David. The concept of cultural crisis. <u>American Anthropologist</u> 48 (4:1), 1946, 534-552, bibl.
[Pp. 547-548, the crises of acculturation.]

17 BONNEY, Rachel Ann. <u>Forms of supratribal Indian interaction in the United States</u>. University of Arizona, Ph.D. dissertation (anthropology) 1975, 295 p.
[Presents a revised diachronic model of revitalization theory (incorporating A. F. C. Wallace's stages); revitalization is a still on-going process, whose earlier forms (pp. 32-41) were religious and comprehensive, and whose later forms are more secular and fragmentary. See especially pp. 5-23, 214-251 for the theory. Based on case studies of modern secular movements.]

18   BURGER, Henry G.   Syncretism, an acculturative accelerator.
        Human Organization 25 (2), 1966, 103-115.
            [An analysis of syncretism into seven types of degrees:
        "quantitative, supplementary, substitutive, phasic, simu-
        lative, simulative-trending, and simulative-enhancing".]

19   CARROLL, Michael P.   Revitalization movements and social struc-
        ture: some quantitative tests.   American Sociological
        Review 40 (3), 1975, 389-401, bibl.
            [Primarily on the Ghost Dance as a model for understand-
        ing the rise and spread of revitalization movements.]

20   COLPE, Carsten.   Krisenkulte und prophetische Bewegungen, und
        Messianismus und Millenarismus, in J. P. Asmussen et al.
        (eds.), Handbuch der Religions-geschichte.   Göttingen:
        Vandenhoeck & Ruprecht 1975, vol. 3, 495-523, bibl.
            [Pp. 502, 510, peyote, Ghost Dance and Shakers discussed
        in a theoretical context.]

21   CRESPY, Georges.   Sociologie et théologie des messianismes.
        Etudes Théologiques et Religieuses (Montpellier) 54 (2),
        1976, 189-210.
            [A theological analysis of the introduction to
        H. Desroche's Dieux d'Hommes, item 171, pp. 1-41.]

22   CRUMRINE, N. Ross.   Anomalous figures and liminal roles.   A
        reconsideration of the Mayo Indian Čapakoba.   Anthropos
        69 (5/6), 1974, 858-873, maps, illus.
            [A study of "ritual clowns" as an example of liminal
        roles which are also adopted by folk prophets and revitali-
        zation cult leaders; as a reply to L. Makarius' item 1513,
        and of her use of his earlier work on the Mayo ritual
        impersonator.]

23   CRUMRINE, N. Ross and MACKLIN, Barbara June.   Sacred ritual vs.
        the unconscious: the efficacy of symbols and structure in
        North Mexican folk saints' cults and general ceremonialism,
        in I. Rossi (ed.), The unconscious in culture: the struc-
        turalism of Claude Levi-Strauss in perspective.   New York:
        E. P. Dutton 1974, 179-197.
            [Uses a trance description of a follower of Niño Fidencio,
        part of the procession ritual on Mayo Lenten rites, a cur-
        ing ritual from a Cuna shaman, and visions of Jesus or God
        by young Mayo men--to discuss Levi-Strauss's theory of the
        unconscious.]

24   DAVENPORT, Frederick Morgan.   Primitive traits in religious
        revivals. A study in mental and social evolution.   New
        York: Macmillan 1905, 323 p., repr. New York: Negro
        Universities Press 1968, 323 p.

[Pp. 32-36, Indian Shakers; pp. 36-44, Ghost Dance; based on J. Mooney, with Davenport's psychological explanations in terms of hypnosis etc.]

25 DE COSTER, Michael. Acculturation. <u>Diogenes</u> 73, 1971, 21-38.
    [Six stages or phases: contact, communication, evaluation or appreciation, total or partial acceptance or rejection, integration and adjustment, and assimilation.]

26 DESROCHE, Henri. Messianismus, in K. Galling (ed.), <u>Die Religion in Geschichte und Gegenwart</u>. Tübingen: J. C. B. Mohr, 3rd. ed. vol. 4, 1960, cols. 895-900, bibl.
    [See also the important introduction to his item 171, pp. 1-41.]

27 DEVEREUX, George and LOEB, Edwin M. Antagonistic acculturation. <u>American Sociological Review</u> 8 (2), 1943, 133-147.
    [Sociological and psychological analysis of positive reactions to means and techniques, coupled with negative reaction to goals and ends; pp. 145-146, Ghost Dance as a regressive reaction.]

28 DOZIER, Edward P. <u>The Hopi-Tewa of Arizona</u> (University of California Publications in American Archaeology and Ethnology 44 (3)). Berkeley and Los Angeles: University of California Press 1954, 259-376.
    [Pp. 298-301, relations with missions and Americans.]

29 DOZIER, Edward P. Differing reactions to religious contacts among North American Indian societies. <u>Akten des 34. Internationalen Amerikanistenkongress...1960</u>. Horn-Wien: Verlag Ferdinand Berger 1962, 161-171.
    [An important classification of the types of adjustment to contact with Christianity, as rejection, assimilation, compartmentalization, fusion, reactive adaptation, stabilized pluralism, or passive or adjustive nativism; omits consideration of independent churches. By an Indian anthropologist.]

30 EATON, Walter H. Alternative meanings of adjustment. <u>American Sociological Review</u> 12, 1947, 75-81.
    [Surveys use of the term; distinguishes between attitudinal and functional adjustment, the latter being easier to observe.]

31 EISTER, Allan W. An outline of a structural theory of cults. <u>Journal for the Scientific Study of Religion</u> 11 (4), 1972, 319-333.
    [Abridged and revised (sic) version of his item 32.]

32   EISTER, Allan W. Culture crises and new religious movements: a paradigmatic statement of the theory of cults, in I. I. Zaretsky and M. P. Leone (eds.), Religious movements in contemporary America. Princeton, N.J.: Princeton University Press 1974, 612-627.
      [Confined to cults in a Western milieu.]

33   ERTLE, Brigitte. Über Ursachen messianischer Bewegungen unter Naturvölkern. Zeitschrift für Ethnologie (Braunschweig) 97 (1), 1972, 61-73.
      [A good survey of the causal theories that have been proposed for the messianic forms of new religious movements by Eliade, Pereira de Queiroz, Jarvie, Bastide, Balandier, Lanternari, etc., and offers criteria for any satisfactory theory. Illustrates from useful surveys of Guaraní "terre-sans-mal" and Santiaade movements, Brazilian rural movements, the Canela messianic movement, and the Pawnee Ghost Dance; Navajo as a "negative instance".]

34   FALLDING, Harold. The sociology of religion: an explanation of the unity and diversity in religion. London, New York, etc.: McGraw Hill 1974, 240 p.
      [Pp. 144-147, the dynamic illustrated in the origins of some native protest movements (Ghost Dance, cargo cults).]

35   FARB, Peter. Man's rise to civilization as shown by the Indians of North America from primeval times to the coming of the industrial state. London: Secker & Warburg 1969; London: Paladin 1971, 332 p., illus., bibl.
      [Ch. 16, "The hopes of the oppressed"--based on Lanternari (1963) and Mooney (1896)--a good survey; ch. 15, "Borrowed cultures", on acculturation.]

36   FENTON, William N[elson]. Cultural stability and change in American Indian societies. Journal of the Royal Anthropological Institute (London) 83 (2), 1953 [appeared 1955], 169-174.
      [Importance of study of Indian conservatism, illustrated from the Iroquois, Klamath, Blackfoot, and Taos Pueblo; p. 172, Handsome Lake religion.]

37   FREER, Kenneth Orville. A study of vision reports in biblical literature. Yale University, Ph.D. dissertation (religion) 1975, 206 p.
      [Concentrated on Daniel 7-12, and on the motifs common to such accounts.]

38   GERLACH, Luther P. and HINE, Virginia H. Five factors crucial to the growth and spread of a modern religious movement. Journal for the Scientific Study of Religion 7 (1), 1968, 23-40.

39   GERLACH, Luther P. and HINE, Virginia H. People, power,
        change: movements of social transformation. Indianapolis:
        Bobbs-Merrill 1970, xxiii + 257 p.
            [Ch. 1, The Pentecostal Movement; ch. 2, Black Power.
        On the internal dynamics of movements.]

40   GREEN, Thomas Aaron, Jr. Yo Soy Indio: an analysis of a con-
        temporary nativistic movement. University of Texas
        (Austin), Ph.D. dissertation (anthropology) 1974, 198 p.
            [On the Tigua of Ysleta del Sur, a Pueblo Indian group
        near El Paso. Not on a specific religious movement, but
        showing nativism as a "stage in a continuum which culmin-
        ates in protonationalism".]

41   GUSFIELD, Joseph R. The study of social movements. Inter-
        national Encyclopedia of the Social Sciences. New York:
        Collier-Macmillan 1968, vol. 14, 445-452.

42   GUSFIELD, Joseph R. Protest, reform and revolt. A reader in
        social movements. New York, London, etc.: John Wiley &
        Sons 1970, 576 p.
            [Includes abridged version of Y. Talmon's Pursuit of the
        millennium (I, item 67) pp. 436-452.]

43   HARRIS, Marvin. Culture, people, nature. An introduction to
        general anthropology. New York: Thomas Y. Crowell (as
        Culture, man and nature, 1971), 2nd ed. 1975, 694 p.,
        illus.
            [Pp. 554-566, revitalization movements, with outlines of
        those among North American Indians (pp. 556-560) and in
        Melanesia (pp. 560-562, cargo forms only), and within
        Christianity (pp. 564-566). A popular treatment.]

44   HARRISON, Michael I. The maintenance of enthusiasm: involve-
        ment in a new religious movement. Sociological Analysis
        (De Kalb, Illinois) 36 (2), 1975, 150-160, bibl.
            [How movements focus and sustain the participants' expe-
        riences of inspiration; based on a study of pentecostalism
        among Catholics in the U.S.A.]

45   HEBERLE, Rudolf Otto. Social movements: an introduction to
        political sociology. New York: Appleton-Century-Crofts
        1951, 478 p., illus., bibl.
            [Introduction (= 19pp) useful as theoretical background
        on the concept of social movements.]

46   HINTON, Thomas B. Pre-conquest acculturation of the Cora.
        The Kiva (Tucson) 37 (4), 1972, 161-168.
            [Freely chosen acculturation during two centuries pre-
        ceding conquest of the Cora in 1722.]

47 HOPPER, Rex D. The revolutionary process: a frame of reference for the study of revolutionary movements. <u>Social
Forces</u> 28 (3), 1950, 270-279.
[In terms of re-establishment of a destroyed social
equilibrium, through a four-stage process of "Mass (individual) excitement...Crowd (collective) excitement and
unrest...Formulation of Issues and Formation of Publics,
and the Institution Stage of Legalization and Societal
Organization".]

48 HULTKRANTZ, Åke. The contribution of the study of North
American Indian religions to the history of religions, in
W. H. Capps (ed.), <u>Seeing with a native eye</u>. (Forum Books)
New York and London: Harper & Row 1976, 86-106.
[Pp. 100-101, research on religious acculturation.]

49 JARVIE, I[an] C. Theories of cargo cults: a critical analysis.
<u>Oceania</u> 34 (1), 1963, 1-31; 34 (2), 1963, 108-136.
[Analyses the causal explanations found in a large range
of writers on such new religious movements, including:
pp. 2-4, J. Mooney and his economic explanation of the
Ghost Dance; pp. 8-9, B. Barber's theory; pp. 9-13,
R. Linton's theory.]

50 JENNINGS, George J. The American Indian ethos: a key for
Christian missions? <u>Missiology</u> (Pasadena, California)
5 (4), 1977, 487-498.
[On the existence of a pan-Indian ethos, and its contrast to the white American ethos, as a factor in the past
failure and future prospects of Christian missions; p. 494,
peyote cult.]

51 JORGENSEN, Joseph Gilbert. <u>The ethnohistory and acculturation
of the northern Ute</u>. Indiana University, Ph.D. dissertation (anthropology) 1964, 568 p.
[Ute religion and Shamanism alone have resisted sweeping
changes, and remain (especially in the Sun and Bear dances)
as means of pan-reservation integration; contrary to the
theories which expect new religious movements among
"culturally deprived" peoples, this people remain as a
"negative instance".]

52 KANTER, Rosabeth Moss. Commitment and internal organization
of millennial movements, in M. Barkun item 5, 219-243.
[On the similarities between millennial movements and
utopian communities (illustrations mainly North American
or European), and the attractions and social functions of
the former.]

Theory

53 KLUCKHOHN, Clyde. Universal categories in culture, in A. L. Kroeber (ed.), Anthropology Today. Chicago: University of Chicago Press 1953, 507-523.
    [P. 514, "accepts psychological generalization in nativistic movements."]

54 LA BARRE, Weston. The Ghost Dance. Origins of religion. Garden City, N.Y.: Doubleday & Co. 1970, 677 p.
    [A psycho-analytic theory of religions as maladaptive retreats from reality, typified in the American Indian Ghost Dances. Valuable for the bibliographic notes appended to each chapter, for the methodological emphases on holistic approaches rather than single-factor analyses (e.g. pp. 292-294), and the collections of material under certain themes (e.g. invulnerability to bullets, etc., pp. 307-310). Otherwise contains short summaries of many new religious movements, including the following North American examples: pp. 206-209, 300-301, etc., Delaware prophets; pp. 227-233, etc., Ghost Dances; pp. 209-211, etc., Handsome Lake; pp. 214-215, 300, Kennekuk; pp. 215-216, 221, 225-227, Prophet Dances; pp. 221-222, 299-301, etc., Indian Shakers; pp. 218-219, 300-301, etc., Smohalla; pp. 211-214, 299-301, etc., Tenskwatawa; pp. 128-129, 157-158, etc., Sun Dance; strangely little on peyotism — in all cases see index also, and under "cult leaders".]

55 LAMAR, Howard R. The new Old West. Yale Alumni Magazine (New Haven) 36 (1), 1972, 6-15, illus.
    [Surveys the new approaches to "frontier" studies abandoning ethno-centric "white" limitations, and using ethnic and cultural studies to see Indians, Chicanos and pioneers in a new light; pp. 7, 9, illustrate this by reference to Handsome Lake, Tenskwatawa, Ghost Dance, and Peyote cult as subjects of a new interest.]

56 LANTERNARI, Vittorio. Nota su alcuni profetismi americani. Rivista di Antropologia (Rome) 65, 1958, 242-248, bibl., Eng. summary.
    [Peyote cult (as Slotkin, 1956) compared with Dream Dance (as Slotkin, 1957) - the former survived by assimilating Christian elements; both movements represent "adjustment nativism" as compared with "irredentistic nativism" of the Ghost Dance; the same distinction is found in Melanesia and New Zealand; the pan-tribalism of movements in North America and Africa.]

57 LANTERNARI, Vittorio et al. A CA book review: The religions of the oppressed: a study of modern messianic cults. Current Anthropology 6 (4), 1965, 447-465.
    [Author's precis, comments on the book by fifteen reviewers, author's reply, bibliography. A comprehensive critique of the first world survey in English.]

58   LANTERNARI, Vittorio. Religione popolare e contestazione.
      Riflessioni storico-sociali sul dissenso religioso.
      Testimonianze (Florence) no. 118=12 (October), 1969,
      708-729.
         [A historical approach to the problem of religious move-
      ments in different societies, from "primal" to "complex".]

59   LANTERNARI, Vittorio. Religions of the Oppressed (see I,
         item 267): Hungarian trans., Gyarmatosítás és Vallási
         Szabadságmozgalmak. Budapest: Kossuth 1972.

60   LAPLANTINE, François. Les trois voix de l'imaginaire: le
         messianisme, la possession et l'Utopie. Etude psychi-
         atrique (Collection "YE"). Paris: Editions Universitaires
         1974, 256 p.
         [By an ethno-psychiatrist, adding the dimension of
      imagination to the explanations of millennialism; ch. 6
      (= pp. 109-148), "L'espérance messianico-révolutionnaire",
      is the section most relevant to this bibliography.]

61   LAUE, James H. A contemporary revitalization movement in
         American race relations: the "Black Muslims". Social
         Forces 42 (3), 1964, 315-323; repr. in B. E. Segal (ed.),
         Racial and ethnic relations: selected readings. New York:
         Thomas Y. Crowell 1966, 445-458.
         [Useful for comparative purposes, and suggests peyotism
      emerges from the same kind of social pressures, and that
      this comparison needs more research.]

62   LAUER, Robert H. (ed.). Social movements and social change.
         Carbondale, etc.: Southern Illinois University Press;
         London and Amsterdam: Feffer Simons Inc. 1976, 292 p.
         [Includes G. Rosen, item 81, pp. 97-106; T. S. Lebra,
      item 63, pp. 127-143.]

63   LEBRA, Takie Sugiyama. Millenarian movements and resocializa-
         tion, in M. Barkun (ed.), item 5, 195-217; repr. in R. H.
         Lauer (ed.), item 62, 127-143.
         [Millenarianisms as inducing a change in individuals
      similar to psychiatric or correctional treatments; illus-
      trations from cargo cults, Ghost Dance, and Handsome Lake
      religion.]

64   LINTON, Ralph. The distinctive aspects of acculturation, in
         R. Linton (ed.), Acculturation in seven American Indian
         tribes. New York: D. Appleton-Century 1940, 501-520;
         repr. Gloucester, Mass.: Peter Smith 1963, same pagination.
         [On nativistic movements as much more frequent under
      acculturative conditions, especially where there is a
      dominance-submission situation, and appearing somewhat

later in contact periods. See especially pp. 502-503, 517-
519. See also his summaries at ends of chapters.]

65   LINTON, Ralph. Nativistic movements. American Anthropologist
      45 (2), 1943, 230-240; repr. in W. A. Lessa and E. Z.
      Vogt, Reader in comparative religion, 1965, 466-474.
      [A pioneer and influential attempt at an anthropological
      typology in terms of revivalist or perpetuative, and
      magical or rational features.]

66   LJUNGDAHL, Axel. What can we learn from non-Biblical prophet
      movements? in H. Biezais (ed.), New religions ... papers
      read at the symposium ... at Åbo ... 1974. Stockholm:
      Almqvist & Wiksell International 1975, 84-91.
      [The causes of prophet movements, mainly psychological
      but also social, with North American Indian movements con-
      sidered along with Taborites, Muslim movements, and flying
      saucer millennialists.]

67   LOVE, Joseph L. La Raza: Mexican Americans in rebellion.
      Trans-Action February 1969, 35-41; repr. in J. H. Burma
      (ed.), Mexican Americans in the United States. A reader.
      Cambridge, Mass.: Schenkman 1970, 459-472, and in John R.
      Howard (ed.), Awakening Minorities: American Indians,
      Mexican Americans, Puerto Ricans. Chicago: Aldine Press
      1970, 105-122.
      [On the Alianza movement; cf. with Swadesh, item 333;
      also on the Allelujahs and Penitentes, and millenarianism.
      Useful for comparative purposes, as a revitalization move-
      ment with millenarian aspects.

68   LUTH, Dietrich. Nativistic movements in three culture areas:
      a test of Slotkin's theory of nationalism. University of
      British Columbia, M.A. thesis 1964.
      [Africa, North America, Oceania.]

69   McLAUGHLIN, Barry (ed.). Studies in social movements. A
      social psychological perspective. New York: The Free
      Press; London: Collier Macmillan Ltd. 1969, 497 p.
      [Includes reprints of A. F. C. Wallace, Revitalization
      movements (I, item 78), pp. 30-52; and Y. Talmon, Pursuit
      of the millennium (I, item 67), pp. 400-427.]

70   MAIR, Lucy [Philip]. Independent religious movements in three
      continents. Comparative Studies in Society and History
      1 (2), 1959, 113-136; repr. in John Middleton (ed.), Gods
      and rituals. Garden City, N.Y.: American Museum of
      Natural History 1967, 307-335; and in her Anthropology and
      Social Change. London: Athlone Press, and New York:
      Humanities Press 1969, 144-172.

[A theoretical analysis of representative millennial
movements as basically religious movements — cargo cults,
Bantu independent churches, and, for North America, the
Ghost Dance (based largely on Moody).]

71 MÜHLMANN, Wilhelm E. (ed.). Rassen-Ethnien-Kulturen: Moderne
Ethnologie (Soziologische Texte, 24). Neuwied/Berlin:
Hermann Luchterhand 1964, 398 p.
[Pp. 323-339, Chiliasmus, Nativismus, Nationalismus —
similar to his Chiliasmus und Nativismus, see I, item 57.]

72 NEWBERY, J. W. E. The relevance of native religion. Monchanin
(Montreal) no. 48=8 (1), 1975, 13-20.
[Paper at Wilfred Laurier University symposium on
'Native religion reconsidered', October 1974: revivals of
drum dance, sacred pipe, purification, prophecy and power,
medicine wheel; relevance for the Indian situation, and for
Western societies.]

73 NORTHROP, Gordon Douglas. Pan-Indianism in the metropolis: a
case study of an emergent ethno-syncretic revitalization
movement. Michigan State University, Ph.D. dissertation
(anthropology) 1970, 679 p.
[Examines the North American Indian Association of
Detroit, from 1940, as a primarily secular form of revitalization, but with religious overtones and Christian borrow-
ings. Pp. 6-11, 16, Ghost Dance and peyotism in relation
to pan-Indianism; pp. 26-96, revitalization in relation to
stress, deprivation, etc.; pp. 620-625, religious dimensions of this movement.]

74 NOWICKA, Ewa. Ruchy millenarystyczne Indian Ameryki Północnej.
Euhemer-Przegląd Religioznowczy 3, 1972, 69-82.
[Millenarian movements of the North American Indians.]

75 OOSTERWAL, Gottfried. New religious movements: a challenge
to mission. Mission-Focus (Elkhart, Indiana) 3 (5), 1975,
1-11.
[A world-wide survey; general characteristics (born in
crisis situations, charismatic leaders, apocalyptic ideas,
urban spread, holistic outlook, lay nature); new attitudes
of acceptance by the churches, despite the shortcomings.
See also his important study Modern Messianic movements...,
I, item 323.]

76 PEARCE, Roy Harvey. The savages of America: a study of the
Indian and the idea of civilization. Baltimore: Johns
Hopkins Press 1953, 252 p.
[The American idea of the "savage" as applied to the
Indians; pp. 232-236, a critical analysis of J. S. French's
novel, item 1452.]

Theory

77 POSERN-ZIELIŃSKA, Mirosława. Koncepcje zbawienia w doktrywach
    ruchów religijno-politycznych Indian Ameryki północnej
    [The concepts of salvation in the doctrines of religious
    political movements of North American Indians]. Etnografia
    Polska 16 (2), 1972, 69-91; Eng. summary (pp. 90-91).
       [These movements are either (a) "soteric millenarianism",
    related to traditional beliefs, and escaping from the hard
    realities through help of an approaching era of abundance
    and happiness, or (b) "soteric eschatologism", related more
    to Christianity, and adjusting to a new way of life; the
    general movement has been from the former to the latter
    type.]

78 QUEIROZ, Maria Isaura Pereira de. Réforme et révolution dans
    les sociétés traditionelles. Histoire et ethnologie des
    mouvements messianiques. Paris: Editions Anthropos 1968,
    394 p., illus.; Span. trans., Historia y etnologia de los
    movimentos messiánicos.... Mexico City, 1969, 355 p.
       [Pp. 180-192 (Fr. edition) movements in North America —
    chiefly on the Ghost Dance as messianic; Indian Shaker
    Church as non-messianic; based on J. Mooney.]

79 RANGER, T[erence] O[sborn]. Review article: Magic and the
    millennium. African Religious Research (African Studies
    Center, Los Angeles) 3 (2), 1973, 27-33.
       [A historian's highly critical review of the theory and
    methodology of B. R. Wilson's item 371, as ethnocentric,
    identifying magic and religion and overworking the basic
    category of "thaumaturgy" to the point of uselessness.]

80 REICH, Wendy. The uses of folklore in revitalization move-
    ments. Folklore 82 (3), 1971, 233-243.
       [Folklore as an agent of change in revitalization move-
    ments, by creating an ideology for change, an explanation,
    justification and fortification of the movement, illus-
    trated by the peyote and Tangu cults.]

81 ROSEN, George. Social change and psychopathology in the emo-
    tional climate of millennial movements, in R. H. Lauer
    (ed.), item 62, 97-106. Repr. from M. Barkun, item 5,
    153-167.
       [These movements are socio-politico-psychological reac-
    tions to stress, and attempt a solution through creation
    of a new order or by withdrawal from the existing order;
    p. 105 (or 166), passing relation of the thesis to North
    American Indians.]

82 RYAN, Bryce. Die Bedeutung der Revitalizations-bewegungen für
    den sozialen Wandel in den Entwicklungsländern (Ger. trans.
    by H. Sager), in R. König (ed.), Aspekte der Entwicklungs-
    soziologie (Kölner Zeitschrift für Soziologie und

Sozialpsychologie, Sonderheft 13). Köln und Opladen: Westdeutscher Verlag 1969, 37-65.

83 SANFORD, Margaret. Revitalization movements as indicators of completed acculturation. Comparative Studies in Society and History 16 (4), 1974, 504-518.

84 SCHWARTZ, Hillel. The end of the beginning: millenarian studies, 1969-1975. Religious Studies Review 2 (3), 1976, 1-15, bibl. (= pp. 8-15).
    [A bibliographic essay on millennialism as studied in all religions, including new movements in primal societies, and with theoretical value — entered here in spite of its description of my own major article as "waffle".]

85 SIEGEL, Bernard J. and BEALS, Alan R. Conflict and faction-alist dispute. Journal of the Royal Anthropological Institute 90 (1), 1960, 107-117, bibl.

86 SMELSER, Neil J[oseph]. Theory of collective behaviour. London: Routledge and Kegan Paul 1962, xi + 436 p., illus.; New York: Free Press of Glencoe 1963, xi + 436 p., illus.
    [Sometimes applied to the analysis of new religious movements (e.g. by Berkhofer, item 15, for the Seneca) as value-oriented movements.]

87 SPENCER, Robert F. Review of G. Guariglia, Prophetismus und Heilserwartungs-Bewegungen...(1959). American Anthropologist 63, 1961, 596-598.
    [Exhibits a nominalist pushing of definitions too far, and adds little to our understanding through the resultant typology, which is artificial, insufficiently dynamic, and too "Vienna-schoolish" in its historical ethnology.]

88 SPICER, Edward H[olland]. Spanish-Indian acculturation in the Southwest. American Anthropologist 56 (4), 1954, 663-678; also pp. 678-684, two comments by others.
    [Pp. 670-674 are on the Yaqui and Mayo as examples; pp. 675-678, comparative analysis with eastern Pueblos and Athabascans (Navaho).]

89 SPICER, Edward H[olland]. Acculturation. International Encyclopaedia of the Social Sciences. New York: Macmillan/ Free Press, vol. 1, 1968, 21-27, bibl.
    [The emergence of this new field of study in the 1930s; its various sectors of enquiry, including "nativistic movements" (pp. 23-24). Valuable for theoretical orientation in the anthropological sciences.]

90 SPICER, Edward Holland. Acculturation. Encyclopaedia
    Britannica 1972, vol. 1, 83a–84b; references.
    [A simple account, with North American Indian examples.]

91 SPIER, Leslie, SUTTLES, Wayne and HERSKOVITS, M. J. Comment
    on Aberle's thesis of deprivation. Southwestern Journal
    of Anthropology 15, 1959, 84–88.
    [Cf. Aberle, item 1329.]

92 SPINDLER, George [Dearborn] and GOLDSCHMIDT, Walter. Experi-
    mental design in the study of culture change. Southwestern
    Journal of Anthropology 8 (1), 1952, 68–83; repr. Bobbs-
    Merrill Series, A210.
    [Pleads for use of more exact methods (statistical and
    analytical) as in other social sciences; example used is
    Menomini society, where social variables include peyote
    group, and several Catholic groups, including a Holy Name
    society.]

93 SPITZER, Allen and SPITZER, Mary L. Religious reorganization
    among the Montana Blackfeet. Review of Religious Research
    2 (1), 1960, 19–35.
    [No reports of new religious movements, although the Sun
    Dance has been revived for socio-cultural reasons; presents
    a useful classification system in terms of a continuum
    embracing "folk", "cultural", "nominal" and "formal" (i.e.
    orthodox in belief and practice) Catholicism.]

94 STARKLOFF, Carl F. "Evangelization" and Native Americans.
    Studies in the International Apostolate of Jesuits (Jesuit
    Missions, Washington, D.C.) 4 (1), 1975, 1–37.
    [Pp. 2–6, description of the surviving Kennekuk church
    near Horton, Kansas, and its worship; p. 27, the new
    prophet figure in Indian religions; the remainder offers a
    phenomenological analysis of religions, with special refer-
    ence to Indian religions, as a basis for Christian under-
    standing, and is almost identical with his report,
    item 325.]

95 STIPE, Claude Edwin. Eastern Dakota acculturation: the role
    of agents of culture change. University of Minnesota,
    Ph.D. dissertation (anthropology) 1968, 299 p.
    [Missionaries, fur-traders, and government officials —
    threats of force, economic advantages, and assistance of
    half-breeds were more influential factors than the person-
    alities of the white agents.]

96 THOMAS, Prentice Marquet, Jr. Ecological and social correlates
    of religious movements among North American Indians.
    Tulane University, Ph.D. dissertation (anthropology) 1972,
    272 p.

[Explores the correlations between new religious movements and (1) changes in subsistence techniques — high
correlation (2) related changes in occupational roles –
positive correlation (3) intense contact situations, (e.g.
missionary activity and length of foreign domination) —
inhibit acceptance of a movement (4) cultural complexity —
positive connection (5) political complexity — no
association.]

97   THOMAS, Robert K.   The role of the church in Indian adjustment.
     Kansas Journal of Sociology 3 (1), 1967, 20-28.
          [The place of religion in society, and in social change;
     p. 22, the difficulties when there is disparity of power
     between the agents of a new religion and the recipients;
     pp. 22-23, the three examples of successful introduction
     of Christianity — the Yaqui, the Papagos and the Cherokee;
     by a part-Cherokee anthropologist.]

98   TOYNBEE, Arnold J[oseph].   A study of history.   London: Oxford
     University Press 1939.
          [Vol. 5, 328-332, on North American Indian prophet move-
     ments, as reaction to western pressures, and morally
     creative.]

99   TURNER, Harold W[alter].   A new field in the history of
     religions.   Religion: Journal of Religion and Religions
     1 (1), 1971, 15-23.
          [An attempt to present this subject as a new field of
     study with its own working boundaries.]

100   TURNER, Harold W[alter].   Old and new religions among North
      American Indians: missiological impressions and reflec-
      tions.   Missiology 1 (2), 1973, 47-65.
           [Seven theses summarizing the relation of Indians to
      White culture and Christianity; the seventh, pp. 60-64,
      concerns the new religious movements.]

101   TURNER, Harold Walter.   Tribal religious movements, new.
      Encyclopaedia Britannica 1974, vol. 18, 697-705.
           [Pp. 697-701 on theoretical questions and general
      aspects.]

102   VILA VILAR, Luisa.   Aculturación de los grupos indígenas de
      Texas segun la documentación española del siglo XVIII, in
      Actas y memorias, Congreso International de Americanistas
      XXXVI, Sevilla 1964.   Seville, 1966, vol. 2, 161-165.
           [Response to missions showed a wide variety, from
      acceptance to opposition.]

103   VOGET, Fred W. American Indian reformations and acculturation.
      Bulletin 190 (Anthropological Series, 60): (Contributions
      to Anthropology, 1960, Pt. 2.). Ottawa: National Museum
      of Canada 1960, 1-13.
         [With special reference to Handsome Lake, Indian Shakers,
      and peyotism; good theoretical analysis.]

104   VOGET, Fred W. Reflections on acculturation processes and
      stages: a reply to Deward E. Walker, Jr. Northwest
      Anthropological Research Notes 10 (2), 1976, 197-208,
      illus., bibl.
         [Comment on D. E. Walker's item 109.]

105   VOGHT, Martha. Shamans and padres: the religion of the
      Southern Californian mission Indians. The Pacific Histor-
      ical Review (Los Angeles) 36 (4), 1967, 363-373.
         [The Christo-pagan syncretism developed by mission
      Indians.]

106   VOGT, Evon Z. The acculturation of American Indians. Annals,
      American Academy of Political and Social Sciences 311, May
      1957, 137-146; repr. in F. P. Prucha (ed.), The Indian in
      American history. New York: Holt, Rinehart and Winston
      1971, 99-115.
         [A valuable survey, with references to Ghost Dance and
      peyote cult as examples of pan-Indianism.]

107   WALKER, Deward E[dgar], Jr. Some limitations of the renascence
      concept in acculturation: the Nez Percé case. Midcontin-
      ental American Studies Journal 6 (2), 1965, 135-148;
      revised and expanded in S. Levine and N. O. Lurie (eds.),
      item 238 (Penguin ed., 236-256).

108   WALKER, Deward E[dgar], Jr. Conflict and schism in Nez Percé
      acculturation; a study of religion and politics. Pullman,
      Washington: Washington State University Press 1968,
      171 p., maps.
         [Pp. 28-29, 31-39, Tulim syncretist cult from 18th c.;
      pp. 34, 48-52, 87, ipnucililpt neo-primal cult from mid-
      19th c.; pp. 67-72, three independent churches, from 1889;
      pp. 95-123 et passim, two main and other incipient
      Pentecostal sects, with Assemblies of God background;
      pp. 133-139, survey and conclusions; pp. 139-146, com-
      parative findings, of theoretical value.]

109   WALKER, Deward E[dgar], Jr. Stage and statistical models in
      Plateau acculturation. Northwestern Anthropological
      Research Notes 4 (2), 1970, 153-165.
         [A critique of Voget's model of American Indian accult-
      uration, and in favour of statistical models.]

110   WALLACE, Anthony F. C. Study of processes of organization and
      revitalization of psychological and socio-cultural systems,
      based on a comparative study of nativistic revivals. Amer-
      ican Philosophical Society Year-book 1957. 1958, 310-311.
          [Outlines of mathematical theory of organization appli-
      cable beyond the problem of revitalization movements.]

111   WALLACE, Anthony F. C. Revitalization movements, American
      Anthropologist 58 (2), 1956, 264-281; repr. in B.
      McLaughlin (ed.), Studies in social movements. New York
      and London: The Free Press and Collier-Macmillan 1969,
      30-52; and elsewhere.
          [An influential theoretical framework, interpreting
      movements as attempts to relieve strain by remaking
      culture.]

112   WALLACE, Anthony F. C. Mazeway resynthesis: a bio-cultural
      theory of religious inspiration. Transactions of the New
      York Academy of Sciences Series II, 18 (7), 1956, 626-638.
          [Pp. 626-631 specifically on Handsome Lake, especially
      on the question of the change in his whole view of his
      culture during his eight-hour trance; this is discussed in
      terms of the re-organization of the individual's mental
      "mazeway".]

113   WALLACE, Anthony F. C. Stress and rapid personality changes.
      International Record of Medicine no. 2886 = 169 (12),
      1956, 761-774.
          [A detailed comparison of the prophet Handsome Lake and
      Hung-Sui-Tshuen (Taiping revolt in China) to test the
      thesis that rapid personality change in religious prophets
      represents "the organism's response to extreme stress,
      after confusional deterioration has reached a critical
      point" and a physiological mechanism is triggered.]

114   WALLACE, Anthony F. C. The Dekanawidah myth analyzed as the
      record of a revitalization movement. Ethnohistory 5 (2),
      1958, 118-130.
          [Suggests that it derives from a revitalization movement,
      with a schizoid personality accounting for Hiawatha and a
      mythical prophet.]

115   WALLACE, Anthony F. C. Cultural determinants of response to
      hallucinatory experience. AMA Archives of General
      Psychiatry (American Medical Association) 1 (1), 1959,
      58-69.
          [A theoretical account of possession, trance, etc.]

116   WALLACE, Anthony F. C. Exporting the American idea: Quaker
      technology among the Senecas. Saturday Review (New York)
      46 (14), 6 April 1963, 54-56.

[Outlines his revitalization theory with a reference to
Handsome Lake; this movement, and its Quaker stimulation,
taken as a model for current United Nations Third World
development programmes.]

117   WALLACE, Anthony F. C.   Revitalization movements in develop-
      ment, in Richard J. Ward (ed.), The challenge of develop-
      ment: theory and practice. Chicago: Aldine Publishing
      Co. 1967, 448-454.
      [A succinct outline of his revitalization theory;
      pp. 451-453, Handsome Lake movement as an example.]

118   WALLACE, Anthony F. C.   Nativistic movements.   Encyclopaedia
      Britannica 1969, vol. 16, 96^{a-b}.
      [A brief survey, following his own theory and typology,
      involving a culture-area classification based on typical
      forms in each area.]

119   WALLACE, Anthony F. C.
      [See also Vol. 1, items 78-84, for his further theoret-
      ical discussions.]

120   WEIGLE, Marta [=Mary Martha] (comp.). A penitente bibliography.
      Albuquerque: University of New Mexico Press 1976, 162 p.
      [An almost exhaustive bibliography of a long-standing
      and independent folk religious movement among Mexican
      Americans in New Mexico, useful for comparative purposes
      because of the similarity of Mexican American folk cults
      with primal societies' syncretist religions; note espe-
      cially the similarity of Penitente and Yaqui/Mayo Easter
      rites.]

121   WEISER, Neil. The effects of prophetic disconfirmation of the
      committed. Review of Religious Research 16 (1), Fall
      1974, 19-30, notes on movements mentioned, bibl.
      [On the continuation of millennial beliefs as long as
      the need exists, and despite any particular failures in
      the prophecies.]

122   WILKINSON, Paul. Social movement (Key Concepts in political
      science). London: Pall Mall Press; London, New York,
      etc.: Macmillan, 1971, 176 p.
      [Ch. 4 (= pp. 55-79), Religious movement, sect, millen-
      arism: discusses theories of religious development,
      political relevance, etc.]

123   WILLNER, Ann Ruth and WILLNER, Dorothy. The rise and role of
      charismatic leaders. Annals of the American Academy of
      Political and Social Science no. 358, March 1965, 77-88.
      [Their functions in societies undergoing great changes,
      and their use of myths and sacred symbols in support of
      their role.]

124   WILSON, Bryan R[onald].   <u>Magic and the millennium</u>....   (see
         item 371).
         [A massive world survey within a theoretical sociological
         framework based on his earlier study of "sects" in Western
         societies; "revolutionist" and "thaumaturgical" as the two
         main forms in Third World movements, and especially the
         latter, which is interpreted as magical (this, for Wilson,
         is the same as religious). See review, T. O. Ranger,
         item 79.]

125   YINGER, J[ohn] Milton.   <u>The scientific study of religion</u>.
         New York: Macmillan 1970, x + 593 p., illus.
         [Ch. 15, Religion and minority status, includes sections
         on revitalization movements, cargo cults (pp. 317-319),
         North American Indian movements (pp. 319-324), and among
         American Negroes (pp. 324-326).]

126   ZYGMUNT, Joseph F.   When prophecies fail. A theoretical per-
         spective on the comparative evidence, in M. Barkun (ed.),
         item 5, 245-268.
         [The failure of prophecies as leading to the break-up of
         millenarian movements, or to their transformation by
         institutionalization; draws on a wide range of literature.]

General

This is a comprehensive category for items that discuss the movements in a general way, or that refer to more than one movement or
theme, and so are of mixed content as far as the sections of this
volume are concerned. Important material on any particular movement
may therefore be found in this section rather than in its own special
named section; the index of movements, etc., draws the reader's attention to these further items. An exception has been made in the case
of major works on particular movements, which also discuss other
movements in a subsidiary way; it would be unfortunate if such important items were absent from their obvious sections. Again the subject
index of movements takes care of the subsidiary material.

Minor movements, or those on which there is very little literature,
are also included in the "general" section rather than provided with
their own. Thus we include the so-called "Buzzard" or "Southern
Death cult" and the Pan-Indian Ecumenical Conference, but not Yuwipi
or the Sun Dance where the literature is more extensive.

127   ADAMSON, Hoebel E.   The Comanche sun dance and messianic out-
          break of 1873.   American Anthropologist 43, 1941, 301-303.

128   ALEXANDER H[artley] B[urr].   Communion with deity (American),
          in J. Hastings (ed.), Encyclopaedia of Religion and Ethics,
          vol. 3, 1910, 743a-744a.
          [Ghost Dance (Black Coyote and Wovoka), and John Slocum
          (Indian Shaker Church) — their revelations of deity.]

129   ALEXANDER, H[artley] B[urr].   Secret societies (American), in
          J. Hastings (ed.), Encyclopaedia of Religion and Ethics,
          vol. 11, 1920, 305b.
          [Briefly on new movements as hostile to older secret
          societies and traditions: Ojibwa drum religion, Handsome
          Lake, Kennekuk, Tenskwatawa, Smohalla and Wovoka.]

130   AMERICAN HERITAGE, EDITORS OF (including Alvin M. Josephy and
          William Brandon).   The American heritage book of Indians.

New York: American Heritage Publishing Co. 1961, 424 p.,
illus., maps; with William Brandon as author, New York:
Dell Publishing Co. 1964 etc., 384 p., maps.
   [Dell edn., pp. 121-122, Popé's revolt; p. 203,
Tenskwatawa; pp. 328-329, token reference to Ghost Dance
and Wovoka; p. 367, similar reference to Native American
Church.]

131   ANDERSON, Charles A.   Index of American Indian correspondence.
      Journal of the Presbyterian Historical Society 31 (1),
      March 1953, 63-70.
         [14,000 letters from 1833-1893, in library of the
      Presbyterian Historical Society, Witherspoon Building,
      Philadelphia, well indexed by author, Indian tribe and file
      order under general call no. MS/In 25; see the following
      of special relevance to prophets or new movements:
      Kickapoos-Kansas (1846-59, 1850-64, 1883-84), Senecas
      (1843-91), Spokanes (1872-75), and Dakotas (1845-93).]

132   ARISS, Robert.   Indians of Western North America.   (Science
      Series 19:   Anthropology no. 1).   Los Angeles: Los Angeles
      County Museum 1955, 27 p.
         [Pp. 15-16, Plains Indians' "non-material culture" —
      popular outline of vision quest, Sun Dance, peyote cult,
      and 1890 Ghost Dance.]

133   ASTROV, Margot [Luise Therese] (ed.).   The winged serpent: an
      anthology of American Indian prose and poetry.   New York:
      John Day Co. 1946, xi + 366 p., bibl.; repr. as American
      Indian prose and poetry.   New York: Capricorn Books, and
      Toronto: Longmans Canada 1962, 366 p.
         [Pp. 85-86, Smohalla's famous speech on the earth as his
      mother, with comments; pp. 143-145, Ghost Dance: seven
      songs from Mooney, item 508 and comments accepting Spier's
      view of Ghost Dance antecedents being in the N.W. Prophet
      Dance.]

134   BARBEAU, [Charles] Marius.   Fameux Peaux-Rouges d'Amérique du
      Nord-est au Nord-ouest (Collection Indiens d'Amérique).
      Montreal: Librairie Beauchemin 1966, 284 p., illus.
         [Pp. 126-135, Handsome Lake; pp. 255-256, prophet Bini.
      Popular but reliable accounts by an anthropologist.]

135   BARBER, Bernard.   Acculturation and messianic movements.
      American Sociological Review 6 (5), 1941, 663-669, bibl.;
      repr. in W. A. Lessa and E. Z. Vogt (eds.), Reader in
      Comparative Religion.   New York: Harper and Row 1965,
      474-478.
         [Mainly on the Ghost Dance; p. 668, peyote as "an alter-
      native response" of a passive nature; both regarded as
      correlated with widespread deprivation.]

General

136   BARNOUW, Victor. Acculturation and personality among the
       Wisconsin Chippewa (Memoirs, American Anthropological
       Association, 72) = American Anthropologist 52 (4:2), 1950,
       1-152.
           [Pp. 65-68, Shawano cult of Tenskwatawa; pp. 68-70, the
       Ghost Dance; pp. 126-127, peyote cult.]

137   BASS, Altha Leah (Bierbower).
           See SWEEZY, Carl, item 334.

138   BATTEY, Thomas C. The life and adventures of a Quaker among
       the Indians. Boston: Lee and Shepard 1875, xii + 339 p.,
       illus.; repr. Norman: University of Oklahoma Press 1968.
           [Pp. 302-303, Isatai, the young Comanche medicine man,
       with new procedures; early 1870s.]

139   BAUGH, Timothy G. Revitalization movements among the Kiowa
       and Kiowa Apache. Papers in Anthropology (University of
       Oklahoma) 2, Spring 1970, 66-83.
           [Wallace's revitalization theory applied to three
       movements — Daketan's, Ghost Dance and peyote cult; the
       first two failed to restructure society; the third is
       still seeking this goal.]

140   BEALS, Ralph L[eon]. The aboriginal culture of the Cáhita
       Indians (Ibero-Americana, 19). Berkeley and Los Angeles:
       University of California Press 1943, 93 p., map, illus.,
       bibl.
           [Pp. 66-68, Cáhita initiation ceremonies for the Chung-
       ishnish cult, with longer extract in English translation
       from Pérez de Ribas, item 291, and further Spanish extract
       on pp. 83-84, n84; pp. 68-70, modern religious organization
       of the Yaqui and Mayo.]

141   BEAUVAIS, Eugene. La fontaine de jouvence et le Jourdain dans
       la tradition des Antilles et de la Floride. Le Museon
       (Louvain) 3, 1884, 404-429.
           [Especially among the aboriginal Taino of the Caribbean,
       some of whom were in Florida; a traditional millennialism
       corresponding to the search for paradise by the Guaraní,
       etc. in South America.]

142   BENEDICT, Ruth. Patterns of culture. Boston: Houghton
       Mifflin 1959, 291 p.
           [Pp. 85-89, drugs, including peyote, used in the vision
       quest, except among the Pueblos; p. 92, brief reference to
       Ghost Dance, as vision-seeking, not ecstasy-producing.]

143   BILLINGTON, Ray Allen. Westward expansion. A history of the
       American frontier. New York: Macmillan; London: Collier
       Macmillan, 4th ed. 1974, 840 p.

[Pp. 264, 265, 267, Tenskwatawa as "a one-eyed, epileptic
medicine man"; pp. 577-578, brief account of the Ghost
Dance and Wounded Knee.]

144 BLAIR, Emma Helen (ed.). Indian tribes of the Upper Mississippi
Valley and region of the Great Lakes as described by N.
Perrot... B. de la Potherie...M. Marston... and Thomas
Forsyth, United States agent at Fort Armstrong. Cleveland,
Ohio: Arthur H. Clark Co., vol. 2, 1912, 412 p., illus.
[P. 272, prophets; pp. 273-279, Tenskwatawa, based on
T. Forsyth, see item 1451; pp. 280-281, Kennekuk, also
using Forsyth; pp. 297-298, Winnebago "mescal-eaters", i.e.
peyotists, based on Roddy, see item 1083. Also uses
J. Mooney.]

145 BOISSEVAIN, Ethel and ROBERTS, Ralph, III. The minutes and
ledgers of the Narragansett tribe of Indians, 1850-1865;
an intimate glimpse into the economic and social life of
an acculturated Indian tribe on the threshold of detribalization. Man in the Northeast (Rindge, New Hampshire) 7,
1974, 3-28, illus., bibl.
[Of theoretical interest. Also pp. 9, 12, on the
Narragansetts' church, its origins and rebuilding.]

146 BRANDON, William. The last Americans. New York: McGraw
Hill 1974, 553 p., bibl.
[Revision and extension of item 130.]

147 BRANDON, William.
See AMERICAN HERITAGE, EDITORS OF, item 130.

148 BRANT, Charles S. White contact and cultural disintegration
among the Kiowa Apache. Plains Anthropologist 9, 1964,
8-13.
[P. 10, peyote (brief reference); pp. 11-13, Ghost Dance
(more fully).]

149 BROWN, William L. The Mohonk conference. The Southern
Workman 38 (11), 1909, 583-586.
[Discussions of American Indians, the Philippines, Puerto
Rico, and Hawaii, with an assimilation philosophy. See
also ANON, the platform of the Mohonk Conference,
pp. 634-635.]

150 BURLIN, Natalie (Curtis) (ed.). The Indians' book: an offering by the American Indians of...the songs and legends of
their race. New York/London: Harper and Brothers 1907,
xxx + 572 p., plates.
[Pp. 55-56, 109-110, 257-260, the Grass Dance of Plains
Indians; pp. 162-165, 188-193, peyote; pp. 161-162, 201-
202, Hand Game; pp. 41-48, 114-116, 200, Ghost Dance.]

151   BURNETTE, Robert and KOSTER, John. The road to Wounded Knee.
        New York: Bantam Books 1974, 332 p.
            [A Sioux Indian leader (Burnette) and a white journalist
        give the Indian viewpoint; pp. 10, 148-150, Ghost Dance;
        pp. 23, 37, 41, 91, Native American Church; ch. 2 (= pp. 19-
        41), "The rebirth of Indian religion", includes stories of
        healing, yuwipi (pp. 26-28), Sun Dance (pp. 29-31), vision
        quest (31-32), etc.]

151A   BURNS, Robert Ignatius. The Jesuits and the Indian wars of the
        northwest (Yale Western Americana Series, 11). New Haven:
        Yale University Press 1966, 493 p., illus., maps.
            [Pp. 17, 212-213, the Prophet dance from 1830 as a sab-
        batarian syncretism with Christianity; pp. 17-18, the Nez
        Perce and other delegations to St. Louis, and the later
        "fraudulent accounts of their search for the Bible" (cf.
        items 376 and others noted there); p. 365 and index,
        Dreamer religion as a revised "messianic form of the old
        Ghost Dance faith" in the 1870s.]

152   CABBAGE, James Richard. Comparative forms in the call narra-
        tives of Israelite and North American Indian prophets.
        Candler School of Theology, Emory University, Atlanta,
        Georgia, research paper, December 1971. 37 p. Mimeo.
            [Shows similarities and differences; copy held in Depart-
        ment of Religious Studies, Aberdeen University.]

153   CANADIAN GOVERNMENT (Canada Broadcasting Commission). People
        of the Sacred Circle. Toronto: Canada Broadcasting
        Commission 1975, colour film.
            [The Pan-Indian Ecumenical Conference of 1975 on the
        Morley Reserve, Alberta, with 1,500 Indians; on religion,
        culture, language and survival of Indian way of life.
        Broadcast B-3, November 1975, in Man Alive programme.]

154   CARTER, E. Russell. The gift is rich. New York: Friendship
        Press 1955, 117 p., illus.
            [P. 56, brief note of Christian elements in the peyote
        cult, and on the Kennekuk Church, Kickapoo Reservation,
        near Horton, Kansas, as still existing. Chs. 7, 9, appre-
        ciative outline of Indian primal religion.]

155   CATLIN, George. Letters and notes on the manners, customs,
        and condition of the North American Indians. London:
        the author 1841, 2 vols., 264 p. and 266 p., illus; London:
        H. G. Bohn 1845, etc.; many further editions, e.g. 3rd ed.,
        London: D. Bogue 1884, repr. New York: Dover 1973 and
        London: Constable 1973; repr. Barrington, Illinois: Peter
        Woolf 1976.
            [Original and later eds., vol. 2, pp. 98-99, Kennekuk
        and Ahtonwetuck, with Catlin's paintings of them (p. 98,

with the prayer stick illustration, and the traders'
account of Kennekuk's association with a Methodist missionary, reprinted in G. Mallery, item 760), pp. 508-509;
pp. 116-118, Tenskwatawa and Catlin's painting of him;
pp. 214-215, the Sac and Fox berdache custom.]

156   CAZENEUVE, Jean. Spectacles rituels et changement culturel
      dans le Nouveau-Mexique et l'Arizona, in J. Poillon and
      P. Miranda (comps.), Échanges et Communications...offerts
      à Claude Levi-Strauss.... The Hague and Paris: Mouton
      1970, vol. I, 502-511.
         [Pp. 505-506, a shorter version of the interpretation of
      the Yaqui Easter dramas given in his item 1481; pp. 510-
      511, the peyote cult as syncretist, and its future — see
      his item 823.]

157   CHAMBERLAIN, Alexander F. "New religions" among the North
      American Indians, etc. Journal of Religious Psychology 6
      (1), 1913, 1-49, bibl.
         [An important early and wide survey, drawing on primary
      sources, with long quoted extracts; the "etc." covers
      Mexico, Central and South America, an Asian and a
      Philippine movement; curiously the peyote cult is omitted.
      A good introductory overview.]

158   CODERE, Helen. Kwakuitl, in E. H. Spicer (ed.), item 316,
      431-516.
         [The history of Kwakiutl culture change from the 18th c.
      in relation to European contact; pp. 502-503, Kwakuitl
      Anglicanism.]

159   COE, Ralph T. Sacred circles. Two thousand years of North
      American Indian art. Hayward Gallery, London, 7 October
      1976-16 January 1977. London: Arts Council of Great
      Britain 1976, 236 p., illus.
         [Midéwiwin Society, pp. 73, 76, and illustrations
      no. 140a and b (pouches), 160a and b (scrolls), 163
      (medicine bag); Ghost Dance, p. 167 (praying), and illus-
      trations no. 421 (dress), 483 (album of drawings); peyote
      cult, illustration no. 485 (paraphernalia bag).]

160   COLLINS, June McCormick. Growth of class distinctions and
      political authority among the Skagit Indians during the
      contact period. American Anthropologist 52 (3), 1950,
      331-342.
         [P. 340, Slabebtikud's cult in mid-19th c. as an example
      of syncretist cults with formal organization, beliefs
      and rites, introduced by self-appointed Indian
      "missionaries" — set against discussion of contemporary
      changes in Skagit life.]

General

161   CONGREGATIONALIST. Article in The Congregationalist (Boston)
       28 April, 1932.
          [Cited by G. W. Hinman, item 218, as containing account
       of a Zuñi Indian returning home before 1820, with a Spanish
       Bible, and starting a new religion. (The Congregationalist
       was the title used between 1929 and 1934, with other names
       before and since.)]

162   COTTERILL, R. S. The Southern Indians. The story of the
       civilized tribes before removal (The Civilization of the
       American Indian, 38). Norman: University of Oklahoma
       Press 1954 etc., 258 p., illus.
          [Pp. 178-180, 188, the "prophets" in the Creek War,
       1813-1814, under Josiah Francis.]

163   CRANE, K[atherine] E[lizabeth]. See under Dictionary of
       American Biography.

164   CURTIS, Edward S[heriff]. The North American Indian..., ed.
       F. W. Hodge. Prospect, Seattle: E. S. Curtis; Cambridge,
       Mass.: Harvard University Press, 20 vols. 1907-1930;
       repr. New York: Johnson Reprint Corp. 1970; repr., ed.
       J. E. Brown, Millerton, N.Y.: Aperture Press 1972.
          [Vol. 7, pp. 77-78, the Dreamer cult among tribes of
       Columbia; especially the Sanpoil account of its origin,
       and of their dreamer prophet Skolaskin — as background to
       later Christian-influenced developments. Vol. 16, pp. 46-
       47, 53-59, peyote (Tiwa and Keres tribes). Vol. 19,
       pp. 199-213, the peyote cult, with description of the Oto
       rite, four songs (text and musical score) and good
       photos.]

165   DAUGHERTY, Mary Ann. Nativistic religious movements among
       Indians of the United States. University of Arizona,
       Tucson, M.A. thesis (anthropology) 1964.

166   D'AZEVEDO, W. L. (ed.). The Washo Indians of California and
       Nevada (Anthropological Papers, University of Utah, 67).
       Salt Lake City: University of Utah Press 1963; repr. 1971.
          [See papers by Downs, item 176; Leis, item 963; Scotch
       and Scotch, item 1095.]

167   DE ANGULO, Jaime and FREELAND, L. S. A new religious movement
       in northern central California. American Anthropologist
       31 (2), 1929, 265-270.
          [New healer-reformers among the Pomo after a personal
       revelatory experience, rejecting the old shamanist methods
       and with a strict and teetotal ethic, but not hostile to
       the Maru cult; named individuals as examples.]

168   DELORIA, Vine, Jr. Religion and the modern American Indian.
       Current History 67, December 1974, 250-253.
           [A survey article with brief references to the Handsome
       Lake religion (p. 251), the Pan-Indian Ecumenical movement
       (pp. 251-252), the Native American Church (p. 252) and
       Don Juan, the Yaqui medicine man (p. 252).]

169   DENSMORE, Frances. The influence of hymns on the form of
       Indian songs. American Anthropologist 40 (1), 1938,
       175-177.
           [Especially on the paired-phrase pattern in Ghost Dance
       and peyote songs.]

170   DENSMORE, Frances. Native songs of two hybrid ceremonies
       among the American Indians. American Anthropologist
       43 (1), 1941, 77-82.
           [Pp. 78-79, Holy Week among the Yaqui in Arizona near
       Tucson and at Guadalupe; pp. 79-82, Native American
       Church.]

171   DESROCHE, Henri et al. Dieux d'hommes. Dictionnaire des
       messianismes et millénarismes de l'ère chrétienne. Paris,
       the Hague: Mouton 1969, 281 p.
           [Unsigned survey articles, with short bibliographies:
       p. 129, Ghost Dance; p. 137, Hand Game; p. 261, Wovoka.
       See also the important introduction, pp. 1-41, a theoret-
       ical discussion of the origins, typologies, etc., of
       messianism.]

172   DICK, Henry. Report on the 3rd Pan-Indian Ecumenical Con-
       ference, Stoney Reserve, August 1972, to the Commission
       of Home Ministries, General Conference Mennonite Church,
       Newton, Kansas, 31 August 1972. 7 p. Mimeo.
           [Unpublished but contains nothing confidential; the
       observer found difficulty in accepting the form and atti-
       tudes of the Conference, but reports its concerns as
       including the search for Indian identity, the alcohol
       problem, and how to relate to whites who had much to learn
       from Indians.]

173   DICTIONARY OF AMERICAN BIOGRAPHY. London: Oxford University
       Press; New York: Charles Scribner's Sons; 1928-1944.
           [Good outlines of up to one page on the following:
       Skaniadariio (= Handsome Lake): A. C. P[arker], vol. 17,
       194; Smohalla: R. A. W[arner], vol. 17, 371-372; Tecumseh
       (for Tenskwatawa, his brother): K. E. C[rane], vol. 18,
       358-360; Tenskwatawa: K. E. C[rane], vol. 17, 375-376;
       Wovoka: K. E. C[rane], vol. 20, 541.]

174   DORSEY, George A[mos]. The Cheyenne (Field Columbian Museum.
       Publications 90, 103, Anthropological series 9, 1-2).

Chicago: The Museum 1905: vol. 1, Ceremonial organization; vol. 2, The sun dance.
[Vol. 1, pp. 1-5 ff., the pre-contact Great Arrow
prophet, a culture-hero among the Southern Cheyenne, and
founder of Bow-String warrior society; included as an example of the conception of "prophet" in aboriginal
religion.]

175 DORSINFANG-SMETS, Annie. La recherche du salut chez les
     Indiens d'Amérique, in Religions du salut: Annales du
     Centre d'Étude des Religions (Institut de Sociologie
     Solvay, Brussels) 2, 1962, 113-125, illus.
     [Pp. 114-116, Guarani, Tupinamba and Taino (Caribbean)
     search for paradise; pp. 117-118, Ghost Dance; pp. 119-
     125, Midéwiwin and other societies: all as examples of
     indigenous millennial traditions.]

176 DOWNS, James F. Differential response to white contact:
     Paiute and Washo, in W. L. d'Azevedo (ed.), item 166,
     115-137.
     [Pp. 129-130, Washo indifference to the Ghost Dance;
     pp. 132, 133, peyote cult.]

177 DOWNS, James F. The two worlds of the Washo. An Indian tribe
     of California and Nevada. New York: Holt, Rinehart &
     Winston 1966, 113 p.
     [P. 91, "Captain Jim's" nativist revival, 1890s; pp. 93-
     94, "Nativism" (Paiute Ghost Dance) and its small effect
     on the Washo; pp. 102-104, "Peyote, the new way", since
     c. 1932, through a Ute shaman, Lone Bear; then in 1938,
     Franklin York, a Washo, spread it widely. In 1966, Washo
     from San Francisco Bay area were making week-end trips to
     Washo area for the nearest Peyote meetings.]

178 DRAKE, Benjamin. The life and adventures of Black Hawk, with
     sketches of Keokuk, the Sac and Fox Indians and the late
     Black Hawk War. Cincinnati: George Conclin 1838, 252 p.,
     illus; 7th ed., improved, 1844, etc., 288 p., illus.
     [Pp. 177, 206, Wabokieshiek, with the prophet's address
     quoted; p. 208, his reply to the President of the U.S.A.
     after Black Hawk's group had been addressed by the latter.]

179 DRAKE, Samuel Gardner. Biography and history of the Indians
     of North America (commonest title). 1st ed. as Indian
     biography..., Boston, 1832; various titles and many eds.
     including 15th ed. 1860 revised and enlarged as The
     aboriginal races of North America. New York: Hurst & Co.
     1880, 788 p.; 8th ed. repr. as The book of the Indians.
     New York: AMS Press 1976.
     [Includes c. 2 pp. on each of the following prophets:
     (1880 ed.) pp. 398-400, Creek prophets in the 1814 war;

pp. 624-625, Elskwatawa (= Tenskwatawa) — his call through
a vision, and visit to the Creeks in 1811; pp. 658, 659,
descriptions of Wabokieshiek, Sac-Winnebago prophet in the
1830s; note also p. 286, quoting Increase Mather's account
of the vision and call of Squando, the Socokis chief,
c. 1670; from Increase Mather's A brief history... (1676).]

180   DRIVER, Harold E[dson]. Indians of North America. Chicago:
      University of Chicago Press (1961) 1969, xviii + 668 p.,
      illus., maps, bibl.
         [A standard work. Pp. 98-102 and index, and maps 12-14,
      peyote and Native American Church; pp. 420-422, 431, 606,
      Midéwiwin as voluntary secret society; Ghost Dance, see
      index for brief references.]

181   DRUCKER, Philip and HEIZER, Robert F[leming]. To make my name
      good: a re-examination of the southern Kwakiutl potlatch.
      Berkeley and Los Angeles: University of California Press
      1967, 160 p., illus.
         [P. 21, the north Pacific coasts of North America as not
      producing "nativistic" cults; the Indian Shaker Church as
      a different movement; pp. 22-23, the various Christian
      movements — Catholic, Anglican, and Pentecostal.]

182   DRURY, Clifford Merrill (ed.). The diaries and letters of
      Henry H. Spalding and Bowen Smith relating to the Nez
      Perce mission 1838-1842. Glendale, California: Arthur H.
      Clark Co. 1958, 379 p.
         [Pp. 106-109, 140-141, 146-147, 170-171, selections from
      Smith's letters of 1839-1840, with comments on Nez Percé
      religion, indifference to Christianity, and the problems
      of a missionary: as background to D. E. Walker item 359,
      which reproduces extracts.]

183   DU BOIS, Cora Alice. The Feather-Cult of the Middle Columbia
      (General Series in Anthropology, 7). Menasha: George
      Banta Pub. Co. 1938, 45 p., illus., map.
         [Pp. 11-19, Smohalla and contemporary prophets; pp. 20-
      42, Feather Cult; pp. 20-22, new version of longhouse
      religion by Jake Hunt, c. 1904; also includes Indian
      Shakers, passim.]

184   DUSENBERRY, Verne. The Montana Cree: a study in religious
      persistence (Acta Universitatis Stockholmiensis, Stock-
      holm Studies in Comparative Religion, 3). Stockholm:
      Almqvist & Wiksell 1962, 280 p., illus.
         [Pp. 18-27, 75-76, revivals of traditional religion by
      the Cree on Rocky Boy reservation, but with modifications
      from other tribes or Christianity — i.e. renewals rather
      than new movements, especially: pp. 165-172, Spirit Lodge
      (similar to Yuwipi cult), pp. 172-175, Smoke Lodge;

pp. 180–183, Hand Game; pp. 179–180, Painted Tipi cult;
pp. 58, 119, 175–179, Native American Church as the main
new movement; pp. 218, 228, Midéwiwin (similar to the
Ojibwa) till 1938.]

185   DYER, [Mrs.] D. B.   "Fort Reno"; or, Picturesque "Cheyenne and
      Arrapahoe army life" before the opening of Oklahoma.   New
      York: Dillingham 1896, 216 p., plates.
         [Pp. 89–90, peyote; pp. 184–187, Ghost Dance.]

186   ELIADE, Mircea.   Le chamanisme et les techniques archaïques de
      l'extase.   Paris: Payot 1951, 447 p.; Eng. trans., rev.
      and enlarged, Shamanism. Archaic techniques of ecstasy.
      London: Routledge and Kegan Paul, and New York: Bollingen
      Foundation (distributed by Pantheon Books) 1964, xxiii +
      610 p.; repr. Princeton: Princeton University Press 1970,
      xxiii + 610 p.
         [Pp. 314–319, and index, Midéwiwin; pp. 320–322, and
      index, Ghost Dance (in Eng. trans.).]

187   ERDOES, Richard.   The Sun Dance people. The Plains Indians,
      their past and present.   New York: A. A. Knopf 1972,
      218 p., illus.
         [Pp. 178–186, Ghost Dance and Wounded Knee; pp. 99–104,
      Yuwipi cult, with good photos of a Sioux ceremony; pp. 105–
      110 (and see index), Sun Dance at Winner, South Dakota, in
      1967. A popular presentation.]

188   EVANS, David.   North American Indian music.   Journal of
      American Folklore 357 = 90, 1977, 364–371.
         [A useful account of the problem of understanding the
      different aesthetic of Indian culture, with its emphasis
      on timbre, together with valuable reviews of a number of
      recordings, including two albums on peyote songs — see
      items 860, 870 (pp. 369–370).]

189   FARB, Peter.   Ghost Dance and cargo cult.   Horizon (New York)
      11 (2), 1969, 58–65.
         [Using A. F. C. Wallace's theory of revitalization cults,
      analyses "millenarian movements" — Ghost Dance, cargo cults
      of Melanesia, Watch Tower in Africa, Handsome Lake and
      peyote cult.]

190   FEHRENBACH, T. R.   Comanches. The destruction of a people.
      London: George Allen & Unwin 1975, xiv + 557 p., illus.
         [Pp. 533–537, messianism exemplified in Ishatai in
      1874.]

191   FIRE, John/LAME DEER and ERDOES, Richard.   Lame Deer: seeker
      of visions.   New York: Simon & Schuster 1972, 280 p.,
      illus.

[Ch. 13 (= pp. 214-224), peyote cult, in the Cross-Fire, Sioux, form, using a Bible; ch. 14 (= pp. 225-235), personal narration of the Sioux traditional account of the Ghost Dance, and of Wounded Knee.]

192   FISKE, Edward B.   Indians reviving religious heritage.   New York Times 23 August 1972, 43, illus.
        [Report of the 3rd Pan-Indian Ecumenical Conference on Stoney Reserve, Alberta, Summarized in Steiger, item 326, pp. 78-79.]

193   FLANNERY, Regina.   The changing form and functions of the Gros Ventre Grass Dance.   Primitive Man 20 (3), 1947, 39-70.
        [From its introduction 1875-1880, till its decline by 1920:   it filled the gap left by decline of earlier socio-religious dances (e.g. Sun Dance) but was itself social rather than religious, and then declined under further change of Gros Ventre's situation, leaving only vestigial remnants as round dances.]

194   FORBIS, Richard George.   Religious acculturation of the Flat-head Indians of Montana.   University of Montana, M.A. thesis 1950, 107 p.

195   FORD, James Alfred and WILLEY, Gordon R.   An interpretation of the prehistory of the Eastern United States.   American Anthropologist 43 (3:1), 1941, 325-363, bibl.
        [Pp. 357-359 on the "buzzard or Southern cult" as expression of a religious revival during period of decline after early white contacts; possibly similar in purpose to the Ghost Dance; many distinctive cultic artifacts (Mexican influences?) from 16th to 18th centuries, in Mississippi Valley area.]

196   FOREMAN, Grant.   The last trek of the Indians.   Chicago: University of Chicago Press 1946, 382 p., maps.
        [Pp. 207, 213-215, a vivid account of Kennekuk, largely drawn from I. McCoy's item 721, p. 456; pp. 244-247, Ghost Dance, including an account of the Cheyenne medicine man, Porcupine, and the response of the Arapaho and in Oklahoma.]

197   FOSTER, George M.   A summary of Yuki culture.   University of California, Anthropological Records 5 (3), 1944, 155-244, map, illus., bibl.
        [P. 211, n.55, Big Head cult; p. 219, Ghost Dance, Big Head cult and Bole Maru; pp. 219-222, Pentecostal movement as in 1937, the "one really vital force today" — an Indian development, its worship and the text of four hymns.]

198   FRENCH, David. Washo-Wishram, in E. H. Spicer (ed.), item 316.
       [Pp. 392-395, 412-415, on the Washo-Wishram, with
       Shakers, Feather cult and new longhouse religion.]

199   GAMIO, Manuel. Mexican immigration to the United States: a
       study of human migration and adjustment. Chicago: Univer-
       sity of Chicago Press 1930; repr. New York: Dover Publica-
       tions 1971, 262 p.
       [Ch. 8 (= pp. 108-127), Religion: includes new folk
       cults, pp. 122-124, Chapel of our Lord of the Miracles,
       San Antonio; pp. 124-127, El Tiradito (the One Laid Out),
       Tucson.]

200   GAUSTAD, Edwin Scott. Dissent in American religion. Chicago/
       London: University of Chicago Press 1973, 184 p.
       [Pp. 88-89, Ghost Dance; pp. 89-92, peyote cult and
       Native American Church, with their struggles for religious
       freedom. These movements are treated in the section: "The
       misfits. Sinners against society."]

201   GEARING, Fred[erick O.] et al. Documentation history of the
       Fox project 1948-1959. A program in action anthropology.
       Chicago: University of Chicago Press 1960, 426 p.
       [A diverse collection of materials with treatments of
       the three new religious societies among the Fox and
       Mesquakie Indians — the Drum Dance (from 1900), peyote
       (from 1904), and Christian religious groups (from c. 1883) —
       by various researchers. Peyote: pp. 11-12, by N. F.
       Joffe, repr. from item 64; pp. 45-46, 54, 56, 62 (by Lisa
       Peattie), p. 77 (by L. A. Fallers), pp. 99, 107 (by R. W.
       Reitz), p. 144 (by W. B. Miller), pp. 251-252 (by S. Tax).
       Drum Society: pp. 11-12 (by N. F. Joffe), pp. 30-31 (by
       D. Wolfson), pp. 45-46, 54, 55-57 (by L. Peattie), pp. 76-
       77 (by L. A. Fallers), pp. 106-107 (by R. W. Reitz), p. 144
       (by R. W. Miller). Christian missions: pp. 45-46, 54 (by
       L. Peattie), p. 72 (by L. A. Fallers), pp. 107-108 (by
       R. W. Reitz). Midéwiwin or Medicine society: p. 144 (by
       R. W. Reitz). Story of an Ojibwa messiah, similar to
       Wovoka, pp. 56-57 (by L. Peattie). Theory of "action
       anthropology": pp. 167-176 et passim (by S. Tax — on Indian
       acculturation not occurring.); theory of culture contact,
       pp. 408-415 (by F. O. Gearing).]

202   GIBSON, Arrell M[organ]. The Kickapoos: lords of the Middle
       Border (Civilization of the American Indian Series, 70).
       Norman: University of Oklahoma Press 1963, 387 p., bibl.,
       illus., map.
       [Ch. 9, the Kickapoo prophet Kennekuk: historical, with
       almost no reference to his teaching or religious practices;
       facing p. 48, painting of Kennekuk; pp. 48, 57-71,
       Tenskwatawa and Tecumseh.]

203   GILLES, Albert S., Sr. Wer-que-yah, Jesus-man Comanche.
      Southwest Review (Dallas) 53, 1968, 277-291.

204   GILMOUR, John Hamilton. An Indian prophet: a Banning witch
      doctor's foreboding. San Francisco Chronicle June 1892
      [reporting from Palm Springs, 17 June]; repr. in R. F.
      Heizer (ed.), California Indian linguistic records (Univer-
      sity of California Anthropological Records 15 (2)).
      Berkeley and Los Angeles: University of California Press
      1955, 155-156.
         [Several hundred Indians following a young Banning
      prophet in expecting the cataclysmic end of the world, with
      note by H. W. Henshaw comparing this to a similar reaction
      in 1812 after a great earthquake.]

205   GIPSON, Laurence Henry (ed.). The Moravian Indian mission on
      White River (Indiana Historical Collections, vol. 23).
      Indianapolis: Indiana Historical Bureau 1938, 674 p.
         [Pp. 333-334 for Munsee, Delaware prophetess 1805-;
      pp. 392-393, 402-403, 407, Tenskwatawa, "The Prophet".]

206   GOLDENWEISER, Alexander A. The rites of new religions among
      the native tribes of North America. Columbia University,
      M.A. thesis 1904, 85 p.
         [Especially on Smohalla, Tecumseh, Wovoka, Tenskwatawa
      and Kennekuk.]

207   GONZÁLEZ, Nancie L. The Spanish American of New Mexico: a
      distinctive heritage. University of California, Los
      Angeles, Graduate School of Business Administration, Ad-
      vance Report No. 9, Mexican-American Study Project, 1967.
         [The Alianza movement as a nativistic movement under its
      prophet-leader, Tijerina.]

208   GRIFFIN, James B. The De Luna expedition and the "buzzard
      cult" in the southeast. Journal of the Washington Academy
      of Sciences 34 (9), 1944, 299-303.
         [These art forms as the apogee of southeast culture and
      derived from the large number of Mexican Indians with the
      Tristan de Luna expedition. The southeast Indians adopted
      the Mexican art styles.]

209   HAGAN, William T. American Indians (Chicago History of
      American Civilization). Chicago/London: University of
      Chicago Press 1961, etc., 190 p.
         [Pp. 24-25, Delaware prophet; p. 53, Handsome Lake;
      pp. 53, 56-58, Tenskwatawa; pp. 129-134, Ghost Dance;
      pp. 129-130, peyote cult. All brief but reliable outlines
      set within their historical context.]

210   HANDELMAN, Don. The development of a Washo shaman. <u>Ethnology</u>
        6 (4), 1967, 444-464.
        [Life story of Henry Rupert, last surviving shaman
        (b. 1885), as a creative innovator and "cultural broker"
        who developed a new ethic of healing and a coherent
        cosmology beyond traditional Washo forms.]

211   <u>HARPER'S WEEKLY</u>. Dance of the Crow Indians. <u>Harper's Weekly</u>
        27, 1883, 798-799.
        [The traditional Grass Dance as among a small tribe with
        close white contacts, in 1883.]

212   HARRINGTON, John P[eabody] (trans.). A new and original ver-
        sion of Boscana's historical account of the San Juan
        Capistrano Indians of Southern California. <u>Smithsonian
        Institution Miscellaneous Collections</u> 92 (4), 1934, 1-62,
        illus.
        [A translation, with introduction, of a newly discovered
        original manuscript of the description of this Luiseño
        people by the Spanish missionary Jeronimo Boscana (1776-
        1831). On the Indians' god, Chinigchinix (= Chungishnish),
        <u>passim</u>; pp. 16-22, initiation and instruction of children
        into the cult; pp. 12-15, creation and the god, Chinig-
        chinix. See also R. M. Underhill, item 347, 10-11.]

213   HARRINGTON, Mark R. <u>Religion and ceremonies of the Lenape</u>
        (Indian Notes and Monographs, 19). New York: Heye
        Foundation, Museum of the American Indian 1921, 185-190,
        illus.
        [Pp. 185-190, peyote; 190-191, Ghost Dance; 192-199,
        religion in general.]

214   H[ARRINGTON], M[ark] R. New Kiowa collection. <u>The Masterkey</u>
        (Southwest Museum, Los Angeles) 11, 1937, 132.
        [Brief report of acquisition of Kiowa objects, including
        Ghost Dance costumes and peyote paraphernalia.]

215   HAWORTH, J. M.
        See under UNITED STATES. DEPT. OF INTERIOR, item 350.

216   HEIZER, Robert F. A Californian messianic movement of 1801
        among the Chumash. <u>American Anthropologist</u> 43 (1), 1941,
        128-129.
        ["The earliest historical record of such a movement in
        California"; translation of a letter to the Governor of
        North California about an anti-mission movement among the
        Christian Indians at Santa Barbara mission.]

217   HERTZBERG, Hazel W. <u>The search for an American Indian
        identity: modern pan-Indian movements</u>. Syracuse Univer-
        sity Press 1971, 362 p., illus.

[Surveys the first third of 20th c.: Society of
American Indians fraternal movement of 1920s, and "religious pan-Indianism". Ch. 10 (pp. 239-257), The Peyote
Cult; ch. 11 (pp. 259-284), Native American Church; also
see index for peyote, Handsome Lake, Tenskwatawa, Indian
Shaker Church, and Ghost Dance (pp. 10-14, etc.). Note
about ten large photos (unnumbered) of peyote leaders
between pp. 178-179.]

218 HINMAN, George Warren. The American Indian and Christian
     missions. New York and London: Fleming H. Revell Company
     1933, 176 p.
          [Pp. 19-20, peyote cult; p. 23, Ghost Dance; pp. 24-25,
     Indian Shaker Church; with a critical attitude throughout;
     pp. 142-143, Zuñi and Laguna pueblo new religious movement,
     1820s-1850s, including the Black Mask Dance to the Holy
     Ghost.]

219 HODGE, Frederick Webb (ed.). Handbook of American Indians
     north of Mexico = Bulletin, Bureau of American Ethnology
     30 (2), 1910; repr., New York: Rowman and Littlefield
     1971.
          [Brief biographical and historical outlines: pp. 281-
     282, Popé (by Hodge); pp. 309-310, prophets (J. Mooney);
     pp. 602-603, Smohalla (J. Mooney); pp. 729-730, Shawnee
     prophet (J. Mooney).]

220 HOWARD, James H[enri]. Potawatomi mescalism and its relation-
     ship to the diffusion of the peyote cult. Plains
     Anthropologist 7, 1962, 125-135, illus.
          [Pp. 127-130, detailed account of the Midéwiwin-type Red
     Bean society; pp. 130-132, miscellaneous uses of the red
     or mescal bean; pp. 132-134, reconstructed history of the
     two cults, and speculation on the Midéwiwin and mescal
     cults being "polar developments of a widespread super-
     organization of shamans".]

221 HOWARD, J[ames] H[enri]. The Plains Gourd Dance as a revitali-
     zation movement. American Ethnologist 3 (2), 1976, 243-
     259, bibl.
          [Revival of an obsolete dance as a secular form of pan-
     Indian revitalization; p. 256, external similarities to
     peyote forms.]

222 HUGHES, Willis Boldt. Indian messiahs in U.S. history.
     University of Oregon, M.A. thesis 1948, 170 p.

223 HULTKRANTZ, Åke. Pagan and Christian elements in the religious
     syncretism among the Shoshoni Indians of Wyoming, in S.S.
     Hartman (ed.), Syncretism (Scripta Instituti Donneriani
     Aboensis, 3). Stockholm: Almqvist & Wiksell 1969, 14-40.

[Ghost Dances (Tavibo and Wovoka); Sun Dance (Christian elements); peyote and Native American Church.]

224 HULTKRANTZ, Åke. <u>Prairie and Plains Indians</u> (Iconography of Religions, 10:2). Leiden: E. J. Brill 1973, 46 p. + 48 plates, figs.
[Pp. 30-32 and plates 44 to 48, Ghost Dance and peyote cult.]

225 HUNGRY WOLF, Adolf. <u>Good Medicine Companion Issue</u>. Fort Macleod, Alberta: Good Medicine Books n.d. [<u>c</u>. 1972], 32 p.
[Includes Sun Dance, Ghost Dance, etc.]

226 HURDY, John Major. <u>American Indian religions</u>. Los Angeles: Sherbourne Press Inc. 1970, 192 p.
[Ch. 3 (= pp. 65-96), Ghost Dance; ch. 6 (= pp. 131-142), "The sacrament of the bitter herb" (i.e. peyote). A fairly popular account.]

227 HURZELER, Richard Paul. <u>Messianic movements among American aborigines</u>. Columbia University, M.A. thesis 1965, 108 p.
[Includes both North and South America.]

227A ILIFF, Flora Gregg. <u>People of the Blue Water. My adventures among the Walapai and Havasupai Indians</u>. New York: Harper & Brothers 1954, 271 p., illus., map.
[Ch. 8 (= pp. 54-63), The Beautiful Intoxication — how peyote came to the Havasupai via a Kiowa peddler, but no cult resulted; ch. 20 (= pp. 175-181), The Peach Dance, includes pp. 178-180, on possible influence from the Ghost Dance.]

228 <u>INDIAN NEWS</u>. Alberta's Stoney Reserve to host Fourth Indian Ecumenical Conference. <u>Indian News</u> (Ottawa) 16 (2), June 1973, 11; The Indian Ecumenical Conference an international religious gathering, <u>idem</u> 17 (1), October 1974-January 1975, 8, illus.
[An announcement of the 4th Conference in Alberta; and a longer report on the 5th Conference of 1974 with 1100 participants.]

229 JOHNSON, J. B. The Allelujahs: a religious cult in northern New Mexico. <u>Southwest Review</u> (Dallas) 22, 1937, 131-139.
[Spontaneous development of a new cult among Mexican Americans (including Penitentes) in Northern New Mexico, derived from a "Holy Roller" meeting in Utah in 1930, appealing to the strong "Indian strain" in northern New Mexicans, and regarded as analogous to the Shaker religion and the Ghost Dance.]

230 JOSEPHY, Alvin M., Jr. The patriot chiefs: a chronicle of
American Indian resistance. New York: Viking Press
[1961], Compass ed. 1969, 364 p.
[Ch. 3 (= pp. 63-94), Popé and the great Pueblo uprising;
pp. 148-151, Tenskwatawa (same material also in his
article, These lands are ours..., American Heritage 12 (5),
1961, 20-23, 83-84, 85, illus.); pp. 343-344, Ghost Dance.]

231 KLINCK, Carl F[rederick] (ed.). Tecumseh: fact and fiction
in early records: a book of primary source materials.
Englewood Cliffs, N.J.: Prentice-Hall 1961, 246 p.,
illus., bibl.
[Pp. 4-5, Pontiac's account of the Delaware prophet's
(i.e. Neolin's) dream, with introductory note, repr. from
R. De Navarre, item 392A; pp. 6-7, Pontiac's use of this
dream; pp. 32-35, "the emergence of the prophet"
(Tenskwatawa) repr. from B. Drake, item 1447, pp. 86-89;
pp. 35-36, on Tenskwatawa, repr. from B. J. Lossing, The
pictorial field-book of the war of 1812. New York, 1869,
p. 189 note; pp. 36-40, "the ministry of Elskwatawa's
agents", repr. from J. Tanner, item 1466 (1830 ed.),
pp. 155-158, 178-179; pp. 40-41, 49-52, Governor Harrison's
speech about Tenskwatawa, the latter's reply, and
Harrison's letter about the prophet to the Secretary of War
in 1809, repr. from M. Dawson, item 1445A, pp. 83-84, 107-
109, 130-131; a valuable collection of materials.]

232 KRIEGER, Alex D. An inquiry into supposed Mexican influence
on a pre-historic 'cult' in the southern United States.
American Anthropologist 47 (4), 1945, 483-515.
[Supports an indigenous origin for the so-called Buzzard
cult (even if Mexican influence also occurred) and a very
distinctive nature, in full development before De Soto and
De Luna, i.e. pre-1540; possibly a new creative achievement
not prompted by encounter with Caucasians or social
decline.]

233 KROEBER, Alfred L[ouis]. Arapaho religion. Bulletin,
American Museum of Natural History (New York) 18 (4),
1907, 279-454.
[Pp. 319-320, 368-382, the Hand Game; pp. 319, 321-329,
346-349, the Ghost Dance; pp. 320-321, 398-410, peyote
cult.]

234 KROEBER, Alfred Louis. Handbook of the Indians of California =
Bulletin, Bureau of American Ethnology 78, 1925, 995 p.,
illus.; facs. reprint, Berkeley: California Book. Co.
1967.
[Pp. 62-63, 207-208, 269-270, 375-376, 583-584, 868-873,
Ghost Dance; pp. 621, 661, 681, Cáhitan, etc. cult of
Chungishnish; and see index for Kuksu, Jimson-weed, and
Dreamer cults.]

235 KURATH, Gertrude Prokosch. Pan-Indianism in Great Lakes
   tribal festivals. Journal of American Folklore 70,
   1957, 179-182.
   [P. 181, passing reference to Iroquois Longhouse members'
   indifference to the newer dance complexes associated with
   tourists; p. 181, peyote cult meetings held at large intertribal dance meetings or powwows.]

236 LA FARGE, Oliver. The American Indian. New York: Golden
   Press 1960, 213 pp., illus.
   [Pp. 186-193, "Ghosts and visions", surveys new religious movements, especially Ghost Dance and peyote cult,
   in a popular fashion, with good illustrations.]

237 LEIGHTON, Dorothea C. and ADAIR, John. People of the middle
   way: a study of the Zuñi Indians (Behavior Science Monographs). New Haven, Conn.: Human Relations Area Files
   Press 1966, 171 p., illus., bibl.
   [Pp. 20-21, 52-54, religious change among the Zuñi since
   Spanish contact, including interpretations of the Katchina
   cult as syncretistic (E. C. Parsons' early view), and of
   revivals of Zuñi societies and cults since the early 1940s,
   as nativistic reactions to Christianity, etc.; the differential survival of curing as against rain and fertility
   cults.]

238 LEVINE, Stuart and LURIE, Nancy Oestreich (eds.). The American
   Indian today. Deland, Florida: Everett/Edwards Inc.
   (1968) 1972, 229 p., illus., map; Baltimore: Penguin Books
   1970, etc., 352 p., illus., map.
   [Revised and expanded versions of articles in Midcontinent American Studies Journal 6 (2), 1965. Penguin
   ed., pp. 31, 119-120, 165, 176, 193, peyote cult or Native
   American Church; pp. 241-242, the "Christianized prophet
   dance" of the Nez Percé (by D. E. Walker - see also his
   items 108, 1339.]

239 LINDGREN, Gillian. Indians gather at Morley to celebrate 'old
   ways'. Calgary Herald 1 August 1973, illus.; God will
   soon punish the white man. Idem 4 August 1973, illus.
   [A journalist's two articles on the 4th Pan-Indian
   Ecumenical Conference on the Stoney Reserve in 1973, hosted
   by Chief John Snow, the Stoney minister of the United
   Church.]

240 LINDIG, Wolfgang H. and DAUER, Alfons M. Prophetismus und
   Geistertanz-Bewegung bei nordamerikanischen Eingeborenen,
   in W. E. Mühlmann (ed.), Chiliasmus und Nativismus.
   Berlin: Dietrich Reimer (1961) 1964, 41-74, folding map,
   bibl.; Fr. trans., Prophétisme et dance des esprits chez

les indigènes d'Amérique du Nord, in W. E. Mühlmann (ed.),
Messianismes révolutionnaires du Tiers-Monde. Paris:
Gallimard 1968, 40-75.
  [Prophet and Ghost Dance movements summarized, the latter
  (pp. 62-70) as the "classic" North American example; other-
  wise is a survey from Popé onwards.]

241   LINDIG, Wolfgang [H.]. Die Kulturen der Eskimo und Indianer
      Nordamerikas (Handbuch der Kulturgeschichte, Series 2,
      no. 20). Frankfurt am Main: Akademische Verlagsgesell-
      schaft Athenaion 1972, 378 p., illus.
        [Pp. 279-280, Ghost Dance, and photo of Wovoka; pp. 282-
        284, 352, Peyote cult, with map.]

242   LINDQUIST, G[ustavus] E[lmer] E[manuel] (director). The Red
      man in the United States: an intimate study of the social,
      economic and religious life of the American Indian....
      New York: G. H. Doran Co. 1923, 447 p., illus., maps,
      bibl.
        [Pp. 69-76, on peyote ("a terrible menace"); pp. 224-225,
        Ghost Dance ("superstition"); pp. 386-387, Shaker Church.
        By an authority on Indians in a major church-sponsored
        survey.]

243   LONGBOAT, Diane. Conference held on Stony Reservation attracts
      hundreds of Indian delegates. Indian News (Ottawa) 15 (5),
      1972, 4, illus.
        [Report of the 3rd Pan-Indian Ecumenical Conference.]

244   LOWIE, Robert H[arry]. Primitive religion. New York: Live-
      right Pub. Corp. (1924), 2nd ed. 1948, 382 p.; repr. New
      York: Grosset and Dunlap 1952, 363 p.
        [1948 ed., pp. 188-200, 253-257, Ghost Dance (based on
        Mooney); pp. 200-204, peyote; pp. 251-253, early South
        African prophets.]

245   LOWIE, Robert H[arry]. American culture history. American
      Anthropologist n.s. 42, 1940, 409-428.
        [Pp. 423 ff., on religious aspects; pp. 424-425,
        "messianic cults", and pre-contact or non-Christian basis
        of some; p. 425, the great variations over the two
        Americas.]

246   LOWIE, Robert H[arry]. Indians of the plains. Garden City,
      New York: McGraw Hill Book Co. 1954; New York: American
      Museum of Natural History 1963, 259 p.
        [Pp. 199-201, Ghost Dance; pp. 201-204, 222, peyote
        cult; short general summaries.]

246A LUMHOLTZ, Karl [Sofus]. New trails in Mexico: an account of
one year's exploration in northwestern Sonora, Mexico, and
southwestern Arizona, 1901-1910. London: T. Fisher
Unwin 1912, xxv + 411 p., illus., maps.
[Pp. 39-40, a Papago messianic movement c. 1900; extract
repr. in Waddell, item 357, p. 55, which is the fullest
study of the movement.]

247 LURIE, Nancy O[estreich]. Wisconsin: a natural laboratory
for North American Indian Studies. Wisconsin History
Magazine (Madison) 53 (1), 1969, 3-20, illus.
[P. 9, brief outline of religious position: churches,
traditionalists, Drum or Dream Dance and peyote cults.]

248 LURIE, Nancy Oestreich. The world's oldest on-going protest
demonstration: North American Indian drinking patterns.
Pacific Historical Review 40 (3), 1971, 311-332.
[P. 318, Handsome Lake religion and Native American
Church as banning alcohol; Handsome Lake and John Rave
(who helped form Native American Church) were notorious
drunkards before conversion.]

249 McALLISTER, J. Gilbert. Dävéko: Kiowa-Apache medicine man.
With a summary of Kiowa-Apache history and culture by
W. W. Newcomb, Jr. (Bulletin, Texas Memorial Museum, 17).
Austin: Texas Memorial Museum 1970, 61 p., illus.
[Dävéko, c. 1818-1897. P. 12 on the question of the
Ghost Dance/Peyote sequence.]

250 McBETH, Kate [Christine]. Nez Perces since Lewis and Clark.
New York: F. H. Revell Co. 1908, 272 p., illus.
[Pp. 29-34, the Nez Percé delegation to St. Louis in
1832 seeking the Whites' "Book" — as recorded in Christian
Nez Percé oral tradition in the 1880s. By a Presbyterian
missionary for 27 years among the Nez Percé.]

251 MacGREGOR, Gordon. Warriors without weapons. A study of the
society and personality development of the Pine Ridge
Sioux. Chicago: University of Chicago Press 1946, 228 p.,
illus., map, bibl.
[Pp. 100-103, peyote; pp. 98-99, 102, 103, Yuwipi.]

252 MACLEOD, William Christie. The American Indian frontier.
London: Kegan Paul, Trench, Trubner & Co., and New York:
Knopf, 1928, 598 p., bibl.
[Ch. 34 (= pp. 505-521), The Red cry for a Saviour
(Delaware and Shawnee prophets, etc.); ch. 35 (= pp. 522-
532), The Messiah and the Forerunner (Smohalla, Toviko
[= Tavibo], Wovoka, Ghost Dance, peyote). Sympathetic
account.]

253   MALAN, Vernon D. and JESSER, Clinton J. The Dakota Indian
       religion: a study of conflict of values (Bulletin 473,
       Rural Sociology Department, Agricultural Experimental
       Station, South Dakota State College). Brookings, S.D.:
       the Department, February 1959, 64 p., bibl., illus.
       [Pp. 42-50, "marginal religious practices" — Ghost
       Dance, peyote, yuwipi.]

254   MALEFIJT, Annemarie de Waal. Religion and culture. An intro-
       duction to the anthropology of religion. New York:
       Macmillan; London: Collier-Macmillan 1968, 407 p.
       [Pp. 329-332, theory of millenarism; pp. 342-351, millen-
       arism in North America — Ghost Dance and derivatives,
       Prophet Dance, peyote cult.]

255   MARRIOTT, Alice [Lee]. The ten grandmothers (Civilization of
       the American Indian, 26). Norman: University of Oklahoma
       Press 1945, etc., 306 p.
       [Pp. 142-154, [Sons of the Sun] cult of 1881-1882 — new
       beliefs and a new dance dreamed by Eagle Plume; pp. 165-
       172, how Quanah Parker brought peyote to the Kiowa in 1884-
       1885; pp. 196-205, Ghost Dance of 1890-1891 — all in the
       form of imaginative reconstructions.]

256   MARTIN, Paul S[idney], QUIMBY, George I[rving] and COLLIER,
       Donald. Indians before Columbus: twenty thousand years
       of North American history revealed by archaeology. Chicago:
       University of Chicago Press 1947, xxiii + 582 p., illus.,
       map.
       [Pp. 361-366, on evidence for a possible religious re-
       vival, the "Southern Death Cult" in Mississippi Valley and
       S.E. United States, c. 1450-1650, caused by rumours of,
       and incipient contacts with, Spanish invaders of Mexico,
       and De Soto's expedition.]

257   MATHEWS, John Joseph. The Osages: children of the Middle
       Waters (Civilization of the American Indian Series).
       Norman: University of Oklahoma Press 1961, xx + 826 p.,
       illus., maps, bibl.
       [Pp. 735-739, "Disintegration and confusion"; pp. 741-
       759, Ghost Dance, John Wilson, peyotism; pp. 785-786,
       death of Osage's chief (and peyote references); pp. 525-
       538, Christian missions.]

258   MEAD, Margaret. The changing culture of an Indian tribe.
       New York: Columbia University Press 1932, 313 p.
       [The "Antler" group (pseudonym), Mississippi valley, in
       1930; pp. 97, 98, 110, 136, two forms of the Midéwiwin
       surviving but in decline; pp. 27, 106-112, peyote cult's
       development and decline, with healing and funeral rites as

the continuing functions; the peculiar features of this
cult among the "Antlers" are described in detail. Pp. 104-
105, "Holy Roller" Pentecostals' temporary appeal; p. 104,
Mormons' small appeal.]

259   MEREDITH, Howard L.   The Native American factor.   New York:
      Executive Council of the Episcopal Church 1973, 104 p.,
      illus.
         [P. 34, Pan-Indian Ecumenical Conference; p. 39, Ghost
      Dance; p. 40, Native American Church.]

260   MERIAM, Lewis et al.   The problem of Indian administration.
      (Institute for Government Research Studies Administration).
      Baltimore: Johns Hopkins Press 1928, 872 p.; repr. New
      York/London: Johnson Reprint Corporation 1977.
         [Pp. 137, 222, brief references to use of peyote; p. 629,
      Indian Shaker and "Peyote Church" as both inimical to
      health and "reported to be growing".   A very inadequate
      approach, reflecting its date.]

261   MESERVE, Charles F.   A tour of observation among Indians and
      Indian schools in Arizona, New Mexico, Oklahoma and Kansas
      (Publications of the Indian Rights Association, Series 2,
      No. 18).   Philadelphia: Indian Rights Association 1894,
      43 p.
         [Pp. 19-25, the Grass Dance among Plains Indians;
      pp. 22-24, Ghost Dance.]

262   MOONEY, James.   Item 508.
         [Pp. 700-701, Patheske c. 1852/3; pp. 701-704, Tavibo;
      pp. 704-705, Nakaidoklini; pp. 705-706, Potawatomi new
      religion, 1883; pp. 706-707, Cheez-teh-paezh, the Sword-
      bearer, Crow medicine man, 1887.]

263   MOONEY, James.   The Cheyenne Indians.   Memoirs, American
      Anthropological Association (Lancaster, Pennsylvania)
      1 (6), 1907, 357-442, plates 10-12.
         [Pp. 401, 418, 420, Ghost Dance from 1889 but extinct by
      this time; p. 418, 420, briefly on recent introduction of
      the peyote rite and its appeal.]

264   MURIE, James R.   Pawnee Indian societies.   Anthropological
      Papers, American Museum of Natural History 11 (7), 1914,
      543-644.
         [Pp. 630-636, 639, the Ghost Dance; pp. 636-638,
      peyote.]

265   NASH, Philleo.   The place of religious revivalism in the for-
      mation of the intercultural community on Klamath Reserva-
      tion, in Fred Eggan (ed.), Social Anthropology of North

American tribes. Chicago: University of Chicago Press
1937; enlarged edition 1955; repr. 1962, 1972, 377–442.
[The religious revival of 1871–1878 as a nativistic
movement with fantasy restoration of original value-
pattern; uses the deprivation theory; includes Ghost Dance,
pp. 414–419; Earth Lodge cult, pp. 420–425; Dream Dance,
pp. 426 ff.]

266　NEIHARDT, John G[niesenau]. When the tree flowered: the
fictional biography of Eagle Voice, a Sioux Indian.
Lincoln: University of Nebraska Press 1951; repr. Bison
Books 1970, 248 p.
[Ch. 7, Going on vision quest; ch. 15, The Sun Dance;
ch. 29, The girl's road (the Ghost Dance and Wounded Knee).]

267　NETTL, Bruno. North American Indian musical styles. Journal
of American Folklore 67, 1954, 44–56, 297–307, 351–368.
[Pp. 299–300, Ghost Dance songs; pp. 306–307, peyote
cult songs; from a technical musical viewpoint.]

268　NEWCOMB, William W[ilmon], Jr. The culture and acculturation
of the Delaware Indians (Anthropological Papers, Museum of
Anthropology, University of Michigan, 10). Ann Arbor:
the Museum 1956, 141 p., bibl., map.
[Pp. 94–97, Delaware prophets from c. 1750; pp. 109–115,
religious assimilation and peyotism; pp. 123–128, summary
and analysis of acculturation.]

269　NEWSWEEK. Indians: old-time religion. Newsweek 21 May 1973,
51–52, 54, illus.
[On the revival of Indian religions: brief mention of
Indian Ecumenical movement and Sun Dance; fuller references
to Native American Church and a Kiowa meeting at Lawton,
Oklahoma.]

270　NORBECK, Edward. Religion in primitive society. New York:
Harper and Brothers 1961, 318 p.
[Ch. 13 (= pp. 229–266), Religious movements — a useful
world overview: pp. 246–253, peyote; and references — an
elementary outline (largely based on La Barre); pp. 240–
246, Ghost Dance (based on Mooney, Du Bois, Gayton, etc.);
pp. 253–256, cargo cults; pp. 256–262, Mau Mau (based on
Leakey).]

271　NUÑEZ, Theron Aldine, Jr. A comparative study of nativism.
Florida State University, M.A. thesis 1957; as Creek
nativism and the Creek War, 1813–1814, Ethnohistory 5 (1),
1958, 1–47; 5 (2), 1958, 131–175; 5 (3), 1958, 292–301.
[On early Creek prophets.]

272   NYE, Wilbur Sturtevant. Carbine and lance: the story of old
      Fort Sill. Norman: University of Oklahoma Press (1937)
      1943, 345 p., illus.
          [P. 189-191, Isa-tai, Comanche prophet, 1974; pp. 263-
      274, prophets, Ghost Dance, missions.]

273   NYE, Wilbur Sturtevant. Bad medicine and good. Tales of the
      Kiowa. Norman: University of Oklahoma Press 1962, 281 p.,
      illus.
          [Pp. 179-182, Isatai, Comanche prophet.]

274   O'BRODOVICH, L. Plains Cree Sun Dance, 1968. Western
      Canadian Journal of Anthropology (Edmonton) 1 (1), 1969,
      71-87, bibl.

275   PAIGE, Harry W. Songs of the Teton Sioux. Los Angeles:
      Westernlore Press 1970, 210 p., illus., bibl.
          [Includes songs connected with the Ghost Dance, the
      peyote cult and the Yuwipi cult.]

276   PAN-INDIAN ECUMENICAL CONFERENCE. Documents issued in connec-
      tion with a series of annual conferences uniting Indians
      of the U.S.A. and Canada from all religious faiths
      (indigenous, Christian and other) held on the Crow Reser-
      vation, Montana, 1970, and since 1971 on the Stoney
      Reservation, Alberta: e.g., Announcement (2 p.) Report
      and Resolutions (14 p.) of 1970 conference; Announcement
      (3 p.), Report (6 p.), Resolutions (10 p.) and [Verbatim
      statements] (17 p.) of 1971 conference. The Nishnawbe
      Institute, Toronto, acted as organizing base. See further,
      Dick, item 172, Indian News, item 228, and G. Lindgren,
      item 241.

277   PAREDES, J. Anthony. On James' continuity and emergence in
      Indian poverty culture. Current Anthropology 14 (1-2),
      1973, 158-167.
          [P. 162, Midéwiwin "medicine doctor"; p. 163, the Native
      American Church and Native Indian Evangelical Church — all
      fairly brief references.]

278   PARSONS, Elsie [Worthington] Clews. Pueblo Indian religion
      (University of Chicago Publications in Anthropology,
      Ethnological Series). Chicago: University of Chicago
      Press, 2 vols. 1939, 1209 p.
          [Vol. 2, pp. 1029-1030, 1094-1097, peyote at Taos
      pueblo; p. 1137, at Santa Clara; p. 1066, brief reference
      to Popé of San Juan.]

279   PARSONS, Elsie [Worthington] Clews. Notes on the Caddo
      (Memoirs, American Anthropological Association 57) =
      American Anthropologist 43 (3:2), 1941, 1-76, illus., map,
      bibl.

[Pp. 47–50, Ghost Dance; pp. 50–53, peyote; pp. 43–46, Ghost Dance and peyote, passim.]

280   PETERSON, Karen Daniels. The writings of Henry Roman Nose. Chronicles of Oklahoma 42 (4), 1964–65, 458–478.
    [One of seventy-two Plains Indians sent to Ft. Marion, Florida, in 1875 as prisoners of war for three years; later at Carlisle Institute, 1879–1883; his religions were successively Sun Dance, Christianity, and (pp. 476–478) Ghost Dance, and peyote.]

281   POWELL, J[ohn] W[esley]. Report of the Director, in 13th Annual Report, Bureau of American Ethnology 1891–92. Washington, D.C.: Government Printing Office 1896.
    [Pp. xxxi, xxxix, report on W. J. Hoffman's (q.v.) invitation to study Menomini Grand Medicine Society, for comparison with Ojibwa Midéwiwin; pp. xxxii, xxxix, report on J. Mooney's (q.v.) initial work on the Ghost Dance and interview with Wovoka etc.]

282   POWERS, Mabel. The Indian as peacemaker. New York: Fleming H. Revell Co. 1932, 223 p., illus.
    [Pp. 113, 161–164, Handsome Lake; p. 174, Kennekuk and Wovoka.]

283   POWERS, William Keegan. Continuity and change in Oglala religion. University of Pennsylvania, Ph.D. dissertation (anthropology) 1975, 358 p.
    [At Pine Ridge, South Dakota. The Oglala religion at the time of white contact is compared with contemporary practice, especially the Sun Dance, vision quest, sweat lodge, memorial feast and Yuwipi rituals; the relation of these to simultaneous Christian practice.]

284   PRICE, Archibald Grenfell. White Settlers and native peoples. Melbourne: Georgian House; Cambridge: Cambridge University Press 1950, 242 p., illus., maps.
    [Pp. 37–38, 194, "messiah religions" among North American Indians — Tenskwatawa, Smohalla, the two Ghost Dances, the peyote cult; pp. 194–195, interpretation.]

285   PUECH, Henri-Charles (ed.). Histoire des religions, III. Les religions constituées en Asie...Les religions chez les peuples sans tradition écrite. Mouvements religieux nés de l'acculturation (Encyclopédie de la Pleiade, 40). Paris: Gallimard 1976, 1460 p.
    [Includes North American new movements, by W. LaBarre.]

286   RADIN, Paul. The story of the American Indian. New York: Liveright Publishing Corporation 1927; enlarged ed. 1944, 391 p., illus.

[Pp. 366-367, Kennekuk; pp. 368-371, Wovoka and the
Ghost Dance: brief outlines.]

287   RAMSEY, Jarrold.   The Bible in western Indian mythology.
      Journal of American Folklore no. 358 = 90 (October –
      December), 1977, 442-454.
          [Three kinds of assimilation: by incorporation, by
      adaptation, and by mythopoesis (a new creation). P. 447,
      brief reference to Smohalla; p. 454, brief reference to
      Indian Shaker and Native American Churches as going beyond
      the text of the Bible to form new syncretic faiths.]

288   REH, Emma.
          See McNICKLE, item 990.

289   RHODES, Willard.   Acculturation in North American Indian music,
      in S. Tax (ed.), item 336, 127-132.
          [Pp. 128, 132, peyote and Ghost Dance songs (also
      Christian hymns) as borrowing from the musical style of an
      area but "giving nothing in return".]

290   RHODES, Willard.   The Christian hymnology of the North American
      Indians, in A. F. C. Wallace (ed.), Men and cultures.
      Philadelphia: University of Pennsylvania Press 1960,
      324-331.
          [P. 327, peyote cult; pp. 327-329, Shaker church, with
      the music of two songs, and account of the distinct fea-
      tures of Shaker songs, especially the participation of
      women.]

291   RIBAS, Andrés Pérez de.   Historia de los triumphos de nuestra
      Santa Fee entre gentes ... del Nuevo Orbe ....   Madrid:
      A. de Peredes 1645, 3 vols.; repr. as Triunfos [sic] de
      nuestra santa fé ....   Mexico, D. F.: Editorial "Layac"
      1944, 3 vols.
          [By the first missionary in Yaqui territory. Bk. 1,
      ch. 3, pp. 40-41, a Jesuit missionary's description of the
      boys' initiation in the Chungishnish cult among the Cáhita,
      southern California, between 1591-1620; Bk. 1, pp. 138-139,
      comparative absence of idols among the Yaqui; Bk. 2,
      pp. 88-90, 121-128, the first contacts and the mission
      established — as background to the later Yaqui independent
      church.]

292   RICHARDSON, Rupert Norval.   The Comanche barrier to South
      Plains Settlement: a century and a half of savage resis-
      tance to the advancing white frontier.   Glendale,
      California: Arthur H. Clark Co. 1933, 424 p., illus, maps;
      repr. New York: Kraus Reprint Co. 1973.

[P. 39, n55 (= pp. 39-40), history of peyote cult among
the Comanche; pp. 371-382, new "medicine dance" and
Isatai; the causes of Comanche unrest and their defeat.]

293   RICKETTS, Mac Linscott. J. G. Jorgensen, The Sun Dance
Religion. Journal of the American Academy of Religion
41 (2), 1973, 256-259.
[A review from the history of religions viewpoint.]

294   RITZENTHALER, Robert E[ugene]. The Potawatomi Indians of
Wisconsin (Bulletin, Public Museum of the City of Milwaukee
19 (8)). Milwaukee: the Museum 1953, 99-174, illus.
[Pp. 150, 159-161, Dream Dance; pp. 152-153, Medicine
Dance Society; pp. 150, 152, 162-163, peyote cult in the
half-moon form, based on the Stone Lake (= Lake Lucerne)
community east of Crandon.]

295   RUETHER, Rosemary Radford. The radical kingdom. The Western
experience of the Messianic hope. New York and London:
Harper & Row 1970, 304 p.
[Pp. 222-224, Ghost Dance (apocalypticism provoked by
loss of normal way of life) and peyote (mysticism arising
in decline of apocalyptic hopes); p. 225, Nat Turner's
revolt; pp. 227-239, Black Islam.]

296   SANDERS, Thomas E. and PEEK, Walter W. (eds.). Literature of
the American Indian. Beverly Hills: Glencoe Press, and
London: Collier-Macmillan 1973, 534 p.
[Good general survey of new movements, pp. 313-330.
Reprints material on peyote (John Rave), pp. 387-391;
A. Skinner, pp. 366, 384, with introduction, pp. 384-387;
Ghost Dance, pp. 335-358, with introduction pp. 335-337;
the Delaware Prophet, pp. 331-334, from Mooney (1892) and
Parkman (1851); Handsome Lake, pp. 365-374, with intro-
duction pp. 365-367; and the Narragansetts, pp. 375-380
(see items 684, 695).]

297   SCHOOLCRAFT, Henry Rowe. Algic researches ... 1st Series:
Indian tales and legends. New York: Harper & Brothers
1839, 2 vols.
[Vol. 1, pp. 239-248, on Delaware (Lenape) prophet
(Neolin c. 1762): p. 239, "Paradise opened to the
Indians"; pp. 239-240, historic note on source; pp. 240-
248, the tale as told by Pontiac. Schoolcraft could be
called the first American anthropologist. "Algic" is
derived from "Alleghany" and "Atlantic".]

298   SCHOOLCRAFT, Henry R[owe]. Historical and statistical information respecting the history, conditions and prospects of
the Indian tribes of the United States.... Philadelphia:
Lippincott, Grambo and Co. 6 vols. 1851-57; repr. New York:
Paladin Press 1969.

[Vol. 1, pp. 388-401, "The higher Jeesukawin or Sacred Prophetic art: prophets and prophetesses and their symbols; vol. 4, pp. 259-262, Tenskwatawa's speech after return from Canada (1827?) concerning removal to new territory (nothing on religion); vol. 5, pp. 188-189, 416, 434, the Midéwiwin of the Ojibwa, p. 189, Ojibwa prophet.]

299   SCUDDER, Betty Burleigh. From paganism to Christ. World Outlook (Nashville, Tennessee) n.s. 5 (6), 1945, 14-16, illus.
       [Includes hostile accounts of the Ghost Dances and peyote "craze".]

300   SHAKESPEARE, Tom [Senior]. The sky people. New York: Vantage Press 1971, 117 p.
       [P. 92, peyote cult as the only intertribal organization, including perhaps 70% of the people; pp. 97-99, Ghost Dance. A controversial publication of the notes of his uncle, Will Shakespeare.]

301   SHIMKIN, Demitri B. Dynamics of recent Wind River Shoshone history. American Anthropologist 44 (3), 1942, 451-462.
       [Ghost Dance, Mormon contacts, peyote (pp. 457, 459-460); Ghost Dance and peyote as separate and as alternatives.]

302   SHORRIS, Earl. The death of the Great Spirit: an elegy for the American Indian. New York: Simon and Schuster 1971; New American Library (Signet Books) 1972, 205 p.
       [Ch. 3, Native American Church, interpreted as not authentically Indian; ch. 4 (1), Yuwipi cult; pp. 101-103, Ghost Dance; ch. 10, Sun Dance, directed by Lame Deer at Pine Ridge; ch. 9, Hopi traditionalists as represented by radical orthodoxy of Thomas Banyacya: journalistic approach, useful for detail.]

303   SIMONS, Suzanne L. The cultural and social survival of a Pueblo Indian community [Sandie], in H. J. Tobias and C. E. Woodhouse (eds.), Minorities and politics. Albuquerque: University of New Mexico Press 1969, 85-112.
       [P. 89, a nativistic movement in mid-1930s; pp. 104-106, religion, traditional and Catholic.]

304   SKINNER, Alanson [Buck]. Societies of the Iowa, Kansas, and Ponca Indians. Anthropological Papers, American Museum of Natural History 11 (9), 1915, 679-801.
       [Pp. 693-694, 720-721, 758, peyote; pp. 719-720, Ghost Dance.]

305   SKINNER, Alanson [Buck]. Medicine ceremony of the Menomini, Iowa and Wahpeton Dakota = Indian Notes and Monographs, 4. New York: Museum of the American Indian, Heye Foundation 1920, 357 p.

[P. 10, "recently ... the introduction of the so-called
'Peyote religion' has caused members of certain tribes ...
to relax the rigidity of the rules of secrecy," so that
information on the Medicine Dance (among Algonkian and
Sioux tribes) has at last become available; pp. 15-188,
Mitawin Lodge, but nothing on innovating aspects as a new
movement.]

306   SKINNER, Alanson [Buck]. Material culture of the Menomini.=
Indian Notes and Records (Miscellaneous Series, 20).
New York: Museum of the American Indian, Heye Foundation
1921, 478 p., illus.
[Pp. 24, 42-43, peyote; pp. 41-42, the Dreamers, a new
cult.]

307   SKINNER, Alanson [Buck]. Observations on the ethnology of the
Sauk Indians. Bulletin, Public Museum of the City of
Milwaukee 5 (1), 1923, 1-57; 5 (2), 1925, 59-95; 5 (3),
1925, 119-180.
[P. 51, Dream Dance; Ghost Dance prevalent among the
Ioway and Pawnee, but not the Sauk; a semi-Christian
peyote cult has a strong vogue.]

308   SKINNER, Alanson [Buck]. Ethnology of the Ioway Indians.
Bulletin, Public Museum of the City of Milwaukee 5 (4),
1926, 181-354.
[Pp. 248-249, modern religious cults: p. 248, Ghost
Dance, pp. 190, 217, 246, 248-249, 261, peyote.]

309   SKINNER, Alanson [Buck]. The Mascoutens or Prairie Potawatomi
Indians. Bulletin, Public Museum of the City of Milwaukee
6 (1), 1924, 1-262, illus.; 6 (2), 1925, 404-405.
[Pp. 14-15, Tenskwatawa and suppression of Midéwiwin;
pp. 12-13, 15, 232-246, 404-405, the peyote rites and
their origin; pp. 222-227, the Drum Dance ceremony.]

310   SPECK, Frank G[ouldsmith]. Oklahoma Delaware ceremonies,
feasts and dances (Memoirs of the American Philosophical
Society, 7). Philadelphia: American Philosophical
Society 1937, 161 p., illus.
[Pp. 6, 96, 152, peyote rite and its influence briefly
referred to; pp. 15-26, additional notes to the Big House
ceremony and dualogy of symbolism in the Big House rite.
See note on Munsee prophetess at Speck, item 399.]

311   SPECK, F[rank] G[ouldsmith]. Catawba religious beliefs,
mortuary customs, and dances. Primitive Man 12 (2),
1939, 21-57.
[Pp. 21-26, mass takeover of Mormonism by South Carolina
Catawba in the 1880s; balance is on Catawba religion without analyzing out the Mormon contribution.]

312   SPENCE, Lewis. Prophecy (American), in J. Hastings (ed.),
       Encyclopaedia of Religion and Ethics, vol. 10, 1918,
       381-382.
            [Brief references to Popé, Tenskwatawa, Kennekuk,
       Tavibo, Wovoka, Smohalla, Jacinto Can-Ek, and Maria
       Candelaria.]

313   SPENCER, Robert F. Native myth and modern religion among the
       Klamath Indians. Journal of American Folklore 65, 1952,
       217-226.
            [Pp. 219-220, brief reference to 19th c. nativistic
       movements and studies on them; p. 220, Indian Shaker Church
       as now (1948) dying out; pp. 221-226, traditional survivals,
       especially concerning mythology, the culture-hero, and the
       power quest, often syncretized with Christian elements.]

314   SPERLIN, O. B. Two Kutenay women masquerading as men. Or
       were they one? Washington Historical Quarterly (Seattle)
       21, 1930, 120-130.
            [Fullest account of evidence for the Kutenai prophetess
       c. 1812, who possibly carried the prophet dance to the
       N. Athapascans.]

315   SPICER, Edward H[olland]. Cycles of conquest: the impact of
       Spain, Mexico and the United States on Indians in the
       Southwest 1533-1960. Tucson: University of Arizona Press
       1962, 609 p.
            [Ch. 17 (= pp. 502-538), Religious diversification,
       includes independent "Catholic" churches of the Mayos,
       Yaquis, Opatas and Tarahumaras; pp. 272-273, 527-529, the
       Ghost Dance in the southwest, pp. 529-530, Teresa Urrea's
       revolt; pp. 530-531, Dr. Montezuma's influence on the
       Papago and Pima; pp. 532-536, Holy Ground religion;
       pp. 175, 178, 536-537, Native American Church; pp. 75-76,
       Mayo prophet movement. A major study.]

316   SPICER, Edward H[olland] (ed.). Perspectives in American
       Indian culture change. Chicago: University of Chicago
       Press (1961) 1966, x + 549 p., maps, tables.
            [Selections — see under E. H. Spicer, item 1526;
       H. Codere, item 158; D. French, item 198.]

317   SPICER, Edward H[olland]. A short history of the Indians of
       the United States. New York, London, etc.: Van Nostrand
       Reinhold Company (Anvil Books) 1969, 319 p.
            [Good outlines and supporting texts: pp. 41-43, the
       1680 Pueblo revolt and Popé; pp. 47-52, Handsome Lake
       religion; pp. 256-261, selections from the code of Handsome
       Lake; pp. 52-54, the Delaware prophet, and pp. 251-253,
       Heckewelder's description of the teaching (from J. Mooney,
       1896); pp. 54-56, Tenskwatawa, and pp. 266-267, Mooney's

summary of his teaching; p. 56, Kennekuk; pp. 88-90,
Smohalla, and pp. 275-276, his doctrine as given by Mooney;
pp. 90-93, Wovoka and the Ghost Dance, and pp. 280-283,
Indian descriptions as given by Mooney; pp. 105-106, Redbird Smith movement; pp. 119-122, Native American Church,
and pp. 288f., incorporation articles from Slotkin;
pp. 110, 291-295, revival of Hopi religion.]

318   SPINDLER, George Dearborn. Personality and peyotism in
         Menomini Indian acculturation. Psychiatry (Baltimore)
         15 (2), 1952, 151-159.
         [Pp. 152-155, the peyote rites, visions and conversion
      experiences; places the peyote cult on a four-part accul-
      turation continuum as a "transitional" form which is a
      "systematic deviation" from the larger transitional group,
      both as to the personality types who join it, and to the
      socio-cultural forms and functions it represents.]

319   SPINDLER, George Dearborn. Sociocultural and psychological
         processes in Menomini Indian acculturation (University of
         California Publications in Culture and Society, 5).
         Berkeley: University of California Press 1955, 271 p.
         [Among five groups treated are the Dream Dance group
      (nativistic), the "transitionals", and peyote cult.]

320   SPINDLER, George [Dearborn] and SPINDLER, Louise. Dreamers
         without power: the Menomini Indians. (Case Studies in
         Cultural Anthropology). New York: Holt, Rinehart and
         Winston 1971, 208 p., map, illus., bibl.
         [An important study. Pp. 54-62, Midéwiwin or Medicine
      Dance, as post-contact and in decline; pp. 62-68, 72,
      Dream Dance as main traditional (since c. 1879) ceremony;
      pp. 94-140, 189, peyote cult as syncretist (Christian
      elements, pp. 102, 106-109) but nativistic-oriented —
      complementary to Slotkin's reports from same group begin-
      ning about the same time, and with extensive verbatim
      reports by peyotists on conversion, visions, healing etc.;
      pp. 140-169, autobiographies, referring to Dream Dance,
      peyotism and Catholicism; pp. 168-169, summary.]

321   SPINDLER, Louise S. Menomini women and culture change.
         (Memoirs, American Anthropological Association 91) =
         American Anthropologist 64 (1:2), 1962, 1-109.
         [Pp. 18-19, women in Medicine Lodge, Dream Dance, and
      peyote cult; pp. 27-31, the social groupings of which
      peyote is one; pp. 62-69, the peyote cult group.]

322   SPINDLER, Louise [S.]. Menomini witchcraft, in D. E. Walker,
         Jr. (ed.), Systems of North American witchcraft and
         sorcery. Moscow: University of Idaho 1970, 183-220.

General

[Pp. 197-199, three post-contact movements: Midéwiwin, Dream Dance and peyote cult. Pp. 199-205, 210-212, native oriented groups (Midéwiwin and Dream Dance); pp. 205-206, 212-213, peyote cult.]

323 SPRAGUE, Roderick. Easterly orientations: Christian or nativistic. Paper, 3rd Annual Meeting for Historical Archaeology, 1969; digest in Abstracts in Anthropology 1 (4), 1970, 364-365.
[On the attempt to explain the Plateau Indian rejection of both traditional and Christian burial patterns as due to various nativistic movements; but the Feather Cult practice does not support this.]

324 STARKLOFF, Carl F. The people of the center. American Indian religion and Christianity. New York: Seabury Press (Crossroad Book) 1974, 144 p.
[Pp. 54-64, Sun Dance and current forms; pp. 106-107, peyote; pp. 102, 131-136, 140, various new movements. By a Jesuit missionary scholar.]

325 STARKLOFF, Carl F. Evangelization and Native Americans. Jesuit Missions Newsletter (Washington, D.C.) no. 34, November 1974, 1-6.
[Address to Jesuit Missions Board of Directors, October 1974 at Pine Ridge. Exposition of the spirituality of American Indian religion and its congruence with Christianity; p. 5, the prophet figures; p. 6, lack of interest in Jesus in new religious movements.]

326 STEIGER, Brad. Medicine power: the American Indian's revival of his spiritual heritage and its relevance for modern man. Garden City, N.Y.: Doubleday & Co. 1974, 226 p., illus.
[Pp. 78-79, Pan-Indian Ecumenical Conference, based on Fiske, item 192; pp. 80-81, 190-199, Native American Church, including W. H. Clark's experience of it; pp. 20-21, 156-159, Ghost Dance influence continuing. Badly reviewed by anthropologists as confusing Indian spirituality with occultism, Eastern mysticism, and spiritualism.]

327 STEINMETZ, Paul B. The sacred pipe among North American Indians as an Indian and Christian phenomenon. University of Aberdeen, M.Litt. thesis 1975, 170 p.
[P. 73, the pipe in the Ghost Dance; pp. 110-111, 122, Christian influence on the Sun Dance; pp. 119-123, growth of the Yuwipi cult and its use of the pipe; pp. 125-127, Half Moon and Cross Fire forms of peyotism on Pine Ridge Reservation; pp. 127-131, controversial peyote meeting held for the author, with the pipe. By a Jesuit missionary among Oglala Sioux.]

328 STERN, Theodore. A Umatilla prophet cult: an episode in
culture change, in A. F. C. Wallace (ed.), Men and cultures:
selected papers, 5th International Congress of Anthropological and Ethnological Sciences. Philadelphia 1956.
Philadelphia: University of Pennsylvania Press 1960,
810 p.
[Pp. 346-350, the Washani cult in northwest Washington
State, c. 1830.]

329 STEWART, Omer C[all]. The peyote religion and the Ghost Dance.
The Indian Historian 5 (4), 1972, 27-30, bibl.
[Criticism of the view that the Ghost Dance preceded and
paved the way for the spread of the peyote cult.]

330 STRONG, William Duncan. Aboriginal society in Southern
California (University of California Publications in
American Archaeology and Ethnology 26). Berkeley: Univer-
sity of California Press 1929, 358 p.
[Pp. 256, etc. (see index), on Chungishnish religion and
its spread in historic times — traditional aspects only.]

331 STRONG, William Duncan. The occurrence and wider implications
of a 'ghost cult' on the Columbia River suggested by carv-
ings in wood, bone and stone. American Anthropologist
45 (2), 1945, 244-261.
[Hypothesizes a cult in the proto-historic period due to
indirect contact, and similar to the "death and revival
cult" in the south-east U.S.A. (see Ford and Willey, item
195). This suggests that Spier's prophet dance (see
item 1336) was not aboriginal.]

332 STURTEVANT, William C. (gen. ed.). Handbook of North American
Indians. 20 vols. Washington, D.C.: Smithsonian Institution 1978-
[A comprehensive encyclopaedia commencing publication
in 1978. See L. J. Bean, item 13, and A. F. C. Wallace,
item 663, in earliest volumes; later volumes include
Aberle (peyote) Jorgensen (Ghost Dance and Sun Dance), etc.
See especially vols. 18-19, biographies, and vol. 20,
general index.]

333 SWADESH, Frances L. The Alianza movement: catalyst for social
change in New Mexico, in June Helm (ed.), Spanish-speaking
people in the United States (Proceedings, 1968 Annual
Spring Meeting, American Ethnological Society). Seattle:
Washington University Press for American Ethnological
Society 1968, 162-177.
[Concludes that it is not a "revitalization" movement
in Wallace's sense, because it operates for change despite
religious factors; cf. J. L. Love, item 67.]

334   SWEEZY, Carl. The Arapaho way: a memoir of an Indian boyhood
       [Edited for posthumous publication by Mrs. Altha Bass.]
       New York: Clarkson N. Potter Inc. 1966, 80 p., illus.
       [Ch. 8 (= pp. 68-76), Arapaho religion — the traditional
       sun dance (pp. 71, 74-75), the Ghost Dance as a "false
       religion" (pp. 72-73), the Native American Church as tak-
       ing place of traditional religion; by an Arapaho.]

335   TALAHAFTEWA et al. Letter to the President of the United
       States, in Arnold M. Rose (ed.), Race, prejudice and dis-
       crimination: readings in intergroup relations in the
       United States. New York: A. A. Knopf 1951, 42-49.
       [Full text of letter to the U.S. President by six Hopi
       traditionalists concerned with renewal of their religion
       and culture; introduction by A. M. Rose.]

336   TAX, Sol (ed.). Acculturation in the Americas. Proceedings
       and selected papers of the XXIX International Congress of
       Americanists. Chicago: University of Chicago Press 1952,
       339 p.; repr. New York: Cooper Square Publications 1967.
       [See J. I. Gamble, item 874; W. Rhodes, item 289; B. J.
       Siegel, item 1102; F. W. Voget, item 355.]

337   TEBBEL, John and JENNISON, Kenneth. The American Indian wars.
       New York: Harper & Brothers 1960, 312 p., illus., map.
       [Pp. 85-86, and index, the Delaware prophet (confused
       with Tenskwatawa); pp. 148-155, Tenskwatawa and Tecumseh;
       pp. 292-294, 298, Wovoka and the Ghost Dancers.]

338   TEDLOCK, Dennis and TEDLOCK, Barbara (eds.). Teachings from
       the American earth. Indian religion and philosophy. New
       York: Liveright, and Toronto: George J. McLeod 1975,
       xxiv + 279 p., figs.
       [An anthology, with good introduction on Indian spirit-
       uality by the editors. Pp. 75-95, repr. from J. Mooney,
       item 508, pp. 777-791 (Doctrine of the Ghost Dance);
       pp. 96-104, repr. of Slotkin, item 1113; pp. 147, 148,
       149 on the Midéwiwin, repr. from Hallowell, item 746,
       p. 25; pp. 236-237, peyote among the Winnebago, repr. from
       Radin, item 1073.]

339   TEIT, James A. The Salishan tribes of the Western Plateaus
       (ed. F. Boas), in 45th Annual Report, Bureau of American
       Ethnology 1927-1928. Washington, D.C.: Government
       Printing Office 1930, 23-396, illus.
       [P. 292, a Thompson Indian prophetess c. 1850 trying to
       rally Indians to drive out the whites, with only a small
       following.]

340   TERRELL, John Upton. Apache chronicle. New York: World
       Publishing Company, and Canada: Nelson, Foster & Scott
       1972, 411 p., illus., map.

[Pp. 347-349, Noch-ay-del-klinne, the Dreamer, and his death in conflict with the army, 1881.]

341 THOMAS, Robert K[nox]. Pan-Indianism. Midcontinent American Studies Journal 6 (2), 1965, 75-83.
[The sense of a wider identity, especially in the Plains area, was assisted by the reservation system and issued in pan-Indian religions such as the Ghost Dance and peyote cult (p. 78); the process of individual acculturation is being reversed, even among urban Indians.]

342 THOMAS, William I. Primitive behaviour. New York: McGraw-Hill 1937, 847 p.
[Pp. 680-701, Prophet dances, Ghost Dance, and peyote cult, based on Spier and Mooney.]

343 THOMPSON, Augustus Charles. Moravian missions. Twelve lectures. London: Hodder and Stoughton 1883, ix + 516 p.; New York: Charles Scribners' Sons 1886.
[Pp. 208-209 on Matthew the "Great Sage" of 1853, repr. in Chamberlain, item 157, p. 29; pp. 317-319, Papunhank and other Delaware prophets in the 18th c.]

343A TOOKER, Elizabeth J. Papagos in Tucson: an introduction to their history, community life and acculturation. University of Arizona M.A. (anthropology) thesis 1952.
[Pp. 23-24, an old Papago's recollections of their messianic movement c. 1900; extract repr. in Waddell, item 357, pp. 55-56.]

344 TRENHOLM, Virginia Cole. The Arapahoes, our people (Civilization of the American Indian, 105). Norman: University of Oklahoma Press 1970, 367 p., illus.
[Pp. 65, 267, 283-293, on the spread of the Ghost Dance among the Arapaho, in contrast to the Cheyenne skepticism and Kiowa rejection, using J. Mooney, etc.; pp. 293-303, peyote cult.]

345 TURNER, Frederick W. III (ed.). The portable North American Indian reader. New York: Viking Press, and Toronto: Macmillan Co. 1973 etc., 628 p.
[See Mountain Wolf Woman, item 1015, at pp. 471-482; Parkman, item 396, at pp. 531-532; Radin, item 1071, at pp. 431-454.]

346 TURNER, Harold Walter. See item 101, p. 701-702.
[An historical survey of N. American movements. See also the following unsigned survey articles in the Micropaedia volumes: vol. 4, 524-525, Ghost Dance; vol. 4, 886, Handsome Lake religion; vol. 5, 334, Indian Shaker Church; vol. 7, 921, peyote.]

347   UNDERHILL R[uth] M[urray]. <u>Ceremonial patterns in the greater</u>
      <u>Southwest</u> (American Ethnological Society Monographs, 13).
      Locust Valley, N.Y.:   J. J. Augustin 1948, xi + 62 p.;
      repr. 1966, 62 p., bibl.
          [Pp. 9-11, cult of the god Chungishnish 16th-18th cen-
      turies, among Cáhita Indians, as possibly an Indian version
      of Christian teachings, with "God, His Mother, and the Boy
      Jesus Christ" providing the sanctions for its moral
      instruction.]

348   UNDERHILL, Ruth M[urray]. <u>Red man's religion</u>. Chicago and
      London: University of Chicago Press 1965, 301 p., bibl.
          [Pp. 2-3, brief description of a peyote meeting; ch. 23
      (= pp. 254-269), on modern religions; a good survey in-
      cluding modern movements influenced by Christianity (see
      index: religious prophets; religion, modern; peyote;
      Ghost Dance, etc).]

349   UNITED STATES.   CONGRESS.
          Note: Indian affairs were originally handled by the
      Department of War, and appear in a few pages of its annual
      reports from 1821; new religious movements do not appear
      until reports from 1877:   see items 383, 551.   Congress
      organized an Office of Indian Affairs under a Commissioner
      in 1834; his annual reports (see item 728) cover the
      Kennekuk movement.   This Office later became the Bureau of
      Indian Affairs under the Department of the Interior (organ-
      ized in 1849), with a Commissioner and a Board of Indian
      Commissioners.   Its annual reports may appear as from the
      Bureau, the Commissioner, or the Board; it also issued
      other reports, documents, occasional publications, and a
      Bulletin.
          Other Indian materials appear in the <u>Congressional Record</u>
      of debates in the House of Representatives and in the
      Senate, and in the reports of the Committee on Appropri-
      ations, or the Committee on Indian Affairs, of both the
      House and the Senate.
          For a list of various government departmental documents
      and publications see Slotkin, item 1111, pp. 175-182; some
      of the more important are included in this bibliography.
      See also <u>idem</u>, Notes (pp. 81-141) and Bibliography (pp. 143-
      187) for materials on Ghost Dance and peyotism, especially
      the reports of Indian agents.

350   UNITED STATES.   DEPARTMENT OF THE INTERIOR.   BUREAU OF INDIAN
      AFFAIRS.   <u>Annual Reports</u>.   Washington, D.C.:   Government
      Printing Office.
          [References in following agency, etc. reports (name of
      agent or author in brackets) to (a) Grass Dance: 1887,
      p. 60, Yankton (J. F. Kinney); 1892, p. 469, Sisseton
      (D. T. Hindman); 1895, p. 204, Santee (J. Clements); 1896,

p. 300, Missionary in Rosebud Reservation (J. F. Cross). (b) Hand Game: 1894, pp. 250-251, Ponca, Pawnee, Otoe and Oakland (J. P. Woolsey). (c) Isatai's Comanche messianic cult: 1874, p. 220, Kiowa and Comanche (J. M. Haworth — a convinced Quaker).]

351 UNITED STATES. DEPARTMENT OF THE INTERIOR. BUREAU OF INDIAN AFFAIRS. Documents and reports, Series 4587, no. 26: Kiowa Indian Agency (by F. E. Leupp). Washington, D.C.: Government Printing Office 1903.
[Pp. 22-23, Ghost Dance and peyote.]

352 VAN DEURSEN, Arie. Der Heilbringer: eine ethnologische Studie über den Heilbringer bei den nord-amerikanischen Indianern.... Groningen and the Hague: J. B. Wolters 1931, 395 p., bibl. (pp. 382-395).
[Includes messiah theme.]

353 VOGET, Fred [W.]. Individual motivation in the diffusion of the Wind River Shoshone Sun Dance to the Crow Indians. American Anthropologist 50 (4), 1948, 634-646.
[Pp. 635, 637-638, 640, 641-642, 645, peyotism, as background of the three Crow leaders involved in revival of the Sun Dance in 1941 — after having lapsed since 1875 among the Crow.]

354 VOGET, Fred [W.]. A Shoshone innovator. American Anthropologist 52 (1), 1950, 53-63.
[John Truhujo's endeavours to introduce into the Sun Dance elements at present integrated in peyote ceremonialism.]

355 VOGET, Fred W. Crow socio-cultural groups, in S. Tax (ed.), item 336, 88-93.
[Four groups with various attitudes to Christianity and to nativism; incidental references to the Sun Dance and to peyotism.]

356 VOGET, Fred W. The American Indian in transition: reformation and accommodation. American Anthropologist 58 (2), 1956, 249-263, bibl.; repr. in D. E. Walker, item 360, pp. 645-657.
[Handsome Lake, peyote, and Shakerism as reformative movements where a prophet brings a revelation from a creator-God, and healing is prominent.]

357 WADDELL, J. O. Mesquite and mountains with money and Messiah: a Papago Indian case of cultural revitalization. Journal of the Steward Anthropological Society (Urbana) 2 (1), 1970, 51-88, map, bibl.

[An important study of the "Israelites", a Papago messianic movement in a well-to-do, educated clan c. 1900,
influenced by a negress preacher connected with J. A.
Dowie of Chicago; includes extracts repr. from K. Lumholtz,
item 246A, at p. 55, E. Tooker, item 343A, at pp. 55-56,
and from the local press.]

358   WALKER, Deward E[dgar], Jr. A survey of Nez Percé religion.
      New York: Board of National Missions, United Presbyterian
      Church in the U.S.A. 1964; also summary by Betty J. Patton,
      12 p. Mimeo.
      [In summary, see p. 2, ipnucililpt movement between
      1810-1820; and pentecostal groups passim; most of this
      survey also in his item 359.]

359   WALKER, Deward E[dgar], Jr. Conflict and schism in Nez Percé
      acculturation: a study of religion and politics. Pullman,
      Washington: Washington State University Press 1968, 171 p.,
      maps.
      [Pp. 28-29, 31-39, Tulim syncretist cult from 18th c.;
      pp. 34, 48-52, 87, ipnucililpt neo-primal cult from mid-
      19th c.; pp. 67-72, three independent churches, from 1889;
      pp. 95-123 et passim, two main and other incipient Pente-
      costal sects, with Assemblies of God background; pp. 133-
      139, survey and conclusions; pp. 139-146, comparative
      findings, of theoretical value. Based on University of
      Oregon Ph.D. dissertation 1964.]

360   WALKER, Deward E[dgar] (ed.). The emergent native Americans:
      a reader in culture contact. Boston: Little, Brown and
      Co. 1972, 818 p.
      [Section 1, acculturation; section 5, "new religions",
      reprints A. F. C. Wallace on Delaware Indians, item 400,
      pp. 344-361; E. H. Spicer on Yaqui, item 1525, pp. 362-
      369; O. C. Stewart on Native American Church and the law,
      item 1144, pp. 382-397; R. N. Rapoport on Christian mis-
      sions to the Navaho, pp. 397-423; F. W. Voget, item 356,
      pp. 645-657; E. Boissevain, item 677, pp. 435-447; ibid.,
      item 678, pp. 658-664 on Narragansetts.]

361   WALLACE, Ben J. Oklahoma Kickapoo culture change. Plains
      Anthropologist 14, May 1969, 107-112.
      [Pp. 109-110, young woman's revival of the Kickapoo
      religion, c. 1935; p. 108, traditionalists sharing in
      peyotism.]

362   WALLACE, Ernest and HOEBEL, E[dward] Adamson. The Comanches:
      lords of the south plains (Civilization of the American
      Indian Series, 34). Norman: University of Oklahoma Press
      1952, xvii + 381 p., illus., maps, bibl.

[Pp. 109, 168, 331-337, 345, peyote among the Comanche; pp. 318-326, Coyote Droppings prophet (= Isatai) and Sun Dance; 343-345, Ghost Dance.]

363 WALLIS, Wilson D[allam]. Messiahs: Christian and pagan: their role in civilization. Boston: Richard G. Badger 1918, 276 p.; Washington, D.C.: American Council of Public Affairs 1943.
[Ch. 5, especially pp. 134-145, 148-149, messiahs of the North American aborigines — rather sketchy and uneven.]

364 WARING, A. J., Jr. and HOLDER, Preston. A pre-historic cere-monial complex in the Southeastern United States. American Anthropologist 47 (1), 1945, 1-34.
[Regard the artifacts as belonging to a single widespread cult, by detailed comparisons — a pre-Columbian cult which swept through the late pre-historic southeast much as the Ghost Dance did in 19th century Plains area. See also on Buzzard cult.]

365 WARREN, William Whipple. History of the Ojibwa nation, based upon traditions and oral statements, in Collections of the Minnesota Historical Society. St. Paul, Minnesota: the Society, vol. 5, 1885, 21-394; repr. as History of the Ojibway nation. Minneapolis: Ross and Haines 1957, 527 p.
[1885 ed., pp. 117-118, 320-325, Tenskwatawa; passim, the Midéwiwin society in the 1850s; by an authority on the Ojibwa, an interpreter who was himself part Ojibwa, and who became a member of the legislature in Minnesota.]

366 WAX, Murray L. Les Pawnees à la recherche du Paradis perdu. Archives de Sociologie des Religions no. 4 = 2 (juillet-décembre), 1957, 113-122.
[The Paviotso Spirit Dance of 1880, spread to the Pawnees as a messianic movement which gave new meaning to their traditional hand game as a means of escape from influence of the whites.]

367 WAX, Murray L. Indian Americans: unity and diversity. Englewood Cliffs, N.J.: Prentice-Hall Inc. 1971, 236 p.
[Pp. 136-138, Handsome Lake; 138-141, Ghost Dance; 141-144, Native American Church — useful surveys in each case.]

368 WHITE, Robert A. Value themes of the Native American tribal-istic movement among the South Dakota Sioux. Current Anthropology 15 (3), 1974, 284-289, with invited comments, 289-303.
[The religious dimensions of recent nativism, passim, and specifically at pp. 288-289, 291.]

369 WHITEWOLF, Jim. Jim Whitewolf. The life of a Kiowa Apache
     Indian (Edited, with introduction and epilogue, by
     Charles S. Brant). New York: Dover Publications, Toronto:
     General Publishing Co., and London: Constable and Company
     1969, 144 p., map.
        [Born late 19th century, his narration was made to the
     editor in 1949. Pp. 17, 42-43, Ghost Dance minimally
     accepted; pp. 31-34, the three religious groups and their
     relationships — Methodist, Baptist and Native American
     Church (the largest); pp. 117-118, 123-126, 133, peyote
     meetings, healing, etc.]

370 WILLOYA, William and BROWN, Vinson. Warriors of the rainbow.
     Healdsburg, California: Naturegraph Press Co. 1962, 94 p.,
     illus.
        [Pp. 62-80 on the Indian messianic tradition; pp. 61-64,
     Ghost Dance; p. 82, and colour plate facing p. 79, peyote.
     Willoya was an Eskimo.]

371 WILSON, Bryan R[onald]. Magic and the millennium. A socio-
     logical study of religious movements of protest among tribal
     and Third-World peoples. London: Heinemann, and New York:
     Harper and Row 1973, 547 p.; Frogmore, St. Albans: Granada
     Publishing Co. (Paladin Books) 1975.
        [A more comprehensive study than Lanternari, with much
     source information in footnotes and bibliography. Pp. 226-
     229, Delaware prophet (Neolin); pp. 229-236, Tenskwatawa;
     pp. 280-283, Smohalla; pp. 283-306, Ghost Dances; pp. 353-
     364, Shakers; pp. 387-397, Handsome Lake; pp. 414-449,
     peyotism. See also index of movements for many lesser
     references in each case, and for other movements — Bole
     Maru, Dream Dance, Dreamer faith, Earth Lodge, Feather
     cult, Ishatai, Kennekuk (as Kanakuk), etc. The whole work
     attempts a theoretical framework of world-wide application;
     see his item 124.]

372 WISE, Jennings C. The Red Man in the New World drama (Edited,
     revised and with an introduction by Vine Deloria, Jr.).
     New York: Macmillan 1971, 418 p.
        [Examines the inter-relations of Indians and whites in
     religion and politics: pp. 189-190, Tenskwatawa; pp. 289-
     290, Ghost Dance; p. 337, peyote (briefly).]

373 WISSLER, Clark. General discussion of shamanistic and dancing
     societies. Anthropological Papers, American Museum of
     Natural History (New York) 11 (12), 1916, 853-876, folding
     table.
        [Mainly on dance, etc. societies of Plains Indians, in-
     cluding the Grass Dance type; an early and rudimentary
     nativism.]

374 WISSLER, Clark. <u>The relation of nature to man in aboriginal America</u>. New York: AMS Press Inc. (1926) 1971, 248 p., maps.
[Pp. 82ff., Sun Dance; pp. 189-193, peyote, and its distribution.]

375 WITHERIDGE, David E. No freedom of religion for American Indians (Guest editorial). <u>Journal of Church and State</u> 18, Winter 1976, 5-19.
[Pp. 15-16, the Ghost Dance; p. 17, peyotism; the whole article surveys the lack of Indian freedom of religion since the early 17th century, and appeals for such freedom.]

376 YOUNG, Egerton R. The red man's search for the white man's book. <u>The Missionary Review of the World</u> n.s. 12 (7), 1899, 513-516, illus.
[The 1831 Nez Percé search for the Bible. See also Bashford, item 1330, which it follows closely, K. McBeth, item 250, and criticism in R. I. Burns, item 151A.]

United States of America

This section excludes Alaska which is included
in the section on Canada.

APACHE MOVEMENTS

There are other Apache movements on which no literature has been
discovered, including independent churches; there is also the Holy
Ground religion of Silas John Edwards (see index) and of course
peyotism which is dealt with in its own special section.

377   BOURKE, John G. The medicine men of the Apache, in 9th Annual
       Report, Bureau of American Ethnology 1887-88. Washington,
       D.C.: Government Printing Office 1892, 451-603, illus.,
       bibl.
       [P. 505, describes the dance of Nakaidoklini, Cibecue
       Apache religious leader of the 1881 revolt.]

377A   BROWN, Lenard E. The Arizona Apache and Christianization: a
       study of Lutheran missionary activity, 1893-1943. Univer-
       sity of Arizona, M.A. thesis 1963, 126 p.
       [As background to Apache movements.]

378   CRUSE, Thomas. Apache days and after. Caldwell, Idaho:
       Caxton Printers 1941, 328 p.
       [Pp. 93-112, the Apache rising in 1883 under "Nakai-
       doklini" (1845?-1883) as religious leader; by a military
       officer (later Brigadier-General) who was involved.]

379   FRAZER, Robert. The Apaches of the White Mountain reservation.
       Philadelphia: Indian Rights Association 1885, 22 p.
       [Pp. 10-11, Nakaidoklini.]

380   GOODWIN, Grenville. White Mountain Apache religion. American
       Anthropologist 40 (1), 1938, 24-37.
       [Pp. 34-36, "new religious cults": Na'ilde of 1881,
       concerned with return of the dead; Dayodiya of 1903-1906,
       syncretistic, with a post-cataclysmic paradise on earth; a
       syncretistic anti-shaman movement since c. 1920; other
       minor movements, but no sign of Ghost Dance influences.]

United States of America

Apache Movements

381   GOODWIN, Grenville and KAUT, Charles R. A native religious
      movement among the White Mountain and Cibecue Apache.
      Southwestern Journal of Anthropology 10 (4), 1954, 385-404.
        [Dahgodiyáh ("they will be raised up") movement 1903-
      1907, as narrated by an Apache participant-observer.]

382   LOCKWOOD, Frank C[ummins]. The Apache Indians. New York:
      Macmillan 1938, xvi + 348 p., plates, maps.
        [Pp. 234-239, Nakaidoklini, his prophecies and neo-
      primal movement, and death during an Apache attack on his
      military captors.]

383   UNITED STATES. DEPARTMENT OF WAR. Annual Report of the
      Secretary of War for the year 1881. Washington, D.C.:
      Government Printing Office 1881, 4 vols.
        [Vol. 1, pp. 140, 143, 153, references to Apache "medi-
      cine man, Nockyldelklinne", in various reports.]

DELAWARE PROPHETS

This term includes a number of named individuals — Papoonan,
Neolin and Wangomend — in the eighteenth century when the Delawares
were still near the eastern seaboard. Sometimes these may be referred
to simply as "the Delaware prophet", or this phrase may mean some
other individual who has remained anonymous, or yet again an unnamed
prophet whom Brainerd met in 1745. A few others such as Keposh and
the "Munsee prophetess" (related to the Delawares) have also been
placed in this section.

384   BEATTY, Charles. Journal of Beatty's trip to Ohio county in
      1766, in Journals of Charles Beatty 1762-1769, edited by
      Guy S. Klett. University Park, Pennsylvania: Pennsylvania
      State University Press 1972, pp. 41-75.
        [Pp. 57-59, 68-69, Neolin, a Delaware prophet.]

385   BRAINERD, David. An account of the life of the Rev. David
      Brainerd.... Boston: D. Henchman 1749, 316 p.; many
      other editions, especially as Memoirs of the Rev. David
      Brainerd...by Rev. Jonathan Edwards...Including his journal,
      now for the first time incorporated with the rest of his
      diary... By Sereno Edwards Dwight. New Haven: S. Converse
      1822, 507 p. Repr. St. Clair Shores, Michigan: Scholarly
      Press 1970, 504 p. Also shortened version, New York:
      Funk and Wagnalls 1884, 1891, lxxx + 354 p.
        [See pp. 237-239 (= pp. 184-185 in 1884 ed.) for
      encounter with a Delaware (?) prophet on Susquehanna River,
      1745.]

386 DEARDORFF, Merle H. Zeisberger's Allegheny River towns: 1767-
     1770. Pennsylvania Archaeologist (Harrisburg, Society for
     Pennsylvania Archaeology) 16 (1), 1946, 2-19.
       [P. 8, Wangomend, a Delaware prophet, 1765-1790s.]

387 DE SCHWEINITZ, Edmund Alexander. The life and times of David
     Zeisberger, the western pioneer and apostle of the Indians.
     Philadelphia: J. B. Lippincott and Co. 1870, 747 p.
       [Pp. 333-335, Wangomend, a Delaware prophet 1765-1790s.]

388 HAYS, John. John Hays' diary and journal of 1760 (Wm. A.
     Hunter, ed.). Pennsylvania Archaeologist (Honesdale,
     Society for Pennsylvania Archaeology) 24 (2), 1954, 63-83.
       [Includes first publication of portions of the diary of
     the companion of Moravian missionary C. F. Post on his
     embassy to Delaware Indians west of Philadelphia: pp. 74-
     75, an Indian cultic ritual, with Post's own description
     in his unpublished journal given in n93, p. 75; pp. 76-77,
     a book of pictures or "Indian Bible" and its use; first
     hand evidence on Delaware prophet movement.]

389 HECKEWELDER, John Gottlieb Ernestus. History, manners and
     customs of the Indian nations who once inhabited Pennsyl-
     vania and the neighbouring states. Philadelphia: Abraham
     Small 1819, 450 p., Ger. trans., Göttingen 1821; Fr.
     trans., Paris 1822; Philadelphia: the Historical Society
     of Pennsylvania (Memoirs, vol. 12), new revised ed. with
     introduction and notes by Wm. C. Reichel, 1876, xiv +
     450 p.
       [Ch. 39: Preachers and prophets: pp. 291-293, Delaware
     prophet (Neolin); pp. 293-295, Munsee prophet, Wangomend;
     pp. 295-299, Tecumseh, but no mention of Tenskwatawa, with
     whom Tecumseh may have been confused (Draper suggests
     this) — the character described seems to refer to the
     prophet.]

390 HULBERT, Archer Butler and SCHWARZE, W[illiam] Nathaniel (eds.).
     See under ZEISBERGER, item 402.

391 HUNTER, Charles E. The Delaware nativist revival of the mid-
     eighteenth century. Ethnohistory 18 (1), 1971, 39-49,
     illus., maps, bibl.
       [The history of the two branches of a nativistic
     religious revival: 1. Papoonan's pacifist movement from
     1752. 2. Wangomend and Neolin with a nationalistic move-
     ment which supported Pontiac's uprising of 1763, and with
     a "Bible" and christianized beliefs. A good survey of the
     primary sources, with extracts.]

Delaware Prophets

392   JACOBS, Wilbur R. Was the Pontiac rising a conspiracy? <u>Ohio State Archaeological and Historical Quarterly</u> 59, 1950, 26-37.
    [On the relation between the Delaware prophet [Neolin] and Pontiac, who took over his message.]

392A JOURNAL OU DICTATION D'UNE CONSPIRATION...ET DU SIEGE DU FORT DE DETROIX...1763. [A contemporary account known as the "Pontiac manuscript", supposed author, Robert de Navarre.] Eng. trans. as <u>Journal or history of a conspiracy...1763</u> (Michigan Pioneer and Historical Society, Historical Collections, 8). Lansing: the Society 1886, 266-339; original French with Eng. trans. by R. Clyde Ford, as <u>Journal of Pontiac's conspiracy 1763</u> (M. Agnes Burton, ed.). Detroit: Speaker-Hines Publishing Co. 1912, 243 p.
    [Pp. 30-32 (1912 ed.), Pontiac's version of prophet Neolin's teaching, in his address of 1763; repr. in H. Peckham, item 397, pp. 115-116, and in M. M. Quaife (ed.), <u>The Siege of Detroit</u>. Chicago: Lakeside Press 1958, 8-17; see also in F. Parkman, item 396, pp. 204ff.]

393   KENNY, James. Journal of James Kenny, 1761-1763 (edited by John W. Jordan). <u>Pennsylvania Magazine of History and Biography</u> (Philadelphia) 37 (1), 1913, 1-201.
    [Pp. 171-173, 175, on new religion led by a Delaware prophet — entries for October 15, 18, Nov. 4 and Dec. 12 1762, by a Quaker in charge of a trading store of the Commissioners for Indian Affairs.]

394   LOSKIEL, George Henry. <u>Geschichte der Mission der Evangelischen Brüder unter den Indianern in Nordamerika.</u> Leipzig, 1789; Eng. trans., <u>History of the mission of the United Brethren among the Indians of North America...</u>. London: The Brethren's Society for the Furtherance of the Gospel 1794.
    [Vol. 2, p. 114, Keposh (born <u>c</u>. 1680), head chief of the Delawares, his three-day coma and vision, with subsequent baptism as Solomon in 1749; as example of Delaware visionary call.]

395   McCULLOUGH, John. Narrative, in Joseph Pritts (ed.), <u>Incidents of border life ... in parts of the middle and western states, etc.</u> Chambersburg, Pennsylvania 1839, 1-98; 2nd ed., revised and altered, as <u>Mirror of olden time border life ...</u> . Abingdon, Va.: S.S. Miles 1849, 455-473; also in Archibald Loudon (comp.), <u>A selection of some of the most interesting narratives of outrages ...</u> . Carlisle, Pennsylvania: A. Loudon (Whitehall) 2 vols. 1808-1811; repr. 1888.

[Pritts, 1849, pp. 466-467, and more fully and with
illustrations in Louden, vol. 2, pp. 272-276; the Delaware
prophet and his followers in a nativistic movement, reported first hand by a white captured as a child by
Indians.]

396 PARKMAN, Francis. The conspiracy of Pontiac and the Indian
war after the conquest of Canada. Boston: Little, Brown
& Co. 1851; 10th revised ed. 2 vols. London: Macmillan
1885 and many further eds., incl. London: J. M. Dent
and New York: E. P. Dutton (Everyman's Library Nos. 302-
303) 2 vols. 1908.
     [Vol. 1, pp. 179-180, 204-207, Delaware prophet's
nativistic movement, exhorting to war, early 1760s;
vol. 2, pp. 282-283, the same prophet exhorting to peace
in 1765. See also sections from vol. 1 reprinted in
Sanders and Peek (eds.), item 296, pp. 331-332, and in
F. W. Turner III (ed.), item 345, pp. 531-532.]

397 PECKHAM, Howard H. Pontiac and the Indian uprising. Princeton:
Princeton University Press 1947, 346 p.
     [Pp. 98-101, on Delaware prophet (Neolin) c. 1762;
pp. 113-116, Pontiac's address on Neolin's teaching.]

398 POST, Christian Frederick. ...Two journals of Western tours,
by Charles [sic] Frederick Post: one to the neighbourhood
of Fort Duquesne (July-September 1758); the other, to the
Ohio (October 1758-January 1759). London: J. Wilkie
1759; repr. in Reuben G. Thwaites (ed.), Early Western
Journals 1748-1765..., Cleveland, Ohio: A. H. Clark Co.
1904, I, pp. 175-291, quoted from Proud's History of
Pennsylvania. Philadelphia 1798, vol. 2, app. pp. 65-
132; also other reprints.
     [The Delaware prophet at Assinisink.]

399 SPECK, Frank G[ouldsmith]. A study of the Delaware Indian
Big House ceremony (Publications, Pennsylvania Historical
Commission, 2). Harrisburg: Pennsylvania Historical Commission 1931, 192 p., illus. (vernacular text dictated by
Witapanóxwe, English translation on facing pages).
     [Pp. 9-10, 62, some details of the peyote rite, adopted
after their move westwards. The Big House ceremony described (see especially pp. 20-25, 51-57) is probably the
reshaped traditional form of the Munsee prophetess of
1805, although she is not discussed since Speck sees the
rites as a traditional and not a "new religion" as does
A. F. C. Wallace, item 400, p. 10.]

Delaware Prophets

400   WALLACE, Anthony F. C.   New religions among the Delaware
         Indians, 1600-1900.   Southwestern Journal of Anthropology
         12 (1), 1956, 1-21; repr. in D. E. Walker (ed.), item 360,
         pp. 344-361.
            [A basic survey article, with sources and theoretical
         analysis.]

401   ZEISBERGER, David.   David Zeisberger's history of the Northern
         American Indians (A. B. Hulbert and W. N. Schwarze, eds.).
         Ohio Archaeological and Historical Society Publications
         (Columbus) 19 (1-2), 1910, 1-189.
            [Pp. 1-12, introduction by editors; pp. 128-133, Indian
         religion; pp. 133-136, the Delaware prophets or preachers
         and their teachings regarded as rivals by Zeisberger.
         Based on his MS of 1779-1780.]

402   ZEISBERGER, David.   Diary of David Zeisberger's journey to the
         Ohio [1767] (A. B. Hulbert and W. N. Schwarze, eds.).
         Ohio Archaeological and Historical Society Publications
         (Columbus) 21 (1), 1912, 1-125.
            [Pp. 21-30, 55, 57, "Indian preachers" (probably included
         Wangomend), their teaching and claims, and Zeisberger's
         discussions with them; p. 25, their "Bible".]

GHOST DANCES

   Both the dances of the period 1869-73 and 1889 onwards have been
included. These are distinguished by the use of capital letters from
the other entirely traditional ancestor-related dances also known as
ghost dances. The literature is extensive and some reference, especially to the second form with its dramatic climax at the massacre of
Wounded Knee, is now mandatory in most discussions of Indian history.
The material on Wounded Knee itself (and now on its namesake, the confrontation of the 1970s) is also extensive and passes over into
military history; the material selected here has some more explicit
connection with the Ghost Dance. The latter, it should be noted,
spread also into Canada.

   Included also are various cults associated with the Ghost Dances
or derivative from them, such as Bole Maru, Big Head and Earth Lodge.

403   ALEXANDER, H[artley] B[urr].   Incarnation (American), in J.
         Hastings (ed.), Encyclopaedia of Religion and Ethics,
         vol. 7, 1914, 185a-186b.

[P. 186a, brief references to Tenskwatawa the prophet
and the Ghost Dance as prepared for by certain features of
Indian religions; based on J. Mooney.]

404　ALEXANDER, Hartley Burr. The world's rim. Lincoln:　Univer-
　　　sity of Nebraska Press (1933), 1953, 259 p.; New York:
　　　Bison Books 1969.
　　　[The Ghost Dance against the background of similar
　　　earlier movements, and a sensitive interpretation of Indian
　　　religion in general:　pp. 182, 223-227.]

405　ANDERSON, John A., HAMILTON, Henry W. and HAMILTON, Jean Tyree.
　　　The Sioux of the Rosebud. A history in pictures (The
　　　Civilization of the American Indian, 111).　Norman:
　　　University of Oklahoma Press 1971, 320 p., 234 photographs.
　　　[Pp. 59-61, 267, 280-281, Ghost Dance; and see index.]

406　ANDRIST, Ralph K. The long death: the last days of the
　　　Plains Indians. London:　Collier-Macmillan 1964; New
　　　York:　Macmillan 1964, 371 p., illus.
　　　[Detailed history of the Plains Indians; pp. 336-341,
　　　Wovoka.]

407　ARIZONA GRAPHIC. The Yava-Supai Indian.　The Arizona Graphic
　　　14, 7 Oct. 1899.
　　　[Contains short paragraph reporting an Indian agent
　　　(McCowan) having seen what was probably a form of Ghost
　　　Dance among the eastern Pai c. 1895.]

408　ARNOLD, Frazer.　Ghost Dance and Wounded Knee.　Cavalry
　　　Journal no. 183 = 43, 1934, 18-20.
　　　[Reproduces Lt. Mann's letter to his brother written
　　　just after Wounded Knee, a vital document for understand-
　　　ing certain phases of the engagement.]

409　BAILEY, Paul [Dayton].　Wovoka, the Indian messiah (Western-
　　　lore Great West and Indian Series, 10).　Los Angeles:
　　　Westernlore Press 1957, 223 p., illus.
　　　[An historical reconstruction of the life and influence
　　　of the founder of the Ghost Dance, well done, and useful
　　　as a basic overall picture.　See following item.]

410　BAILEY, Paul [Dayton].　Ghost Dance Messiah: the Jack Wilson
　　　story.　Los Angeles:　Westernlore Publishers 1970, 206 p.;
　　　published also under the title The Ghost Dance Messiah.
　　　New York:　Tower Publications 1970, 172 p.
　　　[Replacing his item 409, and drawing on information from
　　　E. A. Dyer, Wovoka's amanuensis.]

71

Ghost Dances

411   BARRY, D. F.   The Indian excitement in the Northwest.   Leslie's
        Weekly Illustrated Newspaper 71, 1890-1, 391, 395.
        [The Ghost Dance; see also pp. 369, 372 ("Anon").]

412   BLACK ELK.   Black Elk speaks, being the life story of a holy
        man of the Oglala Sioux (as told to John G. Neihardt).
        New York: W. Morrow & Co. 1932, xv + 280 p., illus.; repr.
        (as told through John G. Neihardt).   Lincoln: University
        of Nebraska Press (Bison Books) 1961 etc., 280 p., illus.;
        repr. New York: Pocket Books 1972, 238 p.; facs. repr. of
        1932 ed., London: Barrie and Jenkins 1972.
        [Chs. 21-25 (Bison Books = pp. 234-276):   the Ghost
        Dance and Wounded Knee as told through a notable poet by
        Black Elk (d. 1950) whose visions were confirmed by the
        Ghost Dance; he participated in this and survived marginal
        engagements at Wounded Knee through his sacred shirt.
        Black Elk's account of Oglala Sioux religion is recorded by
        Joseph Epes Brown in The Sacred Pipe (1953 etc.).]

413   BLAND, Thomas A. (ed.).   A brief history of the late military
        invasion of the home of the Sioux.   Washington, D.C.:
        National Indian Defense Association 1891, 31 p.
        [A partisan defence of the Sioux in the Ghost Dance
        troubles, containing some very valuable letters and inter-
        views.   Bland was pro-Indian, anti-government and editor
        of The Council Fire.]

414   BOURKE, John G.   The Indian messiah.   The Nation 4 Dec. 1890,
        439-440.
        [A letter of 28 Nov. 1890 from a cavalry captain;
        against the background of the Ghost Dance and Wovoka he
        discusses how to break the very real power of Indian
        medicine men, with practical suggestions, including content
        for the curriculum of Carlisle Indian School.]

415   BRANT, Charles S.   Indian-white cultural relations in south-
        western Oklahoma.   Chronicles of Oklahoma 37 (4), 1959-
        60, 433-439.
        [Whites' reactions to the Ghost Dance.]

416   BROWN, D[ee] Alexander.   The Ghost Dance and the battle of
        Wounded Knee.   American History Illustrated (Harrisburg,
        Pennsylvania) 1 (8), 1968, 4-16, illus.
        [A good popular survey, well-illustrated, and with a
        full account of events immediately before the 1890
        "battle".]

417   BROWN, Dee [Alexander]. Bury my heart at Wounded Knee. An
       Indian history of the American West. New York: Holt,
       Rinehart & Winston 1971; three Book Club eds. (Book-of-
       the Month, Playboy, Popular Science) 1971; New York/
       London: Bantam Books 1972, 458 p., illus.
          [Pp. 254-256, Isatai and Quanah Parker; ch. 18 (= pp. 389-
       412) Dance of the Ghosts (pp. 406-412, the Ghost Dance and
       murder of Sitting Bull); ch. 19 (= pp. 413-418) Wounded
       Knee. Based on original research, and provides the Indian
       point of view.]

418   BROWN, Donald N. The Ghost Dance religion among the Oklahoma
       Cheyenne. Chronicles of Oklahoma 30 (4), 1952-3, 408-
       416, illus.
          [An historical account from 1889 to 1891; draws from J.
       Mooney, and A. M. Miller, item 501.]

419   BROWN, Mark H. and FELTON, W. R. The frontier years. L. A.
       Huffman, photographer of the plains. New York: Henry
       Holt and Co. 1955, 272 p., illus.
          [Pp. 123-127, the Ghost Dance and Wounded Knee, based on
       Mooney, and "fair to both Indians and whites".]

420   BURDICK, Usher L[loyd] (ed.). My friend the Indian or Three
       heretofore unpublished chapters of the book published
       under the title of My friend the Indian, by Major James
       McLaughlin. Baltimore: Proof Press 1936, 30 p.
          [McLaughlin's publishers rejected his final three chap-
       ters, containing much of interest for the story of the
       Ghost Dance at Standing Rock, and they were published in
       this pamphlet.]

421   BUSBY, Christopher. Ghost Dance. Man, Myth and Magic 4 (39),
       n.d. [1970-2], 1091-1092, illus.
          [A popular outline.]

422   CHAPMAN, Arthur I.
          See UNITED STATES, DEPARTMENT OF WAR, item 551, 1891,
       pp. 191-194.

423   COLBY, L[eonard] W[right]. The Sioux Indian War of 1890-'91.
       Transactions and Reports of the Nebraska State Historical
       Society (Lincoln) 3, 1892, 144-190.
          [General Colby commanded the Nebraska militia in the
       Sioux campaign. This article is detailed and useful and
       includes several letters of importance, but is inaccurate
       in many respects.]

Ghost Dances

424   COLBY, L[eonard] W[right]. Wanagi Olowan Kin (the Ghost songs
       of the Dakotas). Proceedings and Collections of the
       Nebraska State Historical Society (Lincoln) 2nd series,
       1 (3), 1895, 131-150.
         [Reproduces translations of ghost songs.]

425   CRAWFORD, Isabel [Alice Hartley]. Kiowa: the history of a
       Blanket Indian mission. New York: Fleming H. Revel 1915,
       242 p.
         [P. 28, some Kiowa still dancing the Ghost Dance in
       expectation of the return of the dead.]

426   DANGBERG, Grace M. (ed.). Letters to Jack Wilson, the Paiute
       prophet, written between 1908 and 1911. Bulletin, Bureau
       of American Ethnology 164 (Anthropological Papers 49-56)
       1957, Paper 55, pp. 279-296.
         [Twenty-one letters (or fragments) to Wovoka from
       thirteen different people, asking for advice on spiritual
       or material concerns, and in general confirming Mooney's
       account of Wovoka; with introduction and comments by the
       editor.]

427   DANGBERG, Grace [Melissa]. Wovoka. Nevada Historical Society
       Quarterly 11, 1968, 1-53.
         [A good account; includes chronology of Wovoka's life
       1856-1932 (pp. 25-37), and repr. of letters in item 426
       (pp. 40-52).]

428   DAVIDSON, Robert Nathaniel. A study of the Ghost Dance of
       1889. Stanford University, M.A. thesis 1952, 49 p.

429   DAY, A[rthur] Grove. The sky clears. Poetry of the American
       Indians. New York: Macmillan 1951, 204 p., bibl.;
       Lincoln: University of Nebraska Press c. 1951.
         [Includes brief references to Wovoka and the Ghost
       Dance among the Northern Paiute.]

430   DE FÉLICE, Philippe. L'Enchantement des danses et la magie du
       verbe. Essai sur quelques formes inférieures de la
       mystique. Paris: Ed. Albin Michel 1957, 416 p.
         [Pp. 71-73, Ghost Dance discussed in the context of a
       world-wide study of religious dance.]

431   DELORIA, Ella. Speaking of Indians. New York: Friendship
       Press 1944, x + 163 p.
         [Pp. 79-84, first-hand account of Ghost Dance among the
       Dakota, by old man who had seen it when c. 10 years old;
       author a Christian Yankton Dakota woman anthropologist.]

432   DEVEREUX, George and LOEB, Edwin M. Antagonistic acculturation.
       American Sociological Review 8 (2), 1943, 133-147.
           [Pp. 145-146, Ghost Dance as example of "antagonistic
       acculturation".]

433   DOBYNS, Henry F. and EULER, Robert C. The Ghost Dance of
       1889 among the Pai Indians of north-western Arizona
       (Prescott College Studies in Anthropology, 1). Prescott,
       Arizona: Prescott College Press 1967, vi + 71 p., illus.,
       maps.
           [A detailed history of the adoption of the Ghost Dance
       from the Paiutes, of the skeptical faction among the Pai,
       and of the stresses the latter experienced in the preced-
       ing period. Based on eye-witnesses, oral tradition, and
       extensive use of the local newspaper, Mohave County Miner,
       with many extracts.]

434   DORSEY, James Owen. A study of Siouan cults, in 11th Annual
       Report, Bureau of American Ethnology. Washington, D.C.:
       Government Printing Office 1894, 351-544, illus.
           [P. 544, the new "Messiah craze" (Ghost Dance) as "wilful
       or accidental perversions" of missionary teaching, and to
       be distinguished from traditional Sioux ghost dances and
       lodge. In the 3rd Annual Report...1881-82, at p. 353,
       he reported that the traditional ghost dance had not been
       held for 40 years.]

435   DOUGHERTY, W. E. The recent messiah craze. Journal of the
       Military Service Institution of the United States 12,
       1891, 576-578.
           [Observations of an infantry officer at Pine Ridge during
       the outbreak.]

436   DOWNEY, Fairfax [Davis]. Indian-fighting army. New York: C.
       Scribner's Sons 1941, xii + 329 p.; repr. Fort Collins,
       Colorado: Old Army Press 1971, xii + 329 p., illus., bibl.
           [Pp. 292-306, "Combat with ghosts" — on the Ghost Dance
       and Wounded Knee — by an army officer, justifying the army
       action.]

437   DU BOIS, Cora [Alice]. The 1870 Ghost Dance (Anthropological
       Records 3:1). Berkeley: University of California 1939,
       151 p., figs., plates, map.
           [Full description of Dreamers, Ghost Dance, Earth Lodge,
       Bole Maru and Big Head cults in N. California; Bole Maru
       was the most under Christian influence, and the only one
       that persisted up to the time of writing. See pp. 129-139

for summary and conclusions, also introduction, pp. 1-2;
pp. 1-3 repr. in Heizer and Whipple, item 457,
pp. 496-499.]

438   EASTMAN, Charles Alexander (= Ohiyesa). From the deep woods
to civilization: chapters in the autobiography of an
Indian. Boston: Little, Brown and Co. 1916, etc., x +
206 p., illus.; repr. Barrington, Illinois: Peter Wolff
Books.
[Most of Eastman's writings on Indian history have been
seriously questioned, but his account of the Ghost Dance
at Pine Ridge (where he was agency physician) and of the
Wounded Knee massacre is an outstanding source generally
corroborated by other evidence: see pp. 82-115. See
also next item.]

439   EASTMAN, Elaine Goodale. The Ghost Dance war and Wounded Knee
massacre of 1890-91. Nebraska History (Lincoln) 26 (1),
1945, 26-42.
[Elaine Goodale taught school at Pine Ridge during the
Ghost Dance troubles and later married the Agency physician,
Dr. Charles Eastman, a Santee Sioux. This article, which
includes excerpts from her diary, is a valuable source,
despite its anti-military tone.]

440   FINLEY [Mrs.] James A. The Messiah superstition. Essex
County Mercury (Salem, Massachusetts) 26 Nov. 1890; repr.
in Journal of American Folk-Lore 4, March 1891, 67-68.
[An eye-witness account of a Ghost Dance. Extracts
repr. in item 450, p. 47.]

441   FISKE, Frank. The taming of the Sioux. Bismarck, N.D.:
Bismarck Tribune 1917, 186 p., illus.
[P. 147ff., Jack Wilson (= Wovoka).]

442   FLETCHER, Alice Cunningham. The Indian messiah. Journal of
American Folk-Lore 4 (March), 1891, 57-60; see also "The
Indian Messiah" superstition, as editorial comment,
pp. 61-69.
[On the Ghost Dance.]

443   FRINK, Maurice M. Died here innocent. Outing February 1915,
549-554.
[An article based on personal experience at Pine Ridge
when Wounded Knee was still fresh in the minds of
survivors.]

444   GATSCHET, Albert S. (ed.). Report of an Indian visit to Jack
Wilson, Payute messiah. Journal of American Folk-Lore 6,
1893, 108-111.
[Three Cheyenne Indians went to see Wovoka in 1890 and
reported through two educated Indian intermediaries to
Gatschet, who adds a biographic appendix (p. 111) in which
he claims that Wovoka regarded himself as a chosen messen-
ger but not a messiah. Extracts repr. in item 450,
pp. 44-46.]

445   GAYTON, A[nna] H[adwick]. The Ghost Dance of 1870 in south-
central California. University of California Publications
in American Archaeology and Ethnology (Berkeley) 28 (3),
1930, 57-82, illus., map.
[The diffusion from the northern Western Mono through
the San Joaquin valley; detailed accounts of the dances at
Saganiu and Eshom valley; analysis of the process of
acculturation, showing both innovations and relation to
traditional culture.]

446   GHOST DANCE [film]. Ghost Dance of the Indian nation. New
York: Crow Dog Defense Fund, 251 W 89th. St., 8D, 1974,
16mm. colour film, 60 mins.
[The Ghost Dance ceremony on Rosebud Sioux Indian Reservation, S. Dakota, 1974. "An intimate view without de-
stroying the spiritual atmosphere".]

447   GHOST DANCE [record tape]. Akwesasne Notes, Mohawk Nation,
via Rooseveltown, N.Y. 13683. Reel to reel, 3 3/4 i.p.s.,
15 mins., n.d.
[A discussion with a historian of Indian music about the
origins of the Ghost Dance, its relation to Indian religious tradition, and how its misinterpretation contributed
to the Wounded Knee massacre.]

448   GIFFORD, Edward Winslow. Miwok cults. University of California Publications in American Archaeology and Ethnology
18 (3), 1926, 391-408.
[Pp. 393, 399, 400-402, relation of Ghost Dance of 1870
to Miwok cults.]

449   GIFFORD, Edward Winslow. Southern Maidu religious ceremonies.
American Anthropologist 29, 1927, 214-257.
[On the central California Kuksu or "God-impersonating"
cult: pp. 217, 221, 224-233, 247, 249, 252-257 on the
influences of the Ghost Dance on this cult.]

Ghost Dances

450   GREENWAY, John. The Ghost Dance. Some reflections, with
        evidence, on a cult of despair among the Indians of North
        America. The American West (Palo Alto) 6 (4), 1969,
        42-47, illus.
        [Interprets such movements as unrealistic reactions to
        severe threats to a culture; includes extracts from Finley,
        item 440, at p. 47, Gatschet, item 444, at pp. 44-46, and
        Grinnell, item 452, at pp. 46-47.]

451   GRESHAM, John C. The story of Wounded Knee. Harper's Weekly
        35, 7 Feb. 1891, 106-107.
        [Good firsthand account by a participant military
        officer.]

452   GRINNELL, George Bird. Account of the Northern Cheyennes con-
        cerning the Messiah superstition. Journal of American
        Folk-Lore 4 (12), 1891, 61-67.
        [Pp. 61-67, analysis of the Ghost Dance, by one of the
        best interpreters, with intimate knowledge of Indians;
        pp. 67-68, report of the Ghost Dance by trader's wife at
        Wounded Knee; pp. 68-69, editorial appeal for information.
        Extracts repr. in item 450, pp. 46-47.]

453   GRUBER, Abraham. The Patrick rancheria. The Masterkey (South-
        west Museum, Los Angeles) 37 (1), 1963, 30-34, illus.
        [In Butte County, California; its use by the Maida as a
        centre for the Ghost Dance of 1869-1873.]

454   HANEY, William Edward. An analysis of the influence of
        environment and contact on the form of two millenarian
        movements. Washington State University, M.A. thesis 1965,
        86 p.
        [The Ghost Dance and Melanesian cargo movements.]

455   HANNAHSON, A. E. An Indian dance in the northwest. The Knox
        College Monthly and Presbyterian Magazine (Toronto) 18,
        1894-95, 167-175.
        [On the Ghost Dance.]

456   HEIDENREICH, Charles Adrian. A review of the Ghost Dance
        Religion of 1889-90 among the North American Indians and
        comparison of eight societies which accepted or rejected
        the dance. University of Oregon, Eugene, M.A. thesis
        1967, 104 p.

457   HEIZER, R[obert] F[leming] and WHIPPLE, M. A. (eds.). The
        Californian Indians: a source book. Berkeley and

Los Angeles: University of California Press 1951, 487 p.,
illus., maps; 2nd rev. enlarged ed. 1971, 619 p.
[Reprints: A. L. Kroeber, item 478, at pp. 54–59, 114–
115; also C. Du Bois, item 437 (pp. 1–3), at pp. 496–499.]

458   HERZOG, George. Plains Ghost Dance and Great Basin music.
      American Anthropologist 37 (3), 1935, 403–419, music scores.
      [Great Basin song styles transmitted with the Ghost
      Dance to the Plains Indians and adopted even when the
      Dance was rejected.]

459   HERZOG, George. Special song types of North American Indian
      music. Zeitschrift für vergleichende Musikwissenschaft
      3 (1–2), 1935.
      [Includes study of 33 Ghost Dance songs.]

460   HILL, W[illard] W. The Navaho Indians and the Ghost Dance of
      1890. American Anthropologist 46 (4), 1944, 523–527;
      repr. in W. A. Lessa and E. Z. Vogt, Reader in Comparative
      Religion, 1965, 478–482.
      [The Navaho were quite familiar with the Ghost Dance
      which had elements congruent with their own culture, but
      their great fear of the dead prevented their accepting it;
      appendix (pp. 525–527), reports of individual attitudes.]

461   HITTMAN, Michael. Ghost Dances, disillusionment and opiate
      addiction: an ethnohistory of Smith and Mason Valley
      Paiutes. University of New Mexico, Ph.D. dissertation
      (anthropology) 1973, 195 p., bibl.
      [The Dances of 1870 and 1890, with fresh examination of
      evidence, and of various interpretations in the past.]

462   HITTMAN, Michael. The 1870 Ghost Dance at the Walker River
      reservation: a reconstruction. Ethnohistory 20 (3), 1973,
      247–278.
      [Interpreted as a transformative movement consequent on
      the effects of white contact, rather than as a development
      from earlier Prophet Dances, etc., with the functions of a
      curing rite and an "increase ceremony"; the problem of
      resurrection in a culture with ritual avoidance of the
      dead.]

463   HOWARD, Oliver O[tis]. My life and experiences among our
      hostile Indians. Hartford: A. T. Worthington & Co. 1907;
      repr. New York: Da Capo Press Inc. 1972, 570 p., illus.,
      with introduction by R. M. Utley.
      [Ch. 37 (= pp. 467–485), the "Messiah craze" among the
      Sioux — Indian dreamers and the Ghost Dance.]

Ghost Dances

464 HOWE, Mark Antony De Wolfe. <u>The life and labors of Bishop
     Hare, apostle to the Sioux</u>. New York: Sturgis & Walton
     Co. 1911, 417 p.
          [Contains important material on the Episcopal missionary
     efforts among the Sioux; pp. 235-243, the "Messiah craze".
     See also his article, An apostle to the Sioux...<u>The
     Atlantic Monthly</u> 108, 1911, 359-370.]

465 HOWELLS, William. <u>The heathens: primitive man and his
     religions</u>. Garden City, New York: Doubleday 1948; with
     American Museum of Natural History 1962, 302 p., illus.
          [Pp. 259-269, popular account of the Ghost Dance.]

466 HULTKRANTZ, Åke. <u>The North American Indian Orpheus tradition:
     a contribution to comparative religion</u> (Monograph Series,
     2). Stockholm: Ethnographic Museum of Sweden 1957,
     340 p., bibl.
          [Pp. 124., 145-146, 262-263, 306-307, etc., on Ghost
     Dance in relation to Orpheus tradition; pp. 308-312,
     summary and conclusion.]

467 HYDE, George E. <u>A Sioux chronicle</u> (The civilization of the
     American Indian Series, 45). Norman: University of
     Oklahoma Press 1956, 320 p., illus.
          [Pp. 238-320, Plains Indians' quest for the "Indian
     Christ" or Ghost Dance Messiah — an historical account.]

468 INDIAN RIGHTS ASSOCIATION. <u>Annual Report</u> (Philadelphia).
     See <u>Report</u> 8, 1891, pp. 4-7, 48; 9, 1892, pp. 24-33; 10,
     1893, p. 31.
          [On the Ghost Dance, by a pro-Indian body founded by
     whites in 1882.]

469 INDIAN RIGHTS ASSOCIATION. <u>A crisis in Indian Affairs</u>.
     Philadelphia: Indian Rights Association 1891.
          [On the Ghost Dance.]

470 JAMES, George Wharton. <u>The Indians of the Painted Desert
     region. Hopis, Navahoes, Wallapais, Havasupaid</u>. Boston:
     Little, Brown & Co. 1903, xxi + 268 p., illus. (Repr.
     1904, 1907).
          [Pp. 249-255, the Ghost Dance among the (Havasupai) Pai
     at Cataract Canyon, as reported by a white participant-
     observer.]

471 JOHNSON, W[illis] Fletcher. <u>The red record of the Sioux. Life
     of Sitting Bull and history of the Indian war of 1890-91...
     story of the Sioux nation; their manners and customs, ghost
     dances and Messiah craze...</u>. Philadelphia: Edgewood
     Publishing Co. 1891, 544 p., illus., map; Ger. trans.,

Die blutige Vergangenheit der Sioux..., same publisher
1891, 33-608 p.
[Pp. 168-171, Sitting Bull's involvement in the Ghost
Dance; pp. 257-266, the Ghost Dances, and Porcupine's version of the "new God" or messiah; pp. 267-281, reports of
visits to Wovoka by Porcupine and others; pp. 318-331,
Mrs. C. Weldon's hostility to Matowanatitaka, the Cheyenne
"prophet of the Messiah"; pp. 426-430, Ghost Dances, Hopkins
(the white false messiah), and Indian scout Chapman's report
of visit to Wovoka; pp. 514-516, Bishop W. H. Hare's remarks
on Ghost Dance troubles.]

472   JONES, W. Anoska Nimiwina. Harvard Monthly 28, 1899, 102-111.
      [Title means "the dance of peace"; a vivid and sympa-
      thetic account of what "others scornfully brand as the
      Ghost Dance or Messiah Craze", as observed among the
      Osakie, united with some six other tribes.]

473   JOURNAL OF AMERICAN FOLK-LORE. The ghost dance in Arizona.
      Journal of American Folk-Lore 5 (16), 1892, 65-68.
      [The Pai Ghost Dance adaptation of the typical Indian
      round dance; repr. from "the Mohave Miner and copied in
      the Chicago Inter-Ocean, 25 June, 1891".]

474   KEHOE, Alice B[eck]. The ghost dance religion in Saskatchewan,
      Canada. Plains Anthropologist (Norman, Oklahoma) 13
      (42:1), 1968, 296-304.
      [Forced change emphasizes health problems, and Indian
      religious movements can cure psychosomatic disorders un-
      relieved by Western medicine.]

475   KEHOE, Alice Beck. The Dakotas in Saskatchewan, in Ethel
      Nurge (ed.), The modern Sioux. Lincoln: University of
      Nebraska Press 1970, 149-172.
      [Pp. 162-163, Ghost Dance, surviving in non-millenarian
      form among the few Dakotas on Round Plains Reserve.]

476   KELLEY, W. F. The Indian troubles and the battle of Wounded
      Knee. Transactions and Reports of the Nebraska State
      Historical Society 4, 1892, 30-50.
      [Good article by a newspaper reporter who covered the
      Pine Ridge campaign and participated in the "battle".]

477   KROEBER, Alfred L[ouis]. A Ghost Dance in California. Journal
      of American Folk-Lore 64 = 17, 1904, 32-35.
      [Pre-Wovoka forms among the Karok and Yurok on lower
      Klamath River in the early 1870s. Men, women and children
      participated, dancing in concentric circles until trance
      ensued and then visions of the dead who would return;
      no special place required, and traditional practices

overturned (dogs killed, intercourse banned, nude mixed
bathing encouraged).]

478   KROEBER, Alfred L[ouis]. Elements of culture in native
       California. University of California Publications in
       American Archaeology and Ethnology 13 (8), 1922, 259-328.
            [Pp. 316-321, Ghost Dance of 1890; repr. in Heizer and
       Whipple, item 457, pp. 54-59, 114-115.]

479   KROEBER, A[lfred] L[ouis]. Anthropology. New York: Harcourt
       Brace and Co. Inc. (1923); new ed. rev. 1948, xii + 856 +
       xxxix p., illus., maps.
            [P. 334, the cultural situation of the Ghost Dance —
       halfpage outline; ch. 12, The growth of a primitive reli-
       gion (that of California Indians).]

479A   LAVIOLETTE, Gontran. The Sioux Indians of Canada. Regina:
       the Marian Press 1944, 5-138 p., illus., bibl.
            [Pp. 119-120, the Messiah (i.e. Ghost) Dance near Wood
       Mountain Reserve, Dakota, in 1895 — "the only Messiah
       Dance ever held in Canada". By a missionary of the Catholic
       O.M.I.]

480   LESLIE'S WEEKLY ILLUSTRATED NEWSPAPER. The Sioux of South
       Dakota. Leslie's Weekly Illustrated Newspaper 71, 1890-1,
       369, 372.
            [P. 369, Grass Dance; p. 372, Ghost Dance; see also
       D. F. Barry, pp. 391, 395, Ghost Dance; and J. M.
       McDonough, pp. 476, 479, Ghost Dance; D. Smith, pp. 432,
       437, Ghost Dance.]

481   LESSER, Alexander. Cultural significance of the Ghost Dance.
       American Anthropologist 35 (1), 1933, 108-115; repr. in
       J. M. Yinger (ed.), Religion, society and the individual.
       New York: Macmillan Co. 1957, etc., 490-496.

482   LESSER, Alexander. The Pawnee Ghost Dance Hand Game, a
       study of cultural change (Columbia University Contribu-
       tions in Anthropology, 16). New York: Columbia University
       Press 1933, x + 337 p., diagrams; repr. New York: AMS
       Press 1969.
            [Pp. 1-3, 49-52, cultural status at dawn of Ghost Dance;
       ch. 2 (= pp. 53-104), the Ghost Dance; Ch. 3 (= pp. 105-
       123), cultural significance; pp. 155-157, Ghost Dance hand
       game; pp. 309-337, Ghost Dance and old games compared.]

483   LEUPP, Francis E[llington]. The Indian and his problem. New
       York: C. Scribner's Sons 1910, xiv + 369 p.
            [Pp. 259-260, Ghost Dance. By a Commissioner for Indian
       Affairs.]

484   LIBERTY, Margot.   I will play with the soldiers.   <u>Montana</u>
        (Helena, Montana) 14 (4), 1964, 16-26.
         [Two young Cheyennes who murdered a white, then virtually
        arranged their own death at the hands of white soldiers
        during the Ghost Dance excitement of 1890 — now a tribal
        legend.]

485   LOTT, Milton.   <u>Dance back the buffalo</u>.   Boston: Houghton
        Mifflin Co. 1959; repr. New York: Pocket Books 1968,
        325 p.
         [Historical novel on the Sioux and the Indian Messiah.]

486   McCANN, Frank D., Jr.   Ghost Dance: last hope of Western
        tribes.   <u>Montana</u> (Helena, Montana) 16 (1), 1966, 25-34.
         [A general survey, up to the Sioux dance and Wounded
        Knee.]

487   McDONOUGH, J. M.   The Indian troubles.   <u>Leslie's Weekly Illus-</u>
        <u>trated Newspaper</u> (New York) 71, 1890-1, 476, 479.
         [On the Ghost Dance.   See also Anon, and D. F. Barry in
        same volume.]

488   McGILLYCUDDY, Julia B.   <u>McGillycuddy, agent.   A biography of</u>
        <u>Valentine T. McGillycuddy</u>.   Palo Alto, California: Stan-
        ford University Press, and London: Oxford University Press
        1941, 291 p., illus.
         [As reported by McGillycuddy (formerly agent at Pine
        Ridge) to his second wife.   Ch. 25 (= pp. 258-274), Sitting
        Bull's last battle: McGillycuddy's part in the events
        leading to Wounded Knee, including vain efforts to avert
        troubles; the Ghost Dance, <u>passim</u>.]

489   McKERN, Sharon S. and McKERN, Thomas W.   The peace messiah.
        <u>Mankind</u> (Los Angeles) 2 (9), 1970, 58-69.
         [On Wovoka — a popular historical account.]

490   McLAUGHLIN, James.   <u>My friend the Indian</u>.   Boston: Houghton
        Mifflin 1910, viii + 416 p., plates; new ed. 1926.
         [Pp. 183-222, Ghost Dance.   By the government agent
        assigned to Standing Rock to Westernize the Sioux.]

491   McLAUGHLIN, James.   <u>My friend the Indian, or three heretofore</u>
        <u>unpublished chapters...</u>, edited and prefaced by Usher L.
        Burdick.   Baltimore: the Proof Press 1936, 30 p., illus.
         [Ghost Dance: the aftermath of Sitting Bull's Death,
        etc.   See also at item 420.]

Ghost Dances

492   MACCHIORO, Vittorio [D.]. Zagreus Studi intorno all'orfismo.
       Florence: Vallechi 1930, 626 p., illus.
           [Pp. 291ff., comparison of Ghost Dance and similar
       movements with Orphism.]

493   MACCHIORO, Vittorio D. From Orpheus to Paul. A history of
       Orphism (Studies in Religion and Culture. Schermerhorn
       Lectures, 1). New York: Henry Holt and Co. 1930, 262 p.,
       illus.
           [Pp. 47-48, the prophet of 1762; pp. 53-57, Ghost Dance
       under Wovoka, and then Sitting Bull, as "the best example
       of a religion based on collective visions", similar to
       Orphism.]

494   MARLEY, Everett Leslie. History of Pine Ridge Indian Reser-
       vation. University of Nebraska, M.A. thesis 1935,
       138 p., maps.
           [On the Oglala Sioux of South Dakota, involved in the
       Ghost Dance and the Wounded Knee massacre.]

495   MASON, Bernard S[terling]. Dances and stories of the American
       Indian. New York: A. S. Barnes & Co., 1944, 269 p.,
       illus.
           [Pp. 150-157, clear account of the movements in the
       Ghost Dance, with diagrams.]

496   MATTES, Merrill J. The enigma of Wounded Knee. Plains
       Anthropologist 5, May 1960, 1-11, maps, bibl.
           [Good analysis of published evidence, showing the dif-
       ficulty of establishing the true facts; pp. 2-3, 6, more
       especially on the Ghost Dance.]

497   MAUS, Marion P. The new Indian messiah. Harper's Weekly
       (New York) 34, 6 December 1890, 944.
           [A member of General Miles' staff, Maus observed the
       Ghost Dance in October 1890 when the general visited Pine
       Ridge as a member of the Northern Cheyenne Commission.]

498   MEASER, Forrest W., Jr. Na'ilde: the Ghost Dance of the
       White Mountain Apache. The Kiva (Tucson) 33 (1), 1967,
       15-24.
           [A. F. C. Wallace's revitalization theory applied to the
       1881 Apache movement, which has the 1870 Paiute Ghost
       Dance as antecedent.]

499   MEIGHAN, Clement W. and RIDDELL, Francis A. The Maru cult of
       the Pomo Indians: a California Ghost Dance survival
       (Southwest Museum Papers, 23). Los Angeles: Southwest
       Museum 1972, x + 134 p., illus.

[The revivalistic cult which continues to serve religious and social functions — a derivative from the Ghost Dance through the intermediate Earth Lodge cult; Appendix D (= pp. 111-120), on the Stewart's Point form of Maru under the current prophetess, Elsie Parrish.]

500   MEKEEL, H. S[cudder]. Ghost Dance, in A. L. Kroeber (ed.), Walapai ethnography (Memoirs, American Anthropological Association, 42). Menasha: American Anthropological Association 1935, 198-202.
[The Dance among the Walapai for a few years from 1889; pp. 199-202, verbatim autobiography reporting the Dance.]

501   MILLER, Anna Marti. A history of the Ghost Dance religion among the Indians. University of Oklahoma, M.A. thesis 1935, 94 p.

502   MILLER, David Humphreys. Ghost Dance. New York: Duell, Sloan & Pearce 1959, 318 p., maps.
[A popular historical reconstruction of the dance and the Sioux military conflict, sympathetic to the Indian viewpoint, based on extensive interviews with survivors from the 1890s, oral tradition and local newspapers (see pp. 279-309 for account of sources); pp. 57-59, 76-81, 232, etc., on young Black Elk (who later "adopted" the author), including origin of ghost shirts in his vision; p. 296, possible use of peyote by Wovoka and others.]

503   MILLER, David Humphreys. Echoes of the Little Bighorn. American Heritage 22 (4), 1971, 28-41, illus.
[Pp. 37-41, interview with Dewey Beard, a Sioux Ghost Dancer who was not at Wounded Knee, together with a general historical survey.]

504   MILLER, Joseph (comp. and ed.). The Arizona story ... from original newspaper sources. New York: Hastings House 1952, 345 p., illus.
[Pp. 333-334, the Ghost Dance among the Pai in 1891; extract in Dobyns and Euler, item 433, pp. 5-6.]

505   MILLER, Virginia Peek. The Yuki: culture contact to allotment. University of California, Davis, Ph.D. dissertation (anthropology) 1973, xvi + 386 p., maps.
[Northern California Indians with late contact with whites; after Methodist ministers acting as Indian Agents had attempted conversion, there were new religious movements in the 1870s combining Methodist and 1870 Ghost Dance elements, as the latter arrived in the form of the Earth

85

Ghost Dances

> Lodge, Bole Maru and Big Head cults; the main result was
> a great, though somewhat temporary, turning to Methodism;
> see pp. 211-228, 241, 339-341, 349-350.]

506 MINNEAPOLIS INSTITUTE OF ARTS. I wear the Morning Star.
Minneapolis: the Institute 1976.
[Describes an exhibition related to the Ghost Dance.]

507 MINTON, Maurice M. The Indian messiah. The Illustrated
American (New York) 13 December 1890, 7.

508 MOONEY, James. The Ghost-dance religion and the Sioux out-
break of 1890 = 14th Annual Report, Bureau of American
Ethnology, 1892-93, Pt. 2. Washington, D.C.: Government
Printing Office 1896, 641-1136, illus.; repr. with new
preface and introduction by B. Fontana, La Casa Escuela,
Glorieta, New Mexico: Rio Grande Press 1973, 641-1136;
repr. as The Ghost Dance religion and Wounded Knee. New
York: Dover Publications Inc. 1973, and Magnolia, Maine:
Peter Smith 1973; under original title, abridged, with
introduction by A. F. C. Wallace, Chicago: University of
Chicago Press (Phoenix Books) 1965, 359 p., illus.; also
selections in many readers and anthologies (see D. and B.
Tedlock, item 338); and separately as facsimile of sections
of 1896 ed. on other movements, at Seattle: Shorey Book
Store — The Ghost Dance religion: the Shakers of Puget
Sound, 1966 etc., original pp. 746-763, and The Ghost
Dance religion: Smohalla and his doctrine. 4th ed. 1970,
original pp. 716-745.
[The classic anthropological account with a wealth of
detail, source references, and extracts reprinted.]

509 M[OONEY], J[ames]. Ghost Dance, in F. W. Hodge (ed.), item
715, 491-492.

510 MOONEY, James. The Indian Ghost Dance. Collections of the
Nebraska State Historical Society 16, 1911, 168-186.
[A speech before the Nebraska State Historical Society
in a more popular vein than in the Bureau of American
Ethnology Publication; also remarks on a second occasion.]

511 [MOOREHEAD, Warren King]. Ghost dances in the West. The
Illustrated American 5 (48), 17 Jan. 1891, 326-333, illus.,
music; repr. separately (together with 5, 1891, p. 544 on
official opposition to The Illustrated American petition
on behalf of the Sioux), Ramona, California: Acoma Books
1976, 10 p.

[A remarkably understanding article for its time, based on first hand experience. The rise of the movement, the Sioux form of the dance — details of preparatory sweat lodge, of the dances, songs (with music) and visions, of original features and similarities to Christianity; the tragic outcome due to the whites' treatment of the Sioux, failure to recognize their religious sincerity, and over-reaction through use of the Army. Good etchings.]

512 MOOREHEAD, Warren K[ing]. The Indian messiah and the Ghost Dance. American Antiquarian and Oriental Journal (Chicago, etc.) 13, May 1891, 161-167.
[Personal observations of the Sioux Ghost Dance, with criticism of soldiers at Wounded Knee; by a Philadelphia Post reporter.]

513 MOOREHEAD, Warren K[ing]. The American Indian in the United States: period 1850-1914. Andover: Andover Press 1914, 440 p., illus., maps.
[Ch. 9 (= pp. 99-109), the "Messiah craze"; ch. 10 (= pp. 110-117), the dance — written at Pine Ridge, December 1890; chs. 11-12 (= pp. 118-132), the military, death of Sitting Bull, Wounded Knee (using J. McLaughlin's account of Sitting Bull's arrest, items 490, 491) — all by a sympathetic eye witness. P. 283, missionaries and Ghost Dance; and independent church activities in Oklahoma, 1913.]

514 THE MORMONS have stepped down and out of celestial government — the American Indians have stepped up and into celestial government. Salt Lake City, n.d. [1892], 4 p.
[A Mormon pamphlet relating Mormon messianic prophecies to events under Wovoka at Walker's Lake, Nevada, in March 1900. Extracts given in Mooney, item 508, 1965 ed., pp. 36-37.]

515 MÜLLER, Hans-Peter. Die Geistertanzbewegung unter den nord-amerikanischen Indianern als Entwicklungsproblem. Ein kulturanthropologisch - vergleichende Studie uber Tradition und abweichendes Verhalten (Studien und Materialen der Anthropologischen Forschung, 1:1). Weisbaden: Edition Ethnos - B. Heymann [1978?].
[Publisher's announcement.]

516 NATIONAL INDIAN DEFENCE ASSOCIATION. The Sioux nation and the United States. A brief history of the treaties of 1868,

Ghost Dances

1876, and 1889 between that nation and the United States.
Washington, D.C.: National Indian Defense Association
1891, 32 p.
[Relevant to the Ghost Dance.]

517 NEIHARDT, John G[niesenau]. The song of the Messiah. New
York: Macmillan (1935) 1949, 110 p. Repr. in his Twilight
of the Sioux. The song of the Indian wars. Song of the
messiah (A Cycle of the West, 2). Lincoln: University of
Nebraska Press (Bison Books) 1971, 179 + 110 p.
[The final narrative poem in his "Cycle of the West", a
series of epics on the Indian wars. This deals with last
phase of Indian resistance on the prairies in western S.
Dakota. Sections:- I. The voice in the wilderness.
II. The coming of the word. III. The Dance. IV. The
soldiers. V. Sitting Bull. VI. The Way. Five chiefs
seek the return of the Dead, and find them led by the Holy
One (Christ) and bring the vision back to their tribes —
the outcome in the Battle of Wounded Knee. Very movingly
told.]

518 NEIHARDT, John G[niesenau]. Black Elk speaks.
See under BLACK ELK.

519 NORMAN, John. Ghost Dance. New York: Ballantine 1970,
342 p.
[An historical novel based on the Sioux and the massacre
of Wounded Knee, set against the background of the Ghost
Dance.]

520 OVERHOLT, Thomas W. The Ghost Dance of 1890 and the nature of
the prophetic process. Ethnohistory 21 (1), 1974 [appeared
December 1975] 37-63.
[The interaction between the supernatural, the prophet
Wovoka, his disciples and the peoples affected as seen in
the origin, transmission and alterations in the Dance —
i.e., the dynamics of the prophetic act.]

521 OVERHOLT, Thomas W. Short Bull, Black Elk, Sword and the
"meaning" of the Ghost Dance. Religion: Journal of
Religion and Religions (accepted for publication 1978).

522 PAINTER, C[harles] C[ornelius Coffin]. Cheyennes and Arapahoes
revisited, and a statement of their agreement and contract
with attorneys (Publications of the Indian Rights Association Series 2 (3)). Philadelphia: Indian Rights
Association 1893, 62 p.
[Pp. 10-13, 15, Ghost Dance.]

523 PARK, Willard S. Paviotso shamanism. <u>American Anthropologist</u>
     36 (1), 1934, 98–113.
     [Pp. 98, 109, 113, brief references to connections with
     the Ghost Dance.]

524 PARKER, Z. A. The Ghost Dance at Pine Ridge. <u>Journal of
     American Folk-Lore</u> 4 (13), 1891, 160–162.
     [Repr. from <u>New York Evening Post</u>, 18 April 1891; repr.
     in Paige, item 275, pp. 134–137. A teacher on Pine Ridge
     Reservation describes the dance she saw on 20 June 1890.]

525 PHISTER, Nat P. The Indian messiah. <u>American Anthropologist</u>
     4 (2), 1891, 105–108.
     [The origins of the Ghost Dance among the Paiute in
     Wovoka's teaching (here named Kvit-tsów or Wo-po-káh-tee),
     which is well summarized on the basis of local investiga-
     tion in Nevada; mention of Johnson Sides, a Paiute critic
     of Wovoka and possibly a rival messiah. By an army
     lieutenant.]

526 POWERS, Stephen. <u>The tribes of California</u> (Contributions to
     North American Ethnology, 3). Washington, D.C.: Govern-
     ment Printing Office 1877, 635 p., illus., map.
     [P. 259 on the Ghost Dance among the Modoc, 1874f.]

527 PRAUS, Alexis A. <u>A new pictographic autobiography of Sitting
     Bull</u> (Smithsonian Miscellaneous Collections 123 (6)).
     Washington, D.C.: Smithsonian Institution 1955, 4 p. +
     13 illustrations.
     [A biographic outline and account of the pictographs
     drawn by Sitting Bull.]

528 RED FOX. <u>The memoirs of Chief Red Fox</u> (with an introduction
     by Cash Asher). New York: McGraw-Hill 1971, 208 p.,
     illus., ports.
     [A poetic and personal account of the Wounded Knee
     tragedy; ch. 5 (= pp. 49–57), The Ghost Dance.]

529 REMINGTON, Frederic. The Sioux outbreak in South Dakota.
     <u>Harper's Weekly</u> 1779 = 35, 24 Jan. 1891, 57, 61–62;
     illus. on pp. 108–109, 112.
     [Ghost Dance — the Wounded Knee battle; pp. 61–62 on
     the faith in bullet-proof Ghost shirts, and subsequent
     disillusionment.]

530 RICKER, Eli S. (collector). The Judge Eli S. Ricker Collec-
     tion. Nebraska State Historical Society, Lincoln, Nebraska.
     [Largely interviews with the Sioux, 1850–1900, and many
     of these on the Ghost Dance.]

Ghost Dances

531   ROBINSON, Doane. Some sidelights on the character of Sitting
      Bull. Collections of the Nebraska State Historical Society
      (Lincoln, Nebraska) 16, 1911, 187-192, photo.
            [Brief biography, with his career as a traditional medi-
      cine man and hostility to whites and Christians; his
      identification with the Ghost Dance in 1890, and his per-
      suasion by a woman missionary to disband a dance held on
      8 December.]

532   ROCKEFELLER, Alfred, Jr. The Ghost Dance and the Sioux. The
      Westerners Brand Book (Chicago) 5 (7), 1948, 37, 40.
            [An historical survey preliminary to the following
      doctoral dissertation on the Dance; note, p. 40, brief
      outline of Albert Hopkins, "another messiah", at Pine
      Ridge.]

533   ROCKEFELLER, Alfred, Jr. The Sioux troubles of 1890-1891.
      Northwestern University, Ph.D. dissertation 1949, 202 p.

534   ROSENBERG, Marvin and ROSENBERG, Dorothy. "There are no
      Indians left now but me." American Heritage, June 1964,
      19-23, 106-111, illus.
            [Wovoka, the Ghost Dance, and Sitting Bull's relation
      to the latter.]

535   SAYRE, Robert F. Vision and experience in Black Elk speaks.
      College English (Champaign, Illinois) 32 (5), 1971,
      509-535.
            [Pp. 530-534 on Black Elk's relation to the Ghost Dance
      of 1890; includes history of J. G. Niehardt's relations
      with Black Elk.]

536   SCHMITT, Martin F[erdinand] and BROWN, Dee Alexander. Fighting
      Indians of the West. New York: C. Scribner's Sons 1948.
            [P. 335, Ghost Dance and Wounded Knee.]

537   SCOTT, Hugh Lenox. Some memories of a soldier. New York and
      London: Century Co. 1928, 673 p., illus.
            [Pp. 146-155, the "Messiah" (Wovoka) in relation to the
      Kiowa, Comanche, etc.; Apiatan (=Ahpiatom), a Kiowa who
      opposed the spread of the Ghost Dance in 1891 to the south-
      western plains Indians; interview with Sitting Bull
      (Arapaho, not the Sioux). By the local military officer,
      with a tolerant attitude.]

538   SEYMOUR, Flora Warren. Indian agents of the old frontier.
      New York and London: D. Appleton-Century Co. Inc. 1941,
      402 p., illus.
            [Pp. 379-392, Notes, on Jack Wilson (Wovoka).]

539   SMITH, D.   The Sioux Ghost Dance.   Leslie's Illustrated
        Weekly Newspaper 71, 1890–1891, 432, 437; also The Indian
        troubles, ibid., 456, 461.
          [See also D. F. Barry, J. M. McDonough, and J. Smith in
        same volume.]

540   SMITH, Maurice G.   The Indian office pays a debt.   American
        Anthropologist 33 (2), 1931, 228–229.
          [On Apiatan, the Kiowa who opposed the southwest spread
        of the Ghost Dance: long extract from his letter of 1930
        to the Commissioner of Indian Affairs, on his experience
        of the Dance.]

541   SPENCE, Lewis.   Cheyenne, in J. Hastings (ed.), Encyclopaedia
        of Religion and Ethics, vol. 3, 1910, 514a.
          [Traditional medicine-arrow and Sun dance rites over-
        shadowed by the Ghost Dance from 1890 — but this has "now
        degenerated into...a semi-social character".]

542   SPIER, Leslie.   The Ghost Dance of 1870 among the Klamath of
        Oregon.   University of Washington Publications in
        Anthropology 2 (2), 1927, 39–55.
          [P. 41, map of Ghost Dance spread; pp. 43–52, source and
        details of the Dance; pp. 53–55, the traditional and the
        innovative features.]

543   STANDING BEAR, Luther (E. A. Brininstool, ed.).   My people,
        the Sioux.   Boston and New York: Houghton Mifflin Co.,
        and London: Williams & Norgate 1928, xiv + 288 p., illus.;
        repr. Lincoln: University of Nebraska Press (Bison Books)
        1974.
          [Autobiography of an Oglala Sioux chief, educated at
        Carlisle Indian School, who was reservation school teacher
        at Rosebud Agency during the Ghost Dance troubles, but not
        a dancer.]

544   STEPHEN, Alexander M.   Hopi journal of Alexander M. Stephen
        (ed. by Elsie Clews Parsons).   New York: Columbia Univer-
        sity Press 1936.
          [Vol. 2, pp. 996–997, Hopi traders' description of a
        Havasupai Ghost Dance in Cataract Canyon, as reported by
        T. V. Keam, a settler. See also Stephen's letters as
        quoted in J. Mooney, item 508, p. 813, abr. ed.,
        pp. 55, 57.]

545   STIRLING, M[atthew] W[illiam].   Three pictographic auto-
        biographies of Sitting Bull (with 46 plates) (Smithsonian

Ghost Dances

Miscellaneous Collections, 97 (5)). Washington, D.C.:
Smithsonian Institution 1938, 57 p., 13 plates.
[With introduction by M. W. Stirling, and notes on each
pictograph, gathered from Indian explanations.]

546   SWORD, George. The story of the Ghost Dance. <u>Folk-lorist</u> 1,
1892-93, 28-31.
[Sword was the intelligent and able Indian captain of
the Pine Ridge police. An important source, and also contains translations of some Ghost songs.]

547   THE TIMES. The Red Indians' "Ghost Dance". <u>The Times</u>
(London), 9 December 1890, 14, cols. 2-3.

548   [TURNER, Harold Walter]. Ghost dance. <u>Encyclopaedia
Britannica</u>, 1974, Micropaedia, vol. 4, 524-525.
[Unsigned survey article.]

549   UNITED STATES. DEPARTMENT OF THE INTERIOR. BUREAU OF INDIAN
AFFAIRS. <u>Annual Reports</u>. Washington, D.C.: Government
Printing Office. [References to the Ghost Dance in the
following agency or area reports (name of agent or author
in parentheses): 1890, p. 49, Pine Ridge (H. D. Gallagher);
1891, p. 223, Mission (H. N. Rust), p. 230, Fort Hall
(S. G. Fisher), p. 283, Fort Reck (C. R. A. Scobey),
p. 301, Nevada (C. C. Warner), p. 304, Western Shoshone
(W. I. Plumb), pp. 327-328, Standing Rock (J. McLaughlin),
p. 352, Kiowa, Comanche and Wichita (C. E. Adams), p. 390,
Cheyenne River (P. P. Palmer), pp. 403-405, Crow Creek and
Lower Brule (A. P. Dixon), p. 410, Pine Ridge (C. G.
Penney), p. 427, Yankton (E. W. Foster), p. 476, Shoshone
(J. Fosher); 1892, pp. 669-670, among Cheyennes and
Arapahoes (C. F. Meserve); 1895, p. 198, Tongue River
(G. W. H. Stouch); 1896, p. 250, Cheyenne and Arapaho
(A. E. Woodson); 1901, pp. 163-166, Montana (W. A. Jones).
This list is indebted to Overholt, item 520, pp. 61-63,
and Slotkin, item 1111, pp. 100-103.]

550   UNITED STATES. DEPARTMENT OF THE INTERIOR. BUREAU OF INDIAN
AFFAIRS. <u>61st. Annual report of the Commissioner of
Indian Affairs</u>. Washington, D.C.: Government Printing
Office 1892.
[Many reports from Agents, Commissioners and others on
Ghost Dances and similar movements; for list see Mooney,
item 508, p. 333; for extracts repr. see <u>idem</u> pp. 74-76
(Commissioner Morgan on the causes, from 1891, vol. I,
pp. 132-135), pp. 138-140 (Sioux delegation at Washington,
1891, vol. I, pp. 179-181).]

551 UNITED STATES. DEPARTMENT OF WAR. Annual reports of the
Secretary of War [usually in several volumes]. Washington,
D.C.: Government Printing Office: e.g., for 1877, vol. 1,
p. 630; for 1881, vol. 1, pp. 140–154; for 1888, vol. 1
(reports of Brigadier-General Ruger and special agent
Howard); for 1891, vol. 1, many reports between pp. 130–
251, including Short Bull's sermon at Pine Ridge on the
Ghost Dance (pp. 142–143, and repr. in Mooney, item 508,
1965 ed., pp. 30–31), pp. 177–178, 189–191, military surveys of the situation, and note especially pp. 191–194,
report of War Department scout Arthur I. Chapman's four-
day visit to Wovoka's area and detailed interview with
him; see also Mooney op. cit., pp. 78–80 (General Miles on
causes of the troubles, from pp. 133, 134, 149), and
p. 338 for list of volumes and relevant contents.

552 USEEM, Ruth Marie Hill. The aftermath of defeat: a study of
acculturation among the Rosebud Sioux of South Dakota.
University of Wisconsin, Ph.D. dissertation 1947, 390 p.
["For informed sympathy with native culture shock"
associated with the Ghost Dance, cited by W. La Barre,
item 54, p. 249.]

553 UTLEY, Robert M[arshall]. The last days of the Sioux nation.
New Haven and London: Yale University Press 1963, 314 p.,
illus.
[Pp. 64–71, Wovoka's religion.]

554 VESTAL, Stanley [= Walter Stanley Campbell] (comp.). New
sources of Indian history, 1850–1891: the Ghost Dance —
the Prairie Sioux; a miscellany (The Civilization of the
American Indians, 7). Norman: University of Oklahoma
Press 1934, xix + 351 p., illus., maps.
[Part I: Documents pertaining to the Ghost Dance and
the death of Sitting Bull, = pp. 1–117; especially pp. 61–
72, Mary Collins, a missionary, and 87–89, Chief Little
Wound.]

555 VESTAL, Stanley [= Walter Stanley Campbell]. Sitting Bull,
champion of the Sioux. A biography. Boston and New York:
Houghton Mifflin 1932, xvi + 350 p., illus., bibl.; Norman:
University of Oklahoma Press, 2nd. ed. 1957.
[Ch. 35, Ghost Dance; ch. 36, On guard. Based on
archives and Indian informants, but uncritical in use of
Indian evidence, and pro-Indian. Includes Sitting Bull's
hieroglyphic autobiography and many photos.]

Ghost Dances

556   WATKINS, June E. Messianic movements: a comparative study of
        some religious cults among the Melanesians, Maoris and
        North American Indians. University of Sydney, M.A. thesis
        (anthropology) 1951, 39 + 35 + 33 + 36 + 16 p.
            [The Ghost Dances of 1870 and 1890 are taken as the
        North American representatives, and compared with Hau Hau
        and Pai Marire (Maori) and various New Guinea, Solomon
        Islands and New Hebridean cults.]

557   WATSON, Elmo S. The last Indian war, 1890-91 — a study of
        newspaper jingoism. Journalism Quarterly 20, 1943,
        205-219.
            [An exposure of the inaccurate and provocative part
        played by press correspondents in the Sioux Ghost Dance
        troubles.]

558   WELLMAN, Paul I[selin]. Death on the prairie: the thirty
        years' struggle for the western plains. New York:
        Macmillan 1934, 298 p.; London: W. Foulsham n.d., 253 p.,
        illus., bibl.
            [Ch. 10 (= pp. 227-240), the war with "the Messiah":
        Section 25, The Ghost Dancers.]

559   WELSH, Herbert. The meaning of the Dakota outbreak.
        Scribners Magazine (New York) 9 (4), 1891, 439-452.
            [By the president of the Indian Rights Association, on
        the Sioux rising, the Ghost Dance, and Christianity among
        the Sioux; pp. 446-447 on the messianic doctrine.]

560   WILSON, Bryan R[onald]. Magic and the millennium.... (see
        item 371).
            [Pp. 283-306, Ghost Dances, within his theoretical frame-
        work as a millennial movement for collective redemption.]

HANDSOME LAKE RELIGION

This movement takes its name from its Seneca founder in 1800,
Ganio'dai'io, whose name appears as Handsome Lake when literally
translated into English. It is also known as the Longhouse religion,
from the buildings in which it meets; it may even appear simply as
Seneca religion or Iroquois religion (the wider group including the
Seneca) since its members sometimes erroneously regard it as identical
with their pre-contact traditional forms. It also has considerable
strength in Canada, at Caughnawaga and especially on the Six Nations
Reserve in Ontario.

561   ABRAMS, George. Moving of the fire. A case of Iroquois ritual innovation, in <u>Proceedings of the 1965 Conference on Iroquois Research</u>. Albany: University of the State of New York <u>et al</u>. 1967, 23-24.
[The removal to the new Coldspring Longhouse, Allegany Reservation, by a Seneca graduate student observer.]

562   AKWENS, Aren [= Ray FADDEN]. <u>Sa-ko-ri-on-nie-ni. Our great teacher</u>. St. Regis Mohawk Reservation, Hogansburg, New York: Akwesasne Counsellor Organization 1947, 25 p., illus.
[Handsome Lake's code, with accompanying pictographs and sundry other material.]

563   ALDEN, Timothy. <u>An account of sundry missions performed among the Senecas and Munsees; in a series of letters</u>. New York: J. Seymour 1827, 180 p.
[Pp. 53-62, a Seneca Council of 1818, to revive the teaching of Handsome Lake.]

564   BAUMAN, Richard. An analysis of Quaker-Seneca Councils 1798-1800. <u>Man in the Northeast</u> (Fitzwilliam, New Hampshire) 3, 1972, 36-48.
[Pp. 39, 44, Quaker attitudes to Handsome Lake.]

565   BEAUCHAMP, William M[artin]. The Iroquois white dog feast. <u>The American Antiquarian and Oriental Journal</u> 7, 1885, 235-239.
[A traditional rite, after Handsome Lake's influence; by a Protestant missionary.]

566   BEAUCHAMP, W[illiam] M[artin]. Iroquois notes. <u>Journal of American Folk-Lore</u> 4, 1891, 41-46.
[Pp. 44-46, sympathetic outline of Handsome Lake and the "new religion", with reference to modifications of traditional rites. By a missionary to the Indians.]

567   BEAUCHAMP, William M[artin]. Onondaga notes. <u>Journal of American Folklore</u> 8, 1895, 209-216.
[P. 209, the longhouse on Onondaga reservation.]

568   BEAUCHAMP, William M[artin]. The new religion of the Iroquois. <u>Journal of American Folklore</u> 10, 1897, 169-180.
[On the Handsome Lake religion.]

569   BEAUCHAMP, William M[artin]. <u>A history of the New York Iroquois, now commonly called the Six Nations</u> (Bulletin 329 of University of the State of New York = Bulletin 78,

Handsome Lake Religion

New York State Museum, Archaeology Subseries 9). Albany:
New York State Education Department 1905, 125-461, illus.,
maps, bibl.; repr. Port Washington, N.Y.: Ira J. Friedman
1961, 337 p.; facs. repr. New York: AMS Press 1976,
125-461.
[Pp. 294-295 (Moravian) and 346-348 (early Protestant)
missions to the Iroquois, but Quakers not mentioned;
pp. 380-381, "Ganeodiyo or Handsome Lake"; pp. 381-382,
temperance societies in early 19th c.; p. 391, religious
and other changes — by a long-time missionary to Indians.]

570 BLAU, Harold. The Iroquois white dog sacrifice: its evolu-
tion and symbolism. Ethnohistory (Bloomington, Indiana)
11 (2), 1964, 97-119, bibl.
[Good detail and analysis of a rite that has been influenced by the Handsome Lake religion.]

571 BLAU, Harold. Calendric ceremonies of the New York Onondaga.
New School for Social Research (New York), Ph.D. dissertation (anthropology) 1969, 295 p., illus.
[The religious practices and social organization at the
Onondaga Longhouse; the theology involved; comparisons
with the situation eighty years earlier and with aboriginal
practices. Concludes that Longhouse religion is both
deistic and pantheistic, and its ceremonies identify and
unify Iroquois culture rather than operate efficaciously.
Handsome Lake, passim, but especially at pp. 115-130.]

572 BOYLE, David. The pagan Iroquois. Annual Archaeological
report 1898 in Report of the Minister of Education.
Toronto, 1898, Appendix, pp. 54-211.
[Especially pp. 62-82 on the dances of the so-called
"pagans", after the influence of the Handsome Lake
religion in Ontario.]

573 BOYLE, David. On the paganism of the civilised [sic] Iroquois
of Ontario. Journal of the Anthropological Institute of
Great Britain and Ireland 30=n.s. 3, 1900, 263-273; repr.
in Annual Archaeological Report, Ontario (Toronto) 1901
[appeared 1902], 115-125.
[Includes an account of Handsome Lake, and of Iroquois
religious conservation.]

574 CABBAGE, James Richard. Evidences of Christian influences on
the Seneca prophet, Handsome Lake. Candler School of
Theology, Emory University, Atlanta, Georgia, research
paper, May 1971, 21 p. Mimeo.

[Concludes that these were considerable and contributed important elements in what is a new religion; copy held in Department of Religious Studies, Aberdeen University.]

575   CANADIAN GOVERNMENT (Canadian Film Board). The Longhouse people. New York: Contemporary Films 1964.
[A 23-minute documentary colour film showing healing and rain-seeking ceremonies, and other contemporary activities.]

576   CARPENTER, Edmund S.   Alcohol in the Iroquois dream quest. American Journal of Psychiatry 116 (August), 1959, 148-151.
[The historical and religious background to Handsome Lake's rejection of alcohol as the work of the devil.]

577   CASWELL, Harriet Clark.   Our life among the Indians.   Boston and Chicago: Congregational Sunday School Union and Publishing Society 1892, 321 p., illus.
[Pp. 207ff., Handsome Lake.]

578   CHAFE, Wallace L.   Seneca thanksgiving rituals.   Bureau of American Ethnology Bulletin 183.   Washington, D.C.: Government Printing Office 1961, 301 p.
[2 ceremonial texts in Seneca with translation and commentary — from Longhouse religion at Tonawanda Reservation, 1959; pp. 1-14, introduction.]

579   CHAFE, Wallace L.   Comment on A. F. C. Wallace's "Cultural composition of the Handsome Lake religion", in W. N. Fenton and J. Gulick (eds.), Symposium on Cherokee and Iroquois Culture (Bureau of American Ethnology, Bulletin 180).   Washington, D.C.: Government Printing Office 1961, 153-157.
[Supports and extends Wallace's view of Handsome Lake's religious history.]

580   CLARK, Joshua V[ictor] H[opkins].   Onondaga; or Reminiscences of earlier and later times.   Syracuse: Stoddard and Babcock 2 vols. 1849, illus.
[Vol. 1, pp. 103-109, Con-ya-tau-you (= Handsome Lake) as a "great Prophet'; pp. 106-108, the President's message to Handsome Lake etc., after recently meeting them, as conveyed by Secretary for War, H. Dearborn, in 1802.]

581   CONFERENCE ON IROQUOIS RESEARCH.   Proceedings of the 1965 Conference on Iroquois Research.   Albany: University of the State of New York et al. 1967, 120 p., illus.

Handsome Lake Religion

>   [Pp. 119-120, a record of the first 20 conferences, and
>   their published reports etc.; p. 11, photo of Coldspring
>   Longhouse on Allegany reservation; pp. 13, 15, the new
>   Coldspring Longhouse. See also G. Abrams, item 561.]

582   CONGDON, Charles E.   The Good News of Handsome Lake.   New York
      Folklore Quarterly 23 (4), 1967, 290-297.
          [With quotations from Henry Simmons' diary of 1799,
      reporting at first hand the visions of Handsome Lake as he
      told them; the later history of the Code.]

583   CONVERSE, Harriet Maxwell.   The festival of the sacrifice of
      the white dog as now practised at the Onondaga reservation.
      Journal of American Folklore 1, 1888, 83-85.
          [As background to the Handsome Lake religion.]

584   CONVERSE, Harriet Maxwell.   Über das Grünkorn und den grossen
      Federtanz. der Seneca.   Journal of American Folklore 4,
      1891, 72-78.
          [P. 72, descriptions of the longhouse on Catteraugus
      reservation; pp. 74ff., the great feather and war dances
      as now transferred to the "Great Spirit".]

585   CORNPLANTER, Jesse J. of the Senecas.   Legends of the Longhouse;
      told to Sah-nee-wah the white sister (Mrs. Walter A.
      Henricks).   Philadelphia: J. B. Lippincott 1938, 216 p.,
      illus; repr. Port Washington, N.Y.:   Ira J. Friedman 1963.
          [Seneca folk tales as current in the Handsome Lake
      religion at Tonawanda longhouse.   Pp. 7-9, introduction by
      Carl Carmer on the author, and the value of Iroquois
      poetic myths.]

586   DEARDORFF, Merle H.   The religion of Handsome Lake: its
      origin and development, in W. H. Fenton (ed.), Symposium
      on local diversity in Iroquois culture (Bulletin, Bureau
      of American Ethnology, 149).   Washington, D.C.:   Smith-
      sonian Institution 1951, 79-107.
          [The best shorter historical account.]

587   DEARDORFF, Merle H. and SNYDERMAN, George S. (eds.), A nine-
      teenth century journal of a visit to the Indians of New
      York.   Proceedings of the American Philosophical Society
      (Philadelphia) 100 (6), 1956, 582-612.
          [Pp. 591-594, Handsome Lake, introduction by editors;
      pp. 504-605, selection from John Philip's Journal of visit
      to Indians September 1806, with Halliday Jackson and
      Isaac Bonsall.]

588   DOUGLAS, Frederic Huntingdon. The Iroquois long house (Leaflet
         12). Denver: Denver Art Museum 1930; repr. 1956, 4 p.,
         illus.
           [On the building.]

589   FADDEN, Ray. The visions of Handsome Lake (with editorial
         introduction, pp. 341-343). Pennsylvania History 22 (4),
         1955, 341-358, illus.
           [By a Mohawk Indian who is a Handsome Lake follower and
         who made a bead wampum (belt) telling Handsome Lake's
         story; this article "translates" the wampum.]

590   FENTON, William N[elson]. An outline of Seneca ceremonies at
         Coldspring Longhouse (Yale University Publications in
         Anthropology, 9). New Haven: Yale University Press 1936,
         pp. 3-23.
           [Little specifically on Handsome Lake, but describes the
         rites he influenced.]

591   FENTON, William N[elson]. Tonawanda Longhouse ceremonies:
         ninety years after Lewis Henry Morgan. Bulletin, Bureau
         of American Ethnology 128 (Anthropological Papers 13-18),
         1941, Paper 15, pp. 139-165 + 10 plates.
           [P. 157, on the two dances dedicated by Handsome Lake
         to the Great Spirit. Otherwise as background.]

592   FENTON, William N[elson] (Recorder). Songs from the Iroquois
         Longhouse.... American Indian music from the eastern
         woodlands (Smithsonian Publication 3691). Washington,
         D.C.: Library of Congress, Archive of American Folksong
         Album 6, 1942 [record].

593   FENTON, William N[elson]. Twi-yendagan (Wood eater) takes the
         heavenly path: on the death of Henry Redeye (1864-1946),
         Speaker of the Coldspring Seneca Longhouse. American
         Indian (New York) 3, 1946, 11-15.

594   FENTON, William N[elson] (recorder and ed.). Seneca songs
         from Coldspring Longhouse, by Chauncy Johnny John and
         Albert Jones. Washington, D.C.: Library of Congress,
         Music Division Recording Laboratory, Folk Music of the
         United States, Album 17, 1948, pp. 1-16 [record].

595   FENTON, William N[elson]. Iroquois studies at the mid-century.
         Proceedings, American Philosophical Society 95 (3),
         1951, 296-310.

Handsome Lake Religion

[P. 300a, Handsome Lake — official sanction for his
religion; p. 302, factions (Christian and Longhouse);
p. 304, historical significance of Handsome Lake's Code;
pp. 306-309, Appendix, text of speeches on 4 and 5
October 1848 in the Council of the Six Nations, rehearsing
Handsome Lake's vision and revelation, etc., being notes
taken probably by E. S. Parker and used later both by
Parker and L. H. Morgan in their writings.]

596   FENTON, William N[elson]. Towards the gradual civilization of
the Indian Natives: the missionary and linguistic work of
Asher Wright (1803-1875) among the Senecas of Western New
York. Proceedings of the American Philosophical Society
100 (6), 1956, 567-581, illus.
[Uses the theoretical framework of modern disaster
studies for discussion of the decline and recovery of the
Senecas; Wright was an outstanding American Board missionary
to the Senecas from 1831 to 1875, and while he recognized
some of Handsome Lake's contributions he regarded this
movement as a pagan revival providing a means of resistance
to Christianity — see especially pp. 574-575.]

597   FENTON, William N[elson] (ed.). Seneca Indians by Asher Wright
(1859). Ethnohistory 4 (3), 1957, 302-321.
[Pp. 307-309, a missionary's hostile view of Handsome
Lake.]

598   FENTON, William N[elson]. Long term trends of change among
the Iroquois, in V. F. Ray (ed.), Cultural stability and
cultural change (Proceedings of the 1957 Annual Spring
Meeting of the American Ethnological Society). Seattle:
American Ethnological Society 1957, 30-35, bibl.
[Handsome Lake religion, passim, as the ritual component
of Longhouse culture.]

599   FENTON, William N[elson]. The Seneca Green Corn ceremony.
New York State Conservationist (Albany, N.Y.) Oct.-Nov.
1963, 20-22 and 27-28, illus.
[Detailed account of the Handsome Lake religion's form
of the ceremony.]

600   FENTON, William N[elson]. The Iroquois confederacy in the
twentieth century: a case study of the theory of Lewis H.
Morgan in "Ancient Society". Ethnology 4 (3), 1965,
251-265.
[The hereditary conservative faction of the Six Nations
in Canada focused on Handsome Lake religion and the Longhouse, preventing development of a true political society,
as has happened by contrast in the Seneca nation.]

601   FENTON, W[illiam] N[elson] (ed.). See under A. C. PARKER as
      author, item 629.

602   FENTON, William N[elson] and KURATH, Gertrude P[rokosch]. The
      feast of the dead, or Ghost Dance on Six Nations Reserva-
      tion (in Symposium on local diversity in Iroquois culture).
      Bulletin, Bureau of American Ethnology 149, 1951, 139-165,
      figs.
      [Nothing to do with the Plains Indian/Wovoka Ghost
      Dances, but give detailed account of rites for the dead at
      Onondaga and Sour Springs Longhouses.]

603   FOLEY, Denis. An ethnohistoric and ethnographic analysis of
      the Iroquois from the aboriginal era to the present sub-
      urban era. State University of New York, Albany, Ph.D.
      dissertation (anthropology) 1975, x + 362 p., illus., map.
      [Passim on the Longhouse religion which preserves tradi-
      tional forms of government and amounts to a theocracy;
      especially pp. 98-116 (dreams, death, the Code), pp. 126-
      127 (place of Jesus Christ), pp. 241-269 (curing, death,
      chiefs and councils, the Code), and ch. 7 (= pp. 317-342),
      conclusions.]

604   FOSTER, Michael K. Speaking in the Longhouse at Six Nations
      Reserve, in R. Darnell (ed.), Linguistic diversity in
      Canadian society. Edmonton and Champaign, Illinois:
      Linguistic Research Inc. 1971, 129-154.
      [The forms and ritual nature of the different speaking
      roles in the Longhouse, including the Handsome Lake code
      preacher (pp. 140-141).]

605   FOSTER, Michael K. From the earth to beyond the sky: an
      ethnographic approach to four Longhouse Iroquois speech
      events (Canadian Ethnology Service, Paper 20, National
      Museum of Man, Mercury Series). Ottawa: National
      Museums of Canada 1974, 448 p., maps, tables, bibl.
      [The oral traditions and their variations. Pp. 61-62,
      69, 109-119, 154, 174, Handsome Lake conventions in relation
      to more traditional ceremonies; p. 83, Christian influence;
      pp. 80-83, 126, Handsome Lake's code, and his last words;
      pp. 350-355, 374, 419, sections on Handsome Lake in text
      of a "deacon's" thanksgiving address.]

606   FRISCH, Jack A. Tribalism among the St. Regis Mohawks: a
      search for self-identity. Anthropologica (Ottawa) n.s.
      12 (2), 1970, 207-219.

Handsome Lake Religion

[P. 213, the advent of Handsome Lake religion in the
1930s, and its spread; also pp. 215, 216-217, 218, its
contribution to the Mohawk search for identity and cultural revival.]

607   The Great Law of Peace of the Longhouse People/Kaianerekowa
Hotinonsionne. Mohawk Nation at Akwesasne, via Rooseveltown, N.Y.: White Roots of Peace 1973, n.p. [84 p.],
illus. by J. Fadden.
[The more traditional Iroquois side of Longhouse
religion.]

608   HALE, Horatio. The Iroquois sacrifice of the white dog. The
American Antiquarian and Oriental Journal 7, 1885, 7-14.
[As background to the Handsome Lake religion.]

609   HENDRY, Jean. Iroquois masks and maskmaking at Onondaga.
Bulletin, Bureau of American Ethnology 191 (Anthropology
Papers 68-74), 1964, Paper 74, pp. 349-409 + 14 plates.
[Pp. 366, 371, 374, 405, Handsome Lake religion;
pp. 375-377, relation with the Christian Church.]

610   HENRY, Thomas R[obert]. Wilderness messiah. The story of
Hiawatha and the Iroquois. New York: William Sloane
Associates Inc. 1955, 285 p.
[The story of the Iroquois traditional "prophets":
pp. 27-44, Deganawida and Hiawatha; pp. 44-51, their
matrilineal society; pp. 144-148, religious survivals and
Handsome Lake religion.]

611   HEWITT, J[ohn] N. B. Field studies of the Iroquois in New
York State and in Ontario, Canada. Explorations and
fieldwork of the Smithsonian Institution 1936.
Washington, D.C.: Smithsonian Institution 1937, 83-86,
illuš.
[Pp. 83-84, the teachings of Handsome Lake as forming
neither a "code" nor a "religion" nor as an extension of
the precepts of the League of the Iroquois, but as derivative from mission teaching.]

612   HEWITT, J[ohn] N. B. Skaniadariio, in F. W. Hodge (ed.),
Handbook of American Indians north of Mexico = Bulletin,
Bureau of American Ethnology 30 (2), 1910, 586-587; repr.
New York: Rowman and Littlefield 1971.
[Bibliographical entry, using the Seneca form of the
name for "Handsome Lake".]

613   JACKSON, Halliday. <u>Civilization of the Indian natives: or a
      brief view of the friendly conduct of William Penn towards
      them...; the subsequent care of the Society of Friends...
      since...1795 in promoting their improvement and gradual
      civilization....</u> Philadelphia: M. T. C. Gould 1830,
      120 p.
      [The author was one of three Quaker youths working among
      the Senecas after 1798. This is the best published account
      of the Quaker mission. Pp. 42-51 on Handsome Lake's activ-
      ities 1800-1802. See also Snyderman, item 645, and A. F. C.
      Wallace, item 659.]

613A JACKSON, Halliday. <u>Sketch of the manners, customs, religion
      and government of the Seneca Indians in 1800.</u> Philadelphia:
      M. T. C. Gould 1830, 34 p.
      [The best account of the situation at Cornplanter's town,
      although mentions Handsome Lake only once. Sometimes bound
      with previous item 613.]

614   JACKSON, Halliday. [Journal] A short history of my sojourning
      in the wilderness [1798-1800]. See A. F. C. Wallace,
      item 659.

614A JACKSON, Halliday. <u>Journal of a visit paid to the Indians of</u>
      New York (1806). See George S. Snyderman, item 645.

615   JOHNSTON, Charles Murray (ed.). <u>The valley of the Six Nations.
      A collection of documents</u> (Publications of the Champlain
      Society, Ontario Series, 7). Toronto: the Champlain
      Society 1964, 344 p., illus., map.
      [Section F (= pp. 232-268) Christianity in the Longhouse,
      provides mainly missionary views of the Longhouse religious
      situation among the Iroquois, and on Six Nations Reserve,
      Ontario, between 1782 and 1844; pp. 242-243 on rise of
      Handsome Lake (see P. C. T. White, item 669); p. 242, a
      Mohawk prophet in 1798 (from Samuel Kirkland's diary
      26 Feb. 1800); see also introduction, pp. lxxxiii-lxxxiv,
      lxxxvii, lxxxviii.]

616   KURATH, Gertrude P[rokosch] (recorder). <u>Songs and dances of
      the Great Lakes Indians.</u> Ethnic Folkways Recordings,
      Monographs Series LP 4003, 1956 [record].
      [Iroquois included, hence Longhouse members.]

617   KURATH, Gertrude P[rokosch]. <u>Iroquois music and dance: cere-
      monial arts of two Seneca longhouses</u> = <u>Bulletin, Bureau of
      American Ethnology</u> 1964, 268 p., illus., music texts.

Handsome Lake Religion

> [Transcriptions of choreography, music and song, with
> detailed analyses of working of the ceremonies. Pp. xiv,
> 71, 72, 102, Handsome Lake or Christian influences.]

618   LALLEY, Frank. A visit with the Mohawks. Akwesasne Notes
      (Mohawk Nation, via Rooseveltown, New York) 5 (4), 1973,
      23.
>   [Report by a Jesuit of a recent visit to the Longhouse
> people on the St. Regis Reservation, and the attitude of
> local Catholic priests to them.]

619   McCLELLAND, Joseph. Warning of violence in sovereignty. Free
      Press (London, Ontario) [c. 1969]; repr. in collection of
      his articles by the Anglican Church of Canada, The Indian
      challenge of the 70s, n.d., p. 14, illus.
>   [Criticism by a clan-mother of Six Nations Reserve, of
> the effects of the Handsome Lake Religion in separating
> politics and religion; the current political situation.]

620   MONTOUR, Enos T. Feathered U.E.L.s. Toronto: United Church
      of Canada, Division of Communications 1973, 148 p., illus.
>   [An historical novel by a United Church of Canada Indian
> minister, set in Six Nations Reserve, and including de-
> scription of Longhouse rites, and Deskaheh, its leader,
> but treated as traditional Iroquois religion.]

621   MORGAN, Lewis Henry. League of the Ho-De-No-Sau-Nee or
      Iroquois. Rochester: Sage and Brother; New York:
      Dodd, Mead & Co. 1851, 2 vols.; several further eds.; new
      enlarged ed. New York: Dodd, Mead & Co. 1901, 338 + 332 p.,
      and 2 vols. in 1, 1922; repr. New Haven: Human Relations
      Area Files 1954; New York: Burt Franklin n.d. and 1966,
      as League of the Iroquois, 1966; Gloucester, Mass.: Peter
      Smith 1962; and New York: Citadel Press 1972 (paperback).
>   [Vol. 1, Bk. 2, ch. 3, "The new religion" — Handsome
> Lake; vol. 2, pp. 233–237, notes on religion; an early
> classic.]

622   MÜLLER, Werner. Die Religionen der Waldlandindianer Nord-
      amerikas. Berlin: D. Reimer 1956, 392 p., illus., maps.
>   [Pp. 129ff., the Iroquois festal calendar, ritual and
> mythology, as background to the Handsome Lake religion.]

623   MÜLLER, Werner. Die Religionen der Indianvölker Nord Amerikas,
      in W. Krickeberg et al. (eds.), Die Religionen des Alten
      Amerika. Stuttgart: W. Kohlhammer 1961, 171–267; Eng.
      trans., Pre-Columbian American religions. London:
      Weidenfeld and Nicolson, and New York: Holt, Rinehart
      and Winston 1968, 147–229.

[Pp. 185-192 (Eng. trans.), Iroquois Longhouse religion
of Handsome Lake treated as a revision of traditional
religion (with a duality in the main figures of its mythology) developed under the influence of the whites and
Christianity.]

624   NICHOLAS, Ralph W. Factions, a comparative analysis, in M. P.
       Banton (ed.), Political systems and the distribution of
       power (A.S.A. monographs, 2). London: Tavistock Publica-
       tions, and New York: Praeger 1965, 21-61.
       [Pp. 46-58, Factions and political change (Iroquois):
       Handsome Lake religion passim.]

625   NOON, John Alfred. Law and government of the Grand River
       Iroquois (Viking Fund Publications in Anthropology, 12).
       New York: Viking Fund 1949, 186 p.
       [Pp. 12-33, 44-49, 108-109, on Handsome Lake.]

626   OVERHOLT, Thomas W. Prophecy: the problem of cross-cultural
       comparison. Paper, Annual Meeting, American Academy of
       Religion, San Francisco 1977. Publication in prospect.
       [On Jeremiah and Handsome Lake; a comparative study
       making a new link between Old Testament and anthropological
       studies.]

627   PARKER, A[rthur] C[aswell]. Secret medicine societies of the
       Seneca. American Anthropologist 11 (2), 1909, 161-185,
       illus.; adapted version in item 629.
       [Pp. 162-164, the Handsome Lake religion at first re-
       pressed traditional secret societies, but as it itself
       became traditional, accepted and blended them so that they
       did not have to remain underground.]

628   PARKER, Arthur C[aswell]. Iroquois sun-myths. Journal of
       American Folklore Oct.-Dec. 1910; repr. in Parker, item
       629, pp. 131-136.
       [Survivals, opposed by the Handsome Lake religion.]

629   PARKER, Arthur C[aswell]. The code of Handsome Lake, the
       Seneca prophet (New York State Museum...Museum Bulletin
       163). Albany: University of the State of New York 1913,
       148 p., illus., plates. Repr. in W. N. Fenton (ed.),
       A. C. Parker on the Iroquois... (New York Study Series 2).
       Syracuse: Syracuse University Press 1968, 3rd. set of
       pagination (1-148), illus.
       [The major feature of the Handsome Lake religion; for
       long orally transmitted, and here given in the English
       translation by William Bluesky (Baptist lay preacher)

Handsome Lake Religion

from the Seneca version begun in 1903 by Edward Cornplanter.
Fenton ed.: pp. 32-37 of his introduction on the code and
its recording in writing; pp. 5-15 (of the Code pagination),
Parker's introduction to Handsome Lake religion and its
present effects; pp. 16-19, E. Cornplanter's account of
how the white race came to America and why the Gaíwiioᵉ
became necessary; pp. 20-26, how the Code was given;
pp. 27-80, the Code, or "Great Message" in 130 sections;
pp. 81-104, Parker's field notes on the rites and ceremonies of the Ganio'dai'io religion (on Cattaraugus reservation 1905); pp. 105-106, legend of the coming of death
(related by E. Cornplanter); pp. 107-109, the usual form
of funeral address (related by Skidmore Lay, 1906);
pp. 110-112, ceremonies for the death feast (related by E.
Cornplanter, 1906); pp. 113-130, adapted version of Parker,
item 627; pp. 131-136, repr. of Parker, item 628; pp. 139-
144, key to phonic system and glossary of Seneca words.]

630   PARKER, Arthur C[aswell]. The constitution of the Five Nations;
        or the Iroquois Book of the great law (Bulletin, New York
        State Museum, 184). Albany: the Museum 1916, 158 p.
            [An editing of Indian manuscripts. Pp. 126-132, sketches
        of an Indian Council, 1846, includes J. Johnson's preaching
        the Handsome Lake code.]

631   PARKER, Arthur C[aswell]. The life of General Ely S. Parker.
        Buffalo: Buffalo Historical Society 1919, 346 p., illus.
            [Pp. 18-20, 24-26, 52-53, 202, on Handsome Lake; pp. 244-
        251, part of A. C. Parker's address on Handsome Lake, 1916;
        pp. 251-261, English trans. of Jimmy Johnson's speech on
        Handsome Lake, Grand Council, 1845.]

632   PARKER, Arthur C[aswell]. Red Jacket: last of the Seneca
        (They made America Series). New York & London: McGraw-
        Hill 1952, 229 p., map.
            [Ch. 11 (= pp. 136-147), Handsome Lake; pp. 189-191, his
        unsuccessful charges against Red Jacket; pp. 151, 153,
        Tenskwatawa and the Shawnee defeat at Tippecanoe. A vivid
        historical reconstruction by a scholar of Indian descent.]

633   POSTAL, Susan Koessler. Hoax nativism at Caughnawaga: a con-
        trol case for the theory of revitalization. Ethnology
        (Pittsburgh) 4 (3), 1965, 266-281.
            [In 1916 a Negro from Cleveland, posing as Chief Thunder-
        water, and as Indian, took advantage of the largely Catholic
        Iroquois at Caughnawaga to start a revitalization movement;
        through its failure the Handsome Lake religion arrived in
        1923, as a belated discovery of "the true Indian religion".]

634 POWERS, Mabel. The legacy of Handsome Lake. The Christian Century (Chicago) 84 (2), 1957, 47-48.

635 PUTT, Raymond V. The role of the hereditary chiefs in contemporary Iroquois society: a nativistic movement on the Six Nations Reserve. Napao (Saskatoon) 3 (1), 1971, 11-20, illus., bibl.
     [The history of political and religious factionalism, with sociological explanations. The division between Christian and Longhouse members of the hereditary council interpreted in terms of Linton's and A. F. C. Wallace's theories; Longhouse religion as background.]

636 RENNER, Egon. Sayings of a Seneca. Indiana Beiträge zur Völker-und Sprachenkunde, Archäologie und Anthropologie des indianischen Amerika. Band 1. Berlin: Gebr. Mann Verlag 1973.
     [A conservative member of the Longhouse on current Iroquois problems.]

637 RICCIARDELLI, Alex Frank. Factionalism at Oneida, an Iroquois Indian community. University of Pennsylvania, Ph.D. dissertation (anthropology) 1961, 298 p.
     [On the Thames River, Ontario, Canada; includes the different effects of growing white influence on the two groups, Christians and Longhouse — their leaders competed for control of the whole community.]

638 RIOUX, Marcel. Relations between religion and government among the Longhouse Iroquois of Grand River, Ontario, in Annual Report, National Museum of Canada, for 1950-51 (= Bulletin 126). Ottawa: the Museum 1952, 94-98.
     [Compares the Lower Cayuga and the Onondaga Longhouse adherents — the former having accepted the separation of "church" and state more than the latter, who are more "consciously native".]

639 RIOUX, Marcel. Some medical beliefs and practices of the contemporary Iroquois longhouse of the Six Nations Reserve. Journal of the Washington Academy of Sciences 41 (5), 1951, 152-158.
     [Examples of conservatism and acculturation in connection with sickness, among Handsome Lake adherents.]

640 ROTHENBURG, Diane Brodatz. Friends like these: an ethnohistorical analysis of the interaction between Allegany Senecas and Quakers, 1798-1823. City University of New York, Ph.D. dissertation 1976, 275 p.

Handsome Lake Religion

[As background to the Quaker influence in the Handsome
Lake religion, but not directly on the latter. The Quaker
encouragement of male agriculture and private property;
queries the usual accounts of the influence of Seneca
demoralization and of a "stress" situation, by emphasizing
economic and political factors.]

641   SELDEN, Sherman Ward. The legend, myth and code of Deganaweda
      and their significance to Iroquois culture history.
      Indiana University, Ph.D. dissertation 1966, 247 p.
      [The adoption of Hiawatha by the Iroquois as a culture
      hero to associate with their Handsome Lake religion; since
      his life and nature made him unsuitable, especially in
      Christian eyes, he was replaced by the legendary founder
      of the Code of the Five Nations, Deganaweda, as a messiah
      figure placed among the gods; this myth continues to
      develop to meet changing Iroquois needs.]

642   SHIMONY, Annemarie [Anrod]. The Iroquois fortune-tellers and
      their conservative influence (in Symposium on Cherokee and
      Iroquois Culture, item 20). Bulletin, Bureau of American
      Ethnology (Washington, D.C.) 180, 1961, 207-211.
      [The diagnosis and cure of ill-health or misfortune in
      Longhouse communities preoccupied with these concerns.]

643   SHIMONY, Annemarie Anrod. Conservatism among the Iroquois at
      the Six Nations Reserve (Yale University Publications in
      Anthropology no. 65). New Haven: Yale University Press
      1961, 1-302, bibl.
      [Longhouse orientation and functions in detail; the
      Handsome Lake religion today, showing persistence of
      ancient cultural patterns.]

644   SKINNER, Alanson [Buck]. Review of A. C. Parker, The code of
      Handsome Lake...(1913). American Anthropologist 17 (1),
      1915, 180-184.
      [Outlines the Code; compares it with Peyote and Tenskwa-
      tawa, and considers possible influence of the latter on
      Handsome Lake.]

645   SNYDERMAN, George S. (ed.). Halliday Jackson's Journal of a
      visit paid to the Indians of New York (1806). Proceedings,
      American Philosophical Society 101 (6), 1957, 565-588.
      [Another account of the 1806 visit by Quaker delegation —
      cf. Philip's account in Deardorf and Snyderman's item 587.]

646   SNYDERMAN, George S.   The function of wampum in Iroquois
          religion.   Proceedings, American Philosophical Society
          (Philadelphia) 105 (6), 1961, 571-608.
          [Contemporary Handsome Lake religion, and symbolism of
          wampum.   See also ibid., 98 (6), 1954, 469-494, on general
          functions of wampum.]

647   SPECK, Frank G[ouldsmith].   An ethnologist speaks for the
          pagan Indians.   The Crozer Quarterly (Philadelphia) 18 (3),
          1941, 213-218.
          [Based on the Cayuga Longhouse version of Handsome Lake
          religion.   Presents an outline with statistics, and an
          itemized account of Longhouse beliefs as a basis for
          acceptance "as a Christian discipline".]

648   SPECK, Frank G[ouldsmith].   Midwinter rites of the Cayuga
          Longhouse.   Philadelphia: University of Pennsylvania
          Press 1949, 192 p. + 16 pl.
          [Pp. 17-19, 29-33, 56-57, 152, 155, 157, 164-173, on
          Handsome Lake and Iroquois religion; pp. 127-129, the
          "Fatherless Boy" myth and Christ.]

649   THAYER, W. A.   Extracts from a letter ... dated at Cattaraugus,
          6th of November 1828.   Missionary Herald (Boston) 25 (3),
          1829, 92-94.
          [Relations between Longhouse followers and Christians;
          account of three-day prayer meeting to settle differences
          between two Indian members of the church.]

650   TOLLES, Frederick B.   Nonviolent contact: the Quaker and the
          Indians.   Proceedings, American Philosophical Society
          106 (2), 1963, 93-101.
          [Pp. 99-100 on Quaker influence on Handsome Lake.]

651   TOOKER, Elizabeth J.   Seneca religion and ethnic identity.
          Science on the March (Buffalo Museum of Science, N.Y.)
          40, 1959, 35-39.
          [The Indian features of the Handsome Lake religion in
          its longhouse, food at ceremonies, dance costumes, cere-
          monial dice games, and retention of Seneca as the ritual
          language.   The difficulties for white Americans in under-
          standing Indian values.]

652   TOOKER, Elizabeth [J.].   Three aspects of Northern Iroquoian
          culture change.   Pennsylvania Archaeologist 30 (2), 1960,
          65-71.
          [On cultural changes since the time of the early Jesuits:
          e.g., fewer curing ceremonies and less reliance on dreams.]

Handsome Lake Religion

653   TOOKER, Elizabeth [J.]. On the new religion of Handsome Lake.
       Anthropological Quarterly 41 (4), 1968, 187–200.
            [A critique of Wallace's social disorganization, psycho-
       logical stress theory; suggests the economics of change to
       farming was influential in explaining the specific choices
       from Christian teaching.]

654   TOOKER, Elizabeth [J.]. The Iroquois ceremonial of Mid-winter.
       Syracuse: Syracuse University Press 1970, x + 189 p.,
       illus., map.
            [Pp. 1–6, 103–107, 112–115, 118–119, 147–153, 155–160,
       on Handsome Lake influence.]

655   TOROK, C. H. Structures and factions in Tyendinaga politics.
       Anthropologica n.s. 14 (1), 1972, 31–42.
            [On Tyendinaga Reserve, Hastings County, Ontario. An
       Iroquois band has developed factions without the focus
       of the Handsome Lake religion, and never had a Longhouse.]

656   [TURNER, Harold Walter]. Handsome Lake religion. Encyclopaedia
       Britannica, 1974 ed., Micropaedia, vol. 4, 886.
            [Unsigned survey article.]

657   VOGET, Fred [W.]. Acculturation at Caughnawaga: a note on
       the native-modified group. American Anthropologist 53 (2),
       1951, 220–231.
            [Iroquois (Mohawk) reserve: "native-modified" as one
       of the social groups identified included two subgroups,
       a) followers of Handsome Lake (divided into three factions)
       b) apostates, or with weak ties to a Christian church
       (Catholic or United); pp. 226–229, specially on the Hand-
       some Lake religion.]

658   WALLACE, Anthony F. C. Handsome Lake and the Great Revival in
       the west. American Quarterly 4 (2), 1952, 149–165.
            [The influence of Handsome Lake religion; remarks on
       Mormon missions to the Iroquois.]

659   WALLACE, Anthony F. C. (ed.). Halliday Jackson's Journal to
       the Seneca Indians, 1798–1800. Pennsylvania History
       19 (2), 1952, 117–147; 19 (3), 1952, 325–349; repr. by the
       Pennsylvania Historical and Museum Commission, Harrisburg,
       Pennsylvania, n.d.
            [Jackson and Simmons were Quakers who lived among the
       Seneca 1798–99; Jackson includes his copy of Henry Simmons'
       notes of Handsome Lake's first vision (as told to Simmons
       on the same day), also of the second vision, and his own
       notes on a third vision, together with Simmons' diary nota-
       tions on the day of the first vision.]

660   WALLACE, Anthony F. C.   The institutionalization of cathartic
       and control strategies in Iroquois religious psychotherapy,
       in K. Opler (ed.), Culture and mental health.   New York:
       Macmillan 1959, 63-96.
       [Pp. 90-94, especially, on Handsome Lake and the thera-
       peutic effect on the Seneca.]

661   WALLACE, Anthony F. C.   Cultural composition of the Handsome
       Lake religion, in W. N. Fenton and J. Gulick (eds.),
       Symposium on Cherokee and Iroquois culture = Bulletin,
       Bureau of American Ethnology 180, 1961, 141-151.
       [A compact survey.   Pp. 144-147, Handsome Lake's value
       themes; pp. 147-150, three stages in subsequent history of
       the movement.   See also comment by W. L. Chafe,
       pp. 155-157.]

662   WALLACE, Anthony F. C. (with the assistance of Sheila C. Steen).
       The death and rebirth of the Seneca.   New York: Alfred A.
       Knopf (1970) 1972, 384 p.
       [Includes Handsome Lake; a definitive work.]

663   WALLACE, Anthony F. C.   Origins of the Longhouse religion, in
       B. C. Trigger (ed.), Northeast: Handbook of North American
       Indians, 15 (gen. ed. W. C. Sturtevant).   Washington, D.C.:
       Smithsonian Institution 1978, 442-448.

664   WALLACE, Anthony F. C.   Revitalization movements in development.
       See Ward, item 117.
       [Pp. 451-453, Handsome Lake movement as an example.]

665   WALLACE, Paul A. W.   They knew the Indian: the men who wrote
       the Moravian records.   Proceedings, American Philosophical
       Society 95 (3), 1951, 290-295.
       [A survey of the archives of the Moravian Church in
       America at Bethlehem, Pennsylvania, including accounts of
       J. Heckenwelder and D. Zeisberger in relation to Indians.]

666   WALLACE, Paul A. W.   Indians in Pennsylvania.   Harrisburg:
       Pennsylvania Historical and Museum Commission 1961, 194 p.,
       illus., maps.
       [Pp. 172, 174, 177, brief biographies of Cornplanter,
       Handsome Lake and Papoonhank; pp. 166-168, Handsome Lake
       religion, selection from the Code, and text of prayer by a
       Seneca "Keeper of the Faith", from the Draper MSS.]

667   WEAVER, Sally M.   Medicine and politics among the Grand River
       Iroquois.   A study of the non-conservatives (Publications

Handsome Lake Religion

in Ethnology, 4). Ottawa: National Museums of Canada 1972, xiii + 182 p., maps, illus., bibl.
[A study in medical acculturation. Pp. xi, 3 (map), 15-16, 23-25, 30-37, the approximately 1,500 Longhouse adherents (of the Handsome Lake religion) on Six Nations Reserve, Ontario, and their relation to the non-conservatives (mostly Christians).]

668   WEAVER, S[ally] M. Smallpox or chickenpox: an Iroquois community's reaction to crisis, 1901-1902. Ethnohistory 18 (4), 1972, 361-378.
[Six Nations Reserve, Ontario: includes the relations between Christians and Longhouse members, and their different reactions to the epidemic.]

669   WHITE, Patrick C. T. (ed.). Lord Selkirk's diary, 1803-1804... (Publications of the Champlain Society, 35). Toronto: Champlain Society 1958, xxiii + 359 p., maps; repr. Westport, Connecticut: Greenwood Press 1975.
[Pp. 245-246, on the rise of Handsome Lake; repr. in C. M. Johnston, item 615, pp. 242-243.]

670   WILSON, Edmund. Apologies to the Iroquois. With a study of the Mohawks in high steel by Joseph Mitchell. New York: Farrar, Straus & Cudahy 1960, 310 p., plates; Random House (Vintage Books) 1966.
[Pp. 72-89, Handsome Lake religion; pp. 224-233, Longhouse ceremonies; pp. 116-125, a Mormon conversion.]

671   WITTHOFT, John. Green corn ceremonialism in the eastern woodlands (Occasional Contributions, Museum of Anthropology, University of Michigan, 13). Ann Arbor: University of Michigan Press 1949, 91 p.
[The Longhouse form of the traditional ceremony.]

672   WOLF, Morris. Iroquois religion and its relation to their morals. New York: Columbia University Press 1919, 110 p., bibl.
[Columbia University Ph.D. dissertation (Political Science); a comprehensive study; pp. 59-64, Handsome Lake and the crystallization of many Christian influences; pp. 65-70, religious festivals in 19th c.; p. 71, a summary of Christian influences.]

INDEPENDENT INDIAN CHURCHES

The literature gives little idea of the number of these movements and of the fact that they are still appearing in the 1970s. In contrast to their African counterparts they usually maintain a low profile or may operate in remote areas. It is also difficult to draw a line between those fully independent in origin and those arising within a mission context or under the influence of whites and maintaining a tenuous connection, while virtually independent in operation and in their own self-understanding. This is particularly true of congregations that have arisen in a Baptist or Pentecostal milieu, and even for some Roman Catholics in the southwest pueblos who are not included here. Much of the literature consists of incidental reference or brief outlines and there appears to be no major study in this area. Independent churches originating in Canada or Alaska will be found in that section. It should be noted that the term "church" is used in this group in its proper sense as referring to movements that possess, or may be presumed to possess, a Christology with some semblance of orthodoxy; movements such as the Indian Shaker Church (excepting possibly some of its more recent evangelical forms) and the Native American Church are placed in their own categories; others, where the position is not known, are accepted in their own terms and included.

673   AKWESASNE NOTES. Chicago group moves to store front operations
      after move to correct Indian Center problems fails.
      Akwesasne Notes 5 (4), 1973, 40.
         [Conflict between "Moody-church" faction and those empha-
      sizing Indian socio-cultural concerns.]

674   BAERG, Anna. History of the Indian Bible Church, Denver,
      Colorado. [Newton, Kansas: General Conference Mennonite
      Church, Home Ministries] 1974. 4 p. Typescript.

675   BEST, Mary Agnes. The town that saved a state — Westerly.
      Westerly, Rhode Island: Utter Co. for Westerly, R.I. Com-
      mittee 1943.
         [Pp. 130-133, history of churches in Westerly; p. 131.
      reference to founding the first church "for the Indians at
      Charlestown" by the S.P.G., early 18th century; this may
      relate to the Narragansetts' church, independent from the
      1740s.]

676   BEYNON, William. The Tsimshians of Metlakatla, Alaska.
      American Anthropologist 43 (1), 1941, 83-88.
         [By a Gyitlan Indian (one of the Tsimshian tribes):
      1. On missionary Duncan's Christian community from 1887.

Independent Indian Churches

2. On Tsimshians in British Columbia becoming Methodists
at Port Simpson, where a society set up by the missionary
as "the Christian Band of Workers" (pp. 86-87) seceded as
an independent church, allowing "freedom of interpretation
and emotional expression". No dates given — early 20th c.?]

677 BOISSEVAIN, Ethel. The detribalization of the Narragansett
Indians: a case study. Ethnohistory 3, Summer 1956, 225-
245; repr. in D. E. Walker, item 360, 435-447.
[Specific references to their church, pp. 438, 445, based
on W. F. Tucker, item 701; an example of "successful" detribalization combined with maintenance of identity.]

678 BOISSEVAIN, Ethel. Narragansett survival: a study of group
persistence through adapted traits. Ethnohistory 6 (4),
1959, 347-362; repr. in D. E. Walker, item 360, pp. 658-664.
[Independent church formed by 1750 from Congregationalism,
and continuing to date.]

679 BOISSEVAIN, Ethel. Ecology of the historic settlement of the
Narragansett tribe in Rhode Island. Paper, 3rd Annual
Meeting for Historical Archaeology 1969; digest in Abstracts
in Anthropology 1 (3), 1970, 212.
[The abandoned sixteen-square-mile settlement of the 18th
to 20th centuries, with its Indian church.]

680 BOISSEVAIN, Ethel. The Narragansett people. Phoenix: Indian
Tribal Series 1975, 99 p., illus., map.
[Pp. 37-38, 56, 61, 75, 78-79, Narragansett Indian Church
from the 1740s, set in an outline of the post-contact tribal
history.]

681 BUSWELL, James O. Florida Seminole religious ritual: resistance and change. St. Louis University, Ph.D. dissertation
1972, 449 p.
[Pp. 387-449, independent churches, and their relation
to missions, the Bible, etc.]

682 CHARLESTOWN TOURIST ASSOCIATION. Charlestown, Rhode Island
welcomes you.... Charlestown: the Association n.d.
[1970s?], folding map and information.
[Narragansett independent Indian church — photograph and
map location.]

683 THE CHRIST CHURCH FAMILY (Christ Church, Episcopal, Yankton,
South Dakota).
[This congregational newsletter in the 1950s reported
the activities of a Dakota group which organized their

own Indian services while remaining loosely attached to
Christ Church. These continued in the 1970s as the Dakota
Hall group on an ecumenical basis. See, e.g., vol. 2 (4),
December 1955, Indian Church people have cottage services,
which may be a report of the beginning of this movement.
See also J. Hayes, item 688, and W. R. Hurt, item 690.]

684   EAGLE EYE. Religion or salvation. The Narragansett Dawn
      (Oakland, Rhode Island) 1 (8), 1935; repr. in T. E.
      Sanders and W. W. Peek (eds.), item 296, 375-376.
      [Reflects Narragansetts' religion in a pan-Indian phase.
      See also Princess Red Wing, item 695.]

685   FIFE, Sharon A. Baptist Indian Church: Thlewarle Mekko Sapkv
      Coko. Chronicles of Oklahoma 48 (4), 1970-71, 450-66,
      illus.
      [An independent "House of Prayer" in continuous existence
      since 1858, near Dustin, Oklahoma.]

686   FREEMAN, Ethel Cutler. Culture stability and change among the
      Seminoles of Florida, in A. F. C. Wallace (ed.), Men and
      cultures. Philadelphia: University of Pennsylvania Press
      1959, 249-253.
      [The relation of the different Seminole groups to
      Christianity and "nativistic" reactions; as background to
      independent Seminole Baptist Church.]

687   GARDNER, Richard E. The role of the pan-Indian church in
      urban Indian life. Anthropology UCLA (Los Angeles) 1 (1),
      1969, 14-26.
      [Based on the Los Angeles area, and shows the strengths
      and weaknesses of Indian religious organizations in assist-
      ing assimilation to urban life.]

688   HAYES, James. Christ Church? Dakota people of Yankton. The
      B.C.U. Digest (Yankton, S.D.) 1 (3), 1957, 1-3.
      [The Brotherhood of Christian Unity (or B.C.U.) is an
      Indian men's organization of the Episcopal Church; describes
      the origins and aims of the semi-independent Dakota branch
      of Christ Church, Episcopal, in Yankton.]

689   HICKS, George L. The same north and south: ethnicity and
      change in two American Indian groups, in J. W. Bennett
      (ed.), The new ethnicity: perspectives from ethnology.
      1973 Proceedings, American Ethnological Society. St. Paul,
      New York, etc.: West Publishing Co. 1975, 75-94.

Independent Indian Churches

[On the Catawba and Monhegan. Pp. 78-79, 89, 90, 91, Catawba Mormonism; pp. 86, 89, Monhegan Indian Church in relation to pow-wows and tribal identity. Brief references.]

690 HURT, Wesley R[obert], Jr. The Yankton Dakota Church: a nationalistic movement of northern plains Indians, in G. E. Dole and R. L. Carneiro (eds.), Essays in the science of culture in honor of Leslie A. White. New York: T. Y. Crowell Co. 1960, 269-287.
[A semi-independent Indian branch of Christ Church, Episcopal, in Yankton, South Dakota, founded 1955 and led by a catechist in members' homes.]

691 LAUDIN, Harvey Golden. The Shinnecock powwow: a study of cultural change. New York University, Ph.D. dissertation (anthropology) 1973, 205 p.
[Reported to include "the oldest mission church in the United States established...in 1641", on their reservation on Long Island. The Shinnecock powwow was revived in 1946, partly through Narragansett associations. Their churches would seem similar in function.]

692 LOVE, William DeLoss. Samson Occoni and the Christian Indians of New England. Boston and Chicago: Pilgrim Press 1899, 379 p., illus.
[P. 194, photo of the Narragansett Indian Church; pp. 189-195, history of the independent Indian church at Charlestown, Rhode Island.]

693 PECKHAM, Philip [H.]. The Narragansett Indian Church. The Narragansett Dawn 1 (1), 1935, 8-9.
[By the commissioner of this independent church, outlining its history and pastors since 1750.]

694 PITT, Robert H. Chickahominy and Pamunkey Indians. Southern Workman 38 (10), 1909, 566-567 (repr. from The Religious Herald).
[A Chickahominy congregation with own building in Virginia — virtually an independent Baptist church, dating from 1901.]

695 PRINCESS RED WING. History of the Indian's religion. The Narragansett Dawn (Oakland, Rhode Island) 1 (8), 1935; repr. in T. E. Sanders and W. W. Peek (eds.), item 296, pp. 376-380.
[An idealized view, by the editor of a journal which promoted the Pan-Indian movement. An example, when

compared with Eagle Eye, item 684, of the range of outlook among the Narragansetts who also supported their independent church.]

696   REYBURN, William [D.]. Hopi report. Mission Board, General Conference Mennonite Church (Newton, Kansas) 1960, 13 p. Mimeo, unpublished.
[Includes account of the split among the Hopi Mennonite missionaries which led to the formation of Fred Johnson's independent Hopi church at New Oraibi in 1946; p. 6, mentions "Navaho Indigenous church" and Southwest Indian Bible Conference. Signed Rayburn, for Reyburn.]

697   SCHUSKY, Ernest [L.]. Pan-Indianism in the Eastern United States. Anthropology Tomorrow (University of Chicago Anthropology Club) 6, 1957, 116-123.
[P. 120, on the independent Indian churches receiving financial support from the Narragansetts' August powwow in Charlestown, Rhode Island, and from the Shinnecock Labour Day weekend powwow on Long Island — passing references, but fuller discussion of the functions of these annual powwows in relation to continuing Indian identity.]

698   STEINBRING, Jack. Acculturation phenomena among the Lake Winnipeg Ojibwa of Canada. Verhandlungen des XXXVIII Internationalen Amerikanistenkongresses, Stuttgart-München 1968. Stuttgart-Munich: Klaus Renner 1971, vol. 3, 177-188, bibl.
[Mainly on Alcoholics Anonymous, and its indigenized form, which, through the Christian religious element, may be the equivalent of an independent church. For the religious aspect see his reference to Arthur H. Cain, Alcoholics Anonymous: cult or cure. Harpers Magazine no. 1353=226, Feb. 1963, 48-53.]

699   STEINER, Stan. The new Indians. New York: Harper and Row, and Dell Publishing Co. (Delta Books) 1968, 348 p.
[Ch. 8, "The Christ who never came", especially pp. 110-115, on an independent Baptist church among Creek Indians, Oklahoma, under Rev. Clifford Hill and his Creek Tribal Centralization Committee; pp. 100-105, the relative independence of the Catholics in Isleta Pueblo, New Mexico.]

700   STERN, Theodore. Chickahominy: the changing culture of a Virginia Indian community. Proceedings, American Philosophical Society 96 (2), 1952, 157-225, maps.
[P. 192, how the Chickahominy adopted a Baptist form of Christianity; p. 208, Cedar Grove and Samaria churches;

Independent Indian Churches

      pp. 217-218, Samaria Indian Baptist Church, as forming group 7 (along with the Pamunkey, Tsena Commocko, and Mattaponi Indian Baptist churches) within the Dover Baptist Association of the Southern Baptist Convention, and virtually independent. As an example of successful adaptation to American white culture.]

701   TUCKER, William Franklin. Historical sketch of the town of Charlestown in Rhode Island from 1636 to 1876. Westerly, R.I.: Charlestown Town Council 1877.
      [Pp. 63ff., churches; p. 65 on Narragansett independent Indian Church, Charlestown.]

702   VOGET, Fred [W.]. A Six Nations diary, 1891-1894. Ethnohistory 16 (4), 1969, 345-360, bibl.
      [Pp. 357-358, and note 3 (pp. 359-360), a late 19th century separation from the Anglican Church on Six Nations Reserve, Ontario, by a "Plymouth Brethren" group resentful of white control, probably led by educated Indians, and with own lay preachers.]

703   WALKER, Deward E[dgar], Jr. Sorcery among the Nez Percés, in D. E. Walker (ed.), Systems of North American witchcraft and sorcery. Moscow: University of Idaho, 1970, 267-295.
      [Pp. 282-285, 287, independent Indian Pentecostal sects since the 1940s, with sorcery beliefs as an equivalent to the former Presbyterian beliefs in the devil as an evil power.]

704   WASHBURN, Albert L. Institution building among Oklahoma's traditional Cherokees, in C. M. Hudson (ed.), Four centuries of Southern Indians. Athens: University of Georgia Press 1975, 132-147.
      [Pp. 136-138, Echota Cherokee Indian Baptist Church and the Four Mothers Society (traditional) in co-operation over an Indian-culture school.]

KENNEKUK

    There are many variations on this form of the prophet's name, and also on its main alternative, Kanakuk. This small but notable movement attracted a good deal of attention, often favourable, during the founder's lifetime and most of the literature concentrates on this period, the second quarter of the nineteenth century. A remnant of this "Kickapoo Church" has persisted and in good health to the present day, but the only modern study is that of J. H. Howard, item 715, although other scholars have begun to take an interest in it in the 1970s.

705 ALLIS, Samuel J. Account of the worship of the Kickapoos, as
     conducted by their prophet Kennekuk, in 1834, Leavenworth
     County, Kansas. Missionary Herald (Boston) 1835, 344.
     [See also under J. Dunbar, item 710.]

706 ALLIS, Samuel [J.]. Forty years among the Indians and on the
     eastern borders of Nebraska. Transactions and Reports of
     the Nebraska State Historical Society 2, 1887, 133-166.
        [Pp. 135-136, detailed account of Kennekuk's community
     worship near Fort Leavenworth. See also under Dunbar,
     item 710.]

707 BERRYMAN, Jerome C. A circuit rider's frontier experiences.
     Kansas Historical Quarterly (formerly Kansas Historical
     Society Collections) 16, 1923-25, 177-226.
        [The first Methodist missionary among the Kickapoo, who
     appointed Kennekuk as his assistant; pp. 215-217, the
     deviations in belief and practice that separated them.]

708 CARMAN, J. Neale and POND, Karl S. The replacement of the
     Indian languages of Kansas by English. Transactions of
     the Kansas Academy of Science (Lawrence) 58 (2), 1955,
     131-150.
        [Pp. 144ff., references to missions and the Kennekuk
     Church, and the survival of the Potawatomi language in this
     context.]

709 CUSTER, Milo. Kannekuk or Keeanakuk. The Kickapoo prophet.
     Illinois State Historical Society Journal 11 (1), 1918,
     48-56.
        [Kennekuk's family history and descendents in the
     Kennekuk Church, Brown County, Kansas, in 1906; his prayer
     sticks and teaching, and the later forms of his church
     worship; uses the Kansas oral tradition and manuscript
     materials possessed by the Church; extracts repr. in
     J. H. Howard, item 716, pp. 8, 20-22.]

710 DUNBAR, John, ALLIS, Samuel [J.] et al. Letters concerning the
     Presbyterian Mission in the Pawnee country, near Bellevue,
     Neb., 1831-1849. Kansas Historical Society Collections
     14, 1915-16, 570-784.
        [By two Presbyterian missionaries: pp. 585-587, the
     fullest account of a Kennekuk service, by Dunbar in 1834;
     pp. 693, 695, Allis' account of the new religion in 1835;
     both accounts repr. in J. H. Howard, item 716, pp. 14-17,
     and see also use made by J. T. Irving, item 718.]

Kennekuk

711   FREDERICKSON, Otto F[rovin]. The liquor question among the
      Indian tribes in Kansas, 1804-1881. (Humanistic Studies
      4:4). Lawrence, Kansas: University of Kansas Department
      of Journalism Press 1932, 103 p.
      [P. 31, on Kennekuk's banning of alcohol among his fol-
      lowers. Cited by J. H. Howard, item 716, p. 44.]

712   GARRAGHAN, Gilbert J. Catholic beginnings in Kansas City,
      Missouri: an historical sketch. Chicago: Loyola Univer-
      sity Press 1920, 137 p., illus.
      [Pp. 49-50, postscript no. 3 to letter from Fr. Benedict
      Roux at Kansas City to Bishop Rosati, 24 Nov, 1833, report-
      ing very favourably on Kennekuk's Kickapoos; pp. 53-54, on
      Kennekuk's message to Fr. Roux, 22 Nov. 1833.]

713   HAMILTON, Henry Edward. Incidents and events in the life of
      Gurdon Saltonstall Hubbard. Chicago: Rand McNally 1888,
      189 p., illus.
      [Pp. 162-168, include Hubbard's translation of a sermon
      by the prophet Kennekuk, preached on 17 July 1831, here
      reprinted from the Illinois Monthly Magazine October 1831;
      Hubbard was a pioneer businessman in Illinois.]

714   HOAD, Louise [Green]. Kickapoo Indian trails. Caldwell,
      Idaho: Caxton Printers Ltd. (1944) 1946, 129 p., illus.
      [Pp. 51-53, Kennekuk, including detailed account of his
      death — quoted in J. H. Howard, item 716, pp. 7-8.]

715   HODGE, Frederick Webb (ed.). Handbook of American Indians
      north of Mexico = Bulletin of American Ethnology 30 (1),
      1907; repr. New York: Rowman & Littlefield 1971.
      [P. 650, "Kanekuk", with Catlin's portrait — based on
      J. Mooney, item 508.]

716   HOWARD, James H[enri]. The Kenakuk religion: an early 19th
      century revitalization movement 140 years later. Museum
      News (University of South Dakota Museum, Vermillion) 26
      (11-12), 1965, 1-49, illus.
      [The major study, with full historical account providing
      extracts from contemporary sources (see under Allis,
      Dunbar, Berryman, Catlin, McCoy, and C. A. Murray), and
      detailed study of the surviving movement in the mid-1960s
      near Horton, Kansas. Interpreted as a revitalization move-
      ment uniting Indian elements with much of the Protestant
      ethic and Western liturgical forms, and showing no signs
      of disappearing.]

717 HUBBARD, Gurdon S. Sermon of Kenakuk, preached near Danville,
     Illinois, July 17, 1831. Illinois Monthly Magazine
     (Vandalia) October 1831.
          [Cited as reputed source by J. H. Howard, item 716,
     p. 21. He calls it "Judge James Hall's Magazine".]

718 IRVING, John Treat, Jr. Indian sketches taken during an
     expedition to the Pawnee tribes, 1833. Philadelphia:
     Carey, Lea & Blanchard, 2 vols., 1835; London: John
     Murray, 2 vols., 1835; New York: G. P. Putnam's Sons, 1
     vol. revd. ed. 1888; repr. of 1st American ed. with "the
     new matter of 1888 acknowledged where pertinent", ed.
     J. F. McDermott (American Exploration and Travel Series,
     18). Norman: University of Oklahoma Press 1955, 275 p.,
     illus., map.
          [Pp. 39-42, first-hand description of Kennekuk's Kickapoo
     village; pp. 42-44, the prophet; p. 43, n9, extract from
     W. D. Smith's letter of 1833, see W. D. Smith, item 727.]

719 LUTZ, J. J. The Methodist Mission among the Indian tribes in
     Kansas. Kansas Historical Society Collections (Topeka) 9,
     1905-1906, 160-235.
          [P. 208 includes account of Kennekuk; cited and used by
     J. H. Howard, item 716, p. 5.]

720 McCOY, Isaac. Kickapoos. Annual Register of Indian Affairs
     within the Indian Territory, no. 4. Indian Territory,
     Shawanoe Baptist Mission House: Isaac M'Coy, 1838.
          [P. 67, account of the Kickapoos' economic development
     and the Methodist mission; "Ken-u-kuk" as one of their two
     chiefs. By a Baptist missionary.]

721 McCOY, Isaac. History of Baptist Indian missions. Washington,
     D.C.: W. M. Morrison, and New York: H. & S. Raynor, 1840,
     611 p.; repr. New York and London: Johnson Reprint
     Corporation 1970, with new introduction by R. F. Berkhofer;
     also repr. in J. H. Howard, item 716, pp. 17-18, 25, 28.
          [Pp. 456-458 on Kennekuk, based on first-hand knowledge
     by a Baptist missionary, but critical in attitude; extracts
     repr. in Custer, item 709, pp. 50-51, who questions
     Kennekuk's alleged polygamy.]

722 MOONEY, James. Item 508.
          [Pp. 692-700, Kennekuk: including illus., also R.
     Graham's letter to General Clark (p. 694) and Kennekuk's
     speech to General Clark, 10 February, 1827 (pp. 694-696) —
     these two sources are repr. in J. H. Howard, item 716,
     pp. 2-3 and pp. 9-12.]

Kennekuk

723   MURRAY, Charles Augustus. Travels in North America during the
       years 1834, 1835 and 1836.... London: R. Bentley, 2 vols.
       1839, 2nd ed. 1841.
       [Vol. 2 (1839 ed.), pp. 72-80 (on period of September
       1835), Kennekuk as "the foremost man in Kickapoo", by an
       English traveller; extracts repr. in J. H. Howard, item
       716, 18-19.]

724   REMSBURG, George J. Some notes on the Kickapoo Indians.
       Philatelic West (Superior, Nebraska) April 1907, 325-326.
       [Includes account of Kennekuk's life; used by J. H.
       Howard, item 716, pp. 3, 8.]

725   ROOT, George A. Chief Kennekuk. Horton Tri-County News
       (Horton, Kansas) Anniversary edition, 12, October 1936,
       207-208.
       [Cited and used by J. H. Howard, item 716 pp. 3, 5.]

726   SCHULTZ, George A. An Indian Canaan. Isaac McCoy and the
       vision of an Indian state. Norman: University of Oklahoma
       Press 1972, 230 p.
       [Pp. 169-172, Kennekuk in relation to the Baptist mis-
       sionary I. McCoy (q.v.) and the Methodist J. C. Berryman
       (q.v.), with source references.]

727   SMITH, W. D. Letters from the Shawnee Village, 1833.
       Philadelphia: Presbyterian Historical Society Manuscripts
       Collection.
       [See quotation on Kennekuk in J. T. Irvine, item 718,
       repr. 1955, p. 43, n9 — letter to E. P. Swift, July 29,
       1833.]

728   UNITED STATES. CONGRESS. OFFICE OF INDIAN AFFAIRS. Report
       of the Commissioner of Indian Affairs. Washington, D.C.:
       Government Printing Office annually from 1834.
       [For reports on Kennekuk's Kickapoos and their economic
       development see 1836, p. 392; 1838, p. 506; 1845, pp. 540-
       541 (Agent R. W. Cummins' Fort Leavenworth Agency report.
       Also found in Senate Executive documents 1846, vol. 1,
       pp. 540-541); 1848, p. 446; 1853, p. 247; 1859, p. 512
       (Agent W. P. Badger's report on the death of Kennekuk).]

729   UNITED STATES. DEPARTMENT OF THE INTERIOR. BUREAU OF INDIAN
       AFFAIRS. Indians of the Central plains. Washington, D.C.:
       Government Printing Office 1968, 20 p., illus.
       [P. 12, summary of Kennekuk as "messiah" of the Kickapoo,
       and still expected to return by some Kickapoo.]

Midéwiwin and Drum Religion

730   VAN QUICKEMBORNE, C. T.   Letter of 24 September 1835, in
      Annales de la Propagation de la Foi (Lyon) no. 48=9
      (September), 1836, 99-101.
           [A contemporary account of Kennekuk by a Catholic
      missionary.]

MIDÉWIWIN AND DRUM RELIGION

These two movements are grouped together as belonging to the same
group of peoples. Both are highly traditional but also "neo-primal"
in our own classification. The Midéwiwin is also known as the Medicine
(or Grand Medicine) Society, or Lodge, or again as Mitawit or Mitawini
Lodge. The question as to whether it is pre-contact (and therefore
not on our agenda) or post-contact remains somewhat controversial, but
both viewpoints are included here in the voluminous literature, with
the post-contact view appearing to predominate.

The Drum religion is also referred to as the Drum Dance or cult,
or as the Dream Dance, and is distinct from the Dreamer religion associated with Smohalla among the Wanapim.

731   ARMSTRONG, Benjamin G.   Early life among the Indians.
      Reminiscences... .   Ashland, Wisconsin: A. W. Bowron
      1892, 266 p., illus.
           [Pp. 156-158, on a Sioux prophetess bringing the Drum
      religion to the Cheyenne about 1878; quoted in F. Densmore,
      item 743, p. 151.]

732   BARNOUW, Victor (recorder).   Reminiscences of a Chippewa mide
      priest.   Wisconsin Archaeologist 35 (4), 1954, 83-112.
           [Discursive autobiographical account revealing the
      beliefs and attitudes of a conservative Medicine Dance
      (midé) priest.]

733   BARRETT, S. A.   The dream dance of the Chippewa and Menominee
      Indians of Northern Wisconsin.   Bulletin of the Public
      Museum of the City of Milwaukee 1 (4), 1911, 237-371,
      illus.
           [Pp. 293-301, comparison of the dream dance with the
      Ghost Dance; otherwise an important early description of
      the Drum or Dream Dance.]

734   BLESSING, Fred K.   An exhibition of Midé magic.   The Minnesota
      Archaeologist (Minneapolis) 20 (4), 1956, 9-13.
           [Two examples of skill in magical manipulation by a
      Chippewa medicine man of the Grand Medicine Lodge in
      northern Minnesota in the late 1930s.]

United States of America

Midéwiwin and Drum Religion

735 BLESSING, Fred K. Birchbark Midé scrolls from Minnesota. The
     Minnesota Archaeologist 25, 1963, 91-142, illus.

736 BLOOMFIELD, Leonard. Menomini texts (Publications of the
     American Ethnological Society, 12). New York: G. E.
     Steichert 1928, 607 p.
        [Pp. 52-55, vernacular texts of songs: Dream Dance (with
        English translation), Peyote ("said to be in Pawnee");
        pp. 104-107, narrative of the origin of the Dream Dance
        (with English translation) set in the period of European
        contact.]

737 BRILL, Charles. Indian and free: a contemporary portrait of
     life on a Chippewa reservation. Minneapolis: University
     of Minnesota Press 1974, 144 p., illus.
        [Developed around 160 excellent photographs selected
        from 10,000 taken in 1964-1969 by a white photographer.
        P. 24, story of Midéwiwin origins; pp. 38-39, photos of
        Midéwiwin leaders; pp. 100-101, 114, 117, Midéwiwin or
        Grand Medicine Society; pp. 102-103, the Society's creation
        myth.]

738 CLIFTON, James A. Sociocultural dynamics of the Prairie
     Potawatomi Drum cult. Plains Anthropologist 14 (May),
     1969, 85-93, fig.
        [Founded 1872 by prophetess Wananikive, among Santee
        Dakota, and now spread as a unitive cult among the Potawa-
        tomi; plan of ceremonial grounds.]

739 CLIFTON, James A. Potawatomi leadership roles: on Okama and
     other influential personages, in W. Cowan (ed.), Papers of
     the Sixth Algonquian Conference 1974 (Canadian Ethnology
     Service, Paper 23). Ottawa: National Museums of Canada
     1974, 42-99, bibl.
        [Pp. 80-89, leadership in late 19th and 20th c. Dream
        Dance religion.]

740 COLEMAN, Bernard [Sister]. The religion of the Ojibwa of
     Northern Minnesota. Primitive Man (Washington, D.C.) 10,
     1937, 33-57.
        [Pp. 43-50, Midéwiwin; by a Catholic nun.]

741 DENSMORE, Frances. Chippewa music = Bulletin, Bureau of
     American Ethnology 45, 1910, 216 p., illus.
        [Pp. 13-118, the Midéwiwin — its beliefs, healing, degrees
        and songs, with drawings, photos and music texts; a depth
        study of the songs and music as expressing the religion.]

Midéwiwin and Drum Religion

742 DENSMORE, Frances. Chippewa music — II = Bulletin, Bureau of
American Ethnology 53, 1913, 341 p., illus.
[Pp. 142-148, the Drum presentation ceremony: pp. 142-
143, the new Ojibwa "Drum religion", more concerned with
social relations than the Midéwiwin society.]

743 DENSMORE, Frances. Menominee music = Bulletin, Bureau of
American Ethnology 102, 1932, 230 p., illus.
[Pp. 150-183, the Drum religion — its origin, songs,
ceremonies and teachings, with good photographs.]

744 DEWDNEY, Selwyn. The sacred scrolls of the southern Ojibway.
Toronto and Buffalo: University of Toronto Press for
Glenbow-Alberta Institute 1975, 199 p., illus.
[Midéwiwin or Grand Medicine Society; see index for its
initiation, ceremonies, diffusion and decline — as a new
cult in the 19th c. seeking unsuccessfully to replace
visionary shamanism with some Christian influences.
Pp. 177-179, Epilogue, on the informant, James Red Sky,
and his final reconciliation of his Midéwiwin and Christian
affiliations.]

745 EASTMAN, Charles Alexander [=Ohiyesa]. The soul of the Indian:
an interpretation. Boston and New York: Houghton Mifflin
Co. 1911, 170 p.; repr. New York: Johnson Reprint Corp.
1971 etc., 170 p., illus.
[Pp. 63-74, the "Grand Medicine Lodge" of the Algonquins,
as "indirect result" of Jesuit missions, with "Caucasian
elements", like the Ghost Dance and the "Shawnee prophet
in 1762".]

746 HALLOWELL, A. Irving. Ojibwa ontology, behaviour and world
views, in S. Diamond (ed.), Culture in history: essays in
honor of Paul Radin. New York: Columbia University Press
1960, 19-52; repr. in D. Tedlock and B. Tedlock (eds.),
item 338, pp. 141-178.
[P. 25 (= pp. 147-148) midéwiwin ceremony — especially
on "animated stones".]

747 HICKERSON, Harold. Notes on the post-contact origin of the
Midéwiwin. Ethnohistory 9 (4), 1962, 404-423.
[Interpreted as a Chippewa response to French contacts
in the 17th c., but incorporating aboriginal medicinal
practices.]

748 HICKERSON, Harold. The southwestern Chippewa: an ethnohistorical study (Memoirs, American Anthropological

Midéwiwin and Drum Religion

Association, 92) = <u>American Anthropologist</u> 64 (3:2), 1962,
110 p., bibl., maps.
[Midéwiwin, <u>passim</u> — see index.]

749   HICKERSON, Harold. The sociohistorical significance of two
      Chippewa ceremonials. <u>American Anthropologist</u> 65 (1),
      1963, 67-85.
      [A new sodality, the Midéwiwin (especially pp. 75-82),
      replaced the Feast of the Dead among the Ojibwa, between
      the 17th and 19th centuries, but as an inevitable histor-
      ical process and not as a revivalistic or nativistic reac-
      tion to European pressures or to culture shock, although
      contact did play a part.]

750   HICKERSON, Harold. William T. Boutwell of the American Board
      and the Pillager Chippewa: the history of a failure.
      <u>Ethnohistory</u> 12, 1965, 1-29, bibl.
      [Boutwell was a Presbyterian missionary who observed
      several Midéwiwin ceremonies in the 1830s; pp. 20-21, a
      Midéwiwin lodge council "trial" of Boutwell for purchasing
      land from an individual.]

751   HICKERSON, Harold. <u>The Chippewa and their neighbours: a study</u>
      <u>in ethnohistory</u> (Studies in Anthropological Method). New
      York: Holt, Rinehart and Winston 1970, 133 p., maps,
      bibl.
      [Ch. 4 (= pp. 51-63), Origin of the Midéwiwin, as an
      Ojibwa nativistic reaction to European contact — the early
      history and the evidence for this discussed in detail,
      especially the use of a cross.]

752   HOFFMAN, Walter James. The Midéwiwin or "Grand Medicine
      Society" of the Ojibwa, in <u>Seventh Annual Report, Bureau</u>
      <u>of American Ethnology 1885-1886</u>. Washington, D.C.:
      Government Printing Office 1891, 143-300, illus., map,
      music, texts.
      [A detailed study, treating Midéwiwin as aboriginal and
      opposed to Christianity.]

753   HOFFMAN, Walter James. The Menomini Indians, in <u>14th Annual</u>
      <u>Report, Bureau of American Ethnology 1892-93. Part I.</u>
      Washington, D.C.: Government Printing Office 1896, 11-
      328, illus.
      [Pp. 66-138, the Mitawit or Grand Medicine Society;
      pp. 157-161, Dreamers' Cult from 1880, with extract from
      Rev. Clay MacCauley's lecture (from <u>Japan Daily Mail</u>
      21 March 1893) on his visit to the Dreamers <u>c</u>. 1881 —
      interpreted as a pagan-Christian mixture.]

754   HOWARD, James [Henri]. The Henry Davis drum rite: an unusual
       Drum religion variant of the Minnesota Ojibwa. <u>Plains
       Anthropologist</u> 11, 1966, 117-126, illus.
              [The Drum religion or Dream Dance as an "accommodative"
       revitalization movement modified from the Grass Dance by
       the addition of religious elements, many of them Christian;
       the form described here occurred in 1963 and incorporated
       more Christian elements than any other Drum rite.]

755   KEESING, Felix M. <u>The Menomini Indians of Wisconsin: a study
       of three centuries of cultural change and contact</u> (Memoirs
       of the American Philosophical Society, 10). Philadelphia:
       American Philosophical Society 1939, 261 p.
              [Pp. 48-50, Mitawini Lodge (i.e. Midéwiwin) cult as
       post-contact; pp. 179-182, Dream Dance; pp. 212-217,
       religion; pp. 216-217, peyote.]

756   KINIETZ, W[illiam] Vernon. <u>The Indians of the Western Great
       Lakes, 1615-1760</u> (Museum of Anthropology, Occasional Con-
       tributions, 10). Ann Arbor: University of Michigan Press
       1940, xiv + 427 p., map.
              [P. 215, assertion that the Ojibwa Midéwiwin society was
       pre-contact, despite its use of a cross; based on explorer
       Marquette in <u>Jesuit Relations</u>, vol. 59, p. 103. P. 270,
       extract from Sabrevois de Bleury, item 766; pp. 372-374,
       letter no. 47 of A. D. Raudot, item 763; pp. 328-329, on
       the Medicine Society or Midéwiwin.]

757   LANDES, Ruth. Potawatomi medicine. <u>Transactions of the Kansas
       Academy of Science</u> 66 (4), 1963 (issued 1964), 553-599.
              [Based on field work in 1935-1936 in Kansas; the Midé-
       wiwin, <u>passim</u>; pp. 556, 566, 575, 578, 582, 584-591, the
       Drum or Religion dance as a pro-Christian, anti-shaman
       movement, similar to this dance among the Ojibwa and
       Menomini described by Barrett, item 733; pp. 557, 588,
       592-598, peyote as curing, and introducing confession and
       reformation emphases; the interactions between all three
       movements.]

758   LANDES, Ruth. <u>Ojibwa religion and the Midéwiwin</u>. Madison and
       London: University of Wisconsin Press 1968, 250 p.,
       illus.
              [Based on field work in the 1930s. Pp. 3-67, Ojibwa
       religion (pp. 52-57, curing by Midéwiwin); Part. 2 (pp. 71-
       237), the Midéwiwin society — the first detailed account
       of its organization and ritual since Hoffman, item 752,
       but without discussion of its origins and acculturative
       value.]

Midéwiwin and Drum Religion

759 MAKARIUS, Laura. The crime of ·Manabozo. American Anthro-
pologist 75 (3), 1973, 663-675, bibl.
[Pp. 667-668, 673 (notes), Midéwiwin in relation to the
Algonkian trickster figure, Manabozo.]

760 MALLERY, Garrick. Picture writing of the American Indians,
in 10th Annual Report, Bureau of American Ethnology 1888-
89. Washington, D.C.: Government Printing Office 1893,
3-822, illus.
[Pp. 202-203, bark rolls and pictographs of Ojibwa Midéwiwin; pp. 232-246, ceremonial chant of Midéwiwin society;
pp. 508-510, Midéwiwin ceremonies and lodges; pp. 508-509,
Kennekuk's prayer sticks (illustrated) and traders' account
of Kennekuk's association with Methodist missionary,
quoted from Catlin, item 155, vol. 2, p. 98.]

761 MASSON, L[ouis François] R[odigue] (ed.). Les bourgeois de
la Compagnie du Nord-Ouest, récits de voyages, lettres et
rapports inédits relatifs au Nord-Ouest Canadien. Quebec:
A. Coté, 2 vols., 1889-1890, map.
[Vol. 2, pp. 361-363, trader Grant's account of the
Ojibwa Midéwiwin ceremony in 1804.]

762 MICHON, J. L. La grande médicine des Ojibways. Bulletin de
la Société Suisse des Américanistes 36, 1972, 37-72, illus.,
bibl.

763 RAUDOT, Antoine Denis. Memoir concerning the different Indian
nations of North America. Eng. trans. of selections from
French original published under two different titles, by
W. V. Kinietz in his item 756, 341-410.
[P. 335 for publishing history. Pp. 372-374, Letter
no. 47, "On the Saulteur Jugglers" — i.e. Midéwiwin.]

764 RÖHRL, Vivian. Some observations on the drum society of
Chippewa Indians. Ethnohistory 19 (3), 1972, 219-225.
[History of the Drum Dance on Mille Lacs Lake reserva-
tion, Minnesota; its reinforcement of traditional beliefs
and bilateral kinship ties, and partial replacement of the
Grand Medicine Society.]

765 ROUFS, Tim. Myth in method: more on Ojibwa culture. Current
Anthropology 15 (3), 1974, 307-309.
[Mainly on the Midéwiwin society and ceremony, in the
period 1966-1972.]

United States of America

766   SABREVOIS DE BLEURY, Jacques Charles. Memoir on the savages
       of Canada as far as the Mississippi River (R. G. Thwaites,
       ed.). Wisconsin Historical Collections 16, 1902, 363-376.
          [Pp. 367-368 on the Midéwiwin Dance, as observed about
       1718 by the commandant at Detroit. See W. V. Kinietz,
       item 756, for extract.]

767   SLOTKIN, James S[ydney]. The Menomini powwow (Publications in
       Anthropology, 4). Milwaukee: Milwaukee Public Museum
       1957, 166 p., illus.
          [The Dream Dance in decline — its meetings, offices and
       ideology, with extensive verbatim reports from members.]

768   WRIGHT, Robert Catlin. Indian masonry. Ann Arbor: Tyler
       Publishing Co. 1907, 123 p., illus.
          [Pp. 51-88, the "Ojibwa Grand Medicine Lodge" or
       Midéwiwin.]

PEYOTE, PEYOTISM, AND NATIVE AMERICAN CHURCH

     These terms refer to the largest and most widespread of the new
religious movements among North American Indians, with a history
reaching back for more than a century. It has also been the least
understood and most controversial movement, and has been bitterly opposed by tribal councils, by the churches, the Bureau of Indian
Affairs, and by the many State governments that banned it. Thanks
largely to the interpretations and support of anthropologists these
attitudes are now changing. It is not surprising that the literature
is voluminous, as may be seen from the size of the bibliographies in
two of the major studies — 44 pages in that of Slotkin in 1956, and
26 pages in the 1969 enlarged edition of LaBarre's work of 1938. The
bibliography now offered updates the material, emphasizes the religious aspects of the movement, and divides the items into three groups,
each representing a different focus in peyote studies. The first of
these groups concentrates on the new peyote cult as it developed in
the United States and penetrated into Canada, and on the later in-
corporated forms known as the Native American Church or by similar
titles; it might seem that material on the latter should have been
separated into a distinct group, but this would probably be mislead-
ing rather than helpful.

769   ABERLE, David F[riend]. Review of The Peyote ritual: visions
       and descriptions of Monroe Tsa Toke, by Monroe Tsa Toke,
       Leslie Van Ness Denman and Susan C. Peters. American
       Anthropologist 60 (5), 1958, 953-954.

Peyote,...Native American Church

770   ABERLE, David F[riend]. The peyote religion among the Navaho
       (Viking Fund Publications in Anthropology, 42). Chicago:
       Aldine Press 1966, xxvi + 469 p., illus., bibl. (pp. 423-
       436).
           [A major study, examining Navaho life before and during
       acceptance of peyote, and giving a full modern history of
       the Navaho. Note especially pp. 193-204, appeal of peyote
       and contrast with Navaho religion; pp. 221-223, summary of
       the opposition; pp. 315-333, a classification of social
       movements.]

771   ABERLE, David F[riend] and STEWART, Omer C[all]. Navaho and
       Ute peyotism: a chronological and distributional study.
       (University of Colorado Studies. Series in Anthropology,
       6). Boulder: University of Colorado Press 1957, ix +
       129 p., maps. Repr. New York: Kraus Reprint 1970.
           [A classic study.]

772   ALBAUGH, Bernard J. and ANDERSON, Philip O. Peyote in the
       treatment of alcoholism among the American Indians.
       American Journal of Psychiatry 131 (11), 1974, 1247-1250.
           [The Native American Church services assist in treatment
       rather than offer a cure.]

772A   AMERICAN INDIAN BAPTIST VOICE. Peyote sentence overturned.
       The American Indian Baptist Voice (Okmulgee, Oklahoma)
       23 (3), 1977, 2.
           [Report of Oklahoma Criminal Court of Appeals upholding
       an Indian's appeal against a two-year prison sentence in
       1975 for possession of peyote. An objective not-
       unsympathetic report in contrast to earlier church
       journals.]

773   AMERICAN INDIAN MAGAZINE. The peyote question. American
       Indian Magazine (Society of American Indians, Washington,
       D.C.) Summer 1918, 67.

774   AMERICAN REVIEW OF REVIEWS. The problem of peyote. The
       American Review of Reviews (New York) 65 (4), 1922,
       437-438.
           [Describes peyote, then reviews several pages of extracts
       from speeches in the Senate and the House of Representa-
       tives in the Congressional Digest and reproduces some of
       these in support of the anti-peyote position.]

775   AMERINDIAN. Use of peyote ruled illegal in ceremonies.
       Amerindian (American Indian Review) (Chicago) 12 (3),
       1964, 2.

[Summary of the 18-page opinion in the California Fourth District Court of Appeals decision against three Navahos; see United States [Courts], item 1186.]

776 APPLEGATE, Richard B. The Datura cult among the Chumash. The Journal of California Anthropology 2 (1), 1975, 7-17.
[On datura as equivalent to peyote in use.]

777 ARIZONA NEWS. Peyote users lose round as Navajo Council strengthens 1940 anti-peyotism measure. Arizona News (Phoenix) 6 July 1956, pp. ?, 4.
[Decided that confiscated peyote must be destroyed, despite claims by a few council members that it is harmless.]

778 ARTH, Malcolm J. A functional view of peyotism in Omaha culture. The Plains Anthropologist (Lincoln, Nebraska) no. 7= 3 (Oct.), 1956, 25-29.

779 ARTHUR, William Reed. Law of drugs and druggists. St. Paul: West Publishing Co. (1940); 4th ed. 1955, 399 p.
[Pp. 127-128, "Poison, use of peyote (pellote) regulated by statute".]

780 ASSOCIATION ON AMERICAN INDIAN AFFAIRS [See also under INDIAN AFFAIRS]. Peyote and the Native American Church of the United States. Supplement No. 41A to Indian Affairs, April 18, 1961, 4 p.

781 BAKER, Fred. Father Peyote's "disciples". Empire Magazine, Sunday Denver Post (Denver, Colorado) 15 (30), 26 July 1964, 4-5, illus.
[By a photographer-journalist who broke Colorado's anti-peyote laws to secure this material.]

782 BALL, Eve. Peyote priest. Frontier Times 40 (6), 1966, 28-30, illus.
[James Kassanovoid, Comanche priest of Native American Church in Oklahoma, with description of the rite.]

783 BARBER, Bernard. A socio-cultural interpretation of the Peyote cult. American Anthropologist 43 (4), 1941, 673-675. Repr. in J. M. Yinger (ed.), Religion, society and the individual. New York: Macmillan 1957, 496-498.

784 BARNARD, Mary. The god in the flowerpot. American Scholar (Washington, D.C.) 32 (4), 1963, 578-596; repr. in Psychedelic Review 1, 1963, 244-251.

Peyote,...Native American Church

[The use of peyote in the peyote cult; the mythology associated with the discovery of peyote in Mexico, and with other "mind-changing" drugs, including soma and mushrooms; the relation of these to shamanism.]

785   BEALS, Kenneth [L.]. The dynamics of Kiowa-Apache peyotism. Papers in Anthropology (University of Oklahoma) 12 (1), 1971, 35-89.
      [Based on an M.A. thesis of same title and university, 1967. A valuable account of the history and ritual, functions (pp. 59-64), ethics (pp. 64-71), Christian opponents and sympathizers (pp. 72-75), and some forty points of change showing decreasing social importance, increasing Western and Christian influence, and more support for pan-Indianism (pp. 77-85).]

786   BEAVER, William T. Peyote and the Hopi. American Anthropologist 54 (1), 1952, 120.
      [A reply to Slotkin's association of peyote with the Hopi (see item 1259), and denying that they have ever had knowledge of it; suggests peyote has been confused with jimsonweed.]

787   BECKER, D. A. Comanche civilization, with history of Quanah Parker. Chronicles of Oklahoma 1, 1923, 243-252.
      [Pp. 251-252, peyote.]

788   BEE, Robert L. Peyotism in North American Indian groups. Transactions of the Kansas Academy of Science 68 (1), 1965, 13-61, illus.
      [Especially on Plains Indians — surveys existing literature.]

789   BEE, Robert L. Potawatomi peyotism: the influence of traditional patterns. Southwestern Journal of Anthropology 22 (2), 1966, 194-205.
      [The peyote cult in the Kansas Potawatomi, with its split in the traditional manner of leadership conflict; peyotists' neutrality as between political actions; overlapping participation by members of the more traditional Drum (see Clifton, item 738) and Bundle societies, peyote cult, and mission churches.]

790   BENEDICT, Ruth. Psychological types in the cultures of the Southwest, in Proceedings of the Twenty-third International Congress of Americanists...New York, Sept...1928. Lancaster, Pennsylvania: Science Press Printing Co. 1930, pp. 572-581.

[On Pueblo Indians, who outlaw "the divine frenzy and
the vision" and have not had a problem with alcohol; Taos,
somewhat marginal in Pueblo culture, has had peyote
(p. 575). Thus shamanism has been ruled out in the Southwest, which is "Apollonian" rather than "Dionysiac", and
this is one of the most abrupt culture breaks in N.
America.]

791   BENZ, Ernst. Neue Religionen. Stuttgart: Ernst Klett Verlag
      1971, 179 p.
           [Ch. 5 (= pp. 68-91), "Der Peyote-Kult der nord-
      amerikanischen Indianer. Native American Church"; by a
      distinguished German historian of religion, after some
      personal contact.]

792   BERGMAN, Robert L. Navajo use of peyote: its apparent safety.
      American Journal of Psychiatry 128 (6), 1971, 695-699.
           [A psychiatrist at Window Rock estimates 30,000 Navaho
      peyote users, and reports the beneficial effects when con-
      trolled within the religious ritual of the cult; see sum-
      mary in W. R. Mackaye, item 988.]

793   BERGQUIST, Laura. Peyote, the strange church of cactus eaters.
      Look (Des Moines) 21 (25), 10 Dec. 1957, 36-41, illus.
           [A journalist's report of participation in a peyote meet-
      ing among the Crow in Montana; many good photographs.]

794   BERLANDIER, Jean Louis. The Indians of Texas in 1830, edited
      by John C. Ewers. Washington, D.C.: Smithsonian Institu-
      tion Press 1969, 209 p., illus., map.
           [P. 62, peyote among the Lipan-Apache, before the Ghost
      Dance.]

795   BISCHOFF, Robert. The peyote cult. Wisconsin Archaeologist
      n.s. 29 (2), 1948, 28-37.
           [Describes the Mexican background and the cult meeting;
      outlines the persecution and misrepresentation met by the
      cult; uses material in the Milwaukee Museum.]

796   BITTLE, William E. The Peyote ritual: Kiowa-Apache. Bulletin
      of the Oklahoma Anthropological Society 2, 1954, 69-78.
           [P. 69, the Ghost Dance and its suppression; pp. 70-71,
      peyote distinguished from "mescal beans" and "mescal
      proper" (agave plant); pp. 71-72, the Kiowa-Apache origin
      myth for the peyote cult; pp. 73-76, the peyote cult
      ritual; pp. 77-78, healing and other functions of peyote —
      all drawing on LaBarre.]

Peyote,...Native American Church

796A   BITTLE, William E.   The curative aspects of peyotism.   Bios
       (Oklahoma City) 31 (3), 1960, 140-148.

797   BLACKBEAR, Joe (Charles S. Brant, recorder).   Joe Blackbear's
       story of the origin of the Peyote religion.   Plains
       Anthropologist 8 (August), 1963, 80-81.
           [A Kiowa Apache's version of an origin myth giving a
       folk explanation of certain aspects of peyote ritual and
       paraphernalia.]

798   BLAKESLEE, Clement.   Some observations of the Indians on Crow
       Creek Reservation, South Dakota.   Plains Anthropologist 2
       (December), 1955, 31-35.
           [P. 33, brief reference to the beginning and the per-
       sistence of the peyote cult.]

799   BLESSING, Fred K.   Discovery of a Chippewa peyote cult in
       Minnesota.   Minnesota Archaeologist (Minneapolis) 23, 1961,
       1-8, bibl.
           [A general introduction to the cult, followed by a very
       favourable account of a small village in the Leech Lake
       area which had practised the cult since the 1920s.]

800   BLOWSNAKE, Sam.
           See under RADIN, item 1071.

801   BOYER, L. Bryce, BOYER, Ruth M. and BASEHART, Harry W.
       Shamanism and peyote use among the Apaches of the Mescalero
       Indian Reservation, in M. J. Harner (ed.), Hallucinogens
       and shamanism.   New York: Oxford University Press 1973,
       53-66, illus., bibl., with editorial introduction,
       pp. 49-52.
           [The unusual case of an Indian people who adopted and
       then rejected the peyote cult (see also pp. 49, 50).   By
       two anthropologists and a psychoanalyst.   The editor's
       introduction places this in the context of cultures under-
       going westernization.   (Abstract in Bulletin of American
       Anthropological Association 1 (3), 1968, 15.)]

802   BRAASCH, W. F., BRANTON, B. J. and CHESLEY, A. J.   Survey of
       medical care among the Upper Midwest Indians.   Journal of
       the American Medical Association 139 (4), 1949, 220-226.
           [P. 225, brief discussion of use of peyote, demanding
       federal restriction as a habit-forming drug.]

803   BRAND, S.   The Native American Church meeting.   Psychedelic
       Review 9, 1967.
           [As cited by J. L. McLaughlin, item 989, p. 7.]

804   BRANT, Charles S.   Peyotism among the Kiowa-Apache and neigh-
       bouring tribes.   Southwestern Journal of Anthropology 6 (2),
       1950, 212-222.
          [The peyote cult as an inter-tribal support for a Pan-
       Indian movement; pp. 212-215, the local origin myth (cf.
       M. E. Opler, item 1048); pp. 215-219, description of a
       rite in Oklahoma in 1949; pp. 219-220, beliefs, and re-
       lations to Christianity and churches; replacement of
       shamanism for healing; the struggle for legal recognition;
       pp. 220-222, sociological aspects.]

805   BRANT, Charles S.   See also under BLACKBEAR, Joe.

806   BRICKMAN, Helen M. et al.   What about peyote? New York: Home
       Missions Council of North America 1941.
          [Anti-peyote.]

807   BRITO, Silvester John/HUNTING BEAR.   The development and change
       of the peyote ceremony through time and space.   Indiana
       University, Ph.D. dissertation (anthropology/folklore)
       1975, xvii + 293 p.
          [Shows that peyotists are aware of changes and how they
       have occurred, and that these form part of the continuing
       adjustment process, strengthening both the peyote cult and
       pan-Indian nationalism.   By a Comanche member of the Native
       American Church, as the first major study by an Indian
       participant; based on the Little Moon ceremony of "Plains"
       or Kiowa-Comanche rites around Oklahoma City and among the
       Wisconsin Winnebago.]

808   BROMBERG, Walter.   Storm over peyote.   Nature Magazine 35
       (October), 1942, 410-412, 444, illus.; p. 410 repr. in
       Schleiffer, item 1314, p. 29.
          [Surveys the differences of opinion among Indians,
       anthropologists, the government Indian Service, and mis-
       sionaries; examines the medical and moral effects, with
       emphasis on the harmful effects, but leaves the question
       open.]

809   BROMBERG, Walter and TRANTER, Charles L.   Peyote intoxication:
       some psychological aspects of peyote rite.   Journal of
       Nervous and Mental Disease 97 (5), 1943, 518-527.
          [An address to the Home Missions Council of North
       America, 1942, by medical doctors: surveys the effects on
       both whites and Indians, and explains the appeal of the
       peyote cult to Indians in terms of an anodyne allaying un-
       conscious anxieties and relieving the pain of culture con-
       flict, assisted by the promise of supernatural power.]

Peyote,...Native American Church

810   BROPHY, William A[loysius], ABERLE, Sophie D. et al. (comps.).
      The Indian. America's unfinished business. Report on the
      Commission on the rights, liberties, and responsibilities
      of the American Indian (Civilization of the American
      Indian Series, 83). Norman: University of Oklahoma Press
      1966, etc., 236 p.
         [Pp. 42, and 43n, 44n, brief references to peyote and
      the law.]

811   BRUCE, H. E. Your religion. A frank discussion on some
      aspects of the peyote drug. News Letter of the National
      Fellowship of Indian Workers (Laurence, Kansas) 40, Autumn
      1949. Reprint, 8 p.

812   BUNZEL, Ruth L[eah]. Introduction to Zuñi ceremonialism, in
      47th Annual Report, Bureau of American Ethnology 1929-1930.
      Washington, D.C.: Government Printing Office 1932, 467-544.
         [P. 489, peyote never adopted in the pueblos (except
      Taos), although Zuñis used jimsonweed to discern evildoers.]

813   BURDETTE, Mary G. (ed.). Young women among blanket Indians.
      The trio at Rainy Mountain. Chicago: Donelly 1895, 60 p.
         [Pp. 47-48, peyote; a publication of the Women's Baptist
      Home Missionary Society.]

814   BURKS, Edward C. Peyote peddler at odds with U.S. New York
      Times 23 June 1960, p. 33L, col. 4.
         [An example of the use of peyote in the non-Indian "drug
      culture" in Greenwich Village, New York City.]

815   CAMPBELL, T. N. Origin of the mescal bean cult. American
      Anthropologist 60 (1), 1958, 156-160.
         [Additional archaeological evidence from Southwestern
      Texas supporting La Barre's case for an ancient southern
      mescal bean cult from which peyotism derived, and against
      J. H. Howard's view of a northern origin.]

816   CANYON RECORDS, PHOENIX. Peyote songs: music of the Native
      American Church of North America (Indian). No. 6054;
      Chants of the Native American Church of North America, III,
      as sung by Wilbur Jack (Paiute-Wasco). No. 6074. Phoenix,
      Arizona: Canyon Records, n.d. and 1971.
         [Two 33 1/3 rpm records; the first containing 14 songs,
      by singers from seven different tribes, the second con-
      taining "morning and occasional songs" from "tribes of the
      far West".]

817　CARDON, B. P.　Peyote and the Native American Church.　<u>Journal of Psychedelic Drugs</u> 1 (2), 1968, 72-76.
　　　[Based on Alice Marriott's description of her experience with peyote, item 994.]

818　CARLSON, G[ustav] G. and JONES, V[olney] H.　Some notes on uses of plants by the Comanche Indians.　<u>Papers of the Michigan Academy of Science, Arts and Letters 1939</u> 25, 1940, 517-542.
　　　[Includes peyote, pp. 522, 537-538.]

819　CARTWRIGHT, Willena D. (comp).　<u>The peyote cult</u> (Leaflet 105) and <u>The peyote cult: ritual equipment</u> (Leaflet 106).　Denver:　Denver Art Museum 1950; repr. 1967, paged 18-20, and 22-24, illus.
　　　[Succinct outlines:　pp. 19-20 being mainly a condensation of O. C. Stewart's description of the Ute rite (see his item 1137); pp. 22-24, the objects used, with illustrations, based on the museum's collection.]

820　CASH, Joseph H. and HOOVER, Herbert T. (eds.).　<u>To be an Indian: an oral history</u>.　New York:　Holt Rinehart and Winston 1971, 239 p., illus.
　　　[Pp. 30-34, interview with Noah White, Winnebago leader in the Native American Church; pp. 35-38, interview with Sterling Snake concerning a peyote meeting; pp. 158, 165, briefer references to peyote cult; see also photos, pp. 1-10.]

821　CASTETTER, E. F. and OPLER, M. E.　The ethnobiology of the Chiricahua and Mescalero Apache.　<u>Bulletin, University of New Mexico, Ethnobiological Series</u> 5 (4), 1936.
　　　[Pp. 54-55, 61, peyote.]

822　CAVAN, Ruth Shonle.
　　　See SHONLE, Ruth.

823　CAZENEUVE, Jean.　Le peyotisme au Nouveau-Mexique, notes sur une nouvelle religion.　<u>Revue Philosophique de la France et de l'Etranger</u> (Paris) 149 (2), 1959, 169-182.
　　　[A general survey of the Mexican background; the peyote cult among the pastoral Navaho and the agricultural Taos pueblo, regarded as a synthesis of the aboriginal and Christian religions, with the latter supplying the ethic and the eschatology; the use of drugs for mystical experiences.]

Peyote,...Native American Church

824   CHAVEZ, Tibo J.   Early witchcraft in New Mexico. El Palacio
       (Santa Fe) 76 (3), 1970, 7-9.
          [When the governor of Isleta Pueblo was tried in 1733 on
          a charge of witchcraft, some evidence was given that he
          had administered peyote to his victims (see p. 8, col. 6,
          but this is only a brief statement).]

825   CHRISTIAN CENTURY. Navajos sentenced for using peyote. The
          Christian Century 79 (50), 12 Dec. 1962, 1506.
          [Judge Hilliard's decision in the San Bernardino Superior
          court. See also items 1186, 1190.]

826   CHRISTIAN INDIAN. Christianity vs. peyote. The Christian
          Indian (Farmington, New Mexico) May 1954; extract repr. in
          Apache Lutheran 32 (7), July 1954.

827   CHURCH AND STATE. Religious use of peyote upheld. Church and
          State (Washington, D.C.) 17 (10), 1964, 3, illus.
          [An unsympathetic editorial in the journal of Protestants
          and Other Americans United for Separation of Church and
          State.]

828   CLARK, David [Sam]. The peyote religion. Navajo Times 8 (25),
          22 June 1967, 4.
          [The President of the Navaho Native American Church de-
          scribes and defends the Church during its struggles for
          legalization. See also on his arrest, item 1022, 29 Feb.
          1968.]

829   CLARK, E. L. Letter. Transmitted to Washington by Special
          Agent E. E. White on 6 July 1888; published in part in
          Slotkin, item 1111, pp. 106-107, and in O. C. Stewart,
          item 1148, p. 213.
          [An early and reliable account of peyote use on the
          Kiowa-Comanche Reservation.]

830   CLARK, Walter Houston. Chemical ecstasy: psychedelic drugs
          and religion. New York: Sheed and Ward 1969, ix + 179 p.
          [Pp. 85-90, peyote and the Native American Church; the
          use of peyote is favourably regarded as "releasing or
          triggering" religious experience.]

831   CLARK, Walter Houston. Pharmacological cults. Encyclopaedia
          Britannica 1974, vol. 14, 200-203.
          [Pp. 200, 202, 203, peyote cult; p. 202, Church of the
          Awakening — a whites' group using peyote sacramentally
          from 1953, until it became illegal, in New Mexico.]

832   CLIGNET, Rémy. Sociologie de la colonisation américaine en
        territoire indien. Cahiers Internationaux de Sociologie
        20 = n.s. 3 (jan.-juin), 1950, 61-89.
        [Pp. 83-84, Navaho Tribal Council and its public and
        personal reasons for the 1954 ban on peyote.]

833   COHEN, Alan. The small grey bird. A study of forms and pat-
        terns in shamanism and ecstatic experience. University of
        Oxford, B. Litt. thesis (Theology) 1976, 223 p.
        [Pp. 108-115, the peyote experience as "making shamanic
        ecstacy generally available rather than supplanting it".]

834   COLLIER, Donald. Peyote, a general study of the plant, the
        cult, and the drug. In United States Congress. Senate
        Committee on Indian Affairs, item 1184, pp. 18,234-18,257,
        bibl.
        [Written in 1932, with bibliography revised to 1937; an
        important paper incorporated in the committee papers.]

835   COLLIER, John. The Indians of the Americas. New York: W. W.
        Norton 1947, 326 p., maps, illus.; abridged ed. as The
        Indians of the Americas: the long hope. New York: The
        New American Library (Mentor Books) 1947 etc., 191 p.
        [Pp. 238-242, peyote.]

836   COLLIER, John. The peyote cult. Science no. 2292=115 (2 May),
        1952, 503-504.
        [The former U.S. Commissioner on Indian Affairs concurs
        with the anthropologists' letter in idem 114, 30 November
        1951, in defending the right to use peyote. See item 954.]

837   COLLINS, John James. Peyotism and religious membership at
        Taos Pueblo, New Mexico. Southwestern Social Science
        Quarterly (Austin, Texas), 48 (2), 1967, 183-191.
        [The three forms of religion found at Taos, and their
        interrelations: pp. 187-188, Kiva aboriginal cult and
        Catholicism; pp. 188-189, Catholicism and the peyotists;
        pp. 189-190, peyotists and the Kiva adherents; pp. 190-
        191, the functions of the peyote cult.]

838   COLLINS, John James. A descriptive introduction to the Taos
        peyote ceremony. Ethnology 7 (4), 1968, 427-449.
        [A very full account of the rite at the only Pueblo
        community to have accepted this cult, first in terms of
        the "specifics" (material, ideological, etc. components),
        and then of ceremonial structure which places the com-
        ponents in context.]

Peyote,...Native American Church

839   COMMONWEAL. Old Coyote protests. Commonweal 9 (21), 27 March
      1929, 585.
           [Reasons for support for Mr. Barney Old Coyote in pro-
      testing against the Wyoming state ban on the sale of
      peyote. See also Hughes, item 913.]

840   CORWIN, Hugh D. Protestant missionary work among the Comanches
      and Kiowas. Chronicles of Oklahoma 46 (1), Spring 1968,
      41-57.
           [P. 45, brief criticism of peyote religion.]

841   CORY, David Munroe. Within two worlds. New York: Friendship
      Press 1955, 177 p.
           [Pp. 155-156, Native American Church as "a corruption of
      Christianity" and peyote intoxication as "not a spiritual
      experience"; estimates 12,000 Navaho now using peyote; less
      hostile than earlier Christian writers.]

842   DAIKER, F. H. Liquor and peyote, a menace to the Indians.
      Report of the 32nd. Annual Lake Mohonk Conference Oct.
      1914. Albany, New York, 1914, 62-68.
           [Extract in W. E. Safford, item 1087, pp. 307-308; also
      pp. 66, 67, 68, in Schleiffer, item 1314, pp. 40-45.]

843   DAILY OKLAHOMAN. Test of Indian worshippers during all-night
      sacrament near Calumet shows no evil effects in peyote.
      Daily Oklahoman (Oklahoma City) 27 April 1919, sec. B, 1-2.

844   DAVIS, Leslie B. Peyotism and the Blackfeet Indians of
      Montana: an historical assessment (Studies in Plains
      Anthropology and History, 1). Browning, Montana: Museum
      of the Plains Indians 1961, 6 p. Mimeo.

845   d'AZEVEDO, Warren L. Delegation to Washington: a Washo
      peyotist narrative. The Indian Historian (San Francisco)
      6 (2), 1973, 4-6.
           [A Washo peyotist's 1954 story of an old treaty.]

846   DE CREDICO, A. C[olorado] U[niversity] prof. performs rites
      of banned "Peyote" cult. Rocky Mountain News (Denver,
      Colorado) 21 October 1948, 33, cols, 4-6.
           [Omer C. Stewart's participation.]

847   DE JACQUES, W. America's newest dope horror. Man to Man
      3 (6), 1952, 8-9, 62-63.
           [On peyote.]

848   DEN HOLLANDER, A[rie] N[icolaas] J[an]. De Peyote-cultus der
Noord-amerikaansche Indianen. Mensch en Maatschappij
(Groningen) 11 (1-2), 1935, 17-19, 123-131.

849   DEN HOLLANDER, A[rie] N[icolaas] J[an]. Americana: Studies
over mensem, deren en een kaktus tussen Rio Grande en
Potomac. Meppel: Boom 1970, 323 p.

850   DENMAN, Leslie van Ness. The peyote ritual. Visions and
descriptions of Monroe Tsa-To-ke. San Francisco:
Grabhorn Press 1957, xvii + 66 p., illus.
[On the Indian artist; see items 1166-1168.]

851   DENSMORE, Frances. Native songs of two hybrid ceremonies among
the American Indians. American Anthropologist 43 (1),
1941, 77-82.
[Holy week ceremonies among the Yaqui at Guadaloupe in
1923 (mainly pp. 78-79), and Native American Church, its
two branches and its songs (mainly pp. 79-82).]

852   DITTMAN, Allen T. and MOORE, Harvey C. Disturbance in dreams
as related to peyotism among the Navaho. American
Anthropologist 59 (4), 1957, 642-649.
[The use of dream material to indicate psychological
disturbance, with results suggesting peyote cultists were
more disturbed than other Navaho.]

853   DOUGLAS, Frederic Huntington. A Cheyenne peyote fan (Material
Culture Notes, 12). Denver: Denver Art Museum 1939, 4 p.

854   DOUGLAS, Frederic Huntington and MARRIOTT, Alice L. Metal
jewelry of the peyote cult (Material Culture Notes).
Denver: Denver Art Museum 1942, illus. pamphlet.

855   DOUGLAS, M[ary] [Margaret] [TEW]. Review of D. F. Aberle,
The peyote religion among the Navaho (1966). Man n.s.
2, 1967, 482-483.
[A perceptive review, concentrating on the interpretation of this religion.]

856   DOUGLAS, Mary [Margaret] [TEW]. The contempt of ritual, I.
New Blackfriars no. 577=49 (June), 1968, 475-482.
[Pp. 477-479 on peyote cult as a model of the Protestant
Reformation — individualistic, moralist, and anti-
ritualist; based on D. Aberle.]

857   DOUGLAS, Mary [Margaret] [TEW]. Natural symbols: explorations
in cosmology. London: Barrie and Rockliff 1970, 177 p.

Peyote,...Native American Church

> [Pp. 12-14, 107-108, peyote among the Navaho (based on
> D. Aberle); see also I, item 19.]

858   DRIVER, Harold E[dson]. The measurement of geographical distribution form. American Anthropologist 41 (4), 1939,
583-588, graphs, tables.
> [P. 588, the distribution of peyote.]

859   DUSTIN, C. Burton. Peyotism and New Mexico. Farmington, New
Mexico: C. B. Dustin 1960; Santa Fe: Vergara Printing
Co., 2nd ed. 1962, 51 p., illus., bibl.
> [A pro-peyote account: pp. 10-15, peyote at Taos, and
> the opposition encountered, with discussion of the accounts
> of Parsons (item 1059) and Lasswell (item 959); pp. 16-24,
> Navaho peyotism, the Navaho Tribal Council 1954 discussion
> (see item 1023), Frank Takes Gun's political efforts for
> the repeal of legal bans (pp. 22-24, extract from the
> McFate decision (see item 1189)); pp. 27-48, the descrip-
> tion of the Navaho peyote rite presented to the Navaho
> Tribal council, and 11 full-page photos (with adequate
> captions) of a rite in 1956 at Fort Battleford, Saskat-
> chewan, from the Saskatoon Star-Phoenix.]

860   DWYER, John D. The mystical cactus. Missouri Botanical Garden
Bulletin (St. Louis, Missouri) 59 (6), 1971, 10-12, illus.
> [A popular survey, with brief quote from D. Weniger
> (item 1214); notes the name "dry whiskey" for peyote, and
> the loss of the vast areas from banks of Rio Grande and
> Pecos Rivers through over-harvesting — p. 12, "ecologically
> the peyote cactus has met a tragic fate".]

861   EASTERLIN, M. Peyote — Indian problem No. 1. Scribner's
Commentator 11 (1), 1941, 77-82.

862   ELKIN, Henry. The northern Arapaho of Wyoming, in R. Linton
(ed.), Acculturation in Seven American Indian tribes. New
York: Appleton-Century 1940, 207-255; repr. Gloucester,
Massachusetts: Peter Smith 1963, 207-255.
> [Pp. 242, 294, 295, 314-315, peyote.]

863   ELLIS, F. G. The mescal intoxicant. Indian School Journal
9 (5), 1909, 31-32.
> [On peyote.]

864   ELLISON, Rosemary. Contemporary Plains and Woodlands metal-
work in German silver. Smoke Signals (Washington, D.C.)
52 (Spring), 1967, 2-26, illus., bibl.

[German silver is an alloy of copper, nickel and zinc, invented in Germany in 2nd decade of 19th c.; peyote cult as the 2nd great stylistic influence on this art among American Indians — pp. 6, 7, 18-19.]

865　EVERETT, Michael W.　Peyotism and the Pueblo Indians of the Southwestern United States.　University of Arizona, Tucson, anthropology paper, 12 May 1967, 33 p.　Typescript.
[Pp. 4-5, peyotism and the Pueblos; pp. 13-18, the problem of Pueblo peyotism at Taos; pp. 19-28, discussion. Copies in Museum of Northern Arizona and Department of Religious Studies, Aberdeen University.]

866　FARMINGTON TIMES HUSTLER.　Navaho Tribal Council to ban use of peyote.　Farmington Times Hustler (Farmington, New Mexico) 7 June 1940, 1.
[A report in a newspaper adjacent to the Navaho Reservation of their Tribal Council decision against religious or other use of peyote, of the same date.]

867　FENTON, William N[elson].　Factionalism at Taos Pueblo, New Mexico.　Bulletin, Bureau of American Ethnology 164 (Anthropological Papers, 49-56), 1957, Paper 56, pp. 297-344, illus.
[Pp. 327-329, the peyote controversy and attempt at suppression.]

867A　FERACA, Stephen E.　Wakinyan:　contemporary Teton Dakota religion (Studies in Plains Anthropology and History, 2). Browning, Montana:　Museum of the Plains Indian 1963, 72 p., illus., bibl.
[Pp. 48-57 on peyotism, its recent spread, its Cross Fire (more Christian) and Half Moon sections and their rites; the relation to the Christian churches, Yuwipi cult and shamanism; controversies surrounding the use of peyote.]

868　FINTZELBERG, Nicholas M.　Peyote paraphernalia (Ethnic Technology Notes, 4).　San Diego:　Museum of Man, Oct. 1969, 5 pp. text + 3 pp. illus.
[A Navaho peyote member's kit in a wooden box, bought by the museum.]

869　FOLKWAYS.　Washo peyote songs:　songs of the American Indian Native Church.　New York:　Ethnic Folkways Library, LP record FE 4384, 1972, with 12 p. booklet.
[Five cycles, each of four songs, recorded in 1954 by W. L. d'Azevedo; notes on the songs, and a reprint of the

Peyote,...Native American Church

        1957 article by A. P. Merriam and W. L. d'Azevedo, item
        1000. See also D. Evans, item 188.]

870   FOLKWAYS. The Kiowa peyote meeting. New York: Ethnic Folk-
        ways Library, triple LP record FE 4601, with 12 p. booklet
        by Harry Smith.
        [Gives an account of Kiowa music, art and peyote rite,
        and a valuable commentary on each song (which remains
        authentic even though recorded outside the rite itself) to-
        gether with a bibliography. See also D. Evans, item 188.]

871   FORTUNE, R[eo] F[ranklin]. Omaha secret societies (Columbia
        University Contributions to Anthropology 14). New York:
        Columbia University Press 1932, vi + 193 p., illus.
        [Pp. 159-162, peyote.]

872   FRANCISCO, Manuel. Man's most potent drink. Sir! A Magazine
        for Males 7 (11), August 1952, 22-23, 54-55.
        [On peyote.]

873   GADDIS, Vincent H. Cult of the sacred cactus. Travel
        (Baltimore & New York) 92 (1), 1948, 16-17, 33, illus.
        [Description of the peyote rite as among the Cheyenne
        in Oklahoma; summary of A. Rouhier's investigations (see
        item 1312); speculation on future use to assist develop-
        ment of supra-normal mental powers.]

874   GAMBLE, J. I. Changing patterns in Kiowa Indian dances, in
        S. Tax (ed.), item 336, 94-104.
        [Pp. 100, 101, passing references to the Sun Dance step
        at peyote meetings.]

875   GEARE, R. I. The consumption of peyote among the Indians.
        Merck's Report (New York) 22 (5), 1913, 9, 110, illus.
        . [A general account, based on Kiowa use; in a pharma-
        ceutical journal.]

876   GIBSON, Fred. More about peyote. Southwestern Monuments
        Monthly Reports (National Park Service) (Coolidge, Arizona),
        March 1936. Mimeo.
        [P. 237, comment on the confusion between peyote and
        "mescal" plants unrelated to cacti; opinion that town of
        Pyote in Texas is named after the cactus peyote; "it looks
        like the Peyote business has picked up and maybe some of
        us will be convinced before it is over, so let's have
        it...".]

877   GILLES, Albert S., Sr.   The Southwestern Indian and his drugs.
      Southwest Review (Dallas) 55 (2), 1970, 196-203.
      [Includes peyote and other hallucinogenics, with emphasis
      on the Comanche.]

878   GILMORE, Melvin R[andolph].   A study in the ethnobotany of
      Omaha Indians.   Collections of the Nebraska State Historical
      Society (Lincoln) 17, 1913, 314-357.
      [Pp. 318-323, sacred plants, including peyote, cedar
      (incense) etc.]

879   GILMORE, Melvin Randolph.   Uses of plants by the Indians of
      the Missouri river region, in 33rd Annual Report, Bureau
      of American Ethnology 1911-1912.   Washington, D.C.:
      Government Printing Office 1919, 43-154, illus.
      [Pp. 104-106, peyote among the Omaha.]

880   GILMORE, Melvin R[andolph].   The Mescal Society among the
      Omaha Indians.   Publications, Nebraska State Historical
      Society (Lincoln) 19, 1919, 163-167, illus.
      [On the peyote cult; note references to Jesus and the
      Bible, pp. 165ff.]

881   GOGGIN, John M[ann].   A note on Cheyenne peyote.   New Mexico
      Anthropologist (Albuquerque) 4 (2), 1940, 26-30; also
      in C. H. Fairbanks et al. (eds.), Indian and Spanish
      selected writings.   Coral Gables, Florida: University of
      Miami Press 1964, 32-35, illus.
      [A detailed description of the peyote rite as conducted
      at El Reno, Oklahoma, for twenty years by Richard
      Goodbear.]

882   GORTON, Bernard E.   Peyote and the Arizona court decision.
      American Anthropologist 63 (6), 1961, 1334-1335.
      [A neurologist/psychologist supports the McFate decision
      (see item 1189) that peyote is not a narcotic.]

883   GREEN, Elizabeth X.   The peyote cult.   Hobbies March 1950,
      142-143, illus.
      [A survey, with brief account of jewellery distinctive
      of peyote cult.]

884   GREEN, Jack.   Peyote, in S. Krim (ed.), The Beats.   Greenwich,
      Connecticut: Fawcett Publications 1960, 94-107.
      [Personal experience of taking peyote, by a white non-
      cultist.]

United States of America

Peyote,...Native American Church

885 GUSINDE, Martin. Der Peyote-Kult: Entstehung und Verbreitung, in Festschrift zum 50 Jährigen Bestandsjubiläum des Missionshauses St. Gabriel (St. Gabrieler Studien 8). Vienna: Missionsdruckerei St. Gabriel 1939, 401-499.
[Covers the cult in Mexico (based on Lumholtz, Bennett and Zingg) and the U.S.A. (its spread, and especially the influence of John Wilson and John Rave). Agrees with La Barre's data, but interprets peyotism from the viewpoint of the Wilhelm Schmidt school as an "ersatz religion". See M. K. Opler, item 1040, for full review.]

886 HALL, J. Lee. Annual report, as Indian Agent of the Kiowa, Comanche and Wichita Agency, Anadarko, Indian Territory, 26 August 1886. See UNITED STATES, item 1193, p. 130.
[The first official notice of the peyote religion; suggested peyote be made contraband.]

887 HALLOWELL, A. Irving. Review of Weston La Barre, The Peyote cult. Psychiatry 3, 1940, 150-151.

888 HAMILTON, Robert. The gospel among the Red Men; the history of Southern Baptist Indian missions. Nashville: Baptist Sunday School Board (Southern Baptist Convention) 1930, 239 p.
[Pp. 26-28, anti-peyote.]

889 HARPER, R. H. American Indians — pagan and Christian. Missionary Review of the World 55, 1932, 395-398.
[Anti-peyote.]

890 HARPER, R. H. The missionary work of the Reformed (Dutch) Church in Oklahoma. Chronicles of Oklahoma 18, 1940, 252-265, 328-347.
[P. 341, anti-peyote.]

891 HARRINGTON, M[ark] R. Peyote outfit. The Masterkey (Southwest Museum, Los Angeles) 18 (5), 1944, 143-144, illus.
[Introductory note on peyote cult instruments; descriptions and illustrations of a rattle and a feather fan added to the museum.]

892 HARRIS, Jack S. The White Knife Shoshoni of Nevada, in R. Linton (ed.), Acculturation in seven American Indian tribes. New York and London: D. Appleton-Century 1940, 39-116; Gloucester, Massachusetts: Peter Smith 1963, 39-116.
[P. 108, peyote, as beginning to be used by individuals but not yet as a ritual; also reference to Ghost Dance.]

893   HAVARD, V.   Report on the flora of western and southern Texas.
       Proceedings of the United States National Museum
       (Washington, D.C.) 8, 1885, 449-533.
            [Pp. 420, 521, peyote used by Mexicans, as observed in
       1880 by an army surgeon — probably the earliest American
       reference.]

894   HAYES, Alden.   Peyote cult on the Goshiute reservation at
       Deep Creek, Utah.   New Mexico Anthropologist (Albuquerque)
       no. 18=4 (2), 1940, 34-36.
            [The spread of the cult to the Goshiute since 1925, in
       two forms: the Western Slope Way (not using tobacco) and
       the Tipi Way (= Native American Church, using tobacco).]

895   HERALD.   Indians retain their right to use peyote bean in
       native sacrament.   Herald (Boston, Massachusetts)
       14 April 1927, 1, cols. 2-3.
            [Reporting failure to re-enact anti-peyote laws in
       Oklahoma State legislature.]

896   HIGGINS, Ethel Bailey.   Peyote (Lophophora Williamsii) the
       sacred mushroom in religious rites of the Indians.   Desert
       Plant Life (Pasadena) 4, 1932-33, 90-91.
            [On peyote as a narcotic and a religion; repr. in
       Schleiffer, item 1314, pp. 27-28.]

897   HILL, Gladwin.   Indian drug rite backed on Coast.   New York
       Times 14 November 1962, p. 52 L+, col. 3.
            [The San Bernardino trial of three Navaho for using
       peyote in a religious rite.]

898   HILL, Gladwin.   Indians on Coast lose peyote case.   New York
       Times 30 November 1962, p. 18 L++, cols. 4-5.   [See also
       items 1186, 1190.]

899   HOEBEL, E. Adamson.   The wonderful herb.   An Indian cult
       vision experience.   The Western Humanities Review (Salt
       Lake City) 3 (2), 1949, 126-130.
            [Based on his own experience with the Cheyenne in
       Montana.]

900   HOME MISSIONS COUNCIL OF NORTH AMERICA.   What about peyote?
       New York: Home Missions Council of North America 1941.
            [A report prepared by a sub-committee.]

901   HOUGHTON, Ruth.   Fort McDermitt Paiute.   University of Oregon,
       M.A. thesis 1968.

United States of America

Peyote,...Native American Church

[Cited by R. M. Wagner, item 1205, p. 393, as showing
results similar to his concerning "relative deprivation"
as correlated with peyotism.]

902 HOWARD, Frankie. Peyote not religious herb but drug, council-
man says. Navajo Times (Window Rock) 7 (27), 7 July 1966,
1, 5; also briefly in idem 8 (25), 22 June 1967, 4.
[A member of the Navaho Tribal Council strongly attacks
Frank Takes Gun (q.v.), the allegedly religious use of
peyote, and the then chairman of the Tribal Council, R. K.
Nakai, who supported freedom of religion in relation to
peyote.]

903 HOWARD, James H[enri]. Omaha peyotism. Museum News (University of South Dakota Museum, Vermillion) 11 (7), 1950,
3-5; repr. in Hobbies 56 (2), 1951, 142.
[How the peyote religion replaced all other forms among
the Omaha Indians at Macy, Nebraska; the form of the rite.]

904 HOWARD, James H[enri]. A Kiowa spear point used in a Kiowa -
Comanche peyote ceremonial. Museum News (University of
South Dakota Museum, Vermillion) 12 (2), 1950, 3-6.

905 HOWARD, James H[enri]. A Tonkawa peyote legend. Museum News
(University of South Dakota Museum, Vermillion) 12 (4),
1951, 1-4.

906 HOWARD, James H[enri]. Pan-Indian culture of Oklahoma.
Scientific Monthly 81 (5), 1955, 215-220.
[P. 218b, peyote as the prime religious expression of
Pan-Indianism, along with standardized war dance, costumes,
use of English, intermarriage, geographic mobility, and
schools — as a final stage in progressive acculturation.]

907 HOWARD, James H[enri]. An Oto-Omaha peyote ritual. Southwestern Journal of Anthropology 12 (4), 1956, 432-436,
illus.
[Charles Whitehorn's peyote rite — the first among the
Oto — and its transmission through keepers during the
20th c. to George Phillips in 1946; its variations from
Plains peyotism, and current dormancy because of the
keeper's "unworthiness".]

908 HOWARD, James H[enri]. The mescal bean cult of the Central
and Southern Plains: an ancestor of the peyote cult?
American Anthropologist 59 (1), 1957, 75-87, bibl.
[Surveys twelve tribes, revealing two different forms
of the pre-contact mescal bean cult: (1) Among the Iowa,

Omaha, Poto, Pawnee, Wichita, etc., resembling the Midéwiwin
society of the Central Algonquins. (2) Among the Apache,
Ponca, and Tonkawa, resembling modern peyote ritual at
many important points not found in the Mexican use of
peyote. The mescal cult therefore paved the way for and
influenced the peyote rites.]

909   HOWARD, James H[enri]. Mescalism and peyote once again.
      Plains Anthropologist 5, 1960, 84-85.
      [A reply to LaBarre's review (item 950) of Howard's
      article, item 908, reasserting the specific contributions
      of the mescal bean cult to the peyote ritual.]

910   HOWARD, James H[enri]. Peyote jokes. Journal of American
      Folklore no. 295=75 (Jan.-March), 1962, 10-14.
      [A particular genre of in-group humour stories told dur-
      ing the Sunday morning meal, often ribald (as reaction
      from the all-night discipline?), sometimes moral; examples
      given, including five from La Barre, item 942.]

911   HOWARD, James H[enri]. Half Moon Way, the peyote ritual of
      Chief White Bear. Museum News (University of South Dakota
      Museum, Vermillion) 28 (1-2), 1967, 1-24, + 13 plates.
      [Claims to be "the most complete and accurate account of
      a peyote ceremonial" — its form, with the sequence and
      meaning of the various acts, as among the Kiowa-Comanche,
      and as understood by the peyote "chief" or ritual leader.
      Based on attendance at over seventy rites, by the Museum's
      director.]

912   HOWARD, James Henri, with LE CLAIRE, Peter et al. The Ponca
      Tribe = Bulletin, Bureau of American Ethnology 195, 1965,
      191 p., illus.
      [Pp. 48, 97, 122, 125, 165 (and see index for many minor
      references), peyote; pp. 60, 97, Medicine Lodge (Midéwiwin);
      p. 104, Christian syncretism in Sun Dance; p. 107, Heduska
      society or Drum religion from 1880; pp. 109-110, 128, 157,
      Ghost Dance; pp. 156-165, differential acculturation and
      pan-Indianism.]

913   HUGHES, William. The perils of peyote. Commonweal 9 (25),
      24 April 1929, 719-720.
      [The director of the Bureau of Catholic Indian Missions
      replying to an editorial (see item 839) and strongly con-
      demning peyote.]

Peyote,...Native American Church

914   HULTKRANTZ, Åke. Conditions for the spread of the peyote cult
          in North America, in H. Biezais (ed.), New Religions
          (Scripta Instituti Donneriani Aboensis). Stockholm:
          Almqvist & Wiksell International 1975, 70-83.
             [Surveys the various views on the place of social and
          acculturative factors, and notes the neglect of the reli-
          gious factor as such; offers his own combination of factors,
          stresses the preformative influence of the vision complex,
          and examines the obstructive factors hindering the spread
          outside the Plains-Prairies areas.]

915   HUOT, M. C. Peyote songs. Transition 23, 1936, 117-119.

916   HURT, Wesley R. Factors in the persistence of peyote in the
          northern Plains. Plains Anthropologist 5, 1960, 16-27;
          repr. Vermillion, South Dakota: Institute of Indian
          Studies, State University of South Dakota, n.d., 12 p.
             [The Native American Church in relation to tribal au-
          thorities, Bureau of Indian Affairs and missions, and to
          economic, social and political factors affecting its
          growth.]

917   HUXLEY, Aldous [Leonard]. The doors of perception. London:
          Chatto & Windus 1954, 63 p.; New York: Harper & Row
          (1954) 1970, 79 p.; new ed. Frogmore, St. Albans: Panther
          Books 1977.
             [A detailed report, together with philosophical reflec-
          tions, of his own experience of mescalin (i.e., partly
          equivalent to peyote), regarded as superior to other drugs
          inducing "self-transcendence"; pp. 55-58, peyote use by
          North American Indians (based on Slotkin).]

918   HUXLEY, Aldous [Leonard]. Island. New York: Harper &
          Brothers 1962, 335 p.; New York: Bantam Books 1963, 295 p.
             [A novel: the use of a peyote-like drug as part of the
          perfect society.]

919   HYLAND, J. E. P. Voodoo in the desert. Desert Magazine (El
          Centro, California) 26 (8), August 1963, 16-18.
             [A sympathetic survey of the use of peyote in ancient
          Mexico, and in the modern Indian cult, with description of
          a rite.]

920   ICKES, Harold L. and SANDOVAL, Santano. Secretary Ickes moves
          to protect minority religious groups at Taos Pueblo.
          Indians at Work (Office of Indian Affairs, Washington, D.C.)
          4 (7), 15 Nov. 1936, 8-13.

[Collier's opposition to Taos Pueblo tribal officers'
attack on Native American Church; pp. 9-13, the official
correspondence.]

921 THE INDEPENDENT. The new mescal religion. The Independent
(Gallup, New Mexico) No. 3413=66 (25 Feb.), 1909, 430-431.
[Anti-peyote: the new religion, its spread, to be com-
batted by moral suasion rather than legal measures.]

922 THE INDEPENDENT. Dr. Salsbury draws bead on use of peyote.
The Independent (Gallup, New Mexico) 17 May 1951, 1.
[Anti-peyote.]

923 INDIAN AFFAIRS.... Peyote and the Native American Church of
the United States. Indian Affairs: Newsletter of the
American Indian Fund and the Association on American Indian
Affairs Inc. (Riverside, New York) No. 41A (Supplement),
April 1961, 4 p.
[A very sympathetic and scholarly survey with explana-
tions of the opposition peyote arouses, and a plea for
freedom for this authentic religion.]

924 INDIAN HELPER. Another habit that kills. Indian Helper
(Carlisle Indian School, Pennsylvania) 14 (25), 1899, 1.
[Anti-peyote; from the main government school for
Indians.]

925 INDIAN HOUSE, TAOS. Comanche peyote songs, vols. 1 and 2,
Nos. IH 2402 Morning songs; Cheyenne peyote songs, vols.,
1 and 2, Nos. IH 2201-2202. Taos, New Mexico: Indian
House 1969, 1975.
[Four 33 1/3 rpm records, each side having three groups
of four widely-sung peyote songs. The sleeves have photos
of singers and drummers, explanatory notes by Tony Isaacs,
and free translations or other indications of the meaning
of each song, but no vernacular text.]

926 INDIAN RIGHTS ASSOCIATION. Annual Report (Philadelphia).
See Report 33, 1915, p. 19; 34, 1916, pp. 37-41; 35, 1917,
pp. 67-68; 36, 1918, pp. 47-49; 37, 1919, pp. 52-54; 40,
1922, pp. 38-39.
[Anti-peyote material from a pro-Indian body founded by
whites in 1882.]

927 INDIAN RIGHTS ASSOCIATION. Peyote: an insidious evil.
Indian Rights Association (Philadelphia) 114, 1919.

Peyote,...Native American Church

928   INDIAN TRUTH. Religious liberty. Indian Truth (Philadelphia,
      Indian Rights Association) 13, December 1936, 2-3.
      [A criticism of Collier's policy on peyote, as in his
      evidence at Congress hearings, 1936; another commentator
      quoted from Taos Pueblo with support for Collier.]

929   INDIAN VOICES. Indians defend use of "vision plant". Indian
      Voices (Tahlequaha, Okla.) Feb.-March 1967, 5-6; repr.
      from Tulsa Daily World.
      [A defence of peyote use, by Allen Dale (Ponca-Omaha
      tribe) as against proposed Oklahoma State legislation that
      would be unduly restrictive.]

930   JACKSON, Clyde L. and JACKSON, Grace. Quanah Parker, last
      chief of the Comanches: a study in Southwestern Frontier
      history. New York: Exposition Press 1963, 184 p., illus.,
      bibl.
      [Ch. 16, Quanah's religion: his relations with
      Christianity and (pp. 152-153) with the Peyote cult.]

931   JACOBSON, O[scar] B[rousse] (ed.). Kiowa Indian art: water
      colour painting in colour by the Indians of Oklahoma [with
      introduction by the editor]. Nice, France: C. Szwedzicki
      1929, 30 colour plates in portfolio.
      [Includes paintings by Monroe Tsa To ke (peyote theme)
      and four others.]

932   JACOBSON, O[scar] B[rousse] and UCEL, Jeanne (eds.). Les
      peintres indiens d'amérique, also Eng. trans., American
      Indian Painters. Nice, France: C. Szwedzicki 2 vols.
      1950, 77 colour plates.
      [Includes paintings with peyote theme by A. Blackowl
      (vol. 1, pl. 15), Tsa To ke (vol. 2, pl. 77), and C.
      Sweezy (vol. 1, pl. 31).]

933   JOFFE, Natalie F. The Fox of Iowa, in R. Linton (ed.),
      Acculturation in seven American Indian tribes. New York:
      Century-Appleton 1940, 259-331; repr. Gloucester,
      Massachusetts: Peter Smith 1963, 259-331.
      [Pp. 295-296, 314-315, 321, peyote cult (more among the
      conservatives) and drum society as two important cults
      whose members still join in the gens festivals.]

934   JOHNSON, W. E. History, use and effects of peyote. Indian
      School Journal 12 (7), 1912, 239-242; 12 (8), 1912,
      289-293.
      [Abstracts of letters from Johnston to Commissioner of
      Indian Affairs, May 4, 1909, and to Commissioner

Peyote,...Native American Church

R. G. Valentine, 29 August 1911, the latter being quoted
in Slotkin, item 1111, p. 129.]

935 JONES, James A[lfred]. The holistic appeal of peyote for the
     American Indian. University of Aberdeen, M. Litt. thesis
     (Religion in Primal Societies) 1976, 120 p.

936 JORGENSEN, Joseph G[ilbert]. Voget's review of [Slotkin's]
     The Peyote Religion: a comment. American Anthropologist
     71 (5), 1969, 909–911.
     [Critical of neglect of Aberle's "relative deprivation"
     thesis; see Voget's reply, idem, 71 (5), 1969, 911.]

937 KACHEL, Arthur Theodore. An American religious community using
     hallucinogens in 1970. Columbia University, Ph.D. dis-
     sertation (religion) 1975, 270 p.
     [A group of young white Americans who founded a community
     on the basis of hallucinogenic religious experience; drug
     use decreased as religious development proceeded. Not on
     Indians, but useful for comparative purposes.]

938 KINNEY, Bruce. A drug peril under religious guise. Native
     American (Phoenix Indian High School, Arizona) 22,
     1 January 1921, 3–5, 7.
     [A highly critical account of peyote cult as a "com-
     mercialized vice" with a "heathen ritual" "veneered with
     an imitation of Christianity"; includes an attack on a
     scientist who assisted the cult, probably James Mooney.]

939 KNEALE, Albert H. Indian agent. An autobiographical sketch.
     Caldwell, Idaho: Caxton Printers 1950, 429 p., illus., maps.
     [Pp. 211–213, peyote.]

940 KOBLER, Turner S. Alice Marriott (Southwest Writers Series,
     27). Austin, Texas: Steck-Vaughn 1969.
     [A biographical and critical account of a writer who
     has presented peyotism sympathetically. See Marriott.]

941 KUNITZ, Stephen Joshua. Navajo drinking patterns. Yale
     University, Ph.D. dissertation (sociology) 1970, 340 p.
     [Reports peyotists in one part of the Navaho Reservation
     had greater success with alcoholics than any other agency.]

942 LA BARRE, Weston. The Peyote cult (Yale University Publica-
     tions in Anthropology, 19). New Haven: Yale University
     Press 1938, 188 p.; Hamden, Conn.: Shoe String Press
     (Anchor Books) (1959), 4th ed. 1976; new enlarged ed.,
     New York: Schocken Books (1969) 4th ed. 1975, 260 p., two
     bibls.

Peyote,...Native American Church

[A straightforward descriptive account of the cult which
became the Native American Church; a doctoral dissertation
that became the standard work from an observer standpoint;
the enlarged editions include his Twenty years of Peyote
studies, Current Anthropology 1 (1), 1960, and a further
chapter, The last five years of peyote studies; the two
bibliographies are extensive; see Appendix 8 for Christian
elements, and Appendix 9 for the Native American Church
and other peyote churches. Ghost Dance — see index; p. 112,
Sons of the Sun Cult among the Kiowa, 1887.

943   LA BARRE, Weston. Note on Richard Schultes' "The appeal of
         peyote". American Anthropologist 41 (2), 1939, 340-342.
         [Correcting Schultes' exclusive emphasis on the healing
      functions, as against the visionary effects.]

944   LA BARRE, Weston. Review of Washo-Northern Paiute peyotism: a
         study in acculturation, by Omer C. Stewart, 1940. American
         Anthropologist 48 (4:1), 1946, 633-635.
         [Critical of the emphasis on Christian elements.]

945   LA BARRE, Weston. A cultist drug-addiction in an Indian
         alcoholic. Bulletin of the Menninger Clinic 5 (2), 1941,
         40-46.
         [Queries the belief that use of peyote is a cure for
      alcoholism.]

946   LA BARRE, Weston. Primitive psychotherapy in native American
         cultures: peyotism and confession. Journal of Abnormal
         and Social Psychology 43 (3), 1947, 294-309, bibl.

947   LA BARRE, Weston. Review of The peyote religion by James S.
         Slotkin, 1956. American Anthropologist 59 (2), 1957,
         359-360.
         [Critical of the author's claim to have closer rapport
      through his membership of the cult.]

948   LA BARRE, Weston. Mescalism and peyotism. American Anthro-
         pologist 59 (4), 1957, 708-711.
         [Critical of J. H. Howard's (1957) views on the location
      of the mescal bean cult, and of his methodology.]

949   LA BARRE, Weston. Review of Navaho and Ute peyotism: a
         chronological and distributional study, by David F. Aberle
         and Omer C. Stewart. American Anthropologist 60 (1), 1958,
         171.
         [Supports the explanation of the spread of peyotism
      through communications, assisted by the psychological
      effects of the stock reduction campaign.]

950 LA BARRE, Weston (et al.). Twenty years of peyote studies.
     Current Anthropology 1, Jan. 1960, 45-60; 2, December 1961,
     501-502; repr. in his The peyote cult, new eds. from 1964.

951 LA BARRE, Weston. (Letters to the editor) A step backward.
     American Anthropologist 66 (5), 1964, 1172.
         [Deploring the decision (here quoted) of the Fourth
     District Court of Appeals in California against the Navaho
     peyote-users. See also item 1186.]

952 LA BARRE, Weston. The narcotics complex of the New World.
     Diogenes (Chicago) no. 48, Winter 1964, 125-138.
         [Discusses a wide range of psychotropic plants (including
     peyote) and intoxicating drinks used ritually in Mesoamerica
     when the Spanish arrived.]

953 LA BARRE, Weston. Religious freedom of Indians again upheld.
     American Anthropologist 67, April 1965, 505.
         [On the Judge Tobriner decision in the California Supreme
     Court in favour of three Navaho peyotists, as following
     the precedent of Judge McFate in a previous Navaho case.
     See also item 1190.]

954 LA BARRE, Weston, McALLESTER, D. P., SLOTKIN, J. S., STEWART,
     O. C. and TAX, Sol. Statement on peyote. Science 2970=
     114, 30 November 1951, 582-583.
         [A defense of the Native American Church as a legitimate
     religious organization, by scholars who have studied it
     intimately. See also J. Collier, item 836.]

955 LA FARGE, Oliver. (Letters to the editor) Defining peyote as
     a narcotic. American Anthropologist 62 (4), 1960,
     687-689.
         [Includes account of the amendment to the New Mexico
     anti-peyote law, and the opposition from churches and the
     Navaho Tribal Council.]

956 LAKE MOHONK CONFERENCE OF FRIENDS OF THE INDIAN. Annual Reports
     no. 32, 1914, pp. 8, 62-76; no. 33, 1915, pp. 7, 75;
     no. 34, 1916, p. 74.
         [Anti-peyote; no. 32, pp. 62-68, see Daiker, item 842.
     An influential series of conferences of Friends of the
     Indian and Other Dependent Peoples, from 1882, for dis-
     cussion of Indian affairs. See also W. L. Brown, item 149.]

957 LANDES, Ruth. The Prairie Potawatomi: tradition and ritual
     in the twentieth century. Madison: University of
     Wisconsin Press 1970, 420 p., illus., bibl.

Peyote,...Native American Church

> [These Potawatomi in 1935 were living on a reservation
> near Mayetta, Kansas, and had preserved much of their
> traditions: Medicine Bundle Societies for group welfare,
> personal "medicine" acquired in the vision quest, a reli-
> gious dance for "rites of passage". Ch. 6 (= pp. 289-316),
> a descriptive and textual account of the peyote cult, for
> personal illness and mental health. See also "peyote" in
> index.]

958   LANTERNARI, Vittorio. Religions of the oppressed. London:
       McGibbon and Kee 1963, etc. (See I, item 267).
       [Ch. 2 (= pp. 63-100), the Peyote Cult.]

959   LASSWELL, Harold D. Collective autism as a consequence of
       culture contact: notes on religious training and the
       peyote cult at Taos. Zeitschrift für Sozialforschung
       (Paris) 4, 1935, 232-247; pp. 246-247, German and French
       summaries.

960   LAURENCE, M. A trip to Quapaw in 1903 (ed. by V. Nieberding).
       Chronicles of Oklahoma 31, 1953-54, 142-167.
       [Pp. 145-152, peyote.]

961   LEHMANN, Herman. Autobiography, in Jonathan H. Jones (comp.),
       A condensed history of the Apache and Comanche Indian
       tribes... . San Antonio: Johnson Bros. Printing Co. 1899.
       [P. 95, a former captive of the Apache in the 1870s, on
       their four-day peyote rite; quoted in O. C. Stewart,
       item 1148, p. 218.]

962   LEHMANN, Herman. Nine years among the Indians, 1870-1879
       (J. M. Hunter, ed.). Austin: Von Boeckman-Jones 1927,
       235 p., illus.
       [P. 80, as above item.]

963   LEIS, Philip E. Washo witchcraft: a test of the frustration-
       aggression hypothesis, in W. L. d'Azevedo (ed.), item 166,
       57-68.
       [Pp. 60-61, 64-65, the peyote cult in relation to
       shamanism with reference to Siskin, item 1106, and Downs,
       item 176.]

964   LEUPP, Francis E[llington]. In Red Man's land: a study of
       the American Indian. New York: Revell 1914, 161 p.
       [P. 136, peyote; by a Commissioner for Indian Affairs.]

965   LEVINE, Stuart. Our Indian minority. Colorado Quarterly
       16 (3), 1968, 297-320.

[Includes comment on Native American Church as the only successful pan-Indian movement, though with varied strength in different areas.]

966   LEVY, Jerrold E. and KUNITZ, Stephen J.   Indian drinking.
      Navajo practices and Anglo-American theories.   New York/
      London: John Wiley and Sons 1974, 257 p.
         [P. 73, alcohol and peyote contrasted; pp. 128-131,
      traditional religion, Native American Church and Christian-
      ity, their statistics and relationships.]

967   LIEBER, Michael D.   Opposition to peyotism among the Western
      Shoshone: the message of traditional belief.   Man n.s.
      7 (3), 1972, 387-396.
         [On the Yomba Reservation, Nevada: peyotism as witch-
      craft and peyote as a narcotic, and why these explanations
      have developed.]

968   LINDQUIST, G[ustavus] E[lmer] E[manuel] et al.   The Indian in
      American life.   New York: Friendship Press 1944, 180 p.,
      maps.
         [Pp. 78-81, "Peyote — as narcotic and cult".   Regrets
      complete change from opposition to tolerance by Indian
      Office Commissioner in 1936 — since it was now regarded as
      a sacramental substance for a religious body.]

969   THE LITERARY DIGEST.   A pernicious Indian "religion".   The
      Literary Digest (New York) 68 (1), 1921, 34.
         [Based on, and quoting from Rev. Bruce Kinney in The
      Christian Herald; strongly criticized in Bischoff, item
      795, p. 32.]

970   LOGAN, Kuyk.   Missionary battles cactus, witchcraft in effort
      to help State Indian band.   The Daily Oklahoman 24 August
      1954, 13.

971   LOGAN, Kuyk.   Indians' peyote has long, weird history.   The
      Daily Oklahoman 25 August 1954, 6.

972   LOGAN, Kuyk.   Cactus is heart of Plains Indian Church.   The
      Daily Oklahoman 26 August 1954, 4.

973   LONG, Haniel.   Piñon country.   New York: Duell, Sloan &
      Pearce 1941, 327 p.
         [Ch. 25 (= pp. 227-239), peyote; mainly among the Navaho
      and in New Mexico; ch. 28 (= pp. 240-253), John Collier,
      the New Deal, and the Navaho — as background to the growth
      of the peyote cult.]

United States of America

Peyote,...Native American Church

974 LOS ANGELES TIMES. [Trial of three Navaho peyotists.] Los
     Angeles Times, 13, 14, 15 and 30 November 1962. [See
     further, items 1186, 1190.]

975 LOWIE, Robert H[arry]. Disease and medicine (American), in
     J. Hastings (ed.), Encyclopaedia of religion and ethics,
     vol. 4, 1911, 735b-736a.
        [The use of peyote among various tribes, often wrongly
     described by Whites as mescal.]

976 LOWIE, Robert H[arry]. Peyote rite, in J. Hastings (ed.),
     Encyclopaedia of religion and ethics, vol. 9, 1917, 815.
        [With special reference to the Arapaho form, and its
     adoption for healing.]

977 LUHAN, Mabel [Ganson] Dodge. Intimate memories. Vol. 3
     Movers and Shakers. London: M. Secker; New York:
     Harcourt Brace and Co. 1936.
        [Ch. 11 (= pp. 265-279), on New York intellectuals try-
     ing peyote, in 1914, leading to unpleasant experiences and
     a suicide.]

978 LURIE, Nancy Oestreich. Esau was an Indian. Badger Folklore
     (Madison, Wisconsin) 3 (1), 1951, 9-11.
        [Includes peyote reference.]

979 McALLESTER, David P[ark]. Peyote music (Viking Fund Publica-
     tions in Anthropology 13). New York: Wenner-Gren
     Foundation 1949, 104 p. + 62 p. of musical scores, bibl.;
     repr. New York: Johnson Reprint 1964.
        [Pp. 11-28, historical outline of peyote use; Comanche
     origin story and rituals; pp. 29-41, meaningful words from
     Comanche texts of 93 peyote songs; pp. 41-45, 24 similar
     Fox, etc. texts, with comments; pp. 43-45, 87-88, Christian
     influences; pp. 46-82, discussion of the songs; pp. 80-82,
     summary of peyote style; pp. 83-88, the Ghost dance and
     peyote style.]

980 McALLESTER, David P[ark]. Pro-peyote. Time 58 (2), 9 July
     1951, 6.
        [Reply to critical brief article in issue of 18 June
     1951, item 1158.]

981 McALLESTER, David P[ark]. Menomini peyote music. Transactions
     of the American Philosophical Society 42 (4), 1952, 681-700.
        [Also printed as Appendix VI to Slotkin, item 1110. Com-
     ments on musical materials collected by Slotkin, and on the

variations among the tribes together with an overriding
distinctive peyote style; gives the musical text and words
for 24 songs.]

982   McALLESTER, David P[ark]. Enemy way music: a study of social
and aesthetic values as seen in Navaho music (Reports of
the Rimrock Project, Value Series, No. 3). Papers of the
Peabody Museum of American Archaeology and Ethnology
(Cambridge, Mass.) 41 (3), 1954, 96 p.
[Pp. 68-69, peyote music, rendered in the Ute rather
than Navaho musical style.]

983   McALLISTER, J. G[ilbert]. Kiowa-Apache tales. Publications
of the Texas Folklore Society, 22, 1949, 141 p.
[Pp. 3, 80, 108-110, on peyote.]

984   McALLISTER, J. G[ilbert]. Peyote, in W. Webb (ed.), Handbook
of Texas. Austin: Texas State Historical Association
1952, vol. 2, 368-370.

985   McCRACKEN, H. L. The Delaware Big House. Chronicles of
Oklahoma 34 (2), 1956, 183-192 + illus.
[P. 192, brief reference to Native American Church annual
tent meeting, as "the only semblance left of Big House
religion". By a Delaware Indian.]

986   McCRAE, William E. Peyote rituals of the Kiowas. Southwest
Review (Dallas) Summer 1975, 217-233.
[Slightly edited transcripts of taped interviews in 1975
with (a) James Silverhorn, peyote "road man" or leader,
and also acting as keeper of four of the Kiowa sacred
bundles (pp. 217-226), and (b) his son-in-law, Rev. R.
Ahhaity, Kiowa minister of United Methodist Church and son
of a peyote "road man", who describes the rites
sympathetically.]

987   MacGREGOR, Gordon. Warriors without weapons. A study of the
society and personality development of the Pine Ridge
Sioux. Chicago: University of Chicago Press 1946,
228 p., illus., map, bibl.
[Pp. 100-103, peyote.]

988   MACKAYE, William R. Navajos use kind of dope in vital religious rite. The Atlanta Journal (Atlanta, Ga.) 12 May
1971, 8-C.
[A sympathetic article (despite its title) which incor-
porates R. L. Bergman's findings as a psychiatrist, in a
paper to the American Psychiatric Association, later
published — see item 792.]

Peyote,...Native American Church

989   McLAUGHLIN, J. L. Peyote: an introduction. Lloydia: the
      Journal of Natural Products (American Society of Pharma-
      cognosy, Cincinnati) 36 (1), 1973, 1-8, illus., bibl.
      [A general introduction to the origins, botanical and
      chemical features, and ritual use of peyote; a paper at a
      pharmaceutical, etc., symposium on peyote at Houston,
      Texas.]

990   McNICKLE, D'Arcy. Peyote and the Indian. Scientific Monthly
      57, Sept. 1943, 220-229, illus.
      [By a Flathead Indian professor of anthropology.]

991   MALOUF, Carling. Gosiute peyotism. American Anthropologist
      n.s. 44 (1), 1942, 93-103, illus.
      [The two forms of peyote cult popular among these
      Shoshone speakers in western Utah — the Tipi Way and the
      Sioux Way; the former rite is described in detail, also
      functions of and attitudes towards peyote among Gosiute,
      who have borrowed the rites intact.]

992   MARGOLIES, Susan. Powwows and peyote help Indians adjust to
      life in the big city. Wall Street Journal (New York)
      15 June 1973, 10.

993   MARRIOTT, Alice L[ee]. Greener fields: experiences among the
      American Indians (Dolphin Books). Garden City N.Y.:
      Greenwood Press (1952) 1962, 232 p.
      [Ch. 8 (= pp. 96-107), The opened door, repr. in slightly
      different form from her item 994.]

994   MARRIOTT, Alice [Lee]. The opened door. The New Yorker
      30 (32), 1954, 80-82, 85-91.
      [A charming popular account of her experiences of peyote
      in South Dakota, when she was ill, and peyote cured her;
      repr. in ch. 8 of her item 993.]

995   MARRIOTT, Alice [Lee] and RACHLIN, Carol K. American Indian
      mythology. New York: Crowell 1968, xii + 211 p., illus.;
      repr. Greenfield, N.J.: New American Library (Mentor
      Books) 1972.
      [Pp. 205-219 (1972 ed.) on peyote cult, as beneficial
      and as harmful.]

996   MARRIOTT, Alice [Lee] and RACHLIN, Carol K. Peyote. New York:
      Crowell 1971, 111 p., illus.; repr. Greenfield, N.J.:
      New American Library (Mentor Books) 1972, x + 128 p.,
      without illus.
      [A very good popular survey, based on personal experience,
      and including the legal aspect.]

997   THE MASTERKEY. Indians' use of peyote upheld. The Masterkey
      (Southwest Museum, Los Angeles) 34 (4), 1960, 168.
      [Report of Judge McFate's decision in the Arizona peyote
      trial — see McFate, in item 1189; quotes Frank Takes Gun
      as claiming 400,000 members for Native American Church.]

998   MASTERS, Robert Edward Lee and HOUSTON, Jean. The varieties
      of psychedelic experience. New York: Holt, Rinehart and
      Winston 1966; New York: Dell Publishing Co. 1966, 326 p.
      [Pp. 40-47, 252, 318, n5, peyote and the Native American
      Church.]

999   MERRIAM, Alan P. Washo peyote songs, in W. L. d'Azevedo and
      A. P. Merriam, Washo-peyote songs: songs of the American
      Indian Native Church - Peyotist. New York: Ethnic Folk-
      ways Library, notes for 12 in. LP album FE 4384, 1972.

1000 MERRIAM, Alan P. and d'AZEVEDO, Warren L. Washo peyote songs.
      American Anthropologist 59, August 1957, 615-641.
      [Religious beliefs' active role in spread of peyotism.]

1001 METHVIN, J[ohn] J[asper]. Andele, or, The Mexican Kiowa
      captive. A story of real life among the Indians. Louis-
      ville: Pentecostal Herald Press 1899, 184 p., plates;
      repr. Anadarko, Oklahoma: Plummer Press 1927, 201 p.,
      illus.
      [Pp. 36-37, an early form of peyote rite among the
      Mescalero Apache about 1867; by a Mexican captive who
      later served J. Mooney as interpreter, etc. Quoted by
      O. C. Stewart, item 1148, p. 218.]

1002 METHVIN, J[ohn] J[asper]. Reminiscences of life among the
      Indians. Chronicles of Oklahoma 5, 1927, 166-179.
      [Pp. 177-178, anti-peyote; by a Methodist missionary.]

1003 MOMADAY, N[atachee] Scott. House made of dreams. New York:
      Harper and Row 1968, 212 p.; New York: New American
      Library (Signet Books) 1969, 191 p.
      [Pp. 101-106, description of a peyote ceremony, with
      prayers, led by "the Priest of the Sun".]

1004 MOONEY, James. The Kiowa mescal rite. Evening Star (Washing-
      ton, D.C.) 4 November 1891, 6, col. 2.
      [This appears to be his first published report on peyote,
      shortly after his first participation in the rite; see also
      following item, two months later.]

Peyote,...Native American Church

1005 MOONEY, James. A Kiowa mescal rattle. American Anthropologist
o.s. 5, Jan. 1892, 64-65.
[P. 65, Christian influence evident; for "mescal" read
"peyote".]

1006 MOONEY, James. Eating the mescal. The Augusta Chronicle
(Augusta, Georgia) Sunday, 24 January 1892, 11, cols. 1-2.
[Description of the peyote ritual and its effects.]

1007 MOONEY, James. The mescal plant and ceremony. Therapeutic
Gazette (Detroit) 3rd series, 20 (1), 1896, 7-11.
[Expanding his earlier summary on September 16, 1895 in
same journal; extract repr. in W. E. Safford, item 1087,
pp. 303-304: the "mescal" really means peyote.]

1008 MOONEY, James. The Kiowa peyote rite. Der Urquell (Leiden)
n.s. 1, 1897, 329-333.

1009 MOONEY, James. Calendar history of the Kiowa Indians, in
17th Annual Report, Bureau of American Ethnology 1895-96.
Part 1. Washington, D.C.: Government Printing Office
1898, pp. 141-468 (distinguish from pagination with
asterisks), illus.
[Pp. L, 237-239, peyote and Kiowa religion, the first
report of peyote in Oklahoma; pp. 201-202, Comanche medicine man (1874 = Isatai); pp. 221-222, 357, 359-360, 374-
376, Ghost Dance: pp. 340-350, new religious movement of
1882 under prophet Patepte; pp. 356-357, its successor
("Sons of the Sun") under Paingya, 1888.]

1010 M[OONEY], J[ames]. Peyote, in F. W. Hodge (ed.), item 219,
p. 237.

1011 MOONEY, James. Statement [1915]. See UNITED STATES. CONGRESS.
HOUSE. COMMITTEE ON INDIAN AFFAIRS, item 1180, pt. 2,
69-74.

1012 MOORE, J. and SCHROER, B. The bitter paste of Dom Apua.
Rocky Mountain Empire Magazine (Denver, Colorado Post,
Sunday supplement) 30 April 1950, 3-4.
[On peyote.]

1013 MOPOPE, S. Peyote paintings, in O. B. Jacobsen (ed.), Kiowa
Indian art. Nice: C. Szwedzicki 1929, plates 12-13.
[By American Indian artists.]

1014 MORGAN, George Robert. <u>Man, plant and religion: peyote trade</u>
      <u>on the Mustang Plains of Texas</u>. University of Colorado,
      Ph.D. dissertation (geography) 1976, xii + 145 p., illus.,
      maps.
      [By "an adopted member of the Native American Church".
      The first report of Indian peyote practices in south Texas,
      and of the peyote traders since the 1870s; contemporary
      trade and the recent Navaho demand; Amada Cárdenas, a
      trader and member of the Native American Church.]

1015 MOUNTAIN WOLF WOMAN. <u>Mountain Wolf Woman, sister of Crashing</u>
      <u>Thunder: the autobiography of a Winnebago Indian</u>
      (Nancy O. Lurie, ed.). Ann Arbor, Michigan: University
      of Michigan Press, and Toronto: Ambassador Books 1961,
      142 p., illus.; repr. 1966; repr. Rexdale, Ontario:
      Ambassador Books 1966.
      [Ch. 5 (= pp. 39-51), conversion to peyote, and pp. 126-
      130, editor's notes; pp. 90-91, and p. 142 note 8 —
      further references to peyote as "a Christian way". A very
      lightly edited tape-recorded account of a typical Winnebago
      (1884-1960); reproduced in F. W. Turner III, item 345,
      pp. 471-482.]

1016 MUMEY, Nolie. The peyote ceremony among the American Indians.
      <u>The Greater Llano-Estacado Southwest Heritage</u> 3 (3),
      1973, 2-5.
      [A general survey reprinted from a medical journal.]

1017 MUNN, Henry. The mushrooms of language, in M. J. Harner (ed.),
      <u>Hallucinogens and shamanism</u>. New York: Oxford University
      Press 1973, 86-122; with editorial comment, 51-52.
      [On shamanistic curing by the Mazatec Indians of
      Oaxaca, Mexico, through psychotropic mushrooms; by a
      participant observer in intimate relation to the community,
      with his defence of these experiences as revelations of
      reality rather than as "hallucinatory" — a position with
      implications for interpretation of the peyote cult.]

1018 MURPHY, Joseph A. Peyote. <u>Native American</u> (Phoenix Indian
      High School, Arizona) 14 (27), 1913, 379-380.
      [The school medical supervisor's hostile report, warning
      against a demoralizing drug habit, which does not deter
      alcoholism as alleged.]

1018A MURRAY, Dan. The peyote ceremony. <u>The Raven Speaks</u> (Dallas)
      4 (10), 1972, 1ff., illus. by the author.
      [An Oto Indian artist describes his experience of the
      peyote rite in its Half-Moon form, and how peyotism is
      assisting in the maintenance of Indian identity.]

163

United States of America

1019   NABOKOV, Peter.   The peyote road.   The New York Times Magazine
       9 March 1969, 30-31, 129-132, 134, illus.; see also p. 129,
       Peyote: legal and illegal (editorial on the law in rela-
       tion to peyote use).
       [A detailed and sympathetic account of his participation
       in a peyote rite on the Navaho Reservation, set in a general
       survey of the use of peyote and especially of its history
       among the Navaho.]

1020   NATIVE AMERICAN CHURCH.   NAC News.   Wittenberg, Wisconsin.
       E.g., 8 and 22 May 1974.
       [A Winnebago peyotists' domestic publication.]

1021   NATIVE NORTH AMERICAN CHURCH OF GOD.   Charter of the Native
       North American Church of God.   State of Kansas, Office of
       the Secretary of State 1925.
       [Probably the incorporation document; cited by R. L.
       Bee, item 788, p. 61.]

1022   NAVAJO TIMES (Window Rock, Arizona).   Articles and letters,
       including e.g. the following from 1962 to 1972 concerning
       the controversies surrounding the use of peyote for reli-
       gious purposes: 1. 3 (30), 8 August 1962, 8 (U.S. Court
       of Appeals rejection of Native American Church plea to
       overrule Tribal Council ban of 1937); 2. 5 (8), 20 February
       1964, 7, 8 (see Frank Takes Gun; reprints Arizona and
       California court decisions); 3. 7 (20), 19 May 1966, 1, 2
       (Chairman Nakai's defence of his pro-peyote stand, and
       reprint of his letters in 1951 against peyote); 4. 7 (26),
       30 June 1966, 1, 4 (denial of making peyote a tribal
       political issue); 5. 7 (27), 7 July 1966, 1, 5 (Howard's
       attack, see item 902); 6. 7 (33), 18 August 1966, 4 (attack
       on the non-religious use of peyote, repr. from Arizona
       Republic); 7. 7 (35), 1 September 1966, 1, 4 (see Frank
       Takes Gun, item 1154); 8. 8 (3), 19 January 1967, 2, 3
       (attack on chairman Nakai and on peyote); 9. 8 (6),
       9 February 1967, 23 (two pro-peyote letters); 10. 8 (8),
       23 February 1967, 23 (peyote is not for Navahos);
       11. 8 (13), 30 March 1967, 3 (anti-peyote); 12. 8 (14),
       6 April 1967, 3 (pro-peyote, as Christian); 13. 8 (25),
       22 June 1967, 4 (see D. S. Clark, item 828, and F. Howard,
       item 902); 14. 8 (26), 29 June 1967, 1 (Bureau of Indian
       Affairs officers recognize and address the Native American
       Church; photo of leaders); 15. 8 (42), 19 October 1967,
       1 (Tribal Council vote to allow religious use of peyote);
       16. 8 (43), 26 October 1967, 7 (editorial reprint of a
       favourable report on peyote made in 1965); 17. 8 (45),

9 Nov. 1967, 4 (editorial on the lifting of the Tribal
Council ban); 18. 8 (49), 7 December 1967, 4 (Texas law
banning religious use of peyote); 19. 9 (7), 15 February
1968, 2, 4 (pro-religious freedom); 20. 9 (8), 22 February
1968, 2 (two anti-peyote letters); 21. 9 (9), 29 February
1968, 1, 15 (D. S. Clark's arrest in Texas — see his
item 828, repr. from the Laredo Times (Texas) 11 February
1968); 22. 9 (11), 14 March 1968, 2 (a peyotist asks for
the study of his church); 23. 9 (23) 6 June 1968, 4
(defence of peyote; criticism of alcohol); 24. 10 (44),
6 November 1969, 2 (history of use of peyote); 25. 10 (48),
4 December 1969, 4 (two letters critical of peyote and
supporting the original Indian religion); 26. 10 (50),
18 December 1969, 20 (repr. of the 1960 McFate decision in
favour of peyote); 27. 11 (10), 5 March 1970, 15 (rejection of pleas by peyotists); 28. 11 (29), 16 March 1970,
2 (peyote church appeal to federal court to secure incorporation in Arizona); 29. 13 (24), 15 June 1972, 1 (Annual
Convention of Native American Church in Tribal Civic Center,
Window Rock).

1023   NAVAJO TRIBAL COUNCIL. Minutes of meetings, 1st-10th June
       1954. Window Rock: Navajo Tribal Council 1954, 343 p.
       Mimeo.
          [Pp. 17-96, peyote discussion on June 1st; p. 146,
       decision to release to the press the full discussions.
       (See also minutes of meeting on 3 June 1940 which banned
       peyote).]

1024   NAVAJO TRIBAL COUNCIL, ADVISORY COMMITTEE. Proceedings of the
       meeting, 1950. Window Rock: Navajo Tribal Council 1950.
       Mimeo.
          [Minutes for May 16-18, dealing with the Native American
       Church.]

1025   NETTL, Bruno. Observations on meaningless peyote song texts.
       Journal of American Folklore 66, 1953, 161-164.
          [The syllabic sequences, the rhythmic patterns, and
       their relationships.]

1026   NETTL, Bruno. Historical aspects of ethnomusicology. American
       Anthropologist 60, 1958, 518-532.
          [P. 523, the changes in peyote style as its music spread
       north to the Plains Indians.]

1027   NEVADA STATE JOURNAL. Nevada Indians assured continued use of
       peyote. Nevada State Journal 13 March 1965, 20; also in
       Inter-Tribal Council of Nevada Inc., Newsletter 2 (1),
       1965, 10-11.

Peyote,...Native American Church

[Evidence presented by the Native Nevada Church and an
anthropologist against a legislative proposal to ban
peyote.]

1028   NEWBERNE, Robert E. L[ee].   Peyote. An abridged compilation
from the files of the Bureau of Indian Affairs. Washington,
D.C.: Government Printing Office 1922, 38 p., illus.;
Lawrence: Haskell Institute, 3rd revised ed. 1935.
[By the Chief Medical Supervisor. Drawn up to provide
materials for Bureau employees and all others engaged in
the fight against peyote. Contains extracts from many
authors, often without source details.]

1029   NEWCOMB, William W[ilmon], Jr. A note on Cherokee-Delaware
pan-Indianism. American Anthropologist 57 (5), 1955,
1041-1045.
[P. 1042, peyote cult in N.E. Oklahoma in 1951.]

1030   NEWCOMB, William W[ilmon], Jr. A re-appraisal of the "Cultural
Sink" of Texas. Southwest Journal of Anthropology 12 (2),
1956, 145-153.
[P. 152, briefly, on the use of peyote as characteristic
of Coahuiltecan culture — found in the arc from Trinity R.,
Texas, to Panuco R., Mexico.]

1031   NEWCOMB, William W[ilmon], Jr. The peyote cult of the Delaware
Indians. Texas Journal of Science 8 (2), 1956, 202-211.

1032   NEWCOMB, W[illiam] W[ilmon], Jr. The Indians of Texas, from
prehistoric to modern times. Austin: University of Texas
Press 1961, 404 p., illus., bibl.
[Pp. 53-54, peyote commonly used in the religion of the
Coahuiltecans.]

1033   NEWSWEEK. Right to hallucinate. Newsweek 60 (6), August 6,
1962, 74, illus.
[Report of the U.S. Court of Appeals upholding the
Navajo Tribal Council ban on peyote, against an action
claiming religious freedom.]

1034   NEW YORK TIMES. Many further articles or news reports concerning peyote; e.g. 12 November 1936, 6 July 1954, 7 December
1960, 14 and 30 November 1962.

1035   NEW YORK TIMES
Court considering use of drug in Indian rite. New York
Times 15 November 1962, 41L++, cols. 5-7.

Peyote,...Native American Church

[Report of the trial of three Navaho for participation
in a peyote rite, in San Bernardino County Superior Court.
See idem, 30 November 1962, for further report, and following item.]

1036 NEW YORK TIMES. Group backs Indians in cactus drug use. New
York Times 7 May 1963, 47, col. 6
[The American Civil Liberties Union decision to appeal
the verdict against the three Navaho for sharing in the
peyote cult rite (see preceding item); the verdict was
based on an analogy with polygamy, ruled illegal in 1879;
for success of appeal see United States [Courts],
item 1190.]

1037 NORTON, R. E. The peyote religion among North American
Indians — problems of explanation. University of Sydney,
B.A. (Hons) thesis (anthropology) 1964.

1038 OKLAHOMA, LEGISLATURE. (a) HOUSE. Journal 2, 1909, 118, 126,
180-181, 211, 353. (b) SENATE. Journal 11, 1927, 573,
594, 907.
[Reports of two unsuccessful attempts to re-introduce
laws against peyote, subsequent to the repeal in 1908 of
the 1899 anti-peyote law. See also under Herald,
item 895.]

1039 OMAHA EVENING WORLD-HERALD. Indian drums beat throughout night:
peyote users faithful to their religion. Omaha Evening
World-Herald 5 Dec. 1938, 3 cols., illus.
[Good reporting by a journalist allowed to attend the
rite in a private house near Winnebago, Nebraska — but only
until 9 pm!]

1040 OPLER, Marvin K[aufmann]. Review of Der Peyote-Kult by Martin
Gusinde (1939). American Anthropologist 42, 1940, 667-669.
[See item 885].
[Appreciative of a "convenient handbook" on peyote which
confirms La Barre's facts, but fails to consider the
socio-cultural dynamics of the cult.]

1041 OPLER, M[arvin] K[aufmann]. The character and history of the
southern Ute peyote rite. American Anthropologist 42 (3),
1940, 463-478.
[Compares the peyote cult at two agency centres: (1) At
Towac it has had wide support since 1931 as a revivalistic
movement, less Christian in form, but with prophetic, curing and moral values. (2) At Ignacio it represents a
belated movement towards Christianity and although active
since 1917 is still opposed by the majority.]

Peyote,...Native American Church

1042 OPLER, Marvin K[aufmann]. The southern Ute of Colorado, in
      R. Linton (ed.), Acculturation in seven American Indian
      tribes. New York: D. Appleton Century 1940, 119-203;
      repr. Gloucester, Mass.: Peter Smith 1963, 119-203.
          [Pp. 188-195, "revitalistic movements" — pp. 188-190,
      Ghost Dance; pp. 190-195, peyote cult.]

1043 OPLER, M[arvin] K[aufmann]. Fact and fancy in Ute peyotism.
      American Anthropologist 44 (1), 1942, 151-159.
          [A reply to O. C. Stewart, item 1135, who criticized
      Opler's article on the southern Ute, item 1041.]

1044 OPLER, M[orris] E[dward]. The influence of aboriginal and
      white contact upon a recently-introduced ceremony, the
      Mescalero peyote rite. Journal of American Folklore 49
      (Jan.-June) 1936, 143-166.
          [The rite flourished from 1870 and had declined by 1910.
      Instead of introducing Christian elements (for reasons,
      see p. 165) Apache values and ideas (expounded in pp. 144-
      148) were retained in modified form as by extending
      shamanism to all participants. Pp. 160-164, detailed
      description of the rite.]

1045 OPLER, Morris E[dward]. The use of peyote by the Carrizo and
      Lipan Apache tribes. American Anthropologist 40 (2),
      1938, 271-285.
          [A reorganized form of a Lipan man's verbatim account of
      the peyote cult as it used to be in two tribes by then
      almost extinct — the gathering of peyote, members' prepara-
      tion for the meeting, the meeting ritual, and the healing
      aspects.]

1046 OPLER, Morris E[dward]. A description of a Tonkawa peyote
      meeting held in 1902. American Anthropologist 41 (3),
      1939, 433-439.
          [Direct report from Mr. Samuel E. Kenoi, a Chiricahua
      Apache, of observation while on a visit to the Tonkawa in
      Texas. Nothing on Christian elements.]

1047 OPLER, Morris E[dward]. Review of: The Peyote Cult by Weston
      La Barre. American Anthropologist 41 (3), 1939, 478-479.
          [General approbation, especially of its many-sided
      approach.]

1048 OPLER, Morris Edward. A Mescalero Apache account of the origin
      of the peyote ceremony. El Palacio (Santa Fe, New Mexico)
      52 (10), 1945, 210-212.

[An origin myth tracing the introduction of peyote to a Lipan Apache, and emphasizing its curing value.]

1049   OPLER, Morris E[dward]. Review of Navaho and Ute peyotism, by David Aberle and Omer C. Stewart, 1957. Ethnohistory 5, 1958, 180-182.
        [Good critical use of wide range of sources; good on chronology and channels of diffusion to the Navaho and Ute, and on differential availability in various areas, but not on the more difficult question of differential appeal — e.g., why 80% in one Navaho district and only 6% in another.]

1050   OPLER, Morris E[dward]. Apache odyssey: a journey between two worlds (Case Studies in Cultural Anthropology). New York: Holt, Rinehart and Winston 1969, 301 p., illus., map.
        [P. 191, brief reference to Silas John Edwards and his "church"; p. 190, photo of members at their sacred ground; pp. 210-217, and index, peyote — detailed descriptions, and stories. All as told to the author by "Chris" (pseudonym), a Chiricahua-Mescalero Apache, in the 1930s.]

1051   OPLER, Morris Edward and OPLER, Catherine H. Mescalero Apache history in the Southwest. New Mexico Historical Review (Santa Fe, New Mexico) 25 (1), 1950, 1-36.
        [P. 35, peyote flourishing during a very difficult period in their history.]

1052   OSMOND, Humphry. "That night in the tepi". The Twentieth Century 1011=170, Autumn 1961, 38-50.
        [An account of an all-night peyote-using service of the Native American Church of North America in Saskatchewan, by a psychiatrist researching into mind-changing substances or "psychedelics" such as mescalin.]

1053   OSMOND, Humphry. Peyote night, in B. S. Aaronson and H. Osmond (eds.), Psychedelics: the uses and implications of hallucinogenic drugs. Garden City, N.Y.: Anchor Books 1970, 67-86; repr. Cambridge, Mass.: Schenkman 1971.
        [A slightly altered version of his item 1052, with extended epilogue (pp. 83-86).]

1054   PAGE, Elizabeth M. In camp and tipi. An Indian mission story. New York: Board of Publications..., Reformed Church in America 1915, 245 p., illus.
        [Pp. 194-198, 202-209, peyote (called mescal): the founding of the cult among the Winnebago c. 1906, breaking the Medicine Lodge monopoly, and claiming to be Christian; the subsequent movement to the mission church.]

Peyote,...Native American Church

1055   PA-NA-RO [= PINERO].   Statement.   American Indian YMCA Bulletin
        8 (4), 1918.
        [The testimony of a Lipan Apache concerning Lipan use of
        peyote in the 1870s; quoted by O. C. Stewart, 1148,
        p. 218.]

1056   PARKER, Arthur C[aswell].   The perils of the peyote poison.
        American Indian Magazine 5 (1), 1917, 12-13.
        [An Indian scholar's attack on peyote as "a dangerous
        drug and harmful narcotic" leading to "mental breakdowns"
        and lowered morality; criticizes anthropologists who
        defend it.]

1057   PARMAN, Donald L.   The Navajos and the New Deal (Yale Western
        Americana, 27).   New Haven and London: Yale University
        Press 1976, 316 p.
        [Pp. 257-260, account of Navajo Tribal Council discussion
        of peyote in 1940, and the 52 to 1 vote against it.]

1058   PARSONS, Elsie [Worthington] Clews.   Kiowa tales (Memoirs of
        the American Folklore Society, 22).   New York: G. E.
        Stechert for the American Folklore Society 1929, 152 p.
        [Pp. 118-120, "White Horse visits Mexico for peyote",
        and subsequent treatment of a sick girl; p. xiii, peyote
        in relation to Kiowa, and to Taos.]

1059   PARSONS, Elsie [Worthington] Clews.   Taos pueblo (General
        Series in Anthropology, 2).   Menasha, Wisconsin: George
        Banta Publishing Company 1936, 121 p. + illus., map.
        [Pp. 62-64, local versions of the introduction of
        peyotism; pp. 64-66, Taos peyote meeting; pp. 66-68, 118-
        120, the resultant local controversies.]

1060   PETRULLO, Vincenzo.   The diabolic root. A study of peyotism,
        the new Indian religion, among the Delaware.   Philadelphia:
        University of Pennsylvania Press 1934, 185 p., illus.,
        diagrams, bibl.; repr. New York: Octagon Books 1975.
        [The first major study, based on a doctoral dissertation;
        pp. 131-174, relation to old Delaware religion and
        Christianity.]

1061   PETRULLO, Vincenzo.   Peyotism as an emergent Indian culture.
        Indians at Work: a newsheet for Indians and the Indian
        Service (Bureau of Indian Affairs, Washington, D.C.)
        7 (8) [printed as 8 (8)], 1940, 51-60, illus.
        [Peyotism as a way of life and profound religion in which
        the effects of peyote are not the chief concern, but rather

the possession of a truly Indian way of bridging the gap
between the old ways and the new; a sympathetic attempt
at interpretation.]

1062   PIERSON, Delavan L. [Mrs.]. American Indian peyote worship.
       The Missionary Review of the World (New York) n.s. 28 (3),
       1915, 201-206, illus.
       [Hostile to this "degrading cult"; based mainly on
       Winnebago peyotists, and includes texts of statements by
       Indians both for and against peyotism.]

1063   POSERN-ZIELIŃSKA, Mirosława. The role of social and economic
       factors in the formation of syncretic religions: the
       example of peyotism [in Polish]. Etnografia Polska 12,
       1968, 304-321.

1064   POSERN-ZIELIŃSKA, Mirosława. Peyotyzm, religia Indian Ameryki
       Północnej. Warsaw: Zaklad Narodowy im Ossolinskich 1972,
       260 p., illus., bibl. (pp. 231-241). English summary.

1065   POWERS, Charles T. The Indian in America — IX: peyote ritual
       a weird affair. Kansas City Star n.d. [soon after
       14 March 1968].
       [Based on use by Navaho.]

1066   PROSSER, Moorman P. The effects of peyote and narcotics upon
       health. The National Fellowship of Indian Workers: News
       Letter no. 11, Jan.-Feb. 1939.

1067   RACHLIN, Carol K. The Native American Church in Oklahoma.
       The Chronicles of Oklahoma (Oklahoma City: Oklahoma
       Historical Society) 42 (3), 1964, 262-272.
       [A useful popular survey, defending the church.]

1068   RACHLIN, Carol K. Tight shoe night: Oklahoma Indians today,
       in S. Levine and N. O. Lurie (eds.), The American Indian
       today. Baltimore: Penguin Books 1970, 160-183.
       [P. 176, the Native American Church as both pan-Indian
       and tribally diversified.]

1069   RADIN, Paul. Personal reminiscences of a Winnebago Indian.
       Journal of American Folklore 26 (102), 1913, 293-318.
       [Pp. 310-313 refer to peyote membership; see also the
       brother's autobiography, under Radin, item 1071.]

1070   RADIN, Paul. A sketch of the peyote cult of the Winnebago: a
       study in borrowing. Journal of Religious Psychology 7 (1),
       1914, 1-22.

Peyote,...Native American Church

[An important detailed account, including the John Rave
rite and its history, the Albert Hensley more Christian
version and its decline, the religious content of the rite,
conversion stories, and conservatives' opposition.]

1071   RADIN, Paul. The autobiography of an American Indian (Univer-
        sity of California Publications in American Archaeology
        and Ethnology 16 (7)). Berkeley: University of California
        Press 1920; with supplementary material as Crashing
        Thunder: the autobiography of a Winnebago Indian. New
        York and London: D. Appleton 1926; orig. ed. repr. as
        The autobiography of a Winnebago Indian. New York: Dover
        Publications 1963, 91 p.; Part I repr. in F. W. Turner
        (ed.), The Portable North American Indian Reader. New York:
        Viking Press, and Toronto: Macmillan Co. 1973, 378-453;
        selections reprinted elsewhere.
        [The Indian is designated only as "S.B." [Sam Blowsnake].
        Pp. 48-67 (= sections 28-35) on his dissolute life, con-
        version to peyote cult, and repudiation of traditional
        practices, but continued respect for his father's teachings
        (given at length, pp. 68-91). Largely translated by Oliver
        Lamere, a Winnebago. (Section on peyote is pp. 431-453
        in Viking Press edition).]

1072   RADIN, Paul. The Winnebago tribe, in 37th Annual Report,
        Bureau of American Ethnology 1915-1916. Washington, D.C.:
        Government Printing Office 1923, 35-551, illus.
        [Pp. 69-74, a peyote follower's account of what the
        "Shawnee prophet" told the Winnebago four generations ago;
        p. 74, recent Winnebago prophets; chs. 10-15, traditional
        religion; ch. 16 (= pp. 388-426), the peyote cult (pp. 389-
        391 being John Rave's account of the cult and his conver-
        sion, repr. in Schleiffer, item 1314, pp. 38-40); plates
        5a and 8d, photos of John Rave and Albert Hensley.]

1073   RADIN, Paul. Monotheism among primitive peoples. London:
        G. Allen & Unwin 1924, 69 p.; Basel: Ethnographical
        Museum; also New York: Bollingen Foundation (Special
        Publications, 4) 1954, 30 p., bibl., footnotes.
        [Includes a short section on peyote among the Winnebago,
        which appears in the repr. by D. and B. Tedlock, item 338,
        pp. 236-237.]

1074   RADIN, Paul. The religious experiences of an American Indian.
        Eranos-Jahrbuch (Zurich) 18, 1950, 249-290; repr. in his
        Primitive man as philosopher. New York: Dover Publica-
        tions 1957, 395-448.

[A Winnebago, John Rave, at a period of personal crisis; born 1860s; became a peyote member, after failing to secure visions in his youth.]

1075 RAGLAND, Hobert D. Missions of the Society of Friends among the Indian tribes of the Sac-Fox agency. The Chronicles of Oklahoma 33 (2), 1955, 169-182, illus.
  [P. 182, peyote worship practised by about half the tribe — Kickapoos, 1925.]

1076 REICHARD, Gladys. The Navaho and Christianity. American Anthropologist 51, 1949, 66-71.
  [Lack of response to Christianity, and lack of their own new movements; cf. with the more recent growth of the peyote cult.]

1077 REKO, Victor A[loisius]. Magische Gifte: Rauschund Betaubungs-mittel der neuen Welt. Stuttgart: F. Enke 1936, vii + 160 p.; 2nd. ed. 1938, xii + 206 p.; 3rd. ed. 1949, xi + 175 p.
  [1st. ed., pp. 39-60, peyote.]

1078 RHODES, Willard. A study of musical diffusion based on the wandering of the opening peyote song. International Folk Music Journal 10, 1958, 42-49.
  [Songs regarded as central to the peyote religious experience; analysis of various versions of the opening song.]

1079 RHODES, Willard (recorder). Navajo peyote song by George Mitchell and Kayah David. Washington: Library of Congress, AFS L41, n.d. [record].

1080 RIDGWAY, James. More lost Indians. The New Republic (Washington, D.C.) 153 (24), 11 Dec. 1965, 19-22.
  [P. 22, the Native American Church and its healing activities in a shack near Pine Ridge, South Dakota.]

1081 RITZENTHALER, Robert E[ugene]. The Potawatomi Indians of Wisconsin. Bulletin, Milwaukee Public Museum 19 (3), 1953, 162-163; idem, 19 (4), 1953, 189.
  [Both on peyote, with description of the half-moon cult.]

1082 RITZENTHALER, Robert E[ugene] and PETERSON, Frederick A. The Mexican Kickapoo Indians (Milwaukee Public Museum, Publications in Anthropology, 2). Milwaukee: the Museum 1956, 91 p., illus., map.
  [Pp. 45-50, religion; p. 50, rejection of peyotism, as well as of Christianity, by the most conservative of all Kickapoo groups.]

Peyote,...Native American Church

1083   RODDY, Thomas R.   The Winnebago Mescal-eaters, in E. H. Blair, item 144.
       [Vol. 2, pp. 281-283, 297-298, peyote: the author, known as "White Buffalo", had intimate knowledge of the Winnebago, and here comments on the peyote cult.]

1084   ROSEMAN, Bernard.   The peyote story.   Hollywood, California: Wilshire Book. Co. (1963) 1968, 92 p., illus.
       [A personal experience of peyote-taking, by a white; appended are: pp. 69-83, extract of Paras. 282-289, with illustrations, on "Narcotics and stimulants", from 38th Annual Report, Bureau of American Ethnology; pp. 85-92, Dan L. Thrapp's interview with A. R. Tippett on Native American Church in Los Angeles Times, Aug. 17, 1967; earlier version of book as 225,000 Indians can't be wrong (The Peyote Story).   Joshua Tree, California: B. Roseman 1963, 44 p., illus. (same text).]

1085   RUBY, Robert H.   The Oglala Sioux: warriors in transition.
       New York: Vantage Press 1955, 115 p.
       [Pp. 44-53, traditional religion; pp. 53-60, detailed description of Pine Ridge peyote cult; pp. 60-62, sweat house; pp. 62-66, Yuwipi cult; pp. 66-71, Half-Moon peyote cult.]

1086   RUBY, Robert H.   I witnessed a service of the Indian peyote cult.   Frontier Times 36 (3:n.s. 19) 1962, 30-31, 40, illus.

1087   SAFFORD, William E[dwin].   An Aztec narcotic.   Journal of Heredity (Washington, D.C.) 6 (7), 1915, 291-311, illus.
       [Economic botanist to U.S. Department of Agriculture. Brief outline of religious use of narcotics; the effects of peyote.]

1088   SAFFORD, William E[dwin].   Peyote, the narcotic mescal button of the Indians.   Journal of the American Medical Association 77, 1921, 1278-1279.

1089   SCHULTES, Richard Evans.   Peyote and the American Indian. Nature Magazine 30 (3), 1937, 155-157; repr. in Literary Digest, 13 November 1937, 24, 26.
       [A brief popular account.]

1090   SCHULTES, Richard Evans.   The appeal of peyote...as a medicine. American Anthropologist 40 (4), 1938, 698-715, illus., bibl.
       [On the peyote vision being incidental and of little significance as against the healing powers; reproduces a Kiowa artist's painting of a peyote leader.]

1091   SCHULTES, Richard Evans. Peyote — an American Indian heritage
from Mexico. El México Antiguo (Mexico, D. F.) 4 (5-6),
1938, 199-208, illus.

1092   SCHUSKY, Ernest L. The right to be Indian. N.p. [Vermillion
and New York?]: Institute of Indian Studies, State University of South Dakota, and Board of National Missions,
United Presbyterian Church 1965, 95 p., bibl.
[Pp. 47, 55-57, 84-86, the Native American Church and
religious freedom; a sympathetic approach.]

1093   SCIENCE NEWS. LSD may become legal. Science News 90 (2),
9 July 1966, 22, col. 2.
[Dr. M. J. Harner considers that legislation will not
stop use of LSD, but that if institutionalized, like peyote
in Native American Church, it could become respectable.]

1094   SCIENCE NEWS LETTER. Peyote button induces religious fervor.
Science News Letter (Baltimore) 493=18, 20 September 1930,
188.
[A half-page report drawn from Dr. Maurice Smith's field
investigations, and archival research at the Bureau of
American Ethnology; e.g., "We observed particularly the
infusion of Christian ideas into the speeches and prayers.
Bible ideas blend simply and naturally in the Indian mind
with the old native theology".]

1095   SCOTCH, Norman A. and SCOTCH, Freda L. Social factors in
hypertension among the Washo, in W. L. d'Azevedo (ed.),
item 166, 69-76.
[A sample of 100 Washo revealed a negative correlation
between peyote cult membership and both hypertension and
alcoholism — i.e. peyotists showed less stress; see
especially pp. 72, 75.]

1096   SCULLY, Bede. The Cheyenne and peyote. Mission Almanac (of
the Seraphic Mass Association). Ashland, Montana:
St. Labre Mission 1941, 6-14.
[By a Catholic missionary.]

1097   SEYMOUR, Flora Warren. Federal favor for fetishism; the
American government and the American Indian. Missionary
Review of the World n.s. 9 (9), 1935, 397-400.
[An attack on the (Collier) policy of religious freedom
for Indians, including freedom for the peyote cult.]

Peyote,...Native American Church

1098   SEYMOUR, Gertrude.   Peyote worship: an Indian cult and a
          powerful drug. Survey (New York) 36 (7), 1916, 181-184;
          repr. American Indian Magazine 4 (2), 1916, 160-163; also
          The Redman 8, Sep. 1915-June 1916, 341-351; and Indian
          School Journal (Chiliceo, Oklahoma) 17 (1), 1916, 16-24.

1099   SHEPARDSON, Mary. Navajo ways in government: a study in
          political process (Memoirs, American Anthropological
          Association 96) = American Anthropologist 65 (3:2), June
          1963, 1-132.
             [From "stateless tribal society" to "domestic independent
          nation" as an example of rapid voluntary change; pp. 17,
          87, 102, 104, Tribal Council's dealing with the peyote
          cult.]

1100   SHEPARDSON, Mary and HAMMOND, Blodwen.   The Navajo Mountain
          community. Social organization and kinship terminology.
          Berkeley and Los Angeles: University of California Press
          1970, 278 p., map.
             [P. 19, on the Native American Church having had no
          impact on this community in the remote northwest of the
          reservation in the early 1960s; pp. 18-19, three missions
          commencing since 1946.]

1101   SHONLE, Ruth [CAVAN]. Peyote, the giver of visions. American
          Anthropologist n.s. 27, 1925, 53-75, bibl., maps.
             [Note pp. 66-70 on the specifically Christian influence
          found in some areas.]

1102   SIEGEL, Bernard J. Suggested factors of culture change at
          Taos Pueblo, in S. Tax, item 336, 133-140.
             [P. 138, passing reference to peyote cult as an escape
          mechanism.]

1103   SIEGEL, Bernard J. and BEALS, Alan R. Pervasive factionalism.
          American Anthropologist 62 (3), 1960, 394-417.
             [Acculturation effects in two communities — Namhalli in
          Mysore State, India, and Taos Pueblo, New Mexico; in the
          latter, peyotism in the 1920s.]

1104   SILVER HORN. Peyote painting, in H. B. Alexander (ed.), Sioux
          Indian painting. Nice, France: C. Szwedzicki 1938, I,
          plate 23.

1105   SIMMONS, Benjamin F. Implications of the court decision on
          peyote for the users of LSD. Journal of Church and State
          11 (1), 1969, 83-91.

[A survey of the legal position of peyotism in various states, and of Federal policy and Navaho Tribal Council prohibition, in relation to the People v. Woody (1964) and Arizona v. Mary Attakai (1960) trials. See items 1186 and 1189.]

1106   SISKIN, Edgar Elias. The impact of the peyote cult upon shamanism among the Washo Indians. Yale University, Ph.D. dissertation (anthropology) 1941, 316 p., illus.
        [On the last Washo shamans and the decline of Shamanism before the growing peyote cult in the 1930s. Widely used by later enquirers for its detailed information.]

1107   SKINNER, Alanson [Buck]. Wisconsin Winnebago collection. Anthropological Papers, American Museum of Natural History 4, 1910, 289-297.
        [P. 389, peyote.]

1108   SKINNER, Alanson [Buck]. Kansa organizations. Anthropological Papers, American Museum of Natural History 11 (9), 1915, 743, 745-775.
        [P. 758, brief paragraph on peyote, and its effect having been to abolish drunkenness.]

1109   SKINNER, Alanson [Buck]. Associations and ceremonies of the Menomini Indians. Anthropological Papers, American Museum of Natural History 13 (2), 1915, 169-215.
        [Pp. 214-215, the introduction of peyote; not a single Menomini convert by the fall of 1913; then refers to W. E. Safford, item 1087.]

1110   SLOTKIN, James S[ydney]. Menomini peyotism: a study of individual variation in a primary group with a homogeneous culture. Transactions of the American Philosophical Society n.s. 42 (4), 1952, 567-700.
        [Pp. 567-606, history, description, interpretation; pp. 606-636, individual verbatim accounts. Appendices: pp. 637-676, notes to chs. 5 to 7; pp. 676-677, peyote trial of 1914; pp. 677-678, notes on "Peyote of Menominee" by S. A. Barrett; pp. 678-680, the 1919 Report of Menomini Agency to Office of Indian Affairs; pp. 680-681, how peyote is obtained; Appendix 6 (= pp. 681-700), Menomini peyote music, by D. P. McAllester, item 981.]

1111   SLOTKIN, James Sydney. The peyote religion: a study in Indian-white relations. Glencoe: Free Press 1956, 195 p., illus., bibliography of over 550 items; repr. New York: Octagon Books 1975; New York: Farrar, Straus & Giroux 1975.

Peyote,...Native American Church

> [A heavily documented account, showing the religious
> expression of Indian nationalism, and giving a more inside
> view than LaBarre, since Slotkin, although a white
> academic, was a member and officer in the Native American
> Church (on which see pp. 57-64 especially); it has been
> called "basically a manual for peyotists". Pp. 100-103
> have a bibliography of Ghost Dance items not in J. Mooney,
> item 508.]

1112   SLOTKIN, James Sydney (ed.). Quarterly Bulletin of the Native
       American Church. January 1955-1958 (ceased). Mimeo.

1113   SLOTKIN, J[ames] S[ydney]. The peyote way. Tomorrow, Quarterly
       Review of Psychical Research (New York) 4 (3), 1956, 64-70;
       abridged version in R. C. Owen (comp.) The North American
       Indians: a sourcebook. New York: Macmillan 1967, 648-
       654; original version repr. in W. A. Lessa and E. Vogt,
       Reader in Comparative religion, 1965, 482-486; also in
       D. Tedlock and B. Tedlock, item 338, pp. 96-104.]

1114   SLOTKIN, J[ames] S[ydney]. Religious defences (the Native
       American Church). Journal of Psychedelic Drugs 1 (2),
       1968, 77-95, illus.
           [Pp. 77-88, repr. of pp. 65-77 of Slotkin, item 1111;
       pp. 89-93, repr. of Plates 1-6 of idem.; pp. 94-95, repr.
       of the most important items as indicated by Slotkin in his
       bibliography, 1956.]

1115   SLOTKIN, James Sydney and STEWART, Omer C[all]. Peyotism.
       Encyclopaedia Britannica 1966, vol. 17, 790^a-791^b.
           [A good survey, including the Christian elements assim-
       ilated, and that peyotists regard themselves as the Indian
       version of Christianity.]

1116   SMITH, H. H. Ethnobotany of the Meskwaki Indians. Bulletin,
       Public Museum of the City of Milwaukee 4 (2), 1928.
           [P. 189, peyote.]

1117   SMITH, Maurice G. Peyote button induces religious fervor.
       Science News-Letter 18, 1930, 188.

1118   SMITH, (Mrs.) Maurice G. (communicated by John R. Swanton).
       A negro peyote cult. Journal of the Washington Academy
       of Sciences (Menasha, Wisconsin) 24 (10), 1934, 448-453.
           [Report of a cult founded by a Negro, John C. Jamieson
       (d. 1926) in Oklahoma; description of the rite, with its
       differences from local Indian forms (e.g., use of whites'
       hymns and the Bible) showing adaptation to the needs of a
       different racial group.]

1119   SNYDER, Walter W. The Native American Church: its origin,
       ritual, doctrine and ethic. Bulletin of the Oklahoma
       Anthropological Society 18, 1969, 13-38, bibl.
           [Published form of a B.D. thesis of the same title for
       Concordia Theological Seminary, Springfield, Illinois.]

1120   SOCIETY OF AMERICAN INDIANS. Resolutions of 6th annual con-
       ference 1916. American Indian Magazine (Oklahoma) 4,
       1916, 223-224.
           [Anti-peyote; by a white-sponsored society founded among
       educated Indians in 1911.]

1121   SOUTH DAKOTA, STATE UNIVERSITY OF: INSTITUTE OF INDIAN
       STUDIES (Vermillion, South Dakota). NAC groups reorganize
       at State meet. Bulletin 13, 15 August 1960; Native Ameri-
       can Church of South Dakota, 40th annual convention, idem 21,
       August 1962, News Report 15; Peyote ruled illegal in
       California, idem 28, February 1964, News Report 19; see
       also Tobriner, in item 1190, reversal of decision.]

1122   SOUTHWESTERNER. Is peyote narcotic? No, say Indians. South-
       westerner 2 (7), 1963; repr. in Newsletter of Bureau on
       Alcoholism, Health and Welfare Building, Regina, Canada,
       11 March 1963. Mimeo.

1123   SPECK, Frank G[ouldsmith]. Notes on the ethnology of the
       Osage Indians. Transactions of the Department of Archae-
       ology, University of Pennsylvania 2 (2), 1907, 159-171.
           [P. 171, peyote.]

1124   SPECK, Frank G[ouldsmith]. Notes on the life of John Wilson,
       the revealer of peyote, as recalled by his nephew, George
       Anderson. General Magazine and Historical Chronicle
       (Philadelphia) 35, 1933, 539-556.
           [A valuable primary source for the origins and details
       of the Wilson "Moon" form of the peyote cult, describing
       his converting revelation and the replacement of the Bible
       by revelations from a personal Peyote.]

1125   SPINDLER, George D[earborn]. Personal documents in Menomini
       peyotism, in B. Kaplan (ed.), Microcard Publications of
       Primary Records in Culture and Personality. Vol. 2 (12).
       Madison, Wisconsin: Microcard Foundation 1958.

1126   SPINDLER, Louise. Witchcraft in Menomini acculturation.
       American Anthropologist 54 (4), 1952, 593-602, bibl.
           [Pp. 595-597, peyote-users as representing the second of
       four stages of acculturation.]

179

Peyote,...Native American Church

1127   SPINDLER, Mary Louise. Women and culture change: a case
        study of the Menomini Indians. Stanford University,
        Ph.D. dissertation (anthropology) 1956, 337 p.
            [Participant peyotists were taken as one of the five
        acculturative categories, and showed greater anxiety and
        greater responsiveness to environmental stimuli.]

1128   STARKLOFF, Carl F. American Indian religion and Christianity:
        confrontation and dialogue. Journal of Ecumenical Studies
        8 (2), 1971, 317-340; repr. in M. E. Marty et al. (eds.),
        New theology no. 9. New York: Macmillan 1972, 121-150.
            [P. 319, brief references to refusal of Native American ·
        Church to allow him to attend, and comment on folly of
        trying to suppress this Indian unifying force.]

1129   STAR-PHOENIX. Photographs of peyote ritual at Fort Battleford.
        Star-Phoenix (Saskatoon, Saskatchewan) October 1956.
            [See photos in C. B. Dustin, item 859, and others in
        O. C. Stewart, item 1145.]

1130   STENBERG, Molly Peacock. The peyote culture among Wyoming
        Indians: a transitional link between indigenous culture
        and an imposed culture. University of Wyoming Publica-
        tions 12 (4), 1946, 85-156, illus., bibl.
            [A comprehensive first-hand study drawing on seven
        years' residence on the Wind River Reservation; pp. 139-
        147, verbatim Indian reports.]

1131   STERLING, William Warren. Trails and trials of a Texas Ranger.
        Norman: University of Oklahoma Press (1959) 1968, 536 p.,
        illus.
            [Pp. 91-92, on the peyote trade as important in southern
        Texas in the 1920s.]

1132   STEVENSON, Matilda Coxe. Ethnobotany of the Zuñi Indians, in
        30th Annual Report, Bureau of American Ethnology 1908-1909.
        Washington, D.C.: Government Printing Office 1915, 31-
        102, illus.
            [P. 41, n2 on J. Mooney finding peyote used by Kiowa
        etc. (1891); in 1894 Mooney brought some to Washington for
        scientific analysis — see report by Prentiss and Morgan,
        item 1310.]

1133   STEWART, Omer C[all]. Indians hold weird rites. Post
        Enquirer (Oakland, California) 4 March 1938, 1, cols. 2-4.
            [On peyote cult.]

1134   STEWART, Omer C[all]. Washo-Northern Paiute peyotism. <u>Pro-
        ceedings, 6th Pacific Science Congress</u> 1939, vol. 4, 65-68.

1135   STEWART, Omer C[all]. The Southern Ute peyote cult. <u>American
        Anthropologist</u> 43 (2:1), 1941, 303-308.
        [A reply to M. Opler, item 1041.]

1136   STEWART, Omer C[all]. <u>Washo-Northern Paiute peyotism: a study
        in acculturation</u> (University of California Publications in
        American Archaeology and Ethnology 40 (3)). Berkeley:
        University of California Press 1944, 63-141.
        [Emphasizes the Christian elements in the cult; it is
        mainly a healing cult, and is hostile to purely socio-
        logical explanations.]

1137   STEWART, Omer C[all]. <u>Ute peyotism: a study of a cultural
        complex</u> (University of Colorado Studies, Series in
        Anthropology: 1). Boulder: University of Colorado Press
        1948, 42 p., illus., tables; repr. New York: Kraus
        Reprint 1972.
        [His Ph.D. dissertation of 1939 summarized; the Ute
        peyote meeting account is reprinted in O. C. Stewart,
        item 1145, pp. 29-47.]

1138   STEWART, Omer C[all]. Pro-peyote. <u>Time</u> 58 (2), 9 July 1951,
        6, 8.
        [Reply to earlier critical articles; see item 1158.]

1139   STEWART, Omer C[all]. Review of: <u>Menomini peyotism</u>, by J. S.
        Slotkin, 1952. <u>American Anthropologist</u> 44 (4), 1953,
        586-587.
        [Brief and favourable.]

1139A   STEWART, Omer C[all]. Peyotism: a modern American religion.
        <u>The Delphian Quarterly</u> (Chicago) 37 (2), 1954, 7-8, 37.
        [The numerical and geographical growth of peyotism to
        some 40,000 participants; description of the rite; its
        advantages and disadvantages for Indians.]

1140   STEWART, Omer C[all]. Peyote. <u>Encyclopedia Americana</u>. New
        York: America Corporation 1954, vol. 21, 700.

1141   STEWART, Omer C[all]. Three gods for Joe. <u>Tomorrow. Quarterly
        Review of Psychical Research</u> (New York) 4, 1956, 71-76.
        [A Northern Paiute who is a shaman, peyotist, and
        Episcopalian.]

Peyote,...Native American Church

1142 STEWART, Omer C[all]. Peyote and Colorado's inquisition law.
The Colorado Quarterly (Boulder) 5 (1), 1956, 79-90.
[The various attempts to ban peyote, from the Mexican
Inquisition laws of 1620 to recent efforts, especially
those of missionaries involving "unintentional slander
because of receiving false information"; details of the
1917 Colorado law and its supporters.]

1143 STEWART, Omer C[all]. Peyote and the Arizona court decision.
American Anthropologist 63 (6), 1961, 1334.
[A brief letter (see also item 882 from B. E. Gorton) on
the decision of Judge Y. McFate (see item 1189) that
peyote is not a narcotic; support for alternative term,
"psychotropic".]

1144 STEWART, Omer C[all]. The Native American Church (peyote
cult) and the law. The Denver Westerners Monthly Roundup
17 (1), 1961, 5-17.
["Best source on recent legal questions"; see repr. in
Westerners Brand Book below.]

1145 STEWART, Omer C[all]. The Native American Church and the law,
with description of peyote religious services. Westerners
Brand Book (Boulder) 17, 1961, 4-47, illus.
[Pp. 4-29 repr. from his item 1144, together with 19 pp.
excerpted from Stewart, item 1137, on Ute peyote meeting;
repr. in D. E. Walker, item 360, pp. 382-397.]

1146 STEWART, Omer C[all]. New bill to outlaw peyote. American
Indian Horizon (New York) 2 (7), 1964, 1, 3.
[Quoting Congressional Record 13 December 1963, Bill
H.R. 9488 to amend Narcotic Drugs Import and Export Act in
order to ban possession or importation of peyote; survey
of attempts at banning by law, and religious use; favour-
able judgement on effects of peyote; the proposed legislation would only remove religious freedom; Judge McFate's
decision referred to.]

1147 STEWART, Omer C[all]. Anthropologists as expert witnesses for
Indians: claims and peyote cases, in American Anthro-
pological Association, Anthropology and the American
Indian. Report of a Symposium, ... San Diego 1970. San
Francisco: Indian Historian Press 1973, 35-42; see also
his discussion, pp. 61-62.
[Pp. 35-39, peyote legal cases; also pp. 43-44, 62-63,
discussion by Mrs. Mary Natani (Winnebago, and an editor
for the Native American Church). See also review in
American Anthropologist 78 (June), 1976, 404.]

1148 STEWART, Omer C[all]. Origin of the peyote religion in the
United States. Plains Anthropologist no. 65=1974, 211-223,
maps, bibl.
[On the problem of relating the peyote cult found in the
now south-west Oklahoma, to the limited sources of the
plant over three hundred miles away around Laredo: the
Lipan Apache, the Carrizo and Tonkawa as intermediaries.
P. 220, on the origins of Christian elements. An authori-
tative survey of early sources, taking the possibility of
Lipan Apache use of peyote back to 1770.]

1149 STEWART, Omer Call. History of the peyote religion.
[A major work, in two or three volumes, of which the
first draft may be completed in 1978. The fruit of a life-
time of study of this subject.]

1150 STRONG, William Duncan. The Indian tribes of the Chicago
region with special reference to the Illinois and the
Potawatomi (Anthropological Leaflet, 24). Chicago: Field
Museum of Natural History, 2nd ed. 1938, 35 p., illus.
[P. 26, peyote cult.]

1151 STUMP, Al. Peyote, the illegal drug that brings you close to
God. Saga: the Magazine for Men (New York) 26 (3), 1963,
46-49, 81-83, illus.
[P. 49 has also photo of Omer C. Stewart, and statement
he made to Saga on peyote.]

1152 TAKES GUN, Frank. Fight to legalize peyote. Desert Magazine
(El Centro, California) February 1960, 32.
[By the then national president of the Native American
Church, a Crow Indian from Montana.]

1153 TAKES GUN, Frank. Letter to the editor. Navajo Times
(Window Rock) 5 (8), 20 February 1964, 7, 8.
[The president of the Native American Church defends the
church and surveys some court cases and decisions in the
struggle to secure religious freedom. Editorial introduction, and reprints of the McFate decision (Arizona 1960,
see item 1189) and the Hilliard decision in California
1963.]

1154 TAKES GUN, Frank. Peyote only for religion. Navajo Times
(Window Rock) 7 (35), 1 September 1966, 1, 4, photo.
[An interview with Frank Takes Gun, national president
of the Native American Church, defending the right use of
peyote. Appended: letters (a) From W. B. Rankin, Acting
Deputy Commissioner, Department of Health, Education and

Peyote,...Native American Church

Welfare, to the president of the Native American Church in
Nebraska; (b) From W. B. Rankin, as Assistant Commissioner
for Planning, to Frank Takes Gun — both concerning recog-
nition of religious use of peyote.]

1155   TAX, Sol. The social organization of the Fox Indians, in
        F. Eggan (ed.), Social Anthropology of North American
        tribes. Chicago: University of Chicago Press (1937)
        1972, 574 p.
           [P. 268, brief summary of peyote among the Fox Indians,
        as a cure-all.]

1156   THURMAN, Melburn D. Supplementary material on the life of
        John Wilson, "the revealer of peyote". Ethnohistory
        20 (3), 1973, 279–287.
           [Wilson's relation to Ghost Dance, the Big Moon peyote
        rite, and Catholicism; Enoch Hoag's form of the peyote
        rite; provides some new data from Oklahoma Historical
        Society sources.]

1157   TILGMAN, Zoe A[gnes] [Stratton]. Quanah, the eagle of the
        Comanches. Oklahoma City: Harlow Publishing Corporation
        1938, viii + 196 p., illus.
           [Pp. 111–121, 133–136, 157, 183, 194, peyote; by the
        wife of a white friend of Quanah Parker.]

1158   TIME. Button, button. Time 57 (25), 18 June 1951, 82–83,
        illus.
           [A critical account of peyote among the Navaho, as
        allegedly offering an escape from their troubles and
        producing deplorable after-effects including sex-crimes.]

1159   TIME. The Church and the cactus. Time 64 (6), 9 August 1954,
        49–50, illus.
           [Report of annual meeting of Native American Church at
        Tama, with 22 delegates from 11 tribes, under Allen P.
        Dale, 5th-time President.]

1160   TIME. The button eaters. Time 73 (7), 16 February 1959, 71,
        illus.
           [Frank Takes Gun, president of the Native American
        Church; his success in securing legalization of the reli-
        gious use of peyote in New Mexico, and the opposition
        attempts to get the Governor to veto the bill.]

1161   TIME. God and peyote. Time 84 (11), 11 September 1964, 64,
        illus.

Peyote,...Native American Church

[The California Supreme Court decision in favour of
three Navaho members of the Native American Church; see
item 1190.]

1162   TIPPETT, Alan R. 45% of Navajos accept Peyote-oriented church.
        Los Angeles Times 17 August 1967.
        [Interviewed by D. L. Thrapp; repr. in B. Roseman, item
        1084, pp. 85-92.]

1163   TIPPETT, Alan R. Report on the San Juan Episcopal Mission to
        the Navaho, Farmington, N.M. For the Committee appointed
        by the Co-ordinating Council December 1967. Mimeo.
        [Pp. 22-30, 87-89, peyote religion from a critical
        Christian viewpoint, by a missionary anthropologist. Con-
        fidential when presented, and unpublished.]

1164   TOBRINER, Mathew O. A similar case but a different decision.
        The Indian Historian (San Francisco) 2 (9), November-
        December 1965, 30.
        [Use of peyote by a white religious group at Palm Springs,
        California held to be illegal by Judge Tobriner, who had
        reversed the decision against Indian users — see United
        States (Courts). Supreme Court of California, item 1190.]

1165   TROIKE, Rudolph Charles. Origins of Plains mescalism.
        American Anthropologist 64 (5:1), 1962, 946-963.
        [Relatively recent development, synthesizing several
        independent complexes; little direct influence of mescal
        cult on peyotism, though both inherit some Plains
        ceremonialism.]

1166   TSA TO KE, Monroe. Monroe Tsa To ke. [San Francisco?] 1953,
        37 p., with mounted illustrations.
        [Introduction by S. C. Peters; catalogue of paintings,
        which include peyote themes.]

1167   TSA TO KE, Monroe. The peyote ritual. Visions and descrip-
        tions. San Francisco: Grabhorn Press 1957, xvii + 66 p.,
        14 colour plates.
        [A noted Kiowa artist, member of peyote cult — his
        paintings and comments on them, giving his interpretations
        of the peyote experience and its meaning to the members.
        See D. F. Aberle's review, American Anthropologist 60 (5),
        1958, 953.]

1168   TSA TO KE, Monroe.
        [See O. B. Jacobsen, items 931, 932; also D. Aberle,
        item 769.]

Peyote,...Native American Church

1169   [TURNER, Harold Walter]. Peyotism. Encyclopaedia Britannica
        1974, Micropaedia, vol. 7, 921.
        [Unsigned survey article].

1170   UNDERHILL, Ruth M[urray]. Peyote (Publication 2). Santa Fe,
        N.M.: San Vincente Foundation Inc. 1948, 14 p. Mimeo.
        [A comprehensive survey: peyote among Huichol and
        Tarahumara, a Kiowa meeting described in detail, variations
        in other tribes, the Native American Church, the pharma-
        cology of peyote.]

1171   UNDERHILL, Ruth M[urray]. Peyote, in Proceedings, 30th
        International Congress of Americanists..., Cambridge...
        1952. London: Royal Anthropological Institute n.d.
        [Pp. 143-148, a peyote healing rite in Texas described,
        with introduction and comments; p. 147, peyote songs.]

1172   UNDERHILL, Ruth M[urray]. The Navajos. Norman: University
        of Oklahoma Press 1956; revised ed. 1967, 288 p., illus.
        [Pp. 247-250, 267-268, peyote and its effects.]

1173   UNDERHILL, Ruth M[urray]. Religion among American Indians.
        Annals of the American Academy of Political and Social
        Science no. 311, May 1957, 127-136; abridged version in
        R. C. Owen (comp.), The North American Indians: a
        sourcebook. New York: Macmillan 1967, 95-108.
        [Pp. 135-136 (= 107-108, 1967 version), peyote and
        Native American Church; "reversion" and "amalgamation"
        in religions.]

1174   UNITED STATES COMMISSION ON CIVIL RIGHTS. American Indian
        civil rights handbook (Clearing House Publication, 33).
        Washington, D.C.: The Commission 1972, 96 p., illus.
        [Section 1, Freedom of belief and expression: pp. 14-
        16, ⊣legal factors related to the use of peyote.]

1175   UNITED STATES. CONGRESS. Congressional Record (67th Congress,
        4th session 1922-23) (Washington, D.C.) 64 (2), Jan. 1923,
        1280-1281.
        [Senate discussion of item of $25,000 in Department of
        the Interior budget for supression of the drug traffic,
        including peyote.]

1176   UNITED STATES. CONGRESS. Congressional Record (67th Congress,
        4th session, 1922-23) (Washington, D.C.) 64 (2), Jan. 1923,
        1362-1363.
        [In the House, a letter from a doctor in Anadarko,
        Oklahoma, criticizing missionaries' misrepresentation of

peyote was read into the Record; also a press report,
"Redskins' 'Superhooch' survives Senate attack",
Washington Post 6 Jan. 1923.]

1177 UNITED STATES. CONGRESS. Congressional Record (Revised
session edition). Washington, D.C.: Government Printers.
  [The official journal. For long list of items relevant
to peyote, see Slotkin, item 1111, pp. 178-179. As
examples, see the next two items. For Federal Bills to
prohibit peyote see especially 53 (7), 6720-6721; 53 (9),
9231; 56 (7), 6469; 56 (11), 11,113-11,115, 11,155;
59 (9), 9149-9151 — all during 1916-1919.

1178 UNITED STATES. CONGRESS. HOUSE. COMMITTEE ON APPROPRIATIONS.
Hearings before the sub-committee on Interior Department
appropriation bill for 1919. Washington, D.C.: Government
Printing Office 1918.
  [Excerpts repr. in UNITED STATES, item 1184, pp. 18258
et seq., which includes much documentary evidence dated
1911. Other relevant Hearings of the same Committee on the
same annual bill between 1922 and 1939 are listed in
Slotkin, item 1111, p. 179.]

1179 UNITED STATES. CONGRESS. HOUSE. COMMITTEE ON APPROPRIATIONS.
Hearings before the Subcommittee on the Department of the
Interior for fiscal year 1936. Washington, D.C.: Office
of Indian Affairs 1936.
  [Pp. 689-699, discussion concerning peyote; repr. in
United States, item 1184, pp. 18225-18231, and in Bulletin,
Bureau of Indian Affairs, April 1935.]

1180 UNITED STATES. CONGRESS. HOUSE. COMMITTEE ON INDIAN AFFAIRS.
Hearings before the Subcommittee on H.R. 2614 to amend
sections 2139 and 2140 of the Revised Statutes.... 65th
Congress, 2nd session. Washington, D.C.: Government
Printing Office, Pt. 1, 21 February 1918; Pt. 2, 23 March
1918.
  [Discussion on peyote, especially Pt. 1, pp. 3-17, 574,
581-582; Pt. 2, pp. 18-193 (including J. Mooney's statement of 1915, pp. 69-74).]

1181 UNITED STATES. CONGRESS. SENATE. COMMITTEE ON INDIAN AFFAIRS.
Hearings before the sub-committee on H.R. 14746, a bill
making appropriations for the fiscal year ending June 30,
1920. Washington, D.C.: Government Printing Office 1919.
  [Includes discussion of peyote.]

Peyote,...Native American Church

1182   UNITED STATES.   CONGRESS.   SENATE.   COMMITTEE ON INDIAN AFFAIRS.
       Survey of conditions of the Indians in the United States.
       Part 18, Navajos in Arizona and New Mexico.   Hearings
       before a subcommittee of the Committee on Indian Affairs...
       71st Congress, 1st session.   Washington, D.C.:   Government
       Printing Office 1932.
         [Includes discussion on peyote.]

1183   UNITED STATES.   CONGRESS.   SENATE.   COMMITTEE ON INDIAN AFFAIRS.
       Survey of conditions of Indians in the United States.
       Hearings before subcommittee, 70th Congress, 2nd session.
       Washington, D.C.:   Government Printing Office 1934, pt. 27,
       14525-14526.
         [Includes discussion of peyote.]

1184   UNITED STATES.   CONGRESS.   SENATE.   COMMITTEE ON INDIAN AFFAIRS.
       Survey of conditions of the Indians in the United States.
       Hearings before subcommittee, 75th Congress, 1st session...
       continuing until end of regular session of 75th Congress.
       Washington, D.C.:   Government Printing Office 1937, pt. 34,
       iv + 17, 423-18, 351, + illus., maps.
         [These hearings were held in Washington, D.C., Arizona
       and New Mexico.   Peyote: pp. 18,164-18,186, 18,190-18,192,
       18,216-18,313; pp. 18,234-18,257 incorporate D. Collier's
       paper on peyote, item 834.]

1185   UNITED STATES.   [COURTS].   DISTRICT COURT, WISCONSIN, EASTERN
       DISTRICT, MILWAUKEE.   United States vs. Mitchell Neck,
       alias Nah-qua-tah-tuck.   Crim. F. No. 280, May 1914.   MS
       only.
         [The trial of the first peyotists on the Menomini
       Reservation, after the arrival of a peyote "missionary".
       Summary in Safford, item 1087, pp. 306-307.]

1186   UNITED STATES [COURTS] DISTRICT COURT OF APPEAL, FOURTH
       DISTRICT, CALIFORNIA.   The People...V. Jack Woody
       et al., ... Cr[iminal case number] 1794, District Court of
       Appeal, Fourth District, California.   December 6, 1963.
       Hearing ... February 28, 1964.   As in California Reporter
       (St. Paul, Minnesota) 35, 1964, 708-719.
         [A full account of the trial of three Navaho members of
       the Native American Church for using peyote, and Judge
       Coughlin's reasons for rejecting their appeal.   See also
       items 897, 898 and 974.]

1187   UNITED STATES.   [COURTS].   DISTRICT COURT, SOUTH DAKOTA,
       WESTERN DIVISION.   United States vs. Harry Black Bear,
       U.S. Congress, Committee on Appropriations 1928, 124-125;

summary of testimony in Daily Pioneer-Times (Deadwood,
South Dakota) 7 September 1916, p. 1, cols. 4-5;
8 September 1916, p. 1, cols. 1-2.
[A peyote case, cited by Slotkin, item 1111, p. 181.]

1188 UNITED STATES. [COURTS]. SUPERIOR COURT OF ARIZONA...COUNTY
OF MARICOPA. State of Arizona vs. Mary Attakai: no. 4098.
Reporter's transcript of proceedings (B. Prochnow, Official
Reporter) Flagstaff, Arizona, July 25-26 1960, Book 1,
pp. 1-90; Book 2, pp. 90-161. MS.
[Hon. Yale McFate, Judge of Superior Court of Arizona...
County of Maricopa. Witnesses: pp. 11-19, Mary Attakai;
pp. 19-40, Frank Takes Gun; pp. 40-126, O. C. Stewart (a
valuable account); pp. 129-151, B. C. Gorton; pp. 155-160,
McFate's decision. Xerox copy in Museum of Northern
Arizona, Flagstaff, MS 124.]

1189 UNITED STATES. [COURTS]. SUPERIOR COURT, COCONINO COUNTY,
FLAGSTAFF, ARIZONA.
Decision of the Honourable Yale McFate in the case of
State of Arizona vs. Mary Attakai No. 4098, Superior Court,
Coconino County, Flagstaff, Arizona, July 26, 1960.
American Anthropologist 63 (6), 1961, 1335-1337.
[An important decision that peyote is not narcotic, and
the State legal ban was unconstitutional; also included in
O. C. Stewart, item 1144, pp. 13-14, and item 1145, pp. 20-
22; also repr. in Navajo Times 10 (50), 18 December 1969,
20, cols. 1-4, and in many other places.]

1190 UNITED STATES. [COURTS]. SUPREME COURT OF CALIFORNIA.
TOBRINER, Mathew O. Opinion of the Supreme Court of
California, in The People v. Jack Woody et al, in Criminal
Case No. 7788, Aug. 24, 1964. Pacific Reporter (St. Paul,
Minnesota) 2nd Series, vol. 394 P.2d, 1964, 813-822; also
in Advance California Records (San Francisco), 11 Sept.
1964, 697-813; repr. in The Indian Historian (San
Francisco) 2 (9), November-December 1965, 23-30, as "Text
of historic peyote decision".
[Rejection of California 4th District Court of Appeal
decision (Crim. No. 1794), and confirming right of Native
American Church to use peyote in religious services. See
also Tobriner, item 1164, for opposite decision in case
of whites.]

1191 UNITED STATES. [COURTS]. SUPREME COURT, MONTANA. State
versus Big Sheep: Montana 219,243P. 1067. Montana
Reports 75, 1926, 219-240; also in Pacific Reporter.
St. Paul: West Publishing Co., vol. 243, 1926, 1068-1073.

Peyote,...Native American Church

> [The appeal from the District Court, Big Horn County;
> judgement was reversed and a new trial ordered in this
> peyote case.]

1192 UNITED STATES. DEPARTMENT OF THE INTERIOR. BOARD OF INDIAN
COMMISSIONERS. Annual reports. Washington, D.C.: Government Printing Office: e.g. No. 41, 1909, 15-16; no. 44,
1912-1913, 9; no. 45, 1913-1914, 13; no. 47, 1916, 9;
no. 60, 1929, 1-26 ("Six decades of Indian progress").
[References to peyote.]

1193 UNITED STATES. DEPARTMENT OF THE INTERIOR. BUREAU OF INDIAN
AFFAIRS. Annual reports. Washington, D.C.: Government
Printing Office: references to the peyote cult listed by
Slotkin, item 1111, in the following agency, etc. reports
(name of agent or author in parentheses): 1886, p. 130,
Kiowa, Comanche and Wichita (J. L. Hall); 1888, pp. 98-99,
Kiowa, Comanche and Wichita (E. E. White); 1889, p. 191,
Kiowa, Comanche and Wichita (W. D. Myers); 1890, p. 180,
Cheyenne and Arapaho (C. F. Ashley), p. 194, Ponca, Pawnee,
Otoe and Oakland (D. J. M. Wood); 1895, p. 122, Pima (J. R.
Young); 1896, p. 250, Cheyenne and Arapaho (A. E. Woodson);
1899, p. 284, Cheyenne and Arapaho (A. E. Woodson), p. 297,
Osage (W. J. Pollock); 1900, p. 339, Osage (O. A. Mitscher);
1903, p. 275, Pawnee School Superintendent (G. I. Harvey);
1905, p. 253, Winnebago (E. S. Hart); 1906, p. 269,
Winnebago (S. A. Tate), p. 321, Ponca school (H. M. Nobel),
p. 322, Sac and Fox (W. C. Kohlenberg), pp. 326-328,
Seger school (R. C. Preston).

1194 UNITED STATES. DEPARTMENT OF THE INTERIOR. BUREAU OF INDIAN
AFFAIRS. Annual reports of the Commissioner of Indian
Affairs. Washington, D.C.: Government Printing Office:
e.g., 1909, 13-14; 1911, 35; 1912, 47-48; 1922, 20; 1923,
20; 1924, 21; 1925, 19.
[On peyote.]

1195 UNITED STATES. DEPARTMENT OF THE INTERIOR. BUREAU OF INDIAN
AFFAIRS. Peyote. Bulletin, Office of Indian Affairs
(Washington, D.C.) 21, 1929, 31 p. Mimeo.
[Effect of peyote on Indians, based on missionaries and
B.I.A. officials: E. B. Putt on mescal; L. E. Sayre;
H. Harms (State chemist); H. W. Wiley; W. E. Dixon's
article, item 1280, summarized; C. E. Shell's experience
of peyote; also Robert D. Hall's affidavit on peyote,
with R. P. Angier's comments to him.]

1196 UNITED STATES. DEPARTMENT OF THE INTERIOR. BUREAU OF INDIAN
AFFAIRS. Documents on peyote. Pt. 1. Washington, D.C.:
Bureau of Indian Affairs, document no. 137817, 18 May 1937.
Mimeo.
[See in conjunction with Senate Bill 1399, 8 Feb. 1937.]

1197 UNITED STATES. DEPARTMENT OF THE INTERIOR. BUREAU OF INDIAN
AFFAIRS. The growing peyote cult and the use of peyote
on the Navajo Indian Reservation. Washington, D.C.:
Bureau of Indian Affairs, document no. 131287, 1940.
Mimeo.

1198 VALLEY NATIONAL BANK. Peyote-using Indians. VNB Agriculture
and Livestock Monthly News Digest (Phoenix, Arizona)
9 (8), August 1962, 2.
[Report of U.S. Court of Appeals support of Navajo Tribal
Council ban, with a few general comments on how hard it is
to enforce. See also item 1209.]

1199 VAUX, G. The pauperism of riches — an Indian paradox. 34th
Annual Report, Lake Mohonk Conference 1916, 69–75.
[P. 74, peyote.]

1200 VESTAL, Paul A[nthony] and SCHULTES, Richard Evans. The economic botany of the Kiowa Indians, as it relates to the
history of the tribe. Cambridge: Harvard University
Botanical Museum 1939, xiii + 110 p., illus., map.
[Pp. 8, 38, 43–45, 79–81, 83–85, peyote.]

1201 VOGEL, Virgil J. American Indian medicine. Norman: University of Oklahoma Press 1970, 583 p.
[Pp. 165–167, 190–191, the medical value and uses of
peyote — both traditional and in the Native American
Church; with source references.]

1202 VOGET, Fred W. Review of The peyote religion among the Navaho
by David F. Aberle. American Anthropologist 70 (1),
1968, 118–121.

1203 VRUWINK, Henry [W.]. Peyote or mescal as a drug and cult,
printed in UNITED STATES, item 1184, pp. 18,309–18,313.
[A paper based on materials gathered by Dr. W. C. Roe,
Rev. G. A. Watermulder and Rev. Henry Sluyter, and sub-
mitted as anti-peyote evidence in Congressional hearings
1936. By a Reformed Church of America minister; see his
further item in Slotkin, item 1111, p. 187.]

Peyote,...Native American Church

1204   WAGNER, Günter. Die Entwicklung und Verbreitung des Peyote-
        Kultes: ein Beitrag zum Problem der Akkulturation.
        Baessler-Archiv (Berlin) 15, 1932, 59-141.
            [Based on a doctoral dissertation, University of Berlin,
        1931, with same title.]

1205   WAGNER, Roland Marshall. Western Navajo peyotism: a case
        analysis. University of Oregon, Ph.D. dissertation
        (anthropology) 1974, 434 p., maps, tables.
            [Two areas — Coppermine and Leche'e — on the Kaibeto
        plateau. Tests seven explanations for peyotism previously
        offered, and finally supplements and expands Aberle's
        "relative deprivation" interpretation. Pp. 354-364, com-
        parison with Christianity.]

1206   WAGNER, Roland M[arshall]. Pattern and process in ritual
        syncretism: the case of peyotism among the Navajo.
        Journal of Anthropological Research 31 (2), 1975, 162-181,
        diagram.
            [An "incorporative" process marks Navaho reaction to
        acculturation over the last three centuries; this is seen
        in the syncretic blending of Navaho primal religion and
        the peyote cult in a meeting near Page and Coppermine in
        1968.]

1207   WAGNER, Roland M[arshall]. Some pragmatic aspects of Navaho
        peyotism. Plains Anthropologist 20, August 1975, 197-205.
            [Criticizes the "flight from reality" explanation of the
        appeal of the peyote cult, by showing its relation to
        immediate practical benefits, and its purpose of dealing
        with and ultimately transforming contemporary social and
        economic conditions.]

1208   WALKER, Sheila S. Ceremonial spirit possession in Africa and
        Afro-America. Forms, meanings and functional significance
        for individual and social groups (Supplements to Numen,
        2nd series, 4). Leiden: E. J. Brill 1972, 179 p.
            [Pp. 74-76, comparison of effects of peyote on Indians
        and whites, based on A. F. C. Wallace, item 115.]

1209   WASHBURN, Wilcomb E. The American Indians and the United
        States. A documentary history. 4 vols. New York:
        Random House 1973, vol. 4.
            [Pp. 2788-2791, Native American Church v. Navajo Tribal
        Council, Circuit Court of Appeals, Tenth Circuit (1959) —
        Judge Huxman's judgement rejecting the suit for an injunc-
        tion against the Tribal Council's ban on peyote, because

the First Amendment to the Constitution guaranteeing
religious freedom did not control tribal authorities, who
hold quasi-sovereignty. See also item 1198.]

1210   WATERMULDER, G. A. Mescal, in 32nd Annual Report, Lake Mohonk
       Conference. Albany, 1914, 68-76.
       [Peyote in relation to Indians; by a Christian pastor.]

1211   WATERS, Frank. The man who killed the deer. Denver,
       Colorado: Alan Swallow (Sage Books) 1942, 311 p.
       [Fiction, with authentic detail. Pp. 81-93, a Pueblo
       Indian's introduction to the Peyote Road; pp. 123-141, his
       further experiences, and persecution of the peyote cult;
       similar to Taos Pueblo.]

1212   WATTS, W. David, Jr. The psychedelic experience: a socio-
       logical study. Beverley Hills, California: Sage
       Publications 1971, 258 p.
       [Appendix I, = pp. 207-214, The drugs, includes peyote;
       Appendix II, = pp. 215-224, Peyotism (a historical survey
       and interpretation, with pharmacology).]

1213   WELSH, Herbert. Peyote: an insidious evil (Publications of
       the Indian Rights Association, Series 2, no. 114).
       Philadelphia: Indian Rights Association 1918.
       [By the Association's president.]

1214   WENIGER, Del. Cacti of the Southwest: Texas, New Mexico,
       Oklahoma, Arkansas and Louisiana. Austin: University of
       Texas Press 1969, xv + 64 + 269 p., illus.
       [Pp. 95-96, missionaries in Mexico as unsuccessful in
       eliminating use of peyote; the reasons why it was used.]

1215   WHITMAN, William. The Oto (Columbia University Contributions
       of Anthropology, 28). New York: Columbia University
       Press 1937, xvi + 132.
       [Pp. 127-130, peyote; based on his Ph.D. dissertation,
       Columbia University, 1937.]

1216   WILSON, Bryan R[onald]. Peyote cults, Man, myth and magic
       5 (77), n.d. [1970-2], 2170-2172, illus.
       [Includes Ghost Dance as alleged forerunner.]

1217   WILSON, Bryan R[onald]. Magic and the millennium.... (see
       item 371).
       [Pp. 414-449, peyotism, within his theoretical frame-
       work as "an introversionist movement?", with special
       reference to the Navaho (pp. 441-448).]

Peyote,...Native American Church

1218   WISSLER, Clark. Societies and ceremonial associations in the
       Oglala division of the Teton-Dakota. Anthropology Papers,
       American Museum of Natural History (New York) 11, 1912,
       1-99.
          [P. 99, peyote.]

1219   WISSLER, Clark. Indian cavalcade; or, life on the old-time
       Indian reservations. New York: Sheridan House 1938,
       351 p., plates.
          [Pp. 29-30, peyote.]

1220   WUTTUNEE, William I. C. Peyote ceremony. The Beaver: Magazine
       of the North (Winnipeg) Summer 1968, 22-25, illus.
          [Report of his participation in the all-night ceremony
       of the Cree Indians of Red Pheasant Indian Reserve,
       Saskatchewan, in July 1964.]

1221   ZAEHNER, R[obert] C[harles]. Mysticism, sacred and profane.
       An enquiry into some varieties of prae-natural experience.
       New York: Oxford University Press (1957) 1961, 274 p.;
       as a Galaxy Book, 1969.
          [Pp. 23-24, Native American Church; brief discussion of
       its use of peyote, based on A. Huxley, item 917, and in a
       Christian context.]

1222   ZOLOTAREVSKAJA, I. A. Some materials on the assimilation of
       Oklahoma Indians. Plains Anthropologist 6 (Feb.), 1961,
       1-6.
          [Pp. 5-6, Native American Church as a "latent protest
       against Indian Bureau turning Indian life into a perfor-
       mance for tourists", and as destructive of tribal distinc-
       tiveness; by a Soviet anthropologist.]

PEYOTE: TRADITIONAL CULTS IN NORTHERN MEXICO

       A full study of the modern peyote cult inevitably leads back into
its origins in more traditional forms among four tribes in Northern
Mexico - the Coras, Tepehuanes, Tarahumaras, and Huichols, each with
its own vernacular name for the peyote plant. Of these peoples only
the Huichols retain the primitive form of the cult to the present day,
and since the 1960s they have been well served with major studies
and an ethnographic film of the annual pilgrimage to secure the
peyote "buttons" or buds from the top of the plant. The bibliography
does not pursue the subject where it naturally leads at this point,
into the range of hallucinogenic substances used for religious and
healing purposes that seems to have been more extensive among American
Indians of both continents than anywhere else in the world.

1223   ARTAUD, Antonin. Les Tarahumaras (Oeuvres Complètes d'Antonin Artaud, 9). Paris: Gallimard 1971; Eng. trans., The peyote dance (trans. Helen Weaver). New York: Farrar, Straus & Giroux 1976, 105 p.
[Pp. 18-42, his participation in the peyote rite among the Tarahumaras, pp. 43-44, post-script explaining how he wrote the above account; pp. 45-58, 75-83, further accounts of his peyote-inspired experience and beliefs. By a writer whose spiritual turmoil found some answer in a mystical-christian view of peyote.]

1224   BEALS, Ralph L[eon]. Comparative ethnology of northern Mexico before 1750. Ibero-Americana (Berkeley) 2, 1932, 93-225, maps.
[Map 28, p. 215, probable limits of aboriginal peyote cult, in northern Mexico; p. 216, bibliographical references to various uses of peyote in eleven tribes.]

1225   CASTAÑEDA, Carlos. The teachings of Don Juan: a Yaqui way of knowledge. Berkeley and Los Angeles: University of California Press 1968, 196 p.; New York: Ballantine Books 1969, 276 p.; Harmondsworth: Penguin Books 1970, 252 p.; New York: Simon & Schuster 1973 etc.
[Recounts the author's apprenticeship to a Yaqui mystic, and includes the discipline associated with the preparation and use of hallucinogenic plants (peyote, jimsonweed and mushroom); part two explicates Don Juan's world. Nothing to do with Yaqui syncretist churches, or with the peyote cult as such, but shows the place of hallucinogens in the traditional shamanic world.]

1226   CASTAÑEDA, Carlos.
The other well-known works of this author (four volumes to date), on Don Juan, the Yaqui mystic and medicine man who used peyote, etc., are not included on account of their specialized nature and marginal relevance.

1227   DE FÉLICE, Philippe. Poisons sacrés, ivresses divines. Essai sur quelques formes inférieures de la mystique. Paris: Éditions Albin Michel 1936.
[Pp. 183-207, the use of peyote among Mexican Indians, Huichols, Coras, Tepehuanes and Tarahumaras, from a sociological viewpoint.]

1228   DE LA SERNA, Jacinto. Manuel de los Ministros para el conocimiento de sus idolatrías y extirpación de ellas (Documentos inéditos para la Historia de España, vol. 104). Madrid, 1892.

Peyote:...Cults in Northern Mexico

[P. 61, extract, in W. E. Safford, item 1087; pp. 309-310, on Mexican use of peyote in 1626.]

1229 DIGUET, Léon. Contribution à l'étude ethnographique des races primitives du Mexique: la Sierra du Nayarit et ses indigenes. Nouvelles Archives des Missions Scientifiques et Litéraires 9, 1899, 621-625.
[Extract from p. 621 in Safford, item 1087, pp. 305-306. The mythology of peyote among the Indians; the annual pilgrimage and ritual to gather this supreme food of both the soul and the gods, which brings supernatural grace to men.]

1230 DIGUET, Léon. Le "peyote" et son usage ritual chez les Indiens de Nayarit. Journal de la Société des Américanistes de Paris n.s. 4, 1907, 21-29, illus.
[The plant, its botanical and pharmacological history; traditional use and rituals among the Huichols and Coras, especially the ritual pilgrimage to gather peyote and the fifteen staging points and their Huichol names. The bibliography provides the earlier Spanish and the early modern pharmacological items.]

1231 FURST, Peter T. (ed.). Flesh of the gods: the ritual use of hallucinogens. London: George Allen & Unwin; New York: Praeger 1972, xvi + 304 p., illus., bibl.; Fr. trans., La chair des dieux: l'usage ritual de psychédéliques (Collection "Science Ouverte"). Paris: Ed. du Seuil 1974, 285 p.
[See P. T. Furst, item 1232; R. E. Schultes, item 1318.]

1232 FURST, Peter T. To find our life: peyote among the Huichol Indians of Mexico, in P. T. Furst (ed.), item 1231, 136-184, illus.
[The early reports of peyote use in northern Mexico, and a full account of the 1968 Huichol peyote pilgrimage in which the author participated.]

1233 FURST, Peter T. An Indian journey to life's source. Natural History (New York) 82 (4), 1973, 34-43, illus.
[The Huichol's annual search for peyote.]

1234 FURST, Peter T. Hallucinogens and culture. (Series in cross-cultural themes). San Francisco: Chandler & Sharp 1976, 194 p., illus.
[Pp. 9-10 and ch. 10 (= pp. 109-119), peyote, the peyote cult and Native American Church; ch. 11 (= pp. 120-133), the Huichol peyote hunt and use.]

1235 FURST, Peter T. and MYERHOFF, Barbara G. Myth as history:
      the jimson weed cycle of the Huichols of Mexico. Antro-
      pologica (Caracas) 17 (junio), 1966, 3-39, illus., bibl.
      [A cycle of stories about Datura Person, who attempts to
      win the Huichols from using peyote. For Span. version see
      item 1236.]

1236 FURST, Peter T. and MYERHOFF, Barbara G. El mito como historia:
      el ciclo del peyote y la datura entre los huichols, in
      S. N. Sittón et al., El peyote y los Huichols. Mexico,
      D.F.: Secretaría de Educación Pública 1972, 192 p., illus.
      [On myths and rituals associated with peyote and datura
      among the Huichol.]

1237 GÁNDOLA, Isabel. El peyote: estudio sobre el uso del peyote,
      entre las tribus huicholes, coras, tepehuanes y tarahumaras.
      Mexico, D.F.: Editorial Orion 1965, 66 p., illus., map.
      [Based on Rouhier, item 1312, Lumholtz, item 1251, and
      Bravo, item 1273; includes botanical pharmaceutical and
      ritual aspects, and the Huichol journey to secure peyote.]

1238 GERSTE, Aquiles. Notes sur la médicine et la botanique des
      anciens Mexicains. Rome: Imprimerie Polyglotte Vaticane
      (1909), 2nd ed. 1910, 191 p.
      [Pp. 68-69, use of peyote for fatigue and also for
      revelatory and prophetic visions.]

1239 HERNÁNDEZ, Francisco. Opera.... Madrid: Ibarra's Heirs 1790.
      [Vol. 3, pp. 70-71 (= Book 15, ch. 25) describe peyote;
      repr. in Schleiffer, item 1314, pp. 30-31. By the
      Emperor's own physician.]

1240 HIJAR Y HARO, Luis. El peyote a través de los siglos. Revista
      Mexicana de Ingeniería y Arquitectura 15 (9), 1937, 543-
      563; idem 15 (11), 1937, 665-692; repr. in his Viajes por
      America. Mexico, D.F., 1940, 60-108.

1241 HOFMANN, A. Mexikanische Zauberdrogen und ihre Wirkstoffe.
      Planta Medica (Stuttgart) 12 (3), 1964, 341-352, illus.
      [Four psychodysleptics (including peyotl) still important
      among the Aztecs, etc. in Mexico, especially in State of
      Oaxaca; these lead to feelings of depersonalization and of
      union with the universe. See Abstracts of Folklore Studies
      3 (4), 1965, no. 548, p. 242.]

1242 INTERCAMBIO.... For those interested in peyotl. Intercambio:
      Organo de la British Chamber of Commerce (Mexico, D.F.)
      188, 1959, 45-51.

Peyote:...Cults in Northern Mexico

1243   KAMFFER, Raúl. Plumed arrows of the Huicholes of Western
          Mexico. Américas (Washington, D.C.) 9 (6), 1957, 12-16.
             [Pp. 14-15, traditional religion; p. 15 includes peyotism
          among Huichol traditional religious activities. Good
          illustrations.]

1244   KLINEBERG, Otto. Notes on the Huichol. American Anthropologist
          36 (3), 1934, 446-460, illus.
             [P. 449 on the most important fiesta, that of peyote in
          January.]

1245   LEONARD, Irving A. (ed. and trans.). Peyote and the Mexican
          Inquisition, 1620. American Anthropologist 44 (2), 1942,
          324-326.
             [The Mexican Inquisition's document banning peyote, in
          Spanish, with English trans. and introduction.]

1246   LEWIS, Norman. The survivors. The Sunday Times Supplement
          (London) 26 April 1970, 33-47, 49, 51-54, 57, 59, 61,
          illus.
             [Huichol Indians' traditional religion surviving,
          assisted by the ritual use of peyote; the conflict with
          Christian missions; features Ramon Medina, the shaman who
          assisted P. T. Furst (q.v.) in his two journeys.]

1247   LUMHOLTZ, Karl [Sofus]. The American cavedwellers: the
          Tarahumaris of the Sierra Madre. Bulletin, American Geo-
          graphical Society 26 (3), 1894, 299-325.
             [Pp. 319-324, Tarahumara peyotism in 19th century, its
          ritual and healing uses; by the Norwegian ethnographer-
          explorer who pioneered the study of Indians in N.-W.
          Mexico.]

1248   LUMHOLTZ, Karl [Sofus]. Tarahumari dances and plant-worship.
          Scribners Magazine 16 (4), 1894, 438-456, illus.
             [Pp. 451-456, the peyote cult in N. Mexico, and Christ-
          ians' recognition of it; with details supplementing Diguet's
          later account, item 1230.]

1249   LUMHOLTZ, Karl [Sofus]. The Huichol Indians of Mexico.
          Bulletin, American Museum of Natural History 10, 1898,
          1-14, 2 plates.
             [Pp. 7-10, Peyote (= hikuli) search, use and ritual.]

1250   LUMHOLTZ, Karl [Sofus]. Symbolism of the Huichol Indians
          (Memoirs, American Museum of Natural History, 3: Anthro-
          pology 2:1), 1900, 1-228, figs., plates, maps.

Peyote:...Cults in Northern Mexico

[The first description of the Huichol peyote pilgrimage,
together with supporting mythology, secured from informants in 1895, but without participation in the journey.
Includes the Huichol hikuli (= peyote), the expedition for
the plant, the January peyote festival, and the relation
of the visions and the cult to fire.]

1251 LUMHOLTZ, Karl [Sofus]. Unknown Mexico: a record of five
years' exploration ... . 2 vols. New York: C. Scribner's
Sons 1902, illus., maps, bibl.; London: Macmillan 1903;
Span. trans., El México desconocido.... 2 vols. New York:
C. Scribner's Sons 1904; repr., Mexico, D.F.: Publica-
ciones Herrerias 1945; repr., Mexico, D.F.: Edition
Nacional 1960.
[Eng. version: Vol. 1, pp. 356-372, Tarahumara peyotism;
vol. 2, pp. 126-136, Huichol peyote pilgrimage (and sum-
mary in Safford, item 1087, p. 30, n3); pp. 375-383, fiesta
of "the miraculous Christ", a syncretistic development.
A fuller account than in previous item.]

1252 MYERHOFF, Barbara G. The deer-maize-peyote symbol complex
among the Huichol Indians of New Mexico. Anthropological
Quarterly 43 (2), 1970, 64-78 (digest in Bulletin, American
Anthropological Association 1 (3), 1968, 96-97.
[Pp. 64-65, on peyote, especially the annual peyote hunt
as a climactic ceremony resolving contradictions in Huichol
life.]

1253 MYERHOFF, Barbara G. Peyote Hunt: the sacred journey of the
Huichol Indians (Symbol, Myth and Ritual Series). Ithaca
and London: Cornell University Press (1974) 1976, 285 p.,
illus., bibl.
[Based on information from a Huichol shaman-priest, Ramon
Medina, and from accompanying him (with P. Furst, q.v.) on
the peyote pilgrimage in 1966.]

1254 MYERHOFF, Barbara G. Organization and ecstasy, in S. F. Moore
and B. G. Myerhoff (eds.), Symbol and politics in communal
ideology. Ithaca and London: Cornell University Press
1975, 33-67.
[Pp. 38-45, the Huichol peyote pilgrimage, by an anthropologist participant.]

1255 ORTEGA, José de. Apostólicos afanes de la Compañía de
Jesús...de su Provincia de México. Barcelona: P. Nadal
1754, 445 p.; repr. as Historia del Nayarit. Mexico, D.F.:
Tipografía de E. Abadiano 1887, 564 p.

Peyote:...Cults in Northern Mexico

[Bk. 1, ch. 3, includes a description of a ritual dance under influence of peyote; Eng. trans. of extract in Schleiffer, item 1314, pp. 31-32.]

1256   RENO, Stephen J. Casteñada and Don Juan: some preliminary observations. Religious Studies 11 (4), 1975, 449-466.
        [A sympathetic analysis of Casteñada's experiences and apprenticeship, from the viewpoint of phenomenology of religion.]

1257   SAHAGÚN, Bernardino de. Historia general de las cosas de Nueva Espana. Many editions, including Mexico City: A. Valdés, 3 vols. 1829-1830; Fr. trans., Histoire générale de les choses de la Nouvelle Espagne. Paris: G. Masson 1880, 898 p.; Eng. trans., General history of the things of New Spain. Santa Fe, New Mexico: School of American Research and University of Utah, 10 vols. 1950-61.
        [Extracts on peyote in Safford, item 1087, p. 308, from Fr. trans., vol. 2, p. 366; and in Schleiffer, item 1314, p. 30, from Eng. trans. (1961), Bk. 11, ch. 7. The peyote passage also in Ger. trans., E. Seler, Die Huichol-Indianer...in Mexico. Berlin: Asher & Behrend 1901, 359. The first serious European account of peyote, by the outstanding 16th c. Spanish chronicler.]

1258   SANTOSCOY, Alberto (comp.). Nayarit. Colección de documentos inéditos, historicos y etnográficos, acerca de la Sierra de ese Nombre. Guadalajara: J. Maria Yguiniz 1899, 68 p., bibl.
        [Cited by P. Furst, item 1231, p. 144, as containing the first published account of the Huichol peyote hunt, by Rosandro Corona.]

1259   SLOTKIN, James S[ydney]. Early eighteenth century documents of peyotism north of the Rio Grande. American Anthropologist 53 (3), 1951, 420-427.
        [Translation of two of the earliest known primary sources, dating from 1716, and from 1720 (full report of court proceedings against Indians taking peyote).]

1260   SLOTKIN, J[ames] S[ydney]. Peyotism, 1521-1891. American Anthropologist 57 (2), 1955, 202-230, map, tables.
        [Invaluable survey of early history and sources, with extracts. Pp. 223-230, bibliography, classified in centuries.]

1261   SLOTKIN, J[ames] S[ydney]. Peyotism, 1521-1891: supplement. American Anthropologist 58, 1956, 184.

[Adding and quoting a primary source concerning "Santa Nina de Peyotes", to his item 1260, also errata in same.]

1262 ZINGG, Robert Mowry. Report of the Mr. and Mrs. Henry Pfeiffer expedition ... The Huichols: primitive artists (Contributions to Ethnography, 1. University of Denver). New York: G. E. Stechert & Co. 1938, lxiv + 826 p., illus., maps, bibl.

[An American ethnologist who was able to support and extend Lumholtz's version of the peyote "hunt", but not to share in the hunt itself. Pp. 403-433, the pilgrimage to secure peyote.]

PEYOTE: BOTANICAL, PHARMACOLOGICAL, PSYCHOLOGICAL, ETC. ASPECTS

The variety of names given to peyote, sometimes erroneously, and the confusions between this and other hallucinogenic plants, can best be approached in botanical and pharmacological terms. Anhalonium Lewinii refers to the carrot-like cactus plant in its older stages, and Lophophora Williamsii to the same plant when younger; Anhalonium Williamsii and other botanical terms also occur. The Aztec term was peyotl, and so it appears in the early Spanish literature. In recent times it has been misnamed as mescal, mescal buttons, dry whiskey, white mule, etc. Although it contains the hallucinogenic alkaloid mescaline it is quite different from the mescal or red bean of the evergreen shrub (Sophora secundiflora) which contains a toxic narcotic alkaloid, and which figured in a mescal bean cult before the peyote cult developed. It is now agreed that peyote itself is non-narcotic.

To add to the confusion the term mescal is also applied to an intoxicating drink (pulque) and a non-intoxicating bread made in Mexico and the southeast U.S.A. from the mescal plant proper (Agave americana). Finally there is datura (Datura Stramonium) also known as jimsonweed (corrupted from Jamestown, Virginia, where the plant is said to have arrived from India); this had ritual and healing uses similar to those of peyote, but in the contiguous areas of northwest Mexico and southern California rather than in the areas where the new peyote cult spread. A fuller study of all these plants and cults is given in LaBarre's main work, item 942; he chooses Lophophora Williamsii as the botanical name.

It should be noted that the psychological studies often reveal how different the effects are for non-Indians who do not share the ritual and cultural context of the peyote cult itself.

Peyote: Botanical,...

1263   BARBER, Carroll G. Peyote and the definition of narcotics.
       American Anthropologist 61 (4), 1959, 641-646.

1264   BARBER, Carroll G. Letters to the Editor: Rejoinder to Maurer.
       American Anthropologist 62 (4), 1960, 685-687.
         [See D. W. Maurer, item 1301. Peyote is a "narcotic"
       according to popular usage of this term; social and cul-
       tural research on peyote is as important as laboratory,
       pharmacological and medicinal research.]

1265   BARRON, Frank et al. The hallucinogenic drugs. Scientific
       American 210 (4), 1964, 24, 29-37, illus.
         [P. 24, the qualifications of the authors; pp. 29-37,
       survey of physiological and psychological effects of the
       alkaloids; p. 32, brief account of peyote cult.]

1266   BENDER, George A. Rough and ready research — 1887 style.
       Journal of the History of Medicine and Allied Sciences
       23 (2), 1968, 159-166.
         [A member of the Parke, Davis pharmaceutical firm de-
       scribes the firm's search for peyote in 1887-1888, and the
       early researchers of the time.]

1267   BENÍTEZ, Fernando. Los Indios de México: [Part 2] En la
       tierra mágica del peyote (Biblioteca Era. Ensayo).
       Mexico, D.F.: Ediciones ERA 1968, 286 p., illus. Eng.
       trans., In the magic land of peyote (with introduction by
       P. T. Furst) (Texas Pan-American Series). Austin: Univer-
       sity of Texas Press 1975, xxvii + 198 p., + 28 photos by
       P. T. Furst between pp. 68-69; also New York: Warner Books
       1976.
         [A detailed informal account of the Huichol peyote
       pilgrimage and its subsequent Festival of Parched Corn, by
       a well-known Mexican author (not an anthropologist) who is
       the first non-Indian to go on this annual journey (1965?).
       Eng. trans. pp. 53-72 (= Span. pp. 64-83) are a documented
       interruption on the drug craze among Western youth. Note
       pp. 107-118, the first reconstructed accounts of Huichol
       myths of "Noah" and of the corn; and pp. 172-177, his own
       experience of taking peyote. Furst's introduction surveys
       the history of the study of the pilgrimage.]

1268   BENNETT, Wendell C. and ZINGG, Robert M. The Tarahumara, an
       Indian tribe of Northern Mexico. Chicago: University of
       Chicago Press 1935, 412 p., illus.
         [Pp. 252-334 on religion as syncretistic; pp. 135-136,
       253, 291-295, 347, 366-367, peyote, its dance and shamans
       in traditional forms.]

1269 BENZI, Marino. Voisins [sic, for visions] des Huichols sous
      l'effet du peyotl. L'Hygiène Mentale (Supplément de
      L'Encéphale) (Paris) 58 (3), 1969, 61-97.
      [The pre-Christian traditional use; pp. 80-97, detailed
      reports of seven visions, with comments; p. 97, conclusions,
      emphasizing the religious and non-erotic nature of the
      visions; note p. 65, n2 on post-conquest identification of
      Peyotl divinity with Catholic saints or members of the
      Trinity.]

1270 BENZI, Marino. Les derniers adorateurs du peyotl. Croyances,
      coutumes et mythes des Indiens Huichol. Paris: Gallimard
      1972, 446 p., maps, 52 plates, bibl.
      [Ch. 4: the distribution of peyote and its use by
      Mexican Indians; ch. 5, the sacred peyote cycle and pil-
      grimage among the Huichol; ch. 6, peyote visions in Huichol
      experience; pp. 272-283, 318-321 on Christian elements;
      pp. 322-328, 330-333, peyote cult among United States
      Indians, with extract from John Rave's account. The author
      accompanied F. Benítez on the peyote hunt — see latter's
      item, 1267, especially p. 85.]

1271 BERINGER, Kurt. Der Meskalinrausch, seine Geschichte und
      Erscheinungsweise (Monographien aus dem Gesamtgebiete der
      Neurologie und Psychiatrie, 49). Berlin: J. Springer
      1927, 315 p., illus.
      [A comprehensive study from the psychological viewpoint:
      pp. 31-118, reports of tests at the Heidelberg psychiatric
      clinic from 1920; pp. 119-315, 37 first-hand reports by
      individuals taking mescaline.]

1272 BOYER, Jacques. Le peyotl, cactus mexicain qui provoque des
      rêves visuels merveilleux. Nature (Paris) 2706=55, 1927,
      403-406.

1273 BRAVO H, Helia. Las cactáceas de Mexico. Mexico City:
      University Press 1937, xiv + 755 p., illus.
      [Includes account of peyote.]

1274 BRIGGS, J. R. Mescale buttons — physiological effects.
      Medical Register 1, 8 April 1887, 276-277; repr. Druggists'
      Bulletin 1 (5), 1887, 78f.
      [A medical doctor's experiments on himself with peyote;
      report of use by Indians.]

1275 BULLETIN ON NARCOTICS. Peyotl. Bulletin on Narcotics (United
      Nations Division on Narcotic Drugs, Geneva) 11 (2), 1959,
      16-29, illus.

Peyote: Botanical,...

[An authoritative account of pharmacology, physiological
and psychological effects, habituation and addiction;
pp. 18, 28, on cultic use.]

1276   CAIRNS, Huntington. A divine intoxicant. The Atlantic
        Monthly (New York & Boston) 144 (5), Nov. 1929, 638-645.
        [Outlines the results of the early experimentation —
        S. W. Mitchell, William James and H. Ellis; reports his
        own experience, especially the visions and their relation
        to art and music; the attempts to have peyote banned, en-
        couraged by missionaries; the future value in psychological
        and physiological experiments.]

1277   CRAHAN, M. E. God's flesh and other precolumbian phantastica.
        The Masterkey (Southwest Museum, Los Angeles) 42 (3),
        1968, 96-103.
        [P. 98, brief reference to peyote; otherwise surveys
        medical and hallucinogenic drugs among Indians; quotes
        Schultes and Wasson.]

1278   CRICHTLEY, Macdonald. Some forms of drug addiction: mescalism.
        British Journal of Inebriety (London) 28 (3), 1931, 99-
        108, bibl.
        [A neurologist's report on the effects of peyote on him-
        self and colleagues, describing the emotional content as
        "amazement, awe, interest and delight", but asserting pro-
        longed use becomes addictive and harmful.]

1279   DIGUET, Léon. Les cactacées utiles du Mexique...(Archives
        d'Histoire Naturelles, 4). Paris: Société Nationale
        d'Acclimation de France 1928 (appeared 1929), 551 p.,
        illus.
        [Includes peyote.]

1280   DIXON, Walter E. The physiological action of the alkaloids
        from Anhalonium Lewinii. Journal of Physiology 25,
        1899-1900, 68-86; summarized in item 1195.
        [On peyote. P. 69, reference to Kiowa, etc.; rest is
        physiological, etc.]

1281   ELLIS, Havelock. Mescal: a new artificial paradise. The
        Contemporary Review (New York) 73 (January), 1898, 130-
        141; also in Smithsonian Institution Annual Report 1898,
        537-548; pp. 131-134 repr. in Schleiffer, item 1314,
        pp. 34-38.
        [An account of his visionary experiences after taking
        peyote as an experiment. A briefer version of the follow-
        ing item.]

1282   ELLIS, Havelock. Mescal: a study of a divine plant. Popular
       Science Monthly (New York) 61 (5), 1902, 52-71.
            [Outlines the history of the investigation of peyote;
       detailed reports of his own experimental consumption and
       of another subject's experience; comparison with effects
       of cannabis, alcohol, etc.; discussion of the visual
       phenomena and of the future use of peyote.]

1283   FERNBERGER, Samuel W. Observations on taking peyote (Anhalon-
       ium lewinii). American Journal of Psychology 34 (2), 1923,
       267-270; idem, 34 (4), 1923, 616.
            [One of the first descriptions of the effects of peyote
       on a trained psychologist, recording distortions of time
       and space, and feeling of inferiority.]

1284   FERNBERGER, Samuel W. Further observations on peyote intoxi-
       cation. Journal of Abnormal and Social Psychology 26 (4),
       1932, 367-378.
            [A psychological and physiological study of the effects
       of peyote, by a group of nine University of Pennsylvania
       faculty members who took the peyote under Indian conditions.

1285   HAVARD, V. Drink plants of the North American Indians.
       Bulletin of the Torrey Botanical Club (Lancaster, Pennsyl-
       vania) 23 (2), 29 Feb. 1896, 33-46.
            [A popular account of his earlier research and of the
       work of others. Cited, and quoted on peyote, by O. C.
       Stewart, item 1148, p. 212.]

1286   HOCH, P. H. Experimental induction of psychoses, in S. Cobb
       (ed.), The biology of mental health and disease (Annual
       Conference of the Millbank Fund, 27). New York: Hoeber
       1952, 539-547.
            [The effect of peyote on non-Indians under clinical
       conditions.]

1287   HUXLEY, Aldous [Leonard]. Mescaline and the other world, in
       L. Cholden (ed.), Proceedings of the Round Table on
       lysergic acid diethylamide and mescaline in experimental
       psychiatry. New York: Grune & Stratton 1956, 46-50.
            [The capacity of peyote to produce a life-enlarging
       sojourn in "the Antipodes of the mind".]

1288   IRELAND, Edward J. Peyote — divine plant of the Southwestern
       Indians. Journal of the New Orleans College of Pharmacy
       6 (5), 1940-42, 4-5, 15.
            [An outline of the pharmacological and psychological
       aspects.]

Peyote: Botanical,...

1289   JAMES, Henry (ed.). Familiar letters of William James. The
       Atlantic Monthly (New York and Boston) 126, July 1920,
       1-15; August 1920, 163-175, 305-317.
          [P. 171, James' own experience of taking peyote, result-
       ing in nothing but nausea.]

1290   KAPADIA, Govind J. and FAYEZ, M. B. E. The chemistry of
       peyote alkaloids. Lloydia: the Journal of Natural
       Products (Cincinnati) 36 (1), 1973, 9ff.
          [A paper at a pharmaceutical, etc., symposium on peyote
       at Houston, Texas; reporting on the latest analysis bring-
       ing the total of identified constituents to 56.]

1291   KARWOSKI, Theodore. Psychophysics and mescal intoxication.
       The Journal of General Psychology 15 (1), 1936, 212-220.
          [Peyote as an aphrodisiac and with varied effects on dif-
       ferent individuals; reports of experiments to establish an
       appropriate methodology for testing peyote effects, leading
       to the three principles of (1) minimal stimulus (2) equi-
       effective stimuli (3) selected subjects.]

1292   KELSEY, F[remont] E[llis]. The pharmacology of peyote. South
       Dakota Journal of Medicine and Pharmacy 12 (6), 1959, 231-
       233; repr. in News Letter of the National Fellowship of
       Indian Workers 72, Spring 1960, 4-5.
          [Its similarity to marijuana and not a true narcotic; its
       visual imagery.]

1293   KLÜVER, Heinrich. Mescal visions and eidetic vision. American
       Journal of Psychology 37 (4), 1926, 502-515, bibl.
          [A personal experimental taking of peyote, from a
       psychological viewpoint; the further experimental
       possibilities.]

1294   KLÜVER, Heinrich. Mescal, the "divine" plant and its psycho-
       logical effects (Psyche Miniatures. General Series, 22).
       London: Kegan Paul, Trench, Trubner & Co. 1928, 111 p.,
       bibl.
          [A brief account of the Tarahumara use of peyote, based
       on Shonle, followed by analysis of peyote visions in
       experimental subjects, changes in sense fields, the
       psychosis of the mescal state, and the importance for
       research.]

1295   KLÜVER, Heinrich. Mescal and mechanisms of hallucinations
       (Phoenix Science Series). Chicago: University of Chicago
       Press (1966) 1969, 108 p., bibl.; a re-issue, with minor
       corrections, of his Mescal. London: Kegan Paul 1928,

111 p., together with his Mechanisms of hallucination,
from Q. McNemar and M. A. Merrill (eds.), Studies in
personality. New York: McGraw Hill 1942, 175-207.
   [Pp. 8, 10-17, brief survey of "mescal buttons" or
peyote, quoting Shonle's account of Tarahumara ceremonies;
otherwise deals with psychological effects; pp. 15-17;
repr. in Schleiffer, item 1314, pp. 32-34.]

1296   KNAUER, Alwyn and MALONEY, William M. A. A preliminary note
       on the psychic action of mescaline, with special reference
       to the mechanism of visual hallucinations. The Journal of
       Nervous and Mental Disease 40 (7), 1913, 425-436.
          [Detailed reports of the hallucinations experienced by
       the authors and other physicians during experimental con-
       sumption of peyote. P. 436 notes the total absence of
       sexual content, and the enormous overestimation of time.]

1297   LEUBA, James H[enry]. The psychology of religious mysticism.
       London: Kegan Paul, Trench, Trubner & Co. Ltd., and New
       York: Harcourt Brace & Co. Inc. 1925, xii + 336 p.
          [Mystical ecstasy as produced by physical means; pp. 18-
       23, alcohol; pp. 23-25, "mescal" (for peyote) based on
       Weir Mitchell's and Havelock Ellis' experiences.]

1298   LEWIN, L[udwig]. Anhalonium lewinii. Therapeutic Gazette
       (Detroit) 12 (4), 1888, 231-237.
          [A very early report by the Berlin scientist after whom
       the peyote cactus was named.]

1299   McGLOTHLIN, William H. Hallucinogenic drugs: a perspective
       with special reference to peyote and cannabis. Psychedelic
       Review (New York) no. 6, 1965, 16-57.

1300   MANGANOTTI, Donatella. La triadi sacra degli antichi Aztechi.
       L'Universo (Firenze, Italy) 46 (3), maggio/giugno 1966,
       501-536, illus., bibl.
          [Summarizes current knowledge of the chemical composition
       and psychedelic effects of peyote and other hallucinogens,
       and gives Italian translations of 16th century Spanish
       writers' descriptions.]

1301   MAURER, D[avid] W. Peyote is not a drug of addiction.
       American Anthropologist 62 (4), 1960, 684-685.
          [A letter in answer to C. G. Barber, item 1264.]

1302   MAURER, David W. and VOGEL, Victor H[ugh]. Narcotics and
       narcotic addiction (American Lecture Series, 513).

Peyote: Botanical,...

Springfield, Illinois: Charles C. Thomas 1954, xv +
303 p.; 2nd ed. 1962, 339 p.
[2nd ed., pp. 123-126, peyote as a non-addictive drug,
its physical and visionary effects, and reports of experimental use by William James and others, see also H. James,
item 1289.]

1303   MELLEN, Chase, III. Reflections of a peyote eater. Harvard
Review 1 (4), 1963, 63-67.
[A Drugs and the Mind Issue.]

1304   MICHAUX, Henri. Misérable miracle (la mescaline). Monaco:
Editions du Rocher 1956, 123 p. Eng. trans., Miserable
miracle (mescaline). San Francisco: City Lights Books
1963, 89 p., illus.
[The author's experiences with mescaline, including 32
autograph pages written while the experience was at its
height; pp. 45-57, comparison with Indian hemp (marijuana);
vivid accounts of "intolerable, unbearable" experiences,
with reflections on the experiments.]

1305   MITCHELL, S[ilas] Weir. Remarks on the effects of Anhelonium
[sic] Lewinii (the mescal button) [i.e. peyote]. British
Medical Journal 2, 5 Dec. 1896, 1625-1629.
[A medical doctor's report of his experiences after
taking peyote — physical unpleasantness, but beautiful
mental visions; also reports less pleasant result by a
colleague, Dr. Eshner.]

1306   NEWSWEEK. Mescal madness. Newsweek 48 (1), 23 Feb. 1953, 92,
94-95, illus.
[On peyote and its experimental values; five photographs
by Leif Geiges attempting to simulate the mental patterns
in the visions described by white peyote users.]

1307   OSMOND, Humphry and SMYTHIES, John [R.]. Schizophrenia: a
new approach. Journal of Mental Science 411=n.s. 375=98,
April 1952, 309-315; see also idem., 418=100, January 1954.
[Especially pp. 311-313, on the close clinical relationship between acute mescaline (i.e. peyote) intoxication
and acute schizophrenia as offering an approach to study of
the latter.]

1308   POPULAR SCIENCE MONTHLY. The mescal ceremony. Popular
Science Monthly 50, 1896, 140.
[Brief report of a paper on the Mexican origin and
physiological effects of peyote, made to the Washington
Chemical Society by James Mooney.]

1309   PRENTISS, D[aniel] W[ebster] and MORGAN, F[rancis] P[atterson].
       Anhalonium Lewinii, a study of a drug with special refer-
       ence to its physiological action on man. Therapeutic
       Gazette (Detroit) 3rd series, 19 (9), 1895, 577-585.
       [Report of the first scientific investigation of the
       effect of peyote on human beings.]

1310   PRENTISS, D[aniel] W[ebster] and MORGAN, Francis P[atterson].
       Mescal buttons (Anhalonium Lewinii): therapeutic uses.
       Therapeutic Gazette (Detroit) 3rd series, 20 (1), 1896,
       4-7; also similarly in Medical Record (New York) 22 August
       1896, 258-266.
       [Despite the mescal terminology, on peyote.]

1311   PRENTISS, D[aniel] W[ebster] and MORGAN, F[rancis] P[atterson].
       The alkaloids of Anhalonium Lewinii (mescal buttons), with
       notes upon therapeutic uses. Transactions of the Medical
       Society of the District of Columbia 1, 1897, 123-127.
       [On peyote.]

1312   ROUHIER, Alexandre. La plante qui fait les yeux émerveillés:
       le peyotl (Echinocactus Williamsii Lem.). Paris: Gaston
       Doin et Cie, 1927, xii + 371 p., illus., map, music, bibl.
       [A comprehensive study with pharmaceutical emphasis;
       includes reports of tests on Europeans experiencing para-
       normal faculties (the latter first published in Revue
       Métaphysique); summary in United States, item 1184,
       pp. 18228-18229.]

1313   RUSBY, H[arry] H[urd]. Mescale buttons. Bulletin of Pharmacy
       (Detroit) 8, 1894, 306.
       [One of the earliest reports on peyote, by a medical
       botanist.]

1314   SCHLEIFFER, Hedwig (comp.). Sacred narcotic plants of the New
       World Indians. An anthology of texts from the sixteenth
       century to date. New York: Hafner Press, and London:
       Collier-Macmillan 1973, 156 p., illus.
       [Pp. 26-49, texts on peyote, including extracts from
       Higgins, item 896; Aberle, item 770; Bromberg, item 808;
       La Barre, item 942; de Sahagún, item 1257 (Eng. trans.);
       Hernandez, item 1239, vol. 3, pp. 70-71; Ortega, item 1255;
       Klüver, item 1295, pp. 15-17; Ellis, item 1281, pp. 131-
       134; Radin, item 1072, pp. 389-391; Daiker, item 842,
       pp. 66-68; Michaux, item 1304, pp. 57-59; Furst, item 1231,
       pp. 145-146.]

Peyote: Botanical,...

1315   SCHULTES, Richard Evans. Peyote and plants used in the peyote
        ceremony. Botanical Museum Leaflets. Harvard University
        4 (8), 1937.

1316   SCHULTES, Richard Evans. Peyote (Lophophora Williamsii) and
        plants confused with it. Botanical Museum Leaflets.
        Harvard University 5 (5), 1937, 61-88, illus., bibl.
            [Lists 16 different botanical names under which peyote
        has been classified, and attempts to remove the confusion,
        due to association of other plants in religious use, and
        the fragmentary and conflicting nature of early Spanish
        records of the use of narcotic plants in Mexico.]

1317   SCHULTES, Richard Evans. Hallucinogens of plant origin: in-
        terdisciplinary studies of plants sacred in primitive
        cultures yield results of academic and practical interest.
        Science 3864=163 (17 Jan.) 1969, 245-254, illus., bibl.
            [A good survey across all cultures; p. 249, mescal bean;
        pp. 250-251, peyote, with briefer references on pp. 247,
        249.]

1318   SCHULTES, Richard Evans. An overview of hallucinogens in the
        Western hemisphere, in P. Furst (ed.), item 1231, 3-54.
            [Pp. 11-17, 32, peyote, and its relation to the mescal
        bean — a useful survey.]

1319   SCHULTES, Richard Evans. For a full bibliography of his many
        relevant writings see the 31 items listed in P. T. Furst
        (ed.), item 1231, pp. 290-292.

1320   SLOSSEN, Edwin E. The peyote paradise. Collier's 84, 27 July
        1929, 44, illus.
            [Quotes Havelock Ellis' experience; also that of
        H. Klüver, and the conversion of an Ingersoll atheist.]

1321   SLOTKIN, James S[ydney] and CUTTING, W. C. Mescalin: an
        answer to cigarettes? the anthropologist; the physician.
        Saturday Review Feb. 6, 1954, 14-15.
            [Both doubt the efficiency of mescalin in the form of
        peyote as an alternative "means of escape" for whites, or
        as introducing A. Huxley's (item 1287) "artificial
        paradise".]

1322   SMITH, Philip B. A Sunday with mescaline. Bulletin of the
        Menninger Clinic 23 (1), 1959, 20-27.
            [Personal report of non-cultic use of mescaline (akin to
        peyote) by a medical doctor; the permanent effect was
        positive.]

1323 SMYTHIES, J[ohn] R. The mescaline phenomena. <u>British Journal</u>
<u>for the Philosophy of Science</u> 3 (12), 1953, 339-347.
[Mescaline, from the peyote cactus, as the only harmless
hallucinogenic drug; the author's scientific experiments,
and extracts from those of others (Prentiss and Morgan,
S. W. Mitchell, H. Ellis, Rouhier, Beringer, etc.) —
stressing the beauty of the visions and the ecstasy of the
experience.]

1324 SODI, Demetrio [= Demetrio Sodi, M.]. Les investigaciones con
plantas alucinantes Mexicanas. <u>Boletin del Centro de</u>
<u>Investigaciones Antropologicas de Mexico</u> (Mexico City) 7,
May 1960, 14-18.
[A general survey with quotations from some 14 authors
on peyote, from Sahagún onwards.]

1325 TAYLOR, Norman. <u>Narcotics: nature's dangerous gifts</u> (Laurel
edition 6270). New York: Dell Publishing Co. (1963)
1970, 222 p.
[Pp. 137-149, mescaline, the "hallucinogenic drug derived from a cactus".]

1326 VALLEY NATIONAL BANK. The controversy revolving around
"peyote". <u>VNB Agriculture and Livestock Monthly News</u>
<u>Digest</u> (Phoenix, Arizona) 7 (4), April 1960, 1-2.
[Summary statement; then quotes Dr. Charles McCammon,
area medical officer, U.S. Public Health Service, Billings,
Montana, that he had experienced nausea and visual effects,
but not "in the sense of seeing people". Also quotes
Dr. James A. McCleary, professor of botany, University of
Arizona, that peyote had marked antibiotic effects on a
wide variety of bacteria.]

1327 WESTON, Ronald. Of transcendental beauty and crawling horror.
<u>Fact</u> (New York) 1 (1), 1964, 30-35, illus.
[On the euphoric effects of peyote on a white "Buddhist
mystic" compared with the horrific experiences resulting
from belladonna.]

1328 WILSON, A. J. C. Ayahuasca, peyotl, yage. <u>Proceedings of the</u>
<u>Society for Psychical Research</u> no. 176=48, 1949, 353-363,
bibl.
[Pp. 353-358, a survey of the reports to date on the
physiological and psychological effects of peyote.]

PROPHET DANCES

This term has been loosely used, but not inappropriately, for movements in many areas; here it is confined to movements in the north-west and the Plateau and mostly in the earlier nineteenth century. There has been controversy as to whether these should be regarded as entirely aboriginal, or as movements developing after some contact with whites, whether the contact was direct or indirect. This latter form of contact has been important elsewhere, as in Melanesia, and more recent opinion seems to favour its relevance to these early Indian movements.

1329   ABERLE, David F[riend]. The prophet dance and reactions to white contact. <u>Southwestern Journal of Anthropology</u> 15 (1), 1959, 74–83.
    [Agrees with Strong, item 331, that the Plateau prophet dance may have been due to indirect and diffused white influences; the possible connection with later Ghost Dances. See Spier <u>et al</u>., item 91, for their comments.]

1330   BASHFORD, J. W. Literature of missions: a romance of modern missions. <u>Missionary Review of the World</u> n.s. 1 (7), July 1888, 481ff.
    [Pp. 481–483, on the Nez Percé-Flathead delegation in 1831 to St. Louis, seeking the white man's "book of heaven" (a possible reflection of earlier new cults — Prophet Dance, Tulim cult); see also Young, item 376.]

1331   LOEB, Edwin M[eyer]. <u>The western Kuksu cult</u> (University of California Publications in American Archaeology and Ethnology 33 (1)). Berkeley: University of California Press 1932, 138 p., map.
    [An early Prophet dance among the peoples of the Plateau and Northwest; nothing especially acculturative.]

1332   LOEB, Edwin M[eyer]. <u>The eastern Kuksu cult</u> (University of California Publications in American Archaeology and Ethnology 33 (2)). Berkeley: University of California Press 1933, pp. 139–231, and large folding table.
    [Similar to previous item.]

1333   MURDOCK, George Peter. Tenino shamanism. <u>Ethnology</u> 4 (2), 1965, 165–171.
    [Pp. 165–166, summary of the Tenino involvement in the Prophet Dance in 19th c. — a Sahaptin-speaking tribe who lived near Columbia River, Oregon.]

1334   RAY, Verne F. The Kolaskin cult: a prophet movement of
1870 in north-eastern Washington. <u>American Anthropologist</u>
38 (1), 1936, 67-75.
[A Sanpoil, etc. cult of the Prophet Dance type, named
after its founder, who had the classic return from "death"
with a revelation from a new god; moral reform, and millennial promises. The founder later repudiated the continuing cult and returned to shamanism.]

1335   SCHAEFFER, Claude E. The Kutenai female berdache: courier,
guide, prophetess and warrior. <u>Ethnohistory</u> 12 (3), 1965,
193-236.
[Early decades of 19th c. in western Montana, Idaho and
British Columbia — a "man-woman" (died 1837); pp. 207-212,
her possible part in dissemination of the early prophet
dance.]

1336   SPIER, Leslie. <u>The Prophet Dance of the northwest and its
derivatives: the source of the Ghost Dance</u> (General Series
in Anthropology, 1). Menasha, Wisconsin: George Banta
Publishing Co. 1935, 74 p., map, illus., bibl.
[Re-opened the Ghost Dance question; traced origins to
pre-Christian British Columbia, through an aboriginal
prophet dance, usually circular, with prophecies of world
renewal, which spread to the Plateau and waxed and waned
under a series of inspired leaders.]

1337   SPIER, Leslie, HERSKOVITS, Melville J. and SUTTLES, Wayne.
Comment on Aberle's thesis of deprivation. <u>Southwestern
Journal of Anthropology</u> 15 (1), 1959, 84-88.
[Rejection of Aberle's suggestion (item 1329) that the
Plateau Prophet Dance may have been a response to indirect
contact with whites in the 18th c., and reassertion of
Spier's original aboriginal thesis of item 1336.]

1338   SUTTLES, Wayne. The Plateau prophet dance among the Coast
Salish. <u>Southwestern Journal of Anthropology</u> 13 (4),
1957, 352-396.
[Summarizes Spier's account (see item 1336) of Plateau
Prophet Dance; gives new data from the Coast Salish, with
reconstruction of the general history. Examines the possibility of Christian influences, and the nature of a
"prophet" (pp. 382f.); indisputably Christian elements
(pp. 386-387).]

1139   WALKER, Deward E[dgar], Jr. New light on the prophet dance
controversy. <u>Ethnohistory</u> 16 (3), 1969, 245-255, bibl.

Prophet Dances

> [Claiming inspiration for the dance from indirect, proto-
> historical influences stemming from Euro-Americans, rather
> than from aboriginal sources.]

1340 WYETH, Nathaniel J[arvis]. The correspondence and journals of
      Captain Nathaniel J. Wyeth, 1831-6. Ed. by F. G. Young.
      (Sources of the History of Oregon, 1 (3-6)). Eugene,
      Oregon, 1899, 262 p.
      [Pp. 247-248, Sahaptin and Yakimas involved in the
      Prophet Dance — cited by D. F. French, item 198, p. 393.]

PUEBLO REVOLT AND POPÉ

This revolt by the Indian village communities of the southwest
against the Spaniards in 1680 seems to have been the first recorded
protest movement with religious dimensions that include features of
some novelty. These, however, are somewhat obscure and the military
aspects tend to overshadow the religious and the religious leader,
Popé, in the sources available. Kindred movements will be found in
the section on North Mexico below.

1341 BANDELIER, A[dolf] F. An outline of the documentary history
      of the Zuñi tribe. Journal of American Ethnology and
      Archaeology (Boston and New York) 3, 1892, 1-115.
      [Pp. 102-115, on the Popé revolt.]

1342 BOWDEN, Henry Warner. Spanish missions, cultural conflict and
      the Pueblo Revolt of 1680. Church History 44 (2), 1975,
      217-228.
      [The difference between the Spanish and the Pueblo
      religious systems and world-views as primary cause of the
      conflict; p. 227, passing reference to Popé.]

1343 CRANE, Leo. Desert drums. The pueblo Indians of New Mexico
      1540-1928. Boston: Little, Brown & Co. 1928, 393 p.,
      illus., map.
      ["A classic account", including the Pueblo revolt.]

1344 DOZIER, Edward P. The Pueblo Indians of North America (Case
      Studies in Cultural Anthropology). New York: Holt,
      Rinehart & Winston 1970, xv + 224 p., maps.
      [Pp. 55-60, the Pueblo revolt of 1680.]

1345 HACKETT, Charles W[ilson]. The revolt of the Pueblo Indians
      of New Mexico in 1680. The Quarterly of the Texas State
      Historical Association 15, October 1911, 99-100, 130-131.
      [A standard account.]

1346   HACKETT, Charles W[ilson] and SHELBY, Charmion C[lair] (eds.).
       Revolt of the Pueblo Indians of New Mexico and Otermin's
       attempted reconquest, 1680-1682 (Coronado Cuarto Centennial
       Publications, vols. 8 and 9). Albuquerque: University of
       New Mexico Press 1942, 262, 430 p.
            [Original contemporary records reproduced, on the revolt
       of 1680 led by the Tewa religious leader, Popé; see index,
       "Popé, El", etc.]

1347   JAMES, Harry C. Pages from Hopi history. Tucson: University
       of Arizona Press 1974, 272 p., illus.
            [Information largely from older Hopi. Pp. 51-54, the
       Pueblo revolt and Popé.]

1348   RYAN, J. C. Revolt along the Rio Grande. San Antonio, Texas:
       The Naylor Company 1964, 234 p., illus., maps.
            [Pp. 81-93, Popé; popular account.]

1349   SILVERBERG, Robert. The pueblo revolt. New York: Weybright
       and Talley 1971, 216 p.
            [Pp. 70-72, 94-98, 111-117, 132-144 concern Popé, the
       religious leader.]

REDBIRD SMITH AND THE NIGHTHAWK KEETOWAH SOCIETY

     This Cherokee movement in the later nineteenth and earlier twen-
tieth century is known by the name of the prime mover, Redbird Smith,
and otherwise as the Nighthawk or "true" Keetowah Society. It was a
movement without either a prophet or visions. It is a pity that the
main study, a master's degree thesis by a part-Cherokee anthropologist,
Robert K. Thomas (see item 1356) remains unpublished.

1350   BUCHANAN, Robert Wayne. Patterns of organization and leader-
          ship among contemporary Oklahoma Cherokees. University of
       Kansas, Ph.D. dissertation (anthropology) 1972, 212 p.
            [Pp. 34-38, 66-68, 72, Redbird Smith movement and the
       current political activities of Lightfoot King, grandson
       of Redbird Smith. The focus is socio-political rather
       than religious.]

1351   EATON, Rachel Caroline. John Ross and the Cherokee Indians.
          Menasha, Wisconsin: G. Banta Publishing Co. 1914, 212 p.
            [Pp. 18-19 on Keetowah revivals, cited in O. C. Seymour,
       item 1355, p. 69.]

Redbird Smith...

1352   JORDAN, Janet Etheridge. Politics and religion in a Western
        Cherokee community: a century of struggle in a white man's
        world. University of Connecticut, Ph.D. dissertation
        (anthropology) 1974, vii + 428 p.
            [In north-east Oklahoma. Chs. 3 and 7 especially for
        the Nighthawk Keetowah Society of Redbird Smith from
        c. 1900, and the 1928 secession of the original "Sacred
        Fire" as the Cherokee Corporate Society — the former as a
        "revivalist revitalization" movement, the latter as "re-
        revivalist". Pp. 56-61 et passim, the semi-independent
        Cherokee Baptist Association (1869-); Ch. 9 (= pp. 296-
        351), a detailed account of return to virtually independent
        Baptist Churches since the 1950s. Pp. 377-384, comparisons
        with Handsome Lake movement. Pp. 384-385, incipient con-
        nections with the pan-Indian Ecumenical movement.]

1353   KILPATRICK, Jack Frederick and KILPATRICK, Anna Gritts. Note-
        book of a Cherokee Shaman (Smithsonian Contributions to
        Anthropology 2 (6)). Washington, D.C.: Smithsonian
        Institution Press 1970, 83-125.
            [P. 83, identification with Redbird Smith movement and
        subsequent dissociation, by a Baptist Christian who con-
        tinued traditional shamanistic medicine.]

1354   LITTLEFIELD, Daniel F., Jr. Utopian dreams of the Cherokee
        fullbloods, 1890-1934. Journal of the West 10 (3), 1971,
        404-427.
            [Pp. 412, 422, 423, 424, Keetowah Society; pp. 424-427,
        Redbird Smith and the Keetowahs. Socio-political history
        with little reference to the religious dimensions.]

1355   SEYMOUR, Otto C. The religion of the Cherokee Indians.
        University of Edinburgh (New College), Ph.D. thesis 1934,
        365 p., illus.
            [Pp. 68-69, 313-330, revival of primal religion by the
        Nighthawks Keetowah Society; p. 314, Redbird Smith;
        pp. 316, 330, his sons; pp. 320-326, his annual memorial
        service, with its account of the origins of the Keetowahs.]

1356   THOMAS, Robert K[nox]. The origin and development of the Red-
        bird Smith movement. University of Arizona, M.A. thesis
        1954, 220 p.
            [By a part-Cherokee anthropologist — "the most exhaus-
        tive and reliable source on the Keetowah Society" in its
        Nighthawk form, and used by J. E. Jordan, item 1352.]

1357 THOMAS, Robert K[nox]. The Redbird Smith movement, in W. N.
Fenton and J. Gulick (eds.), Symposium on Cherokee and
Iroquois culture = Bulletin, Bureau of American Ethnology
180, 1961, 161-166.
[And see F. W. Voget's comment, pp. 167-171.]

1358 TYNER, Howard. The Keetowah Society in Cherokee history.
University of Tulsa (Oklahoma), M.A. thesis 1949.
[Includes the Redbird Smith movement or "true" Keetowah
Society, the Nighthawk Keetowah. Based on secondary
sources, without field work. Cited and used by J. E.
Jordan, item 1352.]

1359 VOGET, Fred W. Comment on Robert K. Thomas' "The Redbird Smith
movement", in W. N. Fenton and J. Gulick (eds.), Symposium
on Cherokee and Iroquois culture = Bulletin, Bureau of
American Ethnology 180, 1961, 167-171.

1360 WAHRHAFTIG, Albert L. The tribal Cherokee population of
eastern Oklahoma. Current Anthropology 9 (5), 1968,
510-518.
[Pp. 513, 514, brief demographic information on Cherokee
churches and stomp grounds (i.e., traditional societies —
Keetowah, Four Mothers, etc.).]

1361 WAHRHAFTIG, Albert L. Institution building among Oklahoma's
traditional Cherokees, in C. M. Hudson (ed.), Four centuries
of southern Indians. Athens: University of Georgia Press
1975, 132-147, bibl.
[Pp. 136-137, 146, the Four Mothers Society co-operating
with Echota Cherokee Indian Baptist Church; p. 146, n.10,
Redbird Smith movement.]

1362 WOODWARD, Grace Steele. The Cherokees (Civilization of the
American Indian Series, 65). Norman: University of
Oklahoma Press 1963, 355 p., illus., maps; repr. 1969.
[Pp. 7-9, Keetowah Society and Redbird Smith; p. 312,
brief reference to the Cherokee-founded "Church in the
Woods" of 1866.]

SHAKER CHURCH (INDIAN)

The Indian Shaker "Church" in the Pacific northwest and extending
into British Columbia is now almost a century old despite predictions
by whites early this century that it would soon be extinct. It has
attracted a more sympathetic attitude from other whites, including
some missionaries, and has had the occasional white member. The

Shaker Church (Indian)

movement tends to divide between those who reject the Christian
Scriptures as unnecessary, and those who accept these and perhaps have
a loose relationship with white evangelicals. The Indian Shakers
should be clearly distinguished from the white Shakers in the eastern
U.S.A., derived from Ann Lee and the Quakers in England, and now almost extinct.

1363   BARNETT, H[omer] G[arner]. Indian Shakers. A messianic cult
          of the Pacific Northwest. Carbondale, Illinois: Southern
          Illinois University Press 1957; repr. as Arcturus Books,
          AB 104, 1972, 378 p., illus., bibl.
          [The major anthropological and historical study, in-
          cluding beliefs and practices, drawing upon information
          from a young sister of Mary Slocum, from church leaders
          and family documents, and secured through participant
          observation.]

1364   BROWN, De Koven. Indian workers for temperance. Collier's,
          the National Weekly 45 (24), 1910, 23–24, illus.
          [Contains two pictures of the new Shaker church at Mud
          Bay, 1910.]

1365   BRYANT, Hilda. The Red Man in America. Olympia, Washington:
          Louis Bruno, State Superintendent of Public Instruction
          1970, 52 p., illus.
          [Reprint of press articles; pp. 35–37, Shaker Church,
          p. 37, Native American Church.]

1366   COLLINS, June McCormick. The Indian Shaker Church: a study
          of continuity and change in religion. Southwestern Journal
          of Anthropology 6, 1950, 399–411.
          [A detailed account based on field work, showing the
          resemblances to and differences from the guardian spirit
          religion of the Skagit and neighbouring Indians; similarly
          examines the relation to Christianity, and the two divi-
          sions in the Shaker church based on desire for or rejection
          of closer relations.]

1367   COLLINS, June McCormick. Valley of the Spirits: the Upper
          Skagit Indians of Western Washington (American Ethnological
          Society Monographs 56). Seattle and London: University
          of Washington Press 1974, 267 p., illus.
          [Based on research from 1940s to 1960s, with incidental
          references to the Indian Shaker Church: see pp. 43, 44,
          150, 172, 194–195, 205, 239–240, 242–243, 246.]

Shaker Church (Indian)

1368   COLSON, Elizabeth. The Makah Indians: a study of an Indian
        tribe in modern American society. Manchester: Manchester
        University Press 1953, 308 p.
            [Shaker Church: see index, and especially pp. 238-239,
        240-241, 244-246, 248, 259-260, 265, 266, 278.]

1369   DE ANGULO, Jaime. The background of the religious feeling of
        a primitive tribe. American Anthropologist 28 (2), 1926,
        352-360.
            [P. 355, an Indian Shaker theological statement about
        Jesus, as given by a Pit River Indian.]

1370   DUFF, Wilson. The impact of the white man, vol. 1 of The
        Indian history of British Columbia (Anthropology in British
        Columbia Memoir 5). Victoria, B.C.: Provincial Museum
        of Natural History and Anthropology 1964, 117 p., illus.,
        bibl.
            [Pp. 87-101, religious changes, including pp. 90-100,
        the Shaker Church, pp. 88-89, prophet cults.]

1371   EELLS, Myron. Ten years of missionary work among the Indians
        at Skokomish, Washington Territory, 1874-1884. Boston:
        Congregational Sunday School and Publishing Society 1886,
        271 p.
            [Chs. 22-27 (= pp. 158-187), detailed first-hand accounts
        of the various individuals and new religious practices
        associated with the beginnings of the Indian Shaker Church —
        especially Big Bill, John Slocum and Billy Clams; by the
        local Congregationalist missionary whose brother was an
        Indian agent.]

1372   ELMENDORF, William W. Skokomish sorcery, ethics and society,
        in D. E. Walker, Jr. (ed.), Systems of North American
        witchcraft and sorcery. Moscow, Idaho: University of
        Idaho 1970, 147-182.
            [Pp. 150-151, 163-164, Shaker religion in relation to
        Shamanism.]

1373   FITZPATRICK, Darleen Ann. The "Shake": the Indian Shaker
        curing ritual among the Yakima. University of Washington
        (Seattle), M.A. thesis 1968, 95 p.

1374   FITZPATRICK, Darleen Ann. A gift from God. A study of the
        Indian Shaker religion in the Pacific northwest. [Under
        consideration for publication, 1978.] MS 318 p., maps,
        illus.
            [An anthropologist's comprehensive study of symbolism,
        doctrine, ritual and social order, with chapters on

219

Shaker Church (Indian)

temperance and healing, and special reference to the
Yakima Shakers. Endorsed by the Shaker Bishop, Harris
Teo.]

1375   GOULD, Richard A. and FURUKAWA, Theodore Paul. Aspects of
ceremonial life among the Indian Shakers of Smith River,
California. Kroeber Anthropological Society Papers
(Berkeley) 31, 1964, 51-67, illus.
[A detailed study of a pan-Indian form of Shakerism —
its history, building, ceremonies, beliefs, Bible usage
(p. 59), and healing rites; in extreme north of California
and marginal to the main Shaker areas.]

1376   GUNTHER, Erna. The Shaker religion of the Northwest, in
Marian W. Smith (ed.), Indians of the Urban North-West.
New York: Columbia University Press 1949, 37-76, illus.
[The fullest account before Barnett's of 1957, covering
history, worship, incorporation, relation to missions and
to shamanism, and internal divisions.]

1377   HARMON, Ray. Indian Shaker Church of The Dalles. Oregon
Historical Quarterly 72 (2), 1971, 148-158, illus.
[The history, layout and rites of a wooden church dating
from c. 1896 near The Dalles.]

1378   THE INDIAN SENTINEL (Washington, D.C., Bureau of Catholic Indian
Missions).
[See issues of 1910, p. 177, and 1913, pp. 37, 40-41,
for examples of references to Indian Shakers.

1379   KEW, John Edward Michael. Coast Salish ceremonial life:
status and identity in a modern village. University of
Washington, Ph.D. dissertation (anthropology) 1970, 367 p.,
[A small reserve village of Musqueam Indians in suburbs
of a large west coast Canadian city. Shaker church services
assist inter-village visiting, healing and personal re-
demptive religious experience; the traditional Spirit
dances in revised forms are the most important ceremonies.]

1380   LEWIS, Claudia. Indian families of the Northwest coast.
Chicago: University of Chicago Press 1970, 224 p.
[A Vancouver Island group, over a ten-year period to
1968. Includes reference to the Shaker Church.]

1381   NOWICKA, Ewa. Indiański Shakeryzm. Etnografia Polska 16 (2),
1972, 133-149, Eng. summary.
[The Indian Shaker Church as a syncretic movement representing a creative response to the disturbing effects of
white contact.]

1382   OBER, Sarah Endicott.   A new religion among the West coast
       Indians.   The Overland Monthly Series 2, 56, 1910, 583-594,
       illus.
           [A remarkably sympathetic account of the Indian Shakers
       by a missionary who had intimate first-hand experience and
       regarded them as "slowly evolving into a Christian
       religion"; the aboriginal and "hypnotic elements" are
       described, with details of conversion and other services,
       and some Shaker written reports are included.]

1383   OLSON, Ronald L[eroy].   The Quinault Indians (University of
       Washington Publications in Anthropology 6 (1)).   Seattle,
       Washington: the University of Washington 1936, 194 p.,
       illus., maps.
           [Pp. 170-174 on Quinault Shakers.]

1384   PETTITT, George A.   The Quileute of La Push 1775-1945 =
       Anthropological Records (University of California Publica-
       tions) 14 (1), 1950, 1-128, 7 plates; repr. in 10-year
       collection, 1960.
           [Pp. 18-20, religion, guardian spirits and shamanism;
       pp. 88-91, current religion; pp. 95-104, Shaker Church;
       pp. 104-105, Assemblies of God.]

1385   POSERN-ZIELIŃSKA, Mirosława.   The sources of relative depriva-
       tion and the origins of the Shakers movement [in Polish].
       Etnografia Polska 19 (2), 1975, 149-181.
           [See also same author, item 77.]

1386   POWELL, Jay V. and JENSEN, Vickie.   Quileute. An introduction
       to the Indians of La Push.   Seattle/London: University of
       Washington Press 1976, 80 p., illus., maps.
           [Pp. 39-43, History of La Push: mostly on the Shaker
       religion from c. 1895; reproduces Indian Agency notice and
       letter of 1905 limiting the number and length of meetings,
       and banning shaking for healing.]

1387   QUIMBY, Lida W.   Puget Sound Shakers.   The State (Tacoma,
       Washington) 7 (6), 1902, 188-189.
           [Outlines the origins and positive influences of the
       Indian Shakers, their survival of opposition and persecu-
       tion, their later degeneration and current relation to the
       churches.]

1388   RAKESTRAW, Charles D.   The Shaker Indians of Puget Sound.   The
       Southern Workman (Hampton Institute, Hampton, Virginia)
       29 (12), 1900, 703-709, illus.

Shaker Church (Indian)

> [A sympathetic account of the origins and rites of the
> Shaker Church, its conversion and healing procedures, and
> its positive moral effects; by a former supervisor of
> Indian schools.]

1389   REAGAN, Albert B. The Shake Dance of the Quileute Indians,
        with drawings by an Indian pupil of the Quileute day
        school. Proceedings of the Indiana Academy of Science
        1908, 71-74, illus.
>   [Reagan was teacher at La Push, 1908-09; outlines the
> history and rite, and quotes the constitution and beliefs
> of the Shaker Church.]

1390   REAGAN, Albert B. Notes on the Shaker Church of the Indian.
        Proceedings of the Indiana Academy of Science 1910,
        115-116.
>   [A continuation of the preceding item, describing the
> acquisition of "power" in terms of hypnotism.]

1391   REAGAN, Albert B. The Shaker Church of the Indians. The
        Southern Workman (Hampton Institute, Hampton, Virginia)
        56 (10), 1927, 447-448.
>   [A brief and sympathetic outline, quoting the official
> aims and beliefs of the Shakers.]

1392   REAGAN, Albert B. Quileute traditions about the organization
        of the Shaker Church.
>   [A manuscript quoted in G. A. Pettitt, item 1384, p. 96,
> n2.]

1393   RICHEN, Marilyn Claire. Leadership and the resolution of con-
        flict in an Indian Shaker Church. University of Oregon,
        Ph.D. dissertation (anthropology) 1974, 168 p.
>   [The resolution of disputes by schisms, and the resultant
> emphasis on secular values through use of courts and con-
> stitutions rather than revelation or the Bible. By a
> student of H. G. Barnett's.]

1394   SACKETT, Lee. The Siletz Indian Shaker Church. Pacific North-
        west Quarterly (Seattle) 64 (3), 1973, 120-126.
>   [The growth and decline of the Shaker congregation at
> Siletz, Oregon: pp. 120-121, antecedent influences of
> Ghost Dance in form of Earth Lodge and Bole Maru cults;
> pp. 121-125, history of Shakers from 1920s to 1969, similar
> to but not identical with E. Gunther's account in her item
> 1376, p. 46; pp. 125-126, four brief biographies of Siletz
> Shakers.]

Shaker Church (Indian)

1395   SCHULZ, John L[awrence]. Deprivation, revitalization and the
        development of the Shaker religion. Northwest Anthropo-
        logical Research Notes 2 (1), 1969, 92-119, bibl.
            [Pp. 92-101, successful application of theories of Aberle
        and A. F. C. Wallace to Shaker religion in general;
        pp. 101-116, inadequacy of same theories to explain Shaker-
        ism on Colville Reservation as found in a depth study.]

1396   SCHULTZ, John Lawrence. Acculturation and religion on the
        Colville Reservation. Washington State University,
        Ph.D. dissertation (anthropology) 1971, 176 p.
            [Progressive Colvilles are almost all Catholics; the
        conservative minority retain a form of their indigenous
        religion; Shakerism and Pentecostalism draw members from
        those in cultural transition since these systems can accom-
        modate a dual and often contradictory set of values.]

1397   SCHULTZ, John L[awrence] and WALKER, Deward E., Jr. Indian
        Shakers on the Colville Reservation. Research Studies
        (Washington State University) 35 (2), 1967, 167-172.
            [Six development phases since introduction of Shakerism
        to a Catholic Indian community in 1914: from dormancy to
        1940, to dominance of new Bible-reading form from 1961;
        the value in assisting acculturation.]

1398   SHAKLEFORD, Elizabeth. History of the Puyallup Indian Reser-
        vation. The College of Puget Sound, Bachelor's degree
        thesis 1918.
            [One of the areas to which the Shaker Church spread,
        but where it never became institutionally established.]

1399   SMITH, Marian W. The Puyallup of Washington, in R. Linton
        (ed.), Acculturation in seven American Indian tribes.
        New York and London: D. Appleton-Century 1940, 3-36.
            [Pp. 30-31, replacement of charismatic shamanist healing
        by Indian Shaker Church healing performed by anyone ful-
        filling the moral requirements.]

1400   SMITH, Marian W. Shamanism in the Shaker Church of Northwest
        America. Man 54, art. 181, August 1954, 119-122, bibl.
            [A scholarly outline, and interpretation as a vitalistic
        non-nativistic movement seeking spiritual power.]

1401   SUTTLES, Wayne. The persistence of intervillage ties among
        the Coast Salish. Ethnology 2, 1963, 512-525.
            [P. 522, in British Columbia the Shaker Church is one
        support of the intervillage community system, and less
        opposed to shamanist and dancing activities than in the

Shaker Church (Indian)

U.S.A.; p. 521 et passim, the continuing winter dances as resembling a nativistic movement.]

1402   TEO, Harris. Indian Shaker Church. Akwesasne Notes
       (Middleton, Conn.) 3 (7), 1971, 47.
           [A letter by the head elder, from White Swan, Washington,
       describing the current situation of this movement — its
       pro-white and more traditional factions, its branches and
       buildings, and its beliefs.]

1403   [TURNER, Harold Walter]. Indian Shaker Church. Encyclopaedia
       Britannica 1974, Micropaedia, vol. 5, 334.
           [Unsigned survey article.]

1404   UPCHURCH, O. C. The Swinomish people and their state. Pacific.
       Northwest Quarterly (Seattle) 27, 1936, 283-310.
           [The attempted rehabilitation of the Swinomish through
       their new tribal constitution. Pp. 293-295, the Shaker
       religion, with description of rites practised in connection
       with the new tribal council, and regarded as a mixture of
       tribal, Catholic and Protestant elements.]

1405   VALORY, Dale. The focus of Indian Shaker healing. Kroeber
       Anthropological Society Papers (Berkeley) 35, 1966, 67-
       112, diagram, bibl.
           [At Smith River, northern California. Detailed account
       of the annual healing convention and its methods of curing,
       now somewhat independent of "Slocum-ism", with verbatim
       testimonies. A valuable study supplementing Barnett,
       item 1363.]

1406   WALHOUSE, Freda. The influence of minority ethnic groups on
       the cultural geography of Vancouver. University of
       British Columbia, M.A. thesis (geography) 1961, 397 p.
           [Ch. 20, Musqueam and Squamish Indians, including Shaker
       Church adherents.]

1407   WATERMAN, T. T. The Shake religion of Puget Sound. Smith-
       sonian Institution Annual Report for 1922. Washington,
       D.C.: Smithsonian Institution 1924, 499-507, illus.
           [On the Indian Shaker church, its Catholic derived
       rituals, Protestant (Congregationalist) ethic, and
       tradition-based healing practices.]

1408   WILSON, Bryan R[onald]. Magic and the millennium...(see
       item 371).
           [Pp. 353-364, Indian Shakers as a "primary example of
       the mutation of the revolutionist response into the thau-
       maturgical pre-occupation".]

SMOHALLA AND THE DREAMER RELIGION

Smohalla the prophet is best known for the oft-quoted reference in which he likens farming to tearing the breast of the Earth, his Mother, and cutting off her hair. His Dreamer religion among the Wanapim should be distinguished from the Dream Dance further east among the Ojibwa and associated peoples. It is very similar to the cult of prophet Luls among the Umatilla about the same time — mid-nineteenth century (see item 528).

1409   CROWDER, Stella I.   The Dreamers.   Overland Monthly Series 2,
          62.   Dec. 1913, 606-609, illus.
          [A sympathetic outline of the life and teaching of
          Smohalla, founder of the Dreamer cult among the Wanapim.]

1410   HAINES, Francis.   The Nez Percés: tribesmen of the Columbia
          Plateau.   Norman: University of Oklahoma Press (1955)
          1972, 364 p., illus.
          [Pp. 192-197, 233, Smohalla's Dreamers' cult, or Too-ats,
          with photo (p. 197), a useful general survey; ch. 6, The
          Macedonian cry — on the 1831 delegation to St. Louis;
          pp. 352-360, bibliographic essay.]

1411   HOWARD, O[liver] O[tis].   Nez Percé Joseph....   Boston: Lee
          and Shepard 1881, 274 p., illus.
          [A brigadier-general's memoirs: pp. 8-9, 45-47, negoti-
          ations for Smohalla to come to meet Howard; pp. 63-67,
          Howard's argument with "the old dreamer" or "Too-hul-hul-
          sote", who stubbornly insisted that the earth was his
          mother and ruler, not Washington (the oft-quoted reference
          to tearing his mother's bosom); pp. 80-83, Smohalla's
          attendance at Fort Simcoe to hear the order to settle on
          a reservation; appeals to Smohalla, his response during a
          Christian service, and final agreement to go to a reserva-
          tion with his followers.   A primary source.]

1412   HUGGINS, E. L.   Smohalla, the prophet of Priest Rapids.   Over-
          land Monthly series 2, 17, Feb. 1891, 208-215.
          [A personal interview with Smohalla in the 1880s by the
          leader of a cavalry unit, and reported with some sympathy,
          although set against a background of the current "Messiah
          Craze" and similar "horribly fantastic conceptions".]

1413   HUNGRY WOLF, Adolf.   Good medicine thoughts.   Fort Macleod,
          Alberta: Good Medicine Books 1972, 32 p.
          [Pp. 16-21, Smohalla and his dreamer people, with quota-
          tions from Capt. Huggins' and Major MacMurray's reports.]

Smohalla and the Dreamer Religion

1414   MacMURRAY, J. W. The "Dreamers" of the Columbia River Valley in Washington Territory. Transactions of the Albany Institute (Albany) 11, 1887, 240-248.
[A first-hand report on Smohalla, by an army major.]

1415   MEACHAM, A[lfred] B[enjamin]. Wigwam and warpath, or the royal chief in chains. Boston: John P. Dale & Co. 1875, 700 p., illus.
[Pp. 155, 156, Smohalla; pp. 165-166, polygamy; pp. 174-177, a moving account of Indians facing problem of polygamy and how dealt with to satisfy both white missionaries and Indian wives and children.]

1416   MEACHAM, A[lfred] B[enjamin]. Another cloud. The Council Fire (Washington, D.C.) 1 (6), 1878, 82.
[An editorial on Smohalla, based on personal contact; pleads for religious freedom and tolerance with firmness, to avoid a military confrontation as with Sitting Bull and the Sioux — the previous "cloud".]

1417   RELANDER, Click (NOW TOW LOOK). Drummers and dreamers the story of Smowhala the prophet and his nephew Puck Hyah Toot, the last prophet of the nearly extinct River people, the last Wanapums. Caldwell, Idaho: Caxton Printers 1956, 345 p., illus., bibl.
[The Wanapums were later known as Sokulk. An important study of Smohalla, and of Puck Hyah Toot (1878 onwards). See review summary by F. H. Rodine, item 1418.]

1418   RODINE, Floyd H. Reviews. Ethnohistory 4 (3) 1957, 326-329.
[A review summary of C. Relander's item 1417 on Smohalla.]

1419   RUBY, Robert H. and BROWN, John A[rthur]. Half-Sun on the Columbia: a biography of Chief Moses (Civilization of the American Indian Series). Norman: University of Oklahoma Press 1965, xix + 377 p., illus., maps, bibl. (pp. 351-364).
[Includes the conflict between Smohalla and Chief Moses.]

1420   SMITH, John. Letter to A. B. Meacham. January 24th 1878. The Council Fire (Washington, D.C.) 1, 1878, 42-43.
[All the Wasco and Wishrams participated in one or other of the revealed religions including the Smohalla cult.]

1421   SPIER, Leslie and SAPIR, Edward. Wishram ethnography = University of Washington Publications in Anthropology (Seattle) 3 (3), 1930, 153-300, illus.

[Pp. 236-251, indigenous religion; pp. 201, 249, 251-254, Smohalla cult as a modification or special expression of old form of revelatory religion prevailing in this whole area, as were also the Ghost Dance, Shakers and Pom-Pom cults. Now majority are converts to Methodism. See Spier, item 542.]

1422   SPINDEN, Herbert J. The Nez Percé Indians (Memoirs, American Anthropological Association 2 (3)). Lancaster: American Anthropological Association 1908.
        [Pp. 260-261, Smohalla; pp. 256-261, Nez Percé religious background.]

1423   W[ARNER], R[obert] A. Smohalla, in D. Malone (ed.), Dictionary of American Biography. London: Oxford University Press, and New York: Charles Scribner's Sons vol. 17, 1935, 371-372, bibl.
        [Smohalla's Dreamer religion as nativistic and responsible for opposition to whites' government.]

1424   WESTERN MAGAZINE. Smohalla, the dreamer prophet (Notable characters in our Indian history, 3). Western Magazine (St. Paul, Minnesota) November 1916, 235-237.

SUN DANCE

This refers to a widespread traditional form that was suppressed by government in the late nineteenth century, and on which there is extensive literature. We have concentrated on the twentieth century revivals, some of which reveal Christianized or syncretistic forms. The most extensive study is that of Jorgensen, item 1431.

1425   AKWESASNE NOTES. Oglala Sun Dance and after Wounded Knee. Akwesasne Notes 5 (4), 1973, 3.

1426   AKWESASNE NOTES. Sun Dance at Rosebud... . Akwesasne Notes 5 (5), 1973, 10.
        [A contemporary account.]

1427   BAUMANN, Peter. Reise zum Sonnentanz: Indianer Zwischengestern und morgen. Berlin: Safari-Verlag 1970, 196 p., illus.
        [Especially on Sioux, Cheyenne, etc. in North and South Dakota reservations.]

Sun Dance

1428   HOEBEL, E. Adamson.   The Comanche sun dance and messianic out-
        break of 1873.   American Anthropologist 43 (2:1), 1941,
        301-303.
        [A wholly new feature for Comanches, the sun dance,
        adopted from other tribes as a vehicle for Isatai's
        messianic prophet movement; the subsequent military disas-
        ter immunized the Comanches against the 1890 Ghost Dance.]

1429   JONES, John Alan.   The rôle of the Sun Dance in Northern Ute
        acculturation.   Columbia University, Ph.D. dissertation
        (sociology) 1950, 102 p.

1430   JONES, J[ohn] A[lan].   The sun dance of the northern Ute.
        Bulletin of the Bureau of American Ethnology 157 (Anthro-
        pology Papers 43-48), 1955, Paper 47, 203-263, bibl.
        [P. 227, Ghost Dance not accepted by Utes, in view of
        their fear of the dead — the Sun Dance was introduced in
        1890 (see pp. 239-241) and was an alternate response for
        the Ute; pp. 228-229, peyote introduced in 1916, but
        stayed underground; also p. 232, as a factional practice
        since 1937; pp. 235-239, shamanism and peyotism; pp. 251-
        259, Christian and nativistic influences in the Sun Dance.]

1431   JORGENSEN, Joseph G[ilbert].   The Sun Dance religion.   Power
        for the powerless.   Chicago and London: University of
        Chicago Press 1972, 360 p., illus., maps.
        [The history of the Dance as a response to Indian
        deprivation, and its modern form among the Utes and Sho-
        shones as a more realistic support for individuals than
        the Ghost Dance, and with some Christian syncretisms (see
        index, and especially pp. 26, 172-173, 210-211, 221);
        peyotism, pp. 172-173, 179, 284 and see index; Ghost Dance,
        passim (see index); theory, see "deprivation" in index.   A
        massive study after prolonged and intimate Indian
        experience.]

1432   LEWIS, Thomas H.   The Oglala (Teton Dakota) Sun Dance: vicis-
        situdes of its structures and functions.   Plains
        Anthropologist 17, 1972, 44-49.
        [Compares the traditional and modern versions of the
        dance — the latter at Pine Ridge, South Dakota, 1967-1970,
        as an example of enforced acculturation, but with social
        functions overshadowing the religious.]

1433   LIBERTY, Margot.   Suppression and survival of the Northern
        Cheyenne Sun Dance.   Minnesota Archaeologist 27 (4), 1965,
        121-143, illus., bibl.

Sun Dance

[A detailed history, 1876-1934; pp. 128-129, peyotism as
in harmony with, but stronger than, the Sun Dance, and the
changes in form achieved by the Cheyenne without the
Christian syncretism seen in the Shoshone dance.]

1434   LIBERTY, Margot. The Northern Cheyenne Sun Dance and the
       opening of the Sacred Medicine 1959. Plains Anthropologist
       12, 1967, 367-380, illus. on pp. 382, 385.
       [Relatively little change since Grinnell's report of
       1910; last opened in 1934; p. 379, shows some Christian
       influence.]

1435   LINTON, Ralph. The Comanche sun dance. American Anthropologist
       37 (3), 1935, 420-428.
       [The traditional form as remembered in 1933 from the
       last performance in 1878; p. 427, one remembered vision
       which claimed to be of Jesus — the Comanche had some
       Christian contact from about 1750.]

1436   MOORE, John Hartwell. A study of religious symbolism among
       the Cheyenne Indians. New York University, Ph.D. dis-
       sertation (anthropology) 1974, 330 p.
       [The symbols in the traditional Sun Dance religion;
       Montana Cheyennes more influenced by Christianity than
       those in Oklahoma.]

1437   NURGE, Ethel. The Sioux Sun Dance in 1962. Actas y Memorias
       XXXVI Congreso Internacional de Americanistas, España
       1964. Seville: Editorial Catolica Española 1966, vol. 3,
       102-114, fig.
       [Detailed description, but very little specifically on
       acculturation aspect.]

1438   RICKETTS, Mac Linscott. Native American traditions. Journal
       of the American Academy of Religion 41 (2), 1973, 256-259.
       [A review of Jorgensen, item 1431, by an historian of
       religion, from the viewpoint of this discipline.]

1439   SHIMKIN, D[emitri] B. The Wind River Shoshone Sun Dance.
       Bulletin, Bureau of American Ethnology 151 (Anthropological
       Papers 33-42). 1953, Paper 41, pp. 397-484 + 8 plates.
       [Pp. 428-437, 466-474 on modern developments (to 1938),
       and on peyote cult.]

1440   VOGET, Fred W. Current trends in the Wind River Shoshone Sun
       Dance. Bulletin, Bureau of American Ethnology 151
       (Anthropological Papers 33-42) 1953, Paper 42, 485-499,
       bibl.

Sun Dance

[Pp. 495–496, et passim, the incorporation of Christian
elements and interpretations.]

1441   WALKER, J. R.   The Sun Dance and other ceremonies of the Oglala
       division of the Teton Dakota.   Anthropological Papers,
       American Museum of Natural History 16 (2), 1917, 55–121.

1442   ZELITCH, Jeffrey.   The Lakota Sun Dance.   Expedition 13 (1),
       1970, 17–23.
       [The Dances of 1969 at Rosebud Reservation and Pine
       Ridge — the former is described.]

1443   ZIMMERLI, D. W.   When the people gather: notes on the Teton
       Dakota Sun Dance.   Pine Ridge Research Bulletin (Public
       Health Service, Pine Ridge, South Dakota) no. 6, 1968.

TENSKWATAWA

   A Shawnee prophet early in the nineteenth century, otherwise known
as Elskwatawa, by his original name of Laulewasikaw, as "the Shawnee
prophet", or simply as "the prophet" or the "brother of Tecumseh";
the term "Shawnee prophet" may also occur in connection with Delaware
prophets in the previous century, or with reference to Kennekuk in
the mid-nineteenth century.   Tenskwatawa has usually been presented
under the shadow of his more famous brother, Tecumseh, the noted
orator and military leader; note, however, the attempt of Golt, item
1454, to give Tenskwatawa his due.

1444   ANDREWS, Edward Deming.   The Shaker mission to the Shawnee
       Indians.   Winterthur Portfolio 7, 1971, 113–128, map,
       illus.
       [A mission of white Shakers from New Lebanon to southern
       Ohio in 1807, which included a desire to meet Tenskwatawa;
       includes the journal of the mission's travels and contacts,
       verbatim.]

1445   [CASS, Lewis].   Hunter's narrative.   North American Review 22,
       Jan. 1826, 94–107.
       [Review article by a state governor on J. D. Hunter's
       Memoirs...., item 1456, questioning its authenticity;
       somewhat favourable description of Tenskwatawa, actually
       written in the latter's presence (see pp. 97, 98, 99, 100),
       with comments on other prophets and explanation of their
       religious experience in terms of the vision quest.]

1445A DAWSON, Moses. Historical narrative of the civil and military
       services of Major-General William H. Harrison.... Cincin-
       nati: M. Dawson (printer) 1824, 464 p.
       [Pp. 83-84, Governor Harrison's speech of 1806 to the
       Delawares on "this pretended prophet", Tenskwatawa;
       pp. 107-109, includes Tenskwatawa's visit and speech to
       Harrison in 1808; pp. 130-131, Harrison's remarks on the
       prophet in a letter to the Secretary of War, 1809. This
       is important primary material, repr. in C. F. Klinck,
       item 231.]

1446   DEAN, Thomas. Journal of Thomas Dean: a voyage to Indiana
       in 1817. Edited by John Candee Dean. Indiana Historical
       Society Publications 6 (2), 1918, 273-345.
       [P. 308, Tenkswatawa as seen by the (white) Shakers in
       Ohio when visited by Quaker Thomas Dean.]

1447   DRAKE, Benjamin. Life of Tecumseh and of his brother the
       prophet. Cincinnati: E. Morgan & Co. 1841, 235 p.;
       Cincinnati: H. S. & J. Applegate 1852, 235 p.; repr. New
       York: Arno Press and New York Times 1969, viii + 235 p.
       [The most reliable biography of Tenskwatawa, being based
       on material from active participants in the 1812-1815 war.
       Note pp. 219-224, Mr. Jefferson's estimate of the prophet
       (from his Correspondence, 10, p. 171), repr. in C. F.
       Klinck, item 231, p. 53.]

1448   DRAPER, Lyman Copeland. Draper manuscript collection. Held
       by the State Historical Society of Wisconsin.
       [Draper (1815-1891) was secretary of the Society, and a
       lifelong collector of materials and information. His 15
       volumes of materials on Tecumseh have references to
       Tenskwatawa passim, and include his own rough notes,
       references to published sources of his information with
       comments, letters from informants, extracts copied from
       some printed sources, clippings of printed materials.]

1449   EGGLESTON, Edward and SEELYE, Lillie Eggleston. Tecumseh and
       the Shawnee prophet. New York: Dodd Mead & Co. 1878,
       332 p.
       [Pp. 105-109, 135-181, 216-223, 320-327, on Tenskwatawa.]

1450   FINLEY, James B[radley] (ed. by D. W. Clark). Life among the
       Indians, or, personal reminiscences and historical inci-
       dents illustrative of Indian life and character. Cincin-
       nati: Cranston & Curts n.d. [1855], 548 p.; many later
       editions.

Tenskwatawa

[By a Methodist settler and missionary who emigrated to
Ohio in 1796; narrative ends c. 1830. Ch. 7, Tecumseh and
his war; ch. 9, Death of Tecumseh. See pp. 187, 189, 197-
198, 204-206, 478-479, passing references to his brother
"the prophet".]

1451   FORSYTH, Thomas. Letter to General William Clark dated
St. Louis December 23, 1812. Also Memorandum (from
Forsyth Papers, vol. 9), in Emma H. Blair (ed.), item 144,
pp. 272-274, 277-283.
[P. 275, portrait of Tenskwatawa; pp. 272-274, the life
of Tenskwatawa; pp. 274, 277-278, his teaching, in 14
"regulations"; pp. 278-279, his influence. Forsyth, as
Indian agent at St. Louis, writing to the Superintendent
of Indian Affairs, would appear to be a primary source,
but the editor regards the reports as "second-hand and
partial". On Forsyth Papers, see also Wisconsin State
Historical Society Report and Collections 6, 1872, 188-
219; and 11, 1888, 316-355.]

1452   FRENCH, James Strange. Elkswatawa [sic]; or The prophet of
the West. A tale of the frontier. New York: Harper and
Brothers 1836, 2 vols.
[A fictionalized account of Tecumseh and Tenskwatawa,
attempting a sympathetic portrayal of the Indian prophet
while showing the victory of civilization over savagery.
See analysis by R. H. Pearce, item 76.]

1453   GALLOWAY, William Albert. Old Chillicothe: Shawnee and
pioneer history; conflicts and romances of the North
territory. Xenia, Ohio: Buckeye Press 1934, 336 p.,
illus., map.
[Chillicothe was a major Shawnee village; cited by
N. W. Schutz, item 1464, pp. 189, etc. Relevant to
Tenskwatawa.]

1454   GOLT, Herbert Charles Walter, Jr. Tecumseh, the prophet and
the rise of the Northwest Indian Confederation. University of Western Ontario, Ph.D. dissertation (history)
1973.
[An attempt to return to primary sources, and so estab-
lish the rightful place of Tenskwatawa in relation to
Tecumseh, who has eclipsed him in most accounts.]

1455   GRAY, Elma E. Wilderness Christians. Ithaca, N.Y.: Cornell
University Press 1956, 354 p., illus.
[Pp. 197-199, Tenskwatawa, as seen by Moravian
missionaries.]

1456   HUNTER, John D[unn]. Memoirs of a captivity among the Indians
        of North America from childhood to the age of nineteen
        years.... London: Longman, Hurst, Ross, Orme and Brown
        1823, 447 p.; edited version repr. New York: Schocken
        Books 1973, 252 p., bibl.
            [Ch. 6 on Indian religion: pp. 225-230, prophets and
        their methods of securing a revelation, with brief refer-
        ence (p. 227) to "Tecumseh and Francis, the celebrated
        Shawanee prophets" as too well "known to require any detail
        in this place". The reference is to Tenskwatawa.]

1457   KENDALL, Edward Augustus. Travels through the northern parts
        of the United States in the years 1807 and 1808. New York:
        I. Riley, 3 vols., 1809.
            [Vol. II, pp. 285-298, Tenskwatawa.]

1458   LAMBERT, John. Travels through lower Canada and the United
        States, in the years 1806, 1807, and 1808 ... . London:
        printed for Richard Phillips, 3 vols. ed., 1810; also eds.
        in 2 vols., 1813, 1814, 1816.
            [Vol. 1, pp. 395-403, Tenskwatawa's message from the
        Great Spirit.]

1459   McKENNEY, Thomas L. and HALL, James. History of the Indian
        tribes of North America, with biographical sketches and
        anecdotes of the principal chiefs.... Philadelphia: E. C.
        Biddle 3 vols. 1836-1844, and many later editions; new
        edition (ed. F. W. Hodge and D. I. Bushnell, Jr.) as The
        Indian tribes.... Edinburgh: J. Grant 3 vols. 1932-34;
        repr. East Ardsley, Yorkshire: E. P. Publications 1972.
            [Vol. 1, pp. 37-49 (new. ed., pp. 75-103), Tenskwatawa
        (and Tecumseh), based largely on B. Drake's materials and
        Governor Harrison's memoirs; vol. 2 (new ed.) pp. 93-95,
        Tenskwatawa's influence on Creek prophets; pp. 406-408,
        derogatory view of Indian prophets, including Tenskwatawa.]

1460   MacLEAN, John Patterson. Shaker mission to the Shawnee Indians.
        Ohio Archaeological and Historical Quarterly (Columbus,
        Ohio) 11, 1903, 215-229.
            [Pp. 222-229 for a more positive picture of Tenskwatawa,
        Shawnee prophet.]

1461   MOONEY, James. Myths of the Cherokee, in 19th Annual Report,
        Bureau of American Ethnology 1897-98. Part I. Washington,
        D.C.: Government Printing Office 1900, 3-548; New York:
        Johnson Reprint Corporation (Landmarks in Anthropology)
        1970, 576 p., illus.

Tenskwatawa

      [Pp. 87-89, 235, Tenskwatawa's influence on Creek
prophets and the Creek war.]

1462   NEW MONTHLY MAGAZINE. Memoir of an American chief. The New
      Monthly Magazine (London) no. 82=14, Nov. 1820, 518-522.
      [Pp. 519b, 520a, 521a, brief references to Tenskwatawa
      and his influence in Shawnee resistance to whites.]

1463   OSKISON, John Milton. Tecumseh and his times: The story of a
      great Indian. New York and London: G. P. Putnam's Sons
      1938, 244 p., map.
      [By an Indian author, and includes Tenskwatawa.]

1464   SCHUTZ, Noel William, Jr. The study of Shawnee myth in an
      ethnographic and ethnohistorical perspective. Indiana
      University, Ph.D. dissertation (anthropology) 1975, 571 p.,
      illus., maps.
      [As background to Tenskwatawa, and on subsequent changes
      from a remote male deity to an active female deity, with
      critical study of the work of his teacher, C. F. Voegelin,
      item 1470, and of Tenskwatawa's information as in Trow-
      bridge, item 1468. Pp. 182-183, 190-193, 494-499, 522-531,
      are especially useful on Tenskwatawa.]

1465   SWANTON, John R[eed]. Religious beliefs and medical practices
      of the Creek Indians, in 42nd Annual Report, Bureau of
      American Ethnology 1924-1925. Washington, D.C.: Govern-
      ment Printer 1928, 473-672 + 6 plates.
      [P. 508, sacred brass plates in the possession of the
      aged Tenskwatawa, regarded by the Creeks as gifts from the
      Great Spirit.]

1466   TANNER, John. A narrative of the captivity and adventures of
      John Tanner..., prepared for press by Edwin James. New
      York: Carvill 1830, 426 p., illus. Abridged ed., Grey
      Hawk. Life and adventures among the Red Indians, ed.
      James Macauley. Philadelphia: J. B. Lippincott 1883,
      xv + 341 p., illus.; repr. as An Indian captivity 1789-
      1822. Works Project Administration California State
      Library, Sutro Branch, Occasional Papers Reprint Series
      no. 20, Part I, May 1940; also repr. Minneapolis: Ross
      and Haines, 1956, 427 p.; Fr. trans., Paris: A. Bertrand
      1835. Ger. trans., Dreissig Jahre unter den Indianern.
      repr. Weimar: Kiepenhauer 1968, 379 p.
      [Tanner, stolen as a child, lived with Ottawa and
      Chippewa Indians in Canada. Pp. 110-113 (1940 ed.),
      Tenskwatawa's teaching and influence on Tanner's group,

repr. in Thatcher, item 1467, pp. 209-214, also in C. F.
Klinck, item 231, pp. 36-39; pp. 137-147, Ais-kaw-ba-wis,
a traditional prophet.]

1467 THATCHER, B[enjamin] B[ussey]. Indian biography, or, an
      historical account of those individuals who have been
      distinguished among the North American Natives ....
      2 vols. 1832, etc.; repr. New York: The Werner Co. 1910,
      350, 338 p., illus.
         [Vol. II, chs. 12 and 14 (= pp. 198-269), Tecumseh and
      the Prophet; pp. 209-214 reprint John Tanner's account,
      item 1466.]

1468 TROWBRIDGE, C[harles] C. Shawnese traditions (V. Kinietz and
      E. W. Voegelin, eds.) (Occasional Contributions from the
      Museum of Anthropology of the University of Michigan, 9).
      Ann Arbor: University of Michigan Press 1939, xxi + 71 p.
         [Pp. vii-xviii, editorial introduction, on Tecumseh and
      Tenskwatawa; pp. 1-59, Shauwanoa traditions (origin
      legend) — an account Trowbridge probably secured from
      Tenskwatawa in 1824 at Detroit or Fort Malden, Ontario;
      pp. 40-43 specifically on religion. This account is an
      important source, and is used critically by N. W. Schutz,
      item 1464.]

1469 TUCKER, Glenn. Tecumseh. Vision of glory. New York and
      Indianapolis: Bobbs-Merrill Co. 1956, 399 p.
         [Pp. 89-110, on Elskwatawa (i.e. Tenskwatawa),
      et passim.]

1470 VOEGELIN, C[arl] F. The Shawnee female deity. Yale University
      Publications in Anthropology 10, 1936, 3-21.
         [Pp. 16-17, the effects of a late 19th century nativistic
      prophetess on Shawnee in Oklahoma; p. 17, brief reference
      to interpretation of Tenskwatawa's prophetic gifts. The
      whole study describes developments after Tenskwatawa; see
      also the critique by his student, N. W. Schutz, item 1464.]

1471 WHITNEY, Edson L. and PERRY, Frances M. Four American Indians:
      King Philip, Pontiac, Tecumseh, Osceola. A book for young
      Americans. New York, etc.: American Book Company 1904,
      240 p., illus.
         [Tecumseh, pp. 117-176; pp. 133-137, the Prophet;
      pp. 144-149, the Prophet's town (i.e. Tenskwatawa).]

1472 WILSON, Bryan R[onald]. Magic and the millenium.... (see
      item 371).

235

Tenskwatawa

[Pp. 229-236, Tenskwatawa — "A prophetic revolutionist response associated with military action".]

1473   WOOD, Norman B.   Lives of famous Indian chiefs... .   Brady Rock, Aurora, Illinois: American Indian Historical Publishing Company 1906, 771 p., illus.
[Pp. 324-334, 344-347, the Prophet of the Shawnee (i.e. Tenskwatawa); pp. 317-361 on Tecumseh (his brother) as setting; p. 339, illustration of the Prophet, from Smithsonian Institution.]

YAQUI AND MAYO CHURCHES AND PROPHETS

The Yaqui and Mayo are adjacent and related Cáhita-speaking tribes in northwest Mexico who have shared a peculiar history both in relation to missions and to the Mexican governments, and who have immigrant settlements in Arizona.   They were extensively Christianized by the Jesuits early in the eighteenth century, but after the suppression of the latter in all Spanish possessions in 1767 the Yaqui and Mayo further developed their new religion in virtual independence of Western Christian influences.   Various subsidiary prophet movements, sometimes associated with resistance to Mexican control, are still appearing and have been included here.   Likewise there are a few accounts of similar religious forms among neighbouring peoples; kindred material will also be found in the final section on Northern Mexico, with its religiously inspired revolts.   The Mayo should be distinguished from the Maya of the Yucatan peninsula, who will be dealt with in volume 4.

1474   BAHTI, Tom.   Southwestern Indian ceremonies.   Las Vegas [Nevada]:   K. C. Publications 1970, 64 p., illus.
[Pp. 54-57, Yaqui Catholic and traditional ceremonies; pp. 58-61, peyote; with coloured illustrations.]

1475   BANNON, John Francis.   The Spanish borderlands frontier 1513-1821.   New York: Holt, Rinehart and Winston 1970, 308 p., maps, bibl.
[Pp. 55-61, earliest missions to the Yaqui and Mayo; pp. 80-86, Pueblo revolt (but little on Popé, etc.).]

1476   BARKER, George C.   The Yaqui Easter ceremony at Hermosillo.   Western Folklore 16, 1957, 256-262 + 2 photographs.

1477   BARKER, George C.   Some aspects of penitential processions in Spain and the American southwest.   Journal of American Folklore 70, 1957, 137-142.
[Includes first-hand report of a Yaqui procession in Arizona in 1955.]

1478   BARKER, George C.   Some functions of Catholic processions in
       Pueblo and Yaqui culture change. American Anthropologist
       60 (3), 1958, 449-455.
           [Compares the Keresan Pueblo observances with the Yaqui
       in Sonora and at Pascua, Arizona — the Yaqui being an ex-
       ample of cultural fusion with the original Spanish
       Catholicism.]

1479   BEALS, Ralph L[eon].   The contemporary culture of the Cáhita
       Indians = Bulletin, Bureau of American Ethnology 142,
       1945, 244 p., illus., bibl., map, figs.
           [Pp. 1-5, summary of Yaqui and Mayo (the surviving
       Cáhita speakers) history since white contact; pp. 190-201,
       the surviving aboriginal "religion of the woods"; pp. 90-
       190, Mayo and Yaqui religious organization, and their
       churches; pp. 202-207, the aboriginal elements surviving
       in the new religious context.]

1480   BROWN, Emily.   The passion at Pascua. Tucson: Chamber of
       Commerce (1941) 1945, 8 p., illus.
           [Descriptive account of events from Ash Wednesday, with
       detailed daily account from Wednesday in Holy Week to
       Easter Sunday.]

1481   CAZENEUVE, Jean.   Les Indiens de la région de Tucson.
       L'Ethnographie (Paris) 51, 1956, 37-44.
           [Focuses on the comparison between two tribes of the
       same stock, both transplanted from their home-territory —
       the Papagos who have maintained their traditional religion,
       and the Yaquis who have abandoned their past and become
       what the author calls Catholics; the Yaqui Easter drama is
       analysed (pp. 39-42).]

1482   CRUMRINE, Lynne Scoggins.   Ceremonial exchange as a mechanism
       in tribal integration among the Mayos of Northwest Mexico
       (University of Arizona, Anthropological Papers, 14).
       Tucson: University of Arizona Press 1969, 52 p., map,
       figs.
           [Includes the patron saint exchange system and the many
       saint's cults within Mayo syncretist Catholicism, and the
       place of the latter in maintaining Mayo identity and re-
       sistance; for specific prophets and movements see p. 35
       (1890 prophets) and p. 37 (1945 and 1957 movements).]

1483   CRUMRINE, Lynne S[coggins].   Mayo Santos: a paradigmatic
       analysis of a sacred symbol, in R. F. Spencer (ed.),
       Forms of symbolic action (Proceedings of the American
       Ethnological Society Annual Meeting 1969). Seattle:
       University of Washington Press 1970, 134-150, bibl.

Yaqui and Mayo Churches...

[Discusses the symbols of crosses, flowers, santos, their variants, and inter-relations in Mayo culture.]

1484   CRUMRINE, L[ynne] S[coggins] and CRUMRINE, N. Ross. Ritual service and blood sacrifice as mediating binary oppositions: a structural analysis of several Mayo myths and rituals. Journal of American Folklore no. 327=83, 1970, 69-76.
       ["Yaqui-Mayo orientation of ceremonial labor" used to test a Levi-Strauss type of structural analysis of "a set of Mayo myths that mediate the life-death and health-sickness oppositions through ritualized giving and sacrifice". Pp. 72-74 are descriptive of Mayo rituals in Holy Week and on the feast-day of San Juan.]

1485   CRUMRINE, N. Ross. The house cross of the Mayo Indians of Sonora, Mexico. A symbol of ethnic identity (University of Arizona, Anthropological Papers, No. 8). Tucson: University of Arizona Press 1964, 57 p., illus.

1486   CRUMRINE, N. Ross. Mayo ritual impersonation: the mask, arousal, and enculturation. Anthropos 63/64 (5-6), 1968-1969, 976-977.
       [Easter ceremonials with ritual impersonations of non-human or a-moral behaviour as a confession and social-reinforcing process.]

1487   CRUMRINE, N. Ross. Čapakoba, the Mayo Easter impersonator: explanations of ritual clowning. Journal for the Scientific Study of Religion 8 (1), 1969, 1-22, bibl.
       [Čapakobam are soldier-clowns in the plays, and represent a liminal anomalous state which serves a mediating function, equivalent to that of trickster figures.]

1488   CRUMRINE, N. Ross. Ritual drama and culture change. Comparative Studies in Society and History 12 (4), 1970, 361-372, bibl.
       [Detailed analysis of a Mayo Easter ceremonial in Sonora, Mexico (based on his Ph.D. dissertation, University of Arizona, 1968); includes comparative material and shows that ritual drama aids adjustment to a dominant society.]

1489   CRUMRINE, N. Ross. "La terra te devorará": un análisis estructural de los mitos de los indígenas Mayo. América Indígena 33 (4), 1973, 1119-1150.
       [A structural analysis of Mayo Indian myths.]

1490 CRUMRINE, N. Ross. God's daughter-in-law, the old man and the olla: an archaeological challenge. The Kiva 39 (3-4), 1974, 277-281.
[Mayo mythologies of death, with burial in pottery ollas; the outcome in the cemetery rituals and Easter rites of the Mayo church.]

1491 CRUMRINE, N. Ross. The Mayo Indians of Sonora: a people who refuse to die (Foreword by E. H. Spicer). Tucson: University of Arizona Press 1977, xiv + 167 p., illus., maps.
[A detailed study of a Mayo community with a syncretist "church" similar to that of the Yaquis, but focused on the new Liohpasko cult (1957-) of Damien Bohoroqui and its effects on Mayo resistance to assimilation. Pp. 5-9, 142-156, theory, on the model of rites of passage and V. W. Turner's "liminal process"; pp. 72-73, saints' healing cults; pp. 73-83, church building, organization and rites; pp. 85-97, Easter ceremonial cycle; pp. 1-4, 121-129 more especially on Bohoroqui's cult; pp. 129-133, San Cayetano cult; p. 8, Indian Shaker Church as parallel example.]

1492 CRUMRINE, N. Ross. Transformational processes and models: with special reference to Mayo Indian myth and ritual, in I. Rossi (ed.), New trends in structural anthropology [reported "expected", as of 1977].

1493 CRUMRINE, N. Ross and CRUMRINE, Lynne S[coggins]. Where Mayos meet mestizos: a model for the structure of culture contact. Human Organization 28 (1), 1969, 50-57, bibl.
[The Mayo churches, passim, in relation to Catholic and Protestant churches.]

1494 CRUMRINE, N. Ross and CRUMRINE, M. Louise. Ritual symbolism in folk and ritual drama. The Mayo Indian San Cayetano Velación, Sonora, Mexico. Journal of American Folklore no. 355=90 (Jan.-Mar.), 1977, 8-28, illus.
[A Mayo ritual symbol focused on the little trickster type of saint, San Cayetano, a powerful curer, and his cult.]

1495 DE GRAZIA, Ted Ettore. De Grazia paints the Yaqui Easter: forty days of Lent in forty paintings, with a personal commentary. Tucson: University of Arizona Press 1968, 92 p., coloured illus.

1496 DENSMORE, Frances. Yuman and Yaqui music = Bureau of American Ethnology Bulletin 110, 1932, xviii + 216 p., illus., music texts.

Yaqui and Mayo Churches...

[Yaqui and Mayo dance songs, especially the Deer Dance, as recorded at Guadalupe village, Arizona — pp. 22-24, and index.]

1497   ERASMUS, Charles John.   The leader vs. tradition: a case study.   American Anthropologist 54 (2:1), 1952, 168-178.
       [A Mayo healer specializing in curing sickness due to witchcraft began in 1945 a local Sinarquismo (= Spanish "Falange") movement, anti-white and mestizo, and in defence of Mayo land against Mexican intruders. He claimed backing of a saint; feasts given in his honour; but Mexican troops easily supressed the movement.]

1498   ERASMUS, Charles J[ohn].   Man takes control: cultural development and American aid.   Minneapolis: University of Minnesota Press 1961, 365 p.
       [Pp. 285-291, Antonio Bacosegua's new movement for healing, and reviving the fiesta system among Mexico Mayo, from 1957.]

1499   ERASMUS, Charles J[ohn].   Culture change in Northwest Mexico, in J. H. Steward (ed.), Contemporary change in traditional societies, vol. 3: Mexican and Peruvian communities.   Urbana: University of Illinois Press 1967, 1-131, illus.
       [Pp. 102-110, Antonio Bacosegua's movement from 1957; p. 106, brief account of "San Francisco's" movement c. 1928.]

1500   FRÍAS, Heriberto.   Tomochic. Novela histórica Mexicana.   Barcelona: Casa Editorial Maucci 1899, 256 p.; and further eds., e.g. Paris 1911; Mexico, D.F.: Editora Nacional 1951, 302 p.
       [Tomochic was the Chihuahua village which drew inspiration from the neighbouring Mayo, Teresa Urrea, in the 1890s, before being destroyed by the Mexican army.]

1501   GIDDINGS, Ruth Warner.   Yaqui myths and legends (University of Arizona Anthropological Papers, 2).   Tucson: the University 1959, 73 p.; same title, Tucson: University of Arizona Press 1969?, 180 p., illus.
       [See stories on the flood, Christ, etc. for Christian influences.]

1502   GILL, Mario.   Teresa Urrea, la santa de Cabora.   Historia Mexicana (Mexico City), October 1956-June 1957, 626-644.
       [A prophet cult among the Mayo of southern Sonora, 1890-1892, led by a girl visionary and other prophets, until she was deported.]

1503   GILL, Mario. Episodios mexicanos: México en la hoguera.
        Mexico, D.F.: Editorial Azteca 1960.
        [Pp. 7-41, Teresa Urrea and the millennial prophets
        among the Mayo in the 1880s-1890s.]

1504   HERBERT, Charles W. Yaqui Easter. Desert Magazine (El Centro,
        California) April 1960, 7-11, illus.
        [A photographic essay.]

1505   HU-DEHART, Evelyn. Development and rural rebellion: pacifi-
        cation of the Yaquis in the late Porfiriato. Hispanic
        American Historical Review 54 (1), 1974, 72-93.
        [On the resistance of the Yaquis — their first revolt
        in 1740; their long struggle from the 1870s until 1910.
        Almost no reference to religion.]

1506   KOSTASH, Janis Mary. Indians on the edge of the Spanish
        empire: the Yaquis and Mapuche in relations to nativistic
        and revitalization theory. Tulane University, M.A. thesis
        1968, 99 p.

1507   KURATH, Gertrude Prokosch. Mexican moriscas: a problem in
        dance acculturation. Journal of American Folklore 62 (1),
        1949, 87-106.
        [Pp. 90-92, 94, 100, 101, Yaqui matachini dances at
        Easter; pp. 92-93, the Mayo matachini; set in a discussion
        of European parallels and influences, and of Indian
        elements.]

1508   KURATH, Gertrude Prokosch. Drama, dance and music, in
        M. Nash (ed.), Handbook of Middle American Indians, vol. 6:
        Social anthropology. Austin: University of Texas Press
        1967, 158-190, illus.
        [Includes the fiestas, etc. of the syncretic religions
        or "churches" of the Yaqui, Mayo, Tarahumara, etc. tribes.]

1509   LA ILLUSTRACIÓN ESPIRITA (Mexico City, D.F.). See issues: 10,
        1 March 1891, 255-258, 281, 360, 267, 269; 11, 1 March
        1892, 313; 12, 1 August 1892, 110.
        [Teresa Urrea, Mayo healer of Cabora, 1889- .]

1510   LOPEZ, Raúl A. Tarahumara ritual aesthetic manifestations.
        The Kiva (Tucson) 37 (4), 1972, 207-233, illus., bibl.
        [Includes the Holy Week dramas akin to those of the
        Yaqui.]

Yaqui and Mayo Churches...

1511   MACKLIN, B[arbara] June and CRUMRINE, N. Ross.   "Santa Teresa",
       El Niño "Santo" Fidencio, and "San" Damian: the structural
       development of three folk saints' movements, northern
       Mexico, in Actas y Memorias, XXXIX Congresso Internacional
       de Americanistas, Lima 1970. Lima: Instituto de Estudios
       Peruanos 1972, vol. 6, 100-109.
          [Teresa Urrea (Mayo, 1880s-1890s), Fidencio Constantino
       (of Nueva León, 1920s), and Damien Bohoroqui (Mayo, 1958).
       Curer-client relationships lead into an innovative and
       restorative movement and a religious cult, and back to the
       clientele form.]

1512   MACKLIN, Barbara June and CRUMRINE, N. Ross.   Three north
       Mexican folk saint movements. Comparative Studies in
       Society and History 15 (1), 1973, 89-105.
          [Expanded version of item 1511.]

1513   MAKARIUS, Laura. The Čapakobam of Sonora, Mexico. Anthropos
       67, 1972, 595-596.
          [On the Mayo ritual clown in the Easter dramatic cycle.]

1514   MALDONADO, Felipe Rojo (ed.). Documentation "Noroeste" (I).
       Estudios Indigenas (CENAPI [=Centro Nacional de Pastoral
       Indigenista] Mexico City) 3 (2), December 1973, 233-250.
          [A collection of materials on Yaqui culture and
       Christianity.]

1515   NAVARRO GARCÍA, Luis. La sublevacíon Yaqui de 1740. Anuario
       de Estudios Americanos (Seville, Spain) 22, 1965, 373-531.
          [Full study of the Yaqui and Mayo uprising of 1740,
       based on Spanish archives; nothing especially on religion,
       but important as background to Yaqui and Mayo religious
       movements.]

1516   PAINTER, Muriel Thayer. The Yaqui Easter ceremony. Tucson:
       Chamber of Commerce 1950, 40 p., illus. 2nd ed. rev. as
       Easter at Pascua village. Tucson: University of Arizona
       Press 1960, 35 p., illus.; republ. as A Yaqui Easter.
       Tucson: University of Arizona Press 1971, 40 p., illus.

1517   PAINTER, Muriel Thayer, SAVALO, Refugio and ALVAREZ, Ignacio
       (eds.). A Yaqui Easter sermon. University of Arizona
       Social Science Bulletin (Tucson) 26 (6), 1955, 4-89, illus.
          [With preface by E. H. Spicer. Pp. 9-20, introduction
       by M. T. Painter; pp. 21-61, sermon of I. Alvarez (text
       with interlinear translation); pp. 61-74, free translation
       of sermon; pp. 74-87, notes on sermon; 87-89, calendar of
       events at Easter. At Pascua, 1941.]

1518   PASO Y TRONCOSO, Francisco.
        See TRONCOSO, Francisco P.

1519   SPICER, Edward H[olland]. The Yaqui Indians of Arizona. The
        Kiva (Arizona Archaeological and Historical Society,
        Tucson) 5 (6), 1940, 21-24.
            [A brief survey, including Easter dances and societies,
        but all dealt with in more detail in later items.]

1520   SPICER, Edward H[olland]. Pascua: a Yaqui village in Arizona
        (University of Chicago Publications in Anthropology.
        Ethnological Series). Chicago: University of Chicago
        Press 1940, xxxi + 319 p., maps, plates.
            [Immigrant Yaquis near Tucson: relations between eco-
        nomics, social organization and religion. Religion is of
        Christian origin, but quite independent of the Catholic
        Church for over a hundred years.]

1521   SPICER, Edward H[olland]. Linguistic aspects of Yaqui accul-
        turation. American Anthropologist 45 (3), 1943, 410-426.
            [Spanish language influences on the Yaqui in Arizona;
        especially pp. 416-419, 423, 424, 425, on the areas of
        ritual and religion. See also J. B. Johnston, pp. 427-
        434 of same issue.]

1522   SPICER, Edward H[olland]. El problema Yaqui. América Indígena
        (Mexico, D.F.) 5 (4), 1945, 273-286, Eng. summary.
            [The problem of Mexican Government planning a withdrawal
        of military occupation, and securing a real understanding
        of Yaqui history and of the sacred-land tradition to
        improve relationships. As background to Yaqui church.]

1523   SPICER, Edward H[olland]. Yaqui villages past and present.
        The Kiva (Arizona Archaeological and Historical Society,
        Tucson) 13 (1), 1947, 2-12 (= whole issue).
            [Surveys history and locations and populations as in
        1940: 10,000 + in 8 Yaqui River settlements and 4,800 in
        11 non-river settlements in Mexico and USA. Useful survey
        of this theme.]

1524   SPICER, Edward H[olland]. Potam, A Yaqui village in Sonora.
        (Memoirs, American Anthropological Association, 77) =
        American Anthropologist 56 (4:2), 1954, 1-220, + illus.,
        maps.
            [One of the eight sacred towns in Sonora State. Ch. 5,
        Church and ceremonial societies; ch. 7, the supernaturals;
        ch. 8, Ceremonials; ch. 9, Patterns of ritual.]

Yaqui and Mayo Churches...

1525   SPICER, Edward H[olland]. Social structure and cultural
        process in Yaqui religious acculturation. American
        Anthropologist 60 (3), 1958, 433-441; repr. in D. E.
        Walker, item 360.
            [Especially on the early Jesuit influence, and on the
        various forms the cross assumed in Yaqui practice.]

1526   SPICER, Edward H[olland]. The Yaqui, in E. H. Spicer (ed.),
        item 316, 7-93, bibl.
            [An important systematic account of Yaqui history and
        culture. Pp. 19-38, Jesuit mission communities; pp. 51-
        52, sacred towns and their churches; pp. 52-58, social
        and religious organization; pp. 58-63, the five main
        cults; pp. 76-81, revival of rituals among immigrants in
        Arizona; pp. 88-91, cultural processes.]

1527   SPICER, Edward H[olland]. El meztizaje cultural en el
        suroeste de Estados Unidos, noroeste de México. Revista
        de Indias (Madrid) 95/96 = enero/junio 1964, 1-26.
            [The different acculturation rates of the Yaqui, Navaho,
        Pueblo and Apache Indians.]

1528   SPICER, Edward H[olland]. La danza Yaqui del Venado en la
        cultura mexicana. América Indígena (Mexico, D.F.) 25 (1),
        1965, 117-139, bibl.
            [The beer dance of the Yaqui, as borrowed by the Ballet
        Folklórico de Mexico.]

1529   SPICER, Edward H[olland]. The Yaqui and Mayo, in E. Z. Vogt
        (ed.), Handbook of Middle American Indians, Vol. 8:
        Ethnology, Part 2. Austin: University of Texas Press
        1969, 830-845, illus., map.
            [Especially pp. 835-844, on Yaqui culture and religion.]

1530   SPICER, Edward H[olland]. Patrons of the poor. Human Organi-
        zation 29 (1), 1970, 12-19.
            [A study of "Navidad", pseudonym for a Yaqui community
        which has maintained its identity and own Catholicism,
        with its annual Easter and other ceremonies; includes
        account of a Protestant missionary's unsuccessful efforts.
        Probably Pascua, on north edge of Tucson.]

1531   SPICER, Edward H[olland]. Contrasting forms of nativism among
        the Mayos and Yaquis of Sonora, Mexico, in W. Goldschmidt
        and H. Hoijer (eds.), The social anthropology of Latin
        America: essays in honour of Ralph Leon Beals (Latin
        American Studies, 14). Los Angeles: Latin American Center,
        University of California, Los Angeles 1970, 104-125.

Yaqui and Mayo Churches...

[Pp. 105-112, Mayo reliance on the supernatural —
millennial movements of Teresa Urrea and Bacasewa; pp. 112-
117, Yaqui reliance on realistic political means of resis-
ting the Mexicans; pp. 117-125, explanation of the difference, in different histories and in consequent social and
cultural integration. The Yaqui church does not figure.]

1532 SPICER, Edward H[olland]. The Yaquis: a cultural history.
      Tucson: University of Arizona Press [expected late 1978],
      illus.
      [Chs. 2 and 4: descriptions and analysis of post-
      Jesuit religious rituals and concepts; Ch. 5, narrative
      account of revival of Yaqui religion in Sonora and Arizona
      in first decades of 20th century. A major study by a life-
      long student of the Yaqui.]

1533 SPICER, Rosamond B. The Easter festival of the Yaqui Indians
      of Pascua, Arizona. University of Chicago, M.A. thesis
      (anthropology) 1939.

1534 TOOR, Frances. The Yaqui festival makers. Mexican Folkways
      (Mexico, D.F.) July 1937, 26-32; see also her Notes on
      Yaqui customs, idem, 52-64.
      [A special Yaqui issue.]

1535 TRONCOSO, Francisco P. Las guerras con las tribus Yaqui y
      Mayo del Estado de Sonora. Mexico, D.F.: Tipografia del
      Departamento de Estado Mayor 1905, 342 p., map.
      [A straightforward history compiled for the government
      as a year-by-year record of military activities against
      the Yaqui and Mayo, 1529-1902, and a good source especially
      for Mayo nativistic movements. Pp. 181-185, Mayo movements
      in 1890 and ensuing violence; p. 193, summary of year 1892;
      pp. 196-199, Teresa Urrea; pp. 199-202, further operations
      in 1892.]

1536 WILDER, Carleton Stafford. The Yaqui Deer Dance: a study in
      cultural change. Bulletin, Bureau of American Ethnology
      186 (Anthropological Papers 63-67), 1963, Paper 66, 145-
      210, + 4 plates.
      [In Pascua, 1939-1940; as an aboriginal survival;
      pp. 157-165, general description of religion in Pascua,
      with plans of church and rameda.]

Yuwipi

YUWIPI

This cult resembles the Sun Dance in having been suppressed and then revived in the twentieth century after a substantial interval. It is also similar in exhibiting some syncretism of Christian elements as well as the survival quality of movements that might seem to have vanished.

1537   FUGLE, Eugene. The nature and function of the Lakota night cults (a study of the Yuwipi and related ceremonies of the Teton).] Museum News (Vermillion, South Dakota) 27 (3-4), 1966, 1-40.

1538   GROBSMITH, Elizabeth S. Wakunza: uses of Yuwipi medicine power in contemporary Teton Dakota culture. Plains Anthropologist no. 64=19, 1974, 129-133.
       [Wakunza, or "supernatural retribution", exercised by animistic spirits as an agent of social control.]

1539   HULTKRANTZ, Åke. Spirit lodge, a North American shamanistic séance, in C.-M. Edsman (ed.), Studies in Shamanism (Scripta Instituti Donneriani Aboensis, 1) Stockholm: Almqvist & Wiksell 1967, 32-68.
       [The Arapaho revival of the Yuwipi cult in the 1950s as a nativistic revitalization movement.]

1540   HURT, Wesley R[obert]. A Yuwipi ceremony at Pine Ridge. Plains Anthropologist (Norman, Oklahoma) no. 10, 1960, 48-52, illus.
       [A description of the final phase of the Dakota curing and foretelling cult — on this occasion for prophecy.]

1541   KEMNITZER, Luis Stowell. Yuwipi: a modern Dakota healing ritual. University of Pennsylvania, Ph.D. dissertation (anthropology) 1968, 219 p.
       [Fourteen performances among Teton Dakota on Pine Ridge Reservation were studied; after 80 years of suppression and apparent disuse, Yuwipi is now the focus of a revival of traditional religion, and of syncretism with Christianity.]

1542   KEMNITZER, Luis S[towell]. Yuwipi. Pine Ridge Research Bulletin No. 10, 1969, 26-33.

1543   KEMNITZER, Luis S[towell]. The cultural provenience of objects used in Yuwipi: a modern Teton Dakota healing ritual. Ethnos 35, 1970, 40-75, bibl.

United States of America

[Among Oglala Sioux of Pine Ridge Reservation, South
Dakota — a neo-primal non-cultic movement of shamans.]

1544   KEMNITZER, L[uis] S[towell].   Structure, content and cultural
        meaning of Yuwipi: a modern Lakota healing ritual.
        American Ethnologist 3 (2), 1976, 261-280, illus.

1545   RUBY, Robert H. Yuwipi: ancient rite of the Sioux.   Montana,
        the Magazine of Western History (Helena) 16 (4), 1966,
        74-79.

Canada, Alaska and Greenland

This section contains those movements that have originated in these areas, including independent churches. While there were new religious developments as early as the late seventeenth century there seems to have been no movement that lasted very long or that spread very widely. This is in striking contrast to movements south of the border with the United States; indeed, the largest and most persistent movements in Canada have come from across the border — the Handsome Lake religion, the peyote cult, the Indian Shaker Church, and also the Ghost Dance which has a marginal survival in Saskatchewan. It is known that nativistic revivals have been occurring in recent times but there appears to be no study of them.

The Pan-Indian Ecumenical Conference is a unique form of movement that includes all traditions — the primal religions, all varieties of Christian churches, and new religious movements such as the Native American Church and others. While it has met on the Stoney Reserve in Alberta since its second annual meeting in 1971, it includes Indians from Alaska to Florida and is not especially Canadian; it is therefore included in our general section above.

Eskimo movements appeared early and again in more recent times, but have not been numerous; they are included in this section.

One imagines that there may well have been more movements among the northern peoples, both Indian and Eskimo, but that these have remained unrecorded on account of their relative isolation or because they have not been subjected to the intensive anthropological scrutiny experienced by the Indians in the United States.

1546 BAILEY, Alfred Goldsworthy. The conflict of European and
       Eastern Algonkian cultures 1504-1700: a study in Canadian
       civilization (Monographic Series, 2). St. John, N.B.:
       New Brunswick Museum 1937, x + 206 p.,; 2nd ed. Toronto:
       University of Toronto Press 1969, xxiii + 218 p., bibl.
          [Pp. 146-147, brief summary of Micmac and other tribes'
       development of new syncretistic religious forms or local
       messiahs, based on the Jesuit Relations (see item 1584)
       and Le Clercq, item 1564.]

1547   BARBEAU, [Charles] Marius. <u>Indian days in the Canadian Rockies.</u>
       Toronto: Macmillan 1923, 208 p., illus.
           [Pp. 11-13, 17-58, 155-156, a semi-fictionalized account
       of Bini, with comments; pp. 11-13, Calf-Child, a Stoney
       Indian medicine-man in the 1920s; based on five narratives
       obtained by the author among Carrier and Gitksan tribes of
       interior of British Columbia.]

1548   BRUEMMER, Fred. The Belcher Islands. <u>The Beaver: A Magazine</u>
       <u>of the North</u> (Winnipeg) no. 302, 1971, 4-13, illus.
           [Includes the religious movement of 1941.]

1549   CALHOUN, [Millard] Fill[more]. Eskimo murders at Hudson Bay.
       <u>Life</u>, June 9, 1941, 14, 16, 18, 22, 24.
           [The Belcher Island Movement, 1941, reported from the
       police files after the first arrests but before the trials.]

1550   DRUCKER, Philip. Native brotherhoods: modern intertribal
       organizations on the Northwest coast. <u>Bulletin, Bureau of</u>
       <u>American Ethnology</u> 169. 1958, 1-197.
           [Pp. 7-77, Alaskan Native Brotherhood, and Sisterhood
       etc., as lay Indian organizations founded by Presbyterians
       from 1912, and becoming non-denominational and widespread;
       pp. 78-152, similar organizations in British Columbia at
       Port Simpson from 1931. Now largely secular societies.]

1551   DRUCKER, Philip. <u>Cultures of the North Pacific Coast.</u> San
       Francisco: Chandler Publishing Co. 1965, xvi + 243 p.,
       illus., maps.
           [Pp. 199-204, William Duncan; p. 204, the split in
       Duncan's Christian Mission Church.]

1552   DRYFOOS, Robert J. (Jr.). The Belcher Island murders: an
       "anti-nativistic" movement. <u>Man in the Northeast</u> (Rindge,
       New Hampshire) 2, 1971, 82-87, bibl.
           [Includes evidence from a participant; the advent of
       Christianity provided the first opportunity of escaping
       from an unsatisfactory life through a new way.]

1553   DUFF, Wilson. <u>The Upper Stalo Indians of the Fraser Valley...</u>
       (Anthropology in British Columbia, Memoir 1). Victoria,
       B.C.: Provincial Museum of Natural History and Anthro-
       pology 1952, 136 p.
           [Pp. 98, 121-122, prophets who spread belief in one
       supreme deity derived from white culture early in 19th c.
       and integrated with aboriginal Stalo culture.]

1554   GODDARD, Pliny Earle. <u>The Beaver Indians</u> (Anthropological
       Papers 10 (4)). New York: American Museum of Natural
       History 1916, pp. 201-293, illus.

[Pp. 226-228, Beaver religion; pp. 228-231, Beaver
prophets in McKenzie Area in "modern times" as initiators
of new religious movements.]

1555   GUBSER, Nicholas J. The Nunamiut Eskimos: hunters of Caribou.
        New Haven & London: Yale University Press 1965, 384 p.
        [Pp. 56-59, a "New Religion" c. 1890s, derivative from
        the Quakers, and non-shamanistic, based on oivaksat [or
        wiivaksat] ideas, or native prophecy of the coming of
        strangers. See also Spencer, item 1581.]

1556   HONIGMANN, John J[oseph]. Ethnography and acculturation of
        the Fort Nelson Slave (Yale University Publications in
        Anthropology, 33). New Haven: Yale University Press,
        and London: Oxford University Press 1946, 169 p.
        [Pp. 132-135, on N. Athabascan prophet cults in later
        19th and 20th centuries.]

1557   HONIGMANN, John J[oseph]. Witch-fear in post-contact Kaska
        society. American Anthropologist 49, 1947, 222-243, bibl.
        [As distinct from aboriginal sorcery of shamans; accul-
        turation dates from early 19th c., and witch-fear probably
        appeared late in 19th c. when introduced diseases spread;
        culture was drastically changing and game was dispersed;
        pp. 239-240, comparisons with other acculturation
        movements.]

1558   HONIGMANN, John J[oseph]. Culture and ethos of Kaska Society
        (Yale University Publications in Anthropology 40). New
        Haven: Yale University Press 1949, 365 p., map, illus.
        [Pp. 47-48, late 19th c. prophet cult with Catholic
        background — its various forms, and similar movements
        among the Bear Lake Sekani and the Taku; pp. 50-53, the
        acculturation process; pp. 317-222, Kaskas' nominal
        Christianity.]

1559   HONIGMANN, John J[oseph]. Social networks in Great Whale
        River. National Museum of Canada, Bulletin 178 1962.
        [Pp. 69-71, on new Eskimo movement of Charlie Ouyerack,
        1941, Flaherty Island, and the Fletcher Island murders.]

1560   JENNESS, Diamond. The Ojibwa Indians of Parry Island, their
        social and religious life (Bulletin, National Museum of
        Canada, 78; Anthropological Series, 17). Ottawa: J. O.
        Patenaude (printer) 1935, 115 p.
        [P. 61, Midéwiwin as newly established, and usually
        referring to witchcraft; pp. 69-78, Potawatomi Midéwiwin
        as brought to Parry Is. — its origin legend, initiation
        rites, and functions as a "secret medical organization
        garbed in the mantle of religion".]

1561   JENNESS, Diamond. The Sekani Indians of British Columbia
       (Bulletin 84; Anthropological Series 20). Ottawa: Canada
       Department of Mines and Resources 1937, 82 p.
       [Ch. 7, pp. 64-67, N. Athabascan tribes with prophet
       cults; pp. 67-79, traditional medicine men, etc.]

1562   JENNESS, Diamond. The Carrier Indians of the Bulkley River.
       Their social and religious life. Bulletin, Bureau of
       American Ethnology 133 (Anthropological Papers 19-26) 1943,
       Paper 25, 469-586 + 11 plates.
       [Pp. 539-559, religion; pp. 546-559, reactions to white
       and Christian contact, especially pp. 551-557, the Bini
       movement — a reconstructed composite account based on the
       discussion of three old men, compared with a second dif-
       ferent account also drawn from contemporary eyewitnesses.]

1563   JENNESS, Diamond. The Indians of Canada (Bulletin 65, Anthro-
       pological Series 15). Ottawa: National Museum of Canada
       1934, 3rd ed. 1955, 452 p., illus., map.
       [Pp. 183-184, brief reference to Handsome Lake and
       similar but short-lived movements; pp. 314-315, Cough
       Child as prophet of a "recent nativisitc revival" on
       Stoney Reserve, Alberta (also known as Calf Child).]

1564   KEHOE, Alice B[eck]. Saskatchewan Indian religious beliefs
       (Saskatchewan Museum of Natural History, Popular Series 7).
       Regina: Department of Natural Resources 1963, 15 p.
       [General information, shamanism, Sun Dance, brief
       reference to the Ghost Dance, Native American Church and
       Baha'i.]

1565   LE CLERCQ, Chrétien. Nouvelle relation de la Gaspésie ...
       moeurs & la religion des sauvages gaspésiens ... . Paris:
       A. Auroy 1691, 572 p.; new ed., idem, 1758. Eng. trans.,
       New relations of Gaspesia, with the customs and religion
       of the Gaspesian Indians (trans. and ed. by W. F. Ganong).
       (Publications of the Champlain Society, 5). Toronto: the
       Champlain Society 1910, 452 p.; repr. New York: Greenwood
       Press 1968.
       [Eng. trans., pp. 229-233, Micmac imitative religions;
       by a French Recollect, a missionary from 1675.]

1566   McCLELLAN, Catharine. Shamanistic syncretism in Southern
       Yukon. Transactions of the New York Academy of Sciences
       Series 2, 19 (2), 1956, 130-137.
       [On Indian shamans' syncretisms using some Christian
       elements in church-like meetings after returning from
       heaven with new rules and powers; pp. 135-136, the Ross
       River shaman-prophet and his visit to heaven. Mostly
       among small Tlingit-speaking groups.]

1567 McKENNAN, Robert A[ddison]. The Chandalar Kutchin (Arctic
     Institute of North America, Technical Paper 17).
     [Montreal]: Arctic Institute of North America 1965, 156 p.,
     illus., maps.
        [Pp. 86-88, Tripp's movement in early 20th c., among
     Natsitkutchin Indians at Arctic village in Alaska; orthodox
     Christian content together with revival of Indian way of
     life.]

1568 M'LEAN, John. Notes of a twenty-five years' service in the
     Hudson's Bay territory. London: R. Bentley, 2 vols.
     1849; repr. Toronto: the Champlain Society, 1 vol. 1932,
     xxxvi + 402 p.
        [Vol. 1, pp. 263-264 (= pp. 159-160 in 1932 ed.), on
     syncretist religion introduced to Carrier Indians, British
     Columbia, c. 1840, by two Oregon Indians.]

1569 MATHIASSEN, Therkel. The material culture of the Iglulik
     Eskimos (Reports of the Fifth Thule Expedition 1921-24,
     vol. 6, no. 1). Denmark: Gyldendal 1928, 242 p., illus.,
     map.
        [P. 235-236, Eskimo new movements.]

1570 MORICE, A[drian] G[abriel]. Are the Carrier sociology and
     mythology indigenous or exotic? Transactions of the Royal
     Society of Canada Section 2, 1892, 109-126, map.
        [Detailed exposition of the Carrier practice of imitating
     other Indian peoples and Europeans; hence their imitation
     of the Europeans' religion in Bini and other cults.]

1571 MORICE, Adrian Gabriel. The history of the northern interior
     of British Columbia (formerly New Caledonia). Toronto:
     William Briggs 1904, 3rd ed. 1905, 368 p., illus.
        [Pp. 225-226, the part-Cree, W. McBean, as preacher, and
     new Carrier religion in 1830s; pp. 238-240, Peni's (=Bini's)
     religion among the Babines, etc., mid-19th century; by a
     Catholic missionary historian.]

1572 OSGOOD, Cornelius. The ethnography of the Great Bear Lake
     Indians, in Annual Report, Department of Mines and
     Resources, National Museum of Canada. Ottawa: National
     Museum of Canada 1931, 31-97, illus., bibl.
        [Pp. 81-87, religion; p. 87, a new "Messiah cult" in
     1925-26, received in the Mackenzie district, Northwest
     Territories, from the Rae Dogribs.]

1573 PATTERSON, Palmer. The colonial parallel: a view of Indian
     history. Ethnohistory 18 (1), 1970, 1-17.
        [Includes "messianism" as one of the aspects of the
     Canadian Indian contact situation, with parallels through-
     out the world.]

1574   PRESBYTERIAN CHURCH IN CANADA. Appendices. <u>Acts and Proceed-
       ings of the General Assembly of the Presbyterian Church in
       Canada</u>, 1905, p. 166.
          [Miss Gillespie's report on a messianic movement, File
       Hills Reserve, near Regina, 1904.]

1575   PRESBYTERIAN CHURCH IN CANADA. Report of the Foreign Missions
       Committee 1907, in <u>Acts and Proceedings of the General
       Assembly of the Presbyterian Church in Canada</u>, 1908,
       Appendix, pp. 185-186.
          [A messianic anti-Christian "Soul Society" among Cree on
       Pipestone Reservation, Manitoba, from about 1903, reported
       by a Cree lay evangelist.]

1576   RAND, Silas Tertius. <u>Legends of the Micmac</u>. New York and
       London: Longmans, Green & Co. 1894, xlvi + 452 p.
          [Pp. 230-231, Abistanaooch's new religion among the
       Micmac <u>c</u>. 1770, and its sudden collapse.]

1577   RASMUSSEN, Knud J[ohan Victor]. <u>The people of the Polar North:
       a record...</u> (compiled and edited by G. Herring). London:
       Kegan Paul, Trench, Trubner & Co. 1908, 358 p., illus.
          [Pp. 250-253, Eskimo "new religion" of 1790 in South
       Greenland: "The Great Revival in Evighedsfjorden"; summary
       in Chamberlain, item 157, 12ff. The author was born and
       grew up among Greenland Eskimos.]

1578   ROHNER, Ronald P. <u>The people of Gilford: a contemporary
       Kwakiutl village</u> (National Museum of Canada Bulletin 225,
       Anthropological Series no. 83). Ottawa: the Museum 1967,
       179 p.
          [P. 146, short-lived indigenous pentecostal movement,
       1942-1944.]

1579   <u>ROYAL CANADIAN MOUNTED POLICE QUARTERLY</u>. The law goes north.
       <u>Royal Canadian Mounted Police Quarterly</u> 9 (2), 1941, 152-
       160, illus.
          [The Belcher Island movement and murders of 1941, from
       the police viewpoint.]

1580   ROYAL CANADIAN MOUNTED POLICE. Eskimo murders — Belcher Island,
       N.W.T. <u>Annual Report of "G" Division, Royal Canadian
       Mounted Police, for year ended March 31, 1942</u>. Ottawa,
       1942.
          [See previous item.]

1581   SPENCER, Robert F. <u>The North Alaskan Eskimo</u> = <u>Bulletin, Bureau
       of American Ethnology</u> 171, 1959, 490 p., illus., maps.
          [Pp. 296-298, development of a new cult (1870s-1880s)
       related to "the strangers in the sky" (=<u>wiivaksat</u>) probably
       referring to the ancestors; also pp. 379, 380-381 similarly.
       And see Gubser, item 1555.]

1582   STEFÁNSSON, Vilhjálmur. My life with the Eskimos (1st ed.
       1941). New York: Collier Books 1962, 1966, 447 p.
       [Pp. 93-98, Christianity as superior magic.]

1583   SWANTON, John R[eed]. Harda texts and myths, Skidegate
       dialect = Bulletin, Bureau of American Ethnology 29,
       1905, 448 p.
       [P. 314, n14 on Bini's (= Peni's) cult, among the
       Carriers.]

1584   THWAITES, R[euben] G[old] (ed.). The Jesuit Relations and
       allied documents...1610-1791. Cleveland: Burrows Brothers
       Company, 73 vols. 1896-1901.
       [Originally published annually in Paris, 1632-1673, by
       Cramoisy: reissued by Canadian Government 1858. Contains
       all available reports, letters, etc., of French Jesuit
       missionaries, 1610-1791. Much material on Indian religions,
       and valuable as background.]

1585   USHER, Jean (FREISAN). The long-slumbering offspring of
       Adam: the evangelical approach to the Tshimshian.
       Anthropologica (Ottawa) 13 (1-2), 1971, 36-62.
       [On William Duncan, the Port Simpson and Metlakatla
       missions of the Church Missionary Society from 1857;
       p. 43 on an individual prophet. Based on primary sources.]

1586   USHER, Jean (FREISAN). William Duncan of Metlakatla. A
       Victorian missionary in British Columbia (Publications in
       History, 5). Ottawa: National Museums of Canada 1974,
       163 p., illus.
       [As background to Tshimshian Independent Church of Port
       Simpson in 20th c.; see p. 96 for pentecostal outbreak in
       Duncan's village, Metlakatla, in 1877, as forerunner of
       later development.]

1587   WILLIAMSON, Robert G. Eskimo underground: Socio-cultural
       change in the Canadian Central Arctic (Instituten for
       Allman och Jamforande Etnografi vid Uppsala Universitet:
       Occasional Papers, 2). Uppsala: the Institute 1974,
       196 p., maps, bibl.
       [Pp. 72-79, Anglicans and Catholic missions in relation
       to Eskimo religion in the Keewatin region; pp. 79-81,
       Eskimo Christian Fellowship as an independent church
       founded 1969.]

Northern Mexico

In anthropological studies the Indian peoples of northern Mexico are usually grouped with those of the United States as belonging to the same cultural area; the present political border is of comparatively recent origin and has been irrelevant through much of post-contact Indian history. Hence this northern area is included in the volume on North America, while movements among the Indians of central and southern Mexico will appear in volume 4, together with the rest of Latin America. This section excludes the Yaqui and Mayo of northwestern Mexico, likewise traditional forms of peyotism, since both these are conveniently treated in their own sections above.

Literature concerning the Indian revolts against the Spaniards in the earlier colonial period period is sparse and not easily accessible; it also tends to concentrate on the political and military aspects and to neglect the religious dimension that was usually present, and often in a neo-primal or syncretistic form. Other literature readily moves over into the sphere of folk religion among the mestizo or ladino population, and we have not drawn the line too strictly at this point for new syncretistic movements of Indian origin may have much in common with what has been called the "Christo-paganism" of the non-Indian population.

1588 ALEGRE, Francisco Javier. Historia de la Compañia de Jesus de Nueva España (E. J. Burrus and F. Zubillaga, eds.). Mexico: J. M. Lara, 3 vols. 1841-1842; Rome: Institutum Historicum Societatis Iesu, 4 vols. 1956-1960.
      [Vol. 2, pp. 271-272, messianic elements in the Tepehuana revolt in Durango, 1616-1618.]

1589 BRENNER, Anita. Idols behind altars. New York: Payson and Clarke 1929, 359 p., illus., bibl.
      [Pp. 20-21, popular healers in the 20th c., especially Fidencio (1928-), set in the context of messianic ideas in Mexico (= ch. 1).]

1590 DUNNE, Peter Masten. Pioneer Jesuits in north Mexico. Berkeley: University of California Press 1944, 227 p., illus.
      [Pp. 123-125, 163, 169, religious aspects of the Tepehuana revolt, 1616-1618, with a religious specialist as a

leader; with source references. From a viewpoint unsympathetic to Indian religion.]

1591 DUNNE, Peter M[asten]. Early Jesuit missions in Tarahumara. Berkeley: University of California Press 1948; repr. (California Library Reprint Series, 14) 1969, 276 p., illus., map, bibl. (= pp. 257-260).
[Pp. 54-80, Tarahumara revolts between 1645 and 1697, with messianic elements.]

1592 FRIED, Jacob. The Tarahumara, in E. Z. Vogt (ed.), Handbook of Middle American Indians, vol. 8: Ethnology, Part 2. Austin: University of Texas Press 1969, 846-870, illus.
[Pp. 860-864, rituals and world view in their syncretist religion, with churcles and fiestas deriving from the 18th c. Jesuit missions.]

1593 GALAVIZ de CAPDEVIELLE, María Elena. Rebeliones de seris et pimas en el siglo XVIII: características y situación. Estudios de Historia Novohispania (Universidad Nacional Autónoma de México, Mexico, D.F.) 1, 1966, 187-213.
[Revolts by Seri and Pima Indians of New Mexico in the 18th c.]

1594 GALAVIZ de CAPDEVIELLE, María Elena. Rebeliones indígenas en el norte del Reino de la Nueva España: siglos XVI y XVII. Mexico, D.F.: Editorial Campesina 1967, 218 p., maps, bibl.
[Brief accounts of some sixty Indian revolts in northern "New Spain", and their causes. Most had religious dimensions involving innovations.]

1595 GRIFFEN, William B. A north Mexican nativistic movement. Ethnohistory 17 (3-4), 1970, 95-116, maps, bibl.
[A revolt with typical nativistic religious features among the Conchos River peoples (now in New Mexico, U.S.A.) in the 17th c.; uses Wallace's revitalization theory.]

1596 GUILLERMO ALDANA, E. Mesa del Nayar's strange Holy Week. National Geographic 139 (6), 1971, 780-795, illus.
[Cora Indians of Mexico in Nayarit State, north of Tepic, with their indigenized rituals derived from 18th c. Jesuit missions; the renewed contact with a Roman Catholic priest from 1969; p. 789, use of peyote as stimulant. Cf. with Yaqui and Mayo independent churches, north of the Cora.]

1597 HUERTA PRECIADO, María Teresa. Rebeliones indígenas en el noreste de México en la época colonial. Mexico, D.F.: Universidad Nacional Autónoma de México 1963, 111 p., bibl. Mimeo.
[A thorough study of Indian revolts, related to the weak Spanish colonization; see also Galaviz de Capdevielle, items 1589, 1590.]

1598   LABARDE, Genevieve. A propósito del libro de Joseph Neumann
       sobre los Tarahumaras. Boletin Bibliografico. Universidad
       Nacional Mayor de San Marcos (Lima) no. 472=18 (April),
       1972, 21ff., map.
       [Includes an outline of Neumann's item 1602, and of the
       rebellions, with attention to the religious aspects.]

1599   MACKLIN, Barbara June. Culture change and structural stability
       in Mexican American culture: a case study. University
       of Pennsylvania, Ph.D. dissertation (anthropology) 1963.
       [El Niño Fidencio of Nueva León, 1920s.]

1600   MACKLIN, Barbara June. El Niño Fidencio: Un estudio del
       curanderismo en Nuevo León, Anuario Humánitas (Monterrey,
       Universidad de Nuevo León, Centro de Estudios Humanisticos)
       1967, 529-563.
       [A folk curer in Nueva León in the 1920s, and the move-
       ment that ensued.]

1601   MACKLIN, Barbara June. Folk saints, healers and spiritist
       cults in Northern Mexico. Revista Inter-america Review
       3 (4), 1974, 351-367.
       [Includes Mayo leaders.]

1602   NEUMANN, Joseph. Révoltes de indiens tarahumara (1626-1724).
       (Trans. from original Latin with introduction and commen-
       taries by Luis Gonzalez R) (Travaux et Mémoires, 24).
       Paris: Institut des Hautes Etudes de l'Amérique Latine
       1969, lxiii + 188 p., maps, bibl. (= pp. xv-xxxiv).
       [The Jesuit missionary to the Tarahumara (1681-1732);
       contains Latin original of his Historia Seditionum (1730),
       with French trans. opposite. P. lv (editor's introduction)
       and pp. 43-44, on the religious specialists ("sorciers")
       and their influence in five revolts — Spanish firearms
       powerless, and Indian dead to rise on third day; pp. 58-65,
       effects of epidemics, and attacks on missions; pp. 43
       n17, 70-71, comment on Neumann's apparent reference to a
       messianic movement. See also Labarde, item 1598.]

1603   RAMOS, Roberto (ed.). Historia de la tercera rebelión tara-
       humara. Chihuahua: Sociedad Chihuahuense de Estudios
       Históricos 1950, 56 p.
       [Edited text of an anonymous document by a priest in
       1691 concerning the revolt which began in 1690.]

1604   RILEY, Carroll L. and HOBGOOD, John. A recent nativistic move-
       ment among the Southern Tepehuan Indians. Southwestern
       Journal of Anthropology 15, 1959, 355-360.
       [Two nativistic movements deriving from visions of the
       Virgin Mary of Guadalupe to young women in 1956 and 1957,
       with rejection of foreign goods and revival of indigenous
       fertility or thanksgiving dances.]

1605   ROMANO, Octavio. <u>Don Pedrito Jaramillo; the emergence of a</u>
        <u>Mexican-American folk-saint</u>. University of California
        (Berkeley) Ph.D. dissertation (anthropology) 1962, 171 p.
            [A healer in south Texas (1829-1907) who conformed to
        the popular image of his type, and whose shrine-grave con-
        tinues as a place of pilgrimage, but whose followers have
        never formed an organized group.]

1606   RUBEL, Arthur J. <u>Across the tracks: Mexican-Americans in a</u>
        <u>Texas city</u>. Austin: University of Texas Press for Hogg
        Foundation for Mental Health 1966, 266 p., illus.
            [Pp. 183-185, Don Pedro Jaramillo, the deceased curan-
        dero, still influential, with shrines (and see index);
        pp. 185-188, El Niño Fidencio, and others using his name.]

1607   SOCIETY OF JESUS. <u>Archivum Romanum Societatis Iesu</u>. Rome.
        Manuscript sources.
            [Mexicana section, vol. 17, pp. 369v-378, messianic
        aspects of the Tarahumara revolt of 1676; cited by
        J. Neumann, item 1602, p. 43.]

Index of Authors and Sources

(The numbers refer to items)

Contributions to symposia, etc., are indexed separately for each author; the colourless category of "Anon." has been replaced by the more informative title of the publication itself, or of the sponsoring body.

Index of Films, Records and Tapes

(These have been included among the literary items).

Index of Main Movements
and Indian Individuals

(Names are given in the common or anglicized form.)

A

ABISTANOOK/ABISTANAOOCH (Micmac), 157, 1576
AIS-KAW-BA-WIS (prophet), 1446
ALCOHOLICS ANONYMOUS (INDIAN), 698
ALIANZA MOVEMENT (Mexican Americans), 67, 207, 333
ALLELUJAHS (Mexican Americans), 67, 229
APACHE MOVEMENTS, 377-383, 498, 797, 961, 962, 1001, 1045, 1048, 1050,
    1051, 1148, 1527. See also NAKAIDOKLINI
APIATAN/AHPIATOM (Kiowa), 537, 540
ASSINISINK PROPHET (Delaware), 393, 398, 400
ATHABASCAN BERDACHE. See KUTENAI BERDACHE

B

BACASEWA, Antonio (Mayo). See BOHOROQUI, Damien (same person)
BACOSEGUA, Antonio (Mayo). See BOHOROQUI, Damien (same person)
BAIYUI/BAIGYA/PAYUI. See SONS OF THE SUN
BANNING PROPHET, 204
BEADE (Munsee prophetess). See MUNSEE PROPHETESS
BEAVER PROPHETS, (McKenzie area, Canada), 1554
BELCHER ISLANDS MOVEMENT (Eskimo), 1549, 1550, 1552, 1579, 1580
BIG HEAD CULT, 197, 437, 505
BINI = PENI (Babines, Carrier and Gitskan), 134, 1547, 1562, 1570,
    1583
BLACK MASK ROUND DANCE TO THE HOLY GHOST (Zuñi), 218
BOHOROQUI, Damien (Mayo). (Otherwise named as BACASEWA or BACOSEGUA,
    Antonio), 315, 1491, 1498, 1499, 1511, 1512, 1531
BOLE MARU CULT, 167, 371, 437, 499, 505, 1394
BOW-STRING SOCIETY (Cheyenne), 174
BUZZARD CULT, 195, 208, 232, 256, 331, 364

C

CALF/COUGH CHILD MOVEMENT (Stoney), 1457, 1563
CANADIAN MOVEMENTS: primarily U.S.A. origin, 474, 475, 479A, 572,
    573, 1052, 1053, 1380; primarily Canadian origin, 1546-1587

CAPTAIN JIM = GUMALANGA (Washo), 177
CARRIER NEW RELIGION. (See also BINI), 1568, 1570, 1571
CATAWBA MORMONISM, 311, 689
CHEEZ-TAH-PAEZH (Crow medicine man), 262
CHEROKEE BAPTIST CHURCH, 704, 1352, 1360, 1361
CHICKAHOMINY BAPTIST CHURCHES, 694, 700
CHINIGCHINIX. See CHUNGISHNISH
CHIPPEWA (=OJIBWA) PROPHET, 298
CHUNGISHNISH (Cahita), 140, 212, 234, 291, 330, 347
CHRISTIAN BAND OF WORKERS (Tshimshians), 1586
CHUMASH MESSIANIC MOVEMENT, 215
"CHURCH IN THE WOODS" (Cherokee), 1362
CHURCH OF THE FIRST-BORN. See FIRST BORN CHURCH OF CHRIST
CONCHOS RIVER REVOLT, 1595
CONSTANTINO, Fidencio (of Nueva León), 1511, 1512, 1589, 1599, 1600, 1606
COUGH or CROW CHILD MOVEMENT. See CALF CHILD MOVEMENT
COYOTE DROPPINGS. See ISATAI
CREEK BAPTIST CHURCHES (Oklahoma), 699
CREEK PROPHETS, 162, 179, 271
CULT OF THE STRANGERS/THE DEAD (Eskimo). See WIIVAKSAT

<u>D</u>

DAHGODIYÁH (Cibecue Apache). See DAYODIYA
DAKETAN'S MOVEMENT, 139
DAKOTA CHURCH (at Yankton), 683, 688, 690
DAVÉKO (Kiowa-Apache), 249
DAYODIYA = DAHGODIYÁH CULT (Apache), 380, 381
DEATH AND REVIVAL CULT. See also BUZZARD CULT
DELAWARE PROPHET (Brainerd's), 385
DELAWARE PROPHETS, 54, 209, 252, 268, 296, 317, 337, 384-402, 665.
   See also NEOLIN, PAPOONAN, and WANGOMEND
DREAM DANCE, 265, 371. See also DRUM RELIGION
DREAMERS' CULT, 151A, 164, 306, 307, 371, 437. See also SMOHALLA
DRUM RELIGION (Chippewa, Potawatomi, Menomini, Fox), 56, 201, 247,
   294, 309, 319-322, 731, 733, 736, 738, 739, 742, 743, 753-55,
   757, 764, 767, 789, 912

<u>E</u>

EARTH LODGE CULT, 265, 371, 437, 499, 505, 1394
EDWARDS, Silas John (Apache). See HOLY GROUND RELIGION
ELSKWATAWA. See TENSKWATAWA
ESKIMO CHRISTIAN FELLOWSHIP, 1587
ESKIMO MOVEMENTS, 1555, 1559, 1569, 1577, 1581, 1586, 1587

<u>F</u>

FEATHER CULT, 183, 198, 323, 371
FILE HILLS MESSIAH (Canada), 1574

MITAWIT or MITAWINI. See MIDÉWIWIN
MIWOK CULTS, 448
MOHAVE MISSION CHURCH, 315
MOHAWK PROPHET (in 1798), 603, 615
MONHEGAN INDIAN CHURCH, 689
"MOONHEAD". See WILSON, John
MUNSEE PROPHETESS (Munsee/Delaware), 205, 310, 399

N

NA'ILDE CULT (Apache), 380, 498
NAKAIDOKLINI / NOKAIDOKLINNY / NOCKYLDELKLINNE (Apache), 262, 340,
    377, 378, 379, 382, 383
NARRAGANSETT CHURCH, 145, 296, 675, 677-680, 682, 684, 691-693, 695,
    697, 701
NATIVE AMERICAN CHURCH. See PEYOTE
NATIVE NORTH AMERICAN CHURCH OF GOD, 1021
NAVAHO INDEPENDENT CHURCHES, 696
NEOLIN (Lenape-Delaware), 231, 296, 297, 371, 384, 389, 391, 392,
    392A, 397
NETLAM'S CULT (Squamish), 1338
NIGHTHAWK SOCIETY. See KEETOWAH SOCIETY
NISHKUNTU. See WILSON, John
NORTH ATHABASCAN PROPHET CULTS (Slave and Sekani), 1556, 1561
NOOKSACK "CHURCH" (Nooksak, Lummi and Skagit), 1338
NUNAMIUT NEW RELIGION (Eskimo), 1555

O

OASLAHDN (Apache). See DAHGODIYÁH
OIVAKSAT (Nunamiut Eskimo), 1555, 1581
OJIBWA MESSIAH, 201
OUYERACK, Charlie (Eskimo), 1559

P

PAINTED TIPI CULT (Cree), 184
PAN-INDIAN ECUMENICAL CONFERENCE. See INDIAN ECUMENICAL CONFERENCE
PAPAGO MESSIANIC MOVEMENT. See ISRAELITES
PAPOONAN / PAPOONHANK / PAPUNHANK (Delaware), 343, 391, 666
PARKER, Quanah (Comanche peyotist), 417, 787, 930, 1157
PARRISH, Elsie, 499
PATEPTE (Kiowa prophet), 1009
PATHESKE (Winnebago), 54, 262
PAVIOTSO SPIRIT DANCE, 366
PENI. See BINI
PENTECOSTAL GROUPS (Apache, Nez Percé, etc.), 108, 181, 197, 258, 358,
    359, 703, 1586
PENTECOSTAL MOVEMENT (Kwakiutl), 1578

Y
_

Z
_